Italian graphic design

Manchester University Press

To buy or to find out more about the books currently available in this series, please go to:
https://manchesteruniversitypress.co.uk/series/studies-in-design-and-material-culture/

STUDIES IN DESIGN & MATERIAL CULTURE

general editors
Sally-Anne Huxtable
Elizabeth Currie
Livia Lazzaro Rezende
Wessie Ling

founding editor
Paul Greenhalgh

Italian graphic design

Culture and practice in Milan, 1930s–60s

Chiara Barbieri

Manchester University Press

Published by Manchester University Press
Oxford Road, Manchester, M13 9PL
www.manchesteruniversitypress.co.uk

British Library Cataloguing-in-Publication Data
A catalogue record for this book is available from the British Library

ISBN 978 1 5261 5113 1 *hardback*
ISBN 978 1 5261 9476 3 *paperback*

First published 2024
Paperback published 2026

The publisher has no responsibility for the persistence or accuracy of URLs for any external or third-party internet websites referred to in this book, and does not guarantee that any content on such websites is, or will remain, accurate or appropriate.

EU authorised representative for GPSR:
Easy Access System Europe – Mustamäe tee 50, 10621 Tallinn, Estonia
gpsr.requests@easproject.com

Typeset
by Cheshire Typesetting Ltd, Cuddington, Cheshire

For my family and friends

Contents

List of figures

Acknowledgements

It is a great pleasure to express my appreciation to those who have contributed to the making of this book. During this journey, I have been assisted by a number of people to whom I owe my most sincere gratitude. First, I would like to thank Sarah Teasley and Jane Pavitt for their help in directing my often-confused thoughts, and for challenging me to look at my own country, history and culture through the eyes of a foreigner. Thanks to a number of colleagues and friends, who helped shape this project through numerous conversations. These include, but are not limited to: Miranda Clow, Lizzy Currie, Spike Sweeting, Alessandra Chessa, Rachel Siobhan Tyler, Jonas Berthod, Davide Fornari, Anna Nyburg, Jessica Kelly and Dora Souza Dias. I am particularly grateful to Carlo Vinti and Jeremy Aynsley for sharing their knowledge and offering invaluable advice. I wish also to thank Kasia Jezowska, Leah Armstrong and the other members of the Design History Writing Group for being my first and most supportive readers.

This book would not have been possible without the cooperation of the staff of the libraries, the archives and the private collections that I have visited over the last ten years. In particular, I would like to thank the staff at the British Library and the National Art Library in London, and at the Biblioteca del Progetto at the Milan Triennale, the Biblioteca Sormani and the Biblioteca Nazionale Braidense in Milan. The Archivio Storico of the Società Umanitaria in Milan has been a uniquely supportive research environment to work in and for this I would like to thank Claudio Colombo for his patience and good humour. Thanks are also due to members of the Aiap who expressed a particular interest in my research project. I wish especially to thank Lorenzo Grazzani and Francesco Ermanno Guida for their kind support and engaged curiosity. My gratitude also goes to Luciana Gunetti for helping me access and navigate my way through the

Archivio Albe e Lica Steiner at the Milan Politecnico. I owe special thanks to Anna Boggeri and Bruno Monguzzi for their hospitality, for showing me their archive and patiently answering my many questions about Studio Boggeri. I am grateful to Angela Persici from the Istituto Pedagogico della Resistenza, whose keen sense of civic responsibility is living proof that the spirit of the Convitto Scuola Rinascita has survived to the present day. Interviews with graphic designers, critics and historians have provided precious insights. Sadly, some of them have since left us, but my memory of our conversations and my gratitude are still alive. Thus, I would like to thank for their indispensable first-hand accounts the late Massimo Dradi, Giancarlo Iliprandi and Gillo Dorfles. Additional thanks go to all those who have granted permission for the reproduction of their images and to the Design History Society for the support I received from the DHS Research Publication Grant. Thanks, too, to Jim McManus for his sharp editorial work and witty minutiae about the English language, and to Niccolò Quaresima for taking good care of the images.

My parents, Carlo and Cristina, and my sister, Livia, have given me unconditional support and unflagging encouragement at every step of the process. I thank my father for his genuine curiosity and my mother for her tireless understanding. My uncle, Giovanni, has turned many moments of discouragement and stress into a good laugh. My friends, Anna, Rachel, Oliver, Miranda, Jonas, Tim, Olivia, Joost and Michaela, made me feel at home in London and became my adoptive family. I look forward to returning the favour and welcoming them in Milan. My husband, Matteo, has taken good care of me and prevented me from going crazy along the way. My sons, Marco and Claudio, were born while I was completing this book. Their smiles have helped me put things in perspective. I am in debt to you all and dedicate this book to all of you.

Abbreviations

ADCM	Art Directors Club Milano
ADI	Associazione per il Design Industriale (Association for Industrial Design)
AGI	Alliance Graphique Internationale
Aiap	Associazione Italiana Artisti Pubblicitari (Italian Association of Advertising Artists)
ANPI	Associazione Nazionale Partigiani d'Italia (National Association of Italian Partisans)
ATAP	Associazione Italiana Tecnici e Artisti Pubblicitari (Italian Association of Advertising Technicians and Artists)
CSDI	Corso Superiore di Disegno Industriale (Graduate Course of Industrial Design)
D&AD	Design & Art Direction
DC	Democrazia Cristiana (Christian Democrats)
EAI	Esposizione dell'Aeronautica Italiana (Italian Aeronautics Exhibition)
HfG	Hochschule für Gestaltung (Institute of Design)
Icograda	International Council of Graphic Design Associations
ICSID	International Council of Societies of Industrial Design
ISIA	Istituto Superiore per le Industrie Artistiche (Higher Institute for the Artistic Industries)
MRF	Mostra della Rivoluzione Fascista (Exhibition of the Fascist Revolution)
PCI	Partito Comunista Italiano (Italian Communist Party)
PNF	Partito Nazionale Fascista (National Fascist Party)
RCA	Royal College of Art

SIA	Society of Industrial Artists
SIAD	Society of Industrial Artists and Designers
TGP	Taller de Grafica Popular (People's Print Workshop)
WoDeCo	World Design Conference

Introduction: drafting Italian graphic design

Five high-relief concrete panels greeted visitors on the portal of the Padiglione della Stampa (Press Pavilion) at the 5th Milan Triennale in 1933 (see figure 0.1). Devised by the artist Mario Sironi and realised by the sculptor Leone Lodi, the panels represented the printing industry with an ambiguous and anachronistic iconography: technical tools and cog wheels were combined with elements of archaic monumentality. Once inside the pavilion and just before entering the Mostra delle Arti Grafiche (Graphic Arts Exhibition), visitors encountered a linotype machine in front of a large-scale photomontage in which the metal types, the letter compartments of the type cases and the composing sticks turned into the skyscrapers and factories of a metropolis (see figure 0.2). The installation conveyed an image of graphic practice in stark contrast with that sculpted on the portal: it connoted graphic practitioners as urban and industrial, at pace with technological progress, embedded in contemporary society and not isolated in a heroic non-time and space, as in Sironi's high reliefs. Both the visual language and technique of the photomontage emphasised impersonality, mechanical reproduction and standardisation. The comparison suggests a shift from an artisanal to an industrial notion of graphic design, and thus attests to a change within graphic practice occurring in Italy at the time.

Milan, 1933, was the place and year of birth of Italian graphic design. Or at least this is what the historiographical canon has told us.[1] Somewhere in between the launch of the magazine *Campo Grafico*, the setting up of Studio Boggeri, the inauguration of the German Pavilion curated by the type designer Paul Renner at the 5th Milan Triennale and the arrival in town of the Bauhausler, Xanti (Alexander) Schawinsky, Italian graphic design was born. As simplistic and anecdotal as the statement might appear, there is some truth in this 'birth certificate'. Yet, a magazine, a graphic design

0.1   View of the portal of the Padiglione della Stampa at the 5th Milan Triennale, 1933.

studio, an exhibition and a foreign designer were but a few elements of a far more complex story. This book tells that story.

In tracing the emergence and articulation of graphic design practice in Milan, this book offers a critical and contextualised history of graphic design in Italy and a historical analysis of the role that graphic design has played in Italian design culture. It opens in the interwar period, adopting the early 1930s as a turning point for Italian graphics; and it concludes in

0.2   Installation shot, Padiglione della Stampa, 5th Milan Triennale, 1933.

the mid-1960s, when graphic designers had attained a better delineated, though still far from secured and uncontested, position within national and international design discourses. Milan is the ideal setting for this story. Its geographical focus stems from the specific geography of Italian design.[2] As the heart of the Italian printing industry since the end of the nineteenth century and the centre of Italy's post-war economic boom, the northern industrial city offered graphic designers an advantageous

environment of economic and industrial structures and cultural organisations that supported the development of the practice and favoured international exchanges.[3] It was in Milan that early design educational initiatives
were undertaken, graphic design studios opened, specialist magazines
launched and professional organisations founded. Obviously, the articulation of graphic design practice did not occur in a vacuum, and the
following pages examine graphic designers' continual adaptation to shifting economic, political and cultural environments, as well as to changing
design discourses over a period of about thirty years: from the Fascist
regime (1922–43), through the war years (1939–45) and post-war reconstruction, to the Italian economic miracle of the 1950s and early 1960s. By
showing how macro historical narratives were experienced in everyday
practice, the book offers a partial history of Italy during the period covered
here, as seen from the perspective of graphic design.

This history looks behind the individual designers, major companies,
iconic visual artefacts and familiar narratives that have populated Italian
graphic design so far, and centres on educational issues, networks, organisational strategies and mediating channels that defined, legitimised,
represented, favoured or hindered the development of graphic design in
Italy. It investigates the ways in which graphic designers negotiated their
collective identity both among themselves and with others. What they
called themselves and how they organised and made their practice visible are further questions tackled here. Building on sociological stances,
I approach professions as historically produced and socially constructed,
and professionalisation as a dynamic process of becoming. In this vein,
the book traces the lineage of Italian graphic design back to typography
and the printing trade. It unpacks the problematic relationship between
graphic design and advertising, from interwar alliance to post-war schism.
It explores the mutually beneficial dialogue with neighbouring fields of
practice, such as photography and exhibition design. Finally, it addresses
the lengthy effort of graphic designers in Milan to negotiate their professional identity and the boundaries of their practice with industrial designers and exponents of the design culture at large.

Given its basic premise that professionalisation is an ongoing process, the book does not presume to offer either a comprehensive history of Italian graphic design or a final assessment of the articulation of
graphic design in Milan. What it does do, however, is to highlight tensions
and contradictions and focus on the struggle of graphic practitioners to
articulate what graphic design was. In adopting an approach that 'combines detailed formalist analysis with contextual understanding of graphic
design in action', the following pages seek to respond to the call for
historians to read graphic design in the cultural context and to open the
discipline to different audiences.[4] Overall, they provide the reader with a
historically integrated, archive-based and outward-looking framework for

the understanding of graphic design history as an integral part of the history of design, visual culture and cultural history.

Locating graphic design in Italian design history

Italian design has been celebrated through scholarly books, glossy catalogues and blockbuster exhibitions. Nevertheless, its history is incomplete and displays a bias towards product design and an emphasis on design production.[5] Graphic design has been downplayed, if not blatantly ignored, in general accounts on Italian design. It still holds a marginal position in the historiography, even if it is gradually gaining greater recognition. When not addressed directly, graphic design has entered the discourse via the attention given to mediation.[6] Since the early 2000s, histories of Italian design have begun drawing attention to advertisements, promotional pamphlets, catalogues and magazines, that is, to the 'symbolic universe where consumers met products', for which graphic designers deserve at least acknowledgement.[7]

Even the most cursory glance through the historiography on Italian graphic design reveals a marked tendency to concentrate on changing graphic styles as exemplified in works, mainly posters, by prominent and almost exclusively male designers, or in the visual communication strategies of mainstream companies. While we know a great deal about a few prominent male designers, information about minor figures, female designers, graphic designers as a group and their professional framework, is inadequate. Current literature includes a plethora of monographic books on celebrities of Italian graphic design, often written by, or in collaboration with, the designers themselves, or their next of kin.[8] These books exhibit a propensity for self-celebration. They repeat well-known anecdotes and report successful stories only. Often richly illustrated, they tend to consider visual artefacts as self-evident sources.

Instead, in a countervailing trend, Italian design historians have, since the mid-2000s, been paving the way towards a critical rewriting of Italian graphic design history; one that moves beyond celebratory hagiography and focuses on design practice, professional networks, mediating channels, technology and designer–client relationships, to challenge existing narratives through a meticulous study of primary literature and archival materials.[9] This book follows in their footsteps. It provides a critical and non-hagiographic study of the history of Italian graphic design and uncovers its contribution to Italy's cultural, social, economic and political fabric. It combines design history with cultural history and social sciences to afford a new reading of everyday practice, professionalisation, vocational training and modernism.

Gendered approaches to Italian graphic design have also appeared since the mid-2010s and significant steps have been taken to redress the gender imbalance in the literature. Monographic publications, exhibitions and awards have brought to light the work of women graphic designers whose presence had been overlooked and contribution underacknowledged. This is the case with Lora Lamm, Lica Covo Steiner – both briefly mentioned in these pages – Anita Klinz and Simonetta Ferrante, among others.[10] But there is still work to be done regarding their experience and representation. The graphic designers discussed in this book are all men. This gendered narrative is a by-product of the book's focus on professionalisation. Many scholars and practitioners in the design fields have remarked upon the system of exclusion on the basis of gender, as well as class, ethnicity and discipline, implicit in the notion of professionalism.[11] In Italy from the 1930s to the mid-1960s, graphic design discourses were male dominated. Nevertheless, I provide some context that contributes to a better understanding of the gendered nature of the practice, by pointing to the access to education and employment for women at the time, as well as their status within the wider Italian socio-cultural context.

Despite its focus on the local, regional and national scene, my study is not confined to the geographical boundaries of the Italian nation-state, but adopts a transnational approach to national design histories.[12] I connect Italian graphic design with Switzerland, Germany, the UK, the US, Mexico and Japan. This network resulted from a meticulous analysis of primary sources and individuals' personal actions that enabled me to map the movement of people, objects and ideas across national borders. In exploring the professionalisation of graphic design as a transnational phenomenon which assumed distinctive characteristics within different local scenarios, I aim to answer the call by design historians Kjetil Fallan and Grace Lees-Maffei 'to produce internationally situated investigations in which national design histories are understood within international contexts'.[13] As such, my focus on graphic design and designers in Milan seeks to improve knowledge about the local and national scene, 'seen as enriching and adding complexity to the debate' on design professionalisation across countries.[14] If, as asserted by design historians Glenn Adamson, Giorgio Riello and Sarah Teasley, professionalisation is an 'implicitly transnational' phenomenon, I provide evidence here that the simultaneous focus on different geographical scales is key for its analysis.[15] Throughout this book, comparative analyses of domestic and international debates and experiences demonstrate that graphic designers from different geographies faced similar issues, shared related experiences and adopted comparable strategies. While establishing the practice locally, Milan's graphic designers also partook in the articulation of a graphic design discourse shared beyond Italy's national borders.

Graphic design in context

At issue, however, is more than just the secondary position of graphic design in Italian design history, and the tendency of previous scholarship to adopt aesthetic perspectives and person-centred approaches with a focus on design celebrities. As the curators of the 5th edition of the Triennale Design Museum in 2012 – *TDM5: Grafica Italiana* – bluntly put it, 'the history of Italian graphics has never been translated, mediated and publicised among people not working in the industry'.[16] In other words, the few publications and exhibitions devoted to it tend to have been written and curated by practitioners-historians, and to have addressed primarily an audience of graphic designers.

Criticism aimed at the inward-looking attitude of graphic design histories has also been made outside Italy.[17] Since the early 2010s, a number of graphic design historians have called for their peers to adopt an outward-looking perspective. According to Rick Poynor, the only chance for graphic design history to become a fully fledged academic discipline is for it 'to be framed and presented in ways that relate to the concerns of viewers who are not designers – that is, most viewers'.[18] Carlo Vinti suggested a similar strategy when asserting that 'what is required is a critical discourse, which is not intended solely for graphic designers; which can speak to a wider public by exploiting the crucial role and relevance of graphics within contemporary culture and economics.'[19] It is from such a perspective that I seek to contribute to the current status of graphic design history. Rooted in the history of design, cultural history, visual and material culture studies and semiotics, I attempt to open the discipline to different audiences in order to avoid confining it to a niche of experts and stakeholders from within the field.

Practice in progress

A sociological stance on design practices is not new to the history of design.[20] In the late 1990s, Jonathan M. Woodham remarked upon the tendency of history of design scholarship to obscure 'much of the wider picture of the professional status of the designer and the role of design in industry through its general focus on successful partnerships between designers and industry'.[21] Meanwhile, the 'wider picture' has been put to the fore as design scholars have investigated the markers paving the path to professionalisation: the setting up of professional organisations, the institution of recognised training and educational standards, the establishment of a self-administered code of conduct and ethics, the identification and articulation of a shared body of skills and knowledge, and the development of a professional network.[22]

Design practices are here understood as 'social practices, enacted, performed and negotiated through media, public institutions and professional organizations'.[23] As ever-evolving social constructs, whose understanding is temporally and spatially specific, design practices are neither fixed nor immutable but constantly in formation: an open-ended work-in-progress. I approach graphic designers as self-conscious actors, drafting and negotiating their collective identity between and across different groups, including neighbouring practices, the industry and the broader public, and constantly re-editing their identity in order to address changing socio-cultural, economic and political environments, adapt to evolving technologies and reflect shifting agendas and design discourses.

The work of a number of sociologists and historians of the profession from the late 1970s onwards affords the theoretical background upon which this book is built. While Magali Sarfatti Larson's analysis of what she calls 'the production of the professional producer' focuses on the power, autonomy and prestige of professions, Andrew Abbott stresses their relational nature, dependence on external factors and vulnerability.[24] Both approaches have been key to developing my argument, in particular Abbott's concept of jurisdictional boundaries in perpetual dispute between neighbouring occupations, which I have applied to graphic designers' conflictual relationship with the adjacent professional fields of advertising and industrial design. Valérie Fournier goes further in developing the concept of professions as continually contested, never completely established, but rather always under ongoing renegotiation.[25] Throughout this book, I draw on Fournier's ideas of the relational nature of professions and of professionalisation as a device of control and identity articulation. Eliot Freidson's definition of professionalism as being 'when an organised occupation gains the power to determine who is qualified to perform a defined set of tasks, to prevent all others from performing that work, and to control the criteria by which to evaluate performance', guided my own approach to the strategies employed by graphic practitioners to establish the social, economic and cultural value of their practice and to obtain the exclusive right to determine how their work should be performed and evaluated.[26]

Vocational schools and professional organisations

Education and organisational strategies are recurring concerns in the literature on the history and sociology of professions. According to Linda Clarke and Christopher Winch, education acts as a gatekeeper, an inclusion–exclusion device that certifies members' competences and expertise, while Sarfatti Larson emphasises the 'democratic potential' of standardised training in the belief that it increases a profession's appeal to outsiders and thereby encourages newcomers.[27] Etienne Wenger's concept of 'communities of practice' also provides a stimulating thinking tool for interrogating education as a situated and social process of identity formation. Learning – and I would add teaching as well – is the 'very process of being engaged in, and participating in developing, an ongoing practice'.[28]

The founding of professional organisations is yet another important stage in the process of professionalisation. 'Until members of an occupation realise their collective existence as a group', sociologist Geoffrey Millerson argued, 'the movement toward professionalisation cannot really begin. Yet, a plea for professional status remains insufficient. The "cause" must be realised and recognised by society, in part or in whole.'[29] Professional bodies promote a sense of community between members, set standards and codes of conduct, offer visibility and improve public understanding of the profession. In chapter 5, I approach organisations as 'internally structured groups that are located in complex networks of intergroup relations characterized by power, status, and prestige differentials'.[30] Drawing on social identity theory, I understand social identities as necessarily defined in comparative terms at a collective level.[31] As such, I explore organisational strategies as a process of self-categorisation during which members identify themselves with an in-group and draw comparisons between this and relevant out-groups from which they differentiate themselves on valued dimensions of comparison.[32]

A word on modernism

The articulation of graphic design practice went hand in hand with critical debates around modernism. Given the ubiquity of the term 'modernism', as well as the ambiguity of its meaning, it is worth clarifying that here it is conceived in the following three ways: as a formal change, as a conceptual shift in design practices and methodologies, and as a vehicle of ideologies and values beyond the design realm.[33]

First, I situate modernism within the history of graphic design and hence understand it as a set of formal guidelines articulated in the interwar period by advocates of the New Typography and later developed in what has become known as International (Typographic) Style.[34] This entailed the adoption of cutting-edge graphic techniques and visual language that favoured photomontage over illustrations, sans-serif over serif typefaces, asymmetrical and grid-based layouts over the centred page. Secondly, I interpret modernism as a move away from the graphic arts tradition towards a new approach to visual communication, one which prioritised design methodology and problem solving over originality and artistic personality, and favoured the design of a comprehensive communication system over sporadic commissions. Thirdly, I also take into consideration the specific belief systems, behavioural concerns and social responsibilities associated with modernism over time, namely its alleged humanist and left-wing stance.

The connotative potential of modernist visual vocabulary is here inter-rogated in light of the integration of modernist imagery and techniques into the propaganda and official culture of the Fascist regime. As we shall see in the first three chapters of this book, modernist design was eminently compatible with Italian Fascism. It furnished the regime with a striking, modern imagery. Benito Mussolini's pluralistic cultural policies also attracted the attention of those who were searching for a way to reconcile modernism with fascism outside Italy – particularly those whose lives were threatened and/or careers hindered under Nazi rules. In chapters 3 and 4, I explore further the ideological malleability of modernism by addressing the rewriting of the Bauhaus legacy in order to advance cultural policies during the Cold War period.

Everyday Fascism

To make my objectives clear, this is not a book about Italian Fascism or fas-cist visual culture. Nevertheless, I wish to suggest that both topics can be seen afresh when viewed through the lens of graphic design and design-ers. The common misconception whereby the terms 'fascism', 'modern art' and 'architecture' were understood as opposed to one another and mutually exclusive has, since the 1980s, been revised by scholarship in history, art and architectural history.[35] Histories of Italian design, and in particular graphic design, are still catching up, as many either betray a cer-tain discomfort in dealing with the shadowy relationship between design and the Fascist regime, or they avoid the issue altogether. A century later, individuals' engagement with Fascism is still a sensitive topic and the silence of literature is often due to the censorship of relatives who prevent the publication of content and images that might link their family members to the regime. With this book, I seek to overcome scholars' reluctance to admit that major figures of Italian graphic design produced works that served as vehicles for fascist propaganda, and their tendency to focus on the formal aspects in order to claim the independence of visual artefacts from any political dimension.[36] To this end, I consider the intended use and patronage of visual artefacts and explore the ways in which graphic designers negotiated their professional identity under the Fascist regime and then re-adapted it to the new political circumstances of post-war Italy.

Rather than pointing fingers, I am interested in showing a more subjective side to Fascism by looking at its impact on everyday life and practice. The complexity of the relationship between professionals and intellectuals and the Fascist regime cannot be reduced to a mere dichot-omy between fascism and antifascism. Instead, account needs to be taken of what historian and cultural critic Ruth Ben-Ghiat has defined as 'a web of tacit regulation [that] kept intellectuals in check and encouraged them to practice self-censorship'.[37] Drawing on perspectives developed by historians of everyday life, the first three chapters of this book look into individual experiences and explore the regime's use of coercion and control over access to social benefits as tools to condition people's attitudes and behaviour, and to set a framework of limits within which they had to navigate their everyday lives during the twenty years of fascist rule.[38] As expressed by historian Paul Corner, 'popular reaction to fascism ... cannot be judged ... by the same criteria that would be applied to popular political reactions under democracy'.[39] These were the considerations that I kept at the forefront of my mind when addressing practitioners' attitudes towards Fascism and the choices they made: from subscribing to the fascist trade unions, to participating in exhibitions sponsored by the regime and designing propaganda.

Graphic design and designers in Milan

For this history of graphic designers in Milan, I have made use of a wide range of sources and documents. Research for each chapter began with a detailed survey of graphic and industrial design, architecture and interior design magazines of the time. As vehicles for a particular message, and as messages in themselves, magazines demand scholars adopt a comparative reading of textual content and visual form.[40] Graphic design magazines were primary media for generating and mediating the self-definition of the practice: they acted as forums for discussion of new ideas and technologies; they were a means of inspiring collective identity and pride, and defining a shared viewpoint; they functioned as instruments for raising readers' educational level and refining their cultural tastes.[41] Beyond the textual content, graphic design magazines also acted as a field for testing the latest technological developments in printing and reproduction, and for experimenting with visual compositions. The shared know-how and visual vocabulary between authors, designers and the readership favoured multiple-level readings and secured the understanding of implicit meanings. Together with magazines, what is to follow is built upon a close reading of a variety of archival materials – from private and business correspondence to meeting minutes, from school syllabi to finance reports, from sales invoices to design sketches – and visual artefacts. These latter are approached as both communication artefacts with their own function and purpose, and also as a visual expression of design methodologies and aesthetic principles.

Organised into five chapters, this book follows a loose chronological structure. The first two chapters focus on the interwar and war periods. The timeframe of chapter 3 spans from the 1930s to the 1950s. The last two chapters explore reconstruction and the post-war period. While the broad chronological timeframe, on one hand, helped bring out various continuities between the interwar and post-war periods, on the other, it also enabled me to highlight and critically address significant changes. In each chapter I address different but mutually relevant aspects of the emergence and articulation of graphic design practice, while gradually introducing the various actors and key players involved in the process: design education is addressed in chapters 1 and 4, everyday design practice and networks are explored in chapters 2 and 5, and mediation is the focus of chapter 3. A series of interrelated case studies bring to light lesser-known narratives and neglected actors of Italian design, while providing an original retelling of well-known stories and offering new perspectives on protagonists of the historiographical canon.

Chapter 1 explores the infancy of graphic design education in interwar Italy and traces the lineage of graphic design back to typography and the printing trade. It centres on the relationship between professionalisation and vocational training, and argues that practitioners' interest in education and agreement on a shared skillset and body of knowledge attest to the gradual articulation of their new collective identity. Focusing on the Scuola del Libro (School of the Book) in Milan, the chapter employs the changing of curricula and graphic output as a lens to reassess the debate on graphic practice and the modernisation of Italian graphics as featured in specialist magazines of the period.

Chapter 2 investigates Studio Boggeri and introduces advertising as an actor in the professionalisation of graphic design. It provides new insights into the complexities of the studio system and examines how and why the studio promoted the spread of modernist techniques – photography above all – and aesthetics in interwar Italy. The chapter explores strategies of self-representation, working and commissioning practices from the studio's foundation in 1933 to the early years of post-war reconstruction. It looks into Boggeri's recruiting strategies and addresses his bias for Swiss-trained practitioners. Grounding Studio Boggeri within the larger socio-cultural context and historical and political circumstances, chapter 2 captures the impact of Fascism on everyday practice.

By exploring the presence of graphic design at the Milan Triennale from 1933 to 1957, chapter 3 traces the gradual articulation, negotiation and mediation of graphic design's public image. It approaches the Triennale, first, as a mediating device between graphic designers, their clients and the general public, and, secondly, as a commissioning body. Chapter 3 also discusses the ways in which exhibition design favoured experimental approaches to graphic design. Covering about twenty-five years, it shows continuity in the drafting of graphic design practice between the interwar and post-war periods. At the same time, it addresses the adaptation of design discourses to changing political circumstances. For instance, it traces the critical debates that gradually associated modernist aesthetics with the notion of 'good taste', while uncovering the malleability of modernist graphics' connotative value. Indeed, an analysis of fascist political exhibitions and propaganda displays brings into question the association of modernist aesthetics with democratic and left-wing ideals.

Building on approaches to design education outlined in chapter 1, chapter 4 suggests that, for Milan's graphic designers, teaching was a means of questioning and then collectively defining their practice. Moreover, it contextualises the case studies of the Scuola del Libro and the Convitto Scuola Rinascita (Rebirth Boarding School) in Milan within a wider international movement to create reform-oriented educational institutes and examines education as a political activity intended to train practitioners who were aware of the social impact of design and capable of assuming responsibility for it. Looking at international design conferences, design organisations, magazines and educational experiences abroad, the chapter shows how in the post-war period education was a key factor in the broader quest to imbue design with social value and cultural meaning.

The last chapter analyses the problematic position of graphic design in between advertising and design. Considering graphic designers' multiple social identities and fields of practice, it investigates graphic designers' changing organisational strategies. To this end chapter 5 addresses conflicts, negotiations, compromises and temporary alliances between the professional associations, the Aiap, Associazione Italiana Artisti Pubblicitari (Italian Association of Advertising Artists) and the ADI, Associazione per il Design Industriale (Association for Industrial Design). While looking at the local scene, it analyses transnational circuits in order to investigate the ways in which Milan's graphic designers participated in, and responded to, the development of a new way of thinking in visual communication shared beyond national borders.

Together, these five chapters uncover one of the long-neglected aspects of Italian design. Recounting the story of the emergence and articulation of graphic design practice in Milan, they show that Italian design history cannot be understood without considering the role that graphic design has played in it. By reading graphic design practice and artefacts in context, this book also suggests that cultural histories of Italy can gain new perspectives from looking through the lens of graphic design and designers.

Notes

1 C. Dradi, *Millenovecentotrentatre: nasce a Milano la grafica moderna* (Milan: Ufficio Stampa Comune di Milano, 1973); S. Bignami (ed.), *1933: un anno del Novecento a Milano* (Geneva; Milan: Skira, 2001); A. Colonetti (ed.), *Grafica e design a Milano, 1933–2000* (Milan: Editrice Abitare Segesta, 2001).

2 J. Foot, *Milan since the Miracle: City, Culture and Identity* (Oxford; New York: Berg, 2001), 109–34; R. Riccini, 'Disegno industriale in Lombardia: un modello per il Made in Italy', in D. Bigazzi and M. Meriggi (eds), *Storia d'Italia. Le regioni dall'Unità a oggi: la Lombardia* (Turin: Einaudi, 2001), pp. 1164–93.

3 G. Montecchi (ed.), *La città dell'editoria: dal libro tipografico all'opera digitale (1880–2020)* (Geneva; Milan: Skira, 2001); P. Ortoleva, 'A geography of the media since 1945', in D. Forgacs and R. Lumley (eds), *Italian Cultural Studies: An Introduction* (New York: Oxford University Press, 1996), pp. 185–98.

4 G. Lees-Maffei, 'Reading graphic design in the expanded field: An introduction', in G. Lees-Maffei and N. P. Maffei (eds), *Reading Graphic Design in Cultural Context* (London: Bloomsbury, 2019), p. 9.

5 M. Dalla Mura and C. Vinti, 'A historiography of Italian design', in G. Lees-Maffei and K. Fallan (eds), *Made in Italy: Rethinking a Century of Italian Design* (London: Bloomsbury, 2014), pp. 35–55.

6 P. Sparke, 'A modern identity for a new nation: Design in Italy since 1860', in Z. G. Barański and R. J. West (eds), *The Cambridge Companion to Modern Italian Culture* (Cambridge; New York: Cambridge University Press, 2001), pp. 265–81; K. Fallan, 'Annus mirabilis: 1954, Alberto Rosselli and the institutionalisation of design mediation', in Lees-Maffei and Fallan (eds), *Made in Italy*, pp. 255–70; C. Rossi, *Crafting Design in Italy: From Post-war to Postmodernism* (Manchester: Manchester University Press, 2015); E. Dellapiana, *Il design e l'invenzione del Made in Italy* (Turin: Einaudi, 2022).

7 M. Piazza (ed.), *La grafica del Made in Italy: comunicazione e aziende del design 1950–1980* (Milan: Edizioni Aiap, 2012), p. 11.

8 For a critique of the emergence of the monograph as a canonical narrative in graphic design history, see J. Drucker, 'Philip Meggs and Richard Hollis: Models of graphic design history', *Design and Culture*, 1:1 (2009), 51–78; T. Triggs, 'Designing graphic design history', *Journal of Design History*, 22:4 (2009), 325–40.

9 See in particular the work of Carlo Vinti which is referred to frequently throughout this book.

10 See R. Riccini (ed.), *Angelica e Bradamante: le donne del design* (Padua: Il Poligrafo, 2017); A. Steiner, *Lica Covo Steiner* (Mantua: Corraini, 2015); L. Lamm and N. Ossanna Cavadini (eds), *Lora Lamm. Grafica a Milano 1953–1963* (Cinisello Balsamo: Silvana Editoriale, 2013); L. Pitoni, *Ostinata bellezza. Anita Klinz, la prima art director italiana* (Milan: Mondadori, 2022); C. Cerritelli and N. Ossanna Cavadini (eds), *Simonetta Ferrante. La memoria del visibile: segno, colore, ritmo e calligrafie* (Cinisello Balsamo: Silvana Editoriale, 2016). Since 2012 the Aiap has promoted a biennial international award open to women designers: AWDA, Aiap Women in Design Award, www.aiap-awda.com.

11 J. Seddon and S. Worden, 'Women designers in Britain in the 1920s and 1930s: Defining the professional and redefining design', *Journal of Design History*, 8:3 (1995), 177–93; J. Seddon, 'Mentioned but denied significance: Women designers and the professionalization of design in Britain, 1920–1951', *Gender and History*, 12:2 (2000), 426–47; G. Beegan and P. Atkinson, 'Professionalism, amateurism and the boundaries of design', *Journal of Design History*, 21:4 (2008), 305–13.

12 K. Fallan and G. Lees-Maffei, 'Introduction: National design histories in an age of globalization', in K. Fallan and G. Lees-Maffei (eds), *Designing Worlds: National Design Histories in an Age of Globalization* (New York: Berghahn Books, 2016), p. 8.

13 K. Fallan and G. Lees-Maffei, 'Real imagined communities: National narratives and the globalization of Design History', *Design Issues*, 32:1 (2016), 12.

14 A. Calvera, 'Local, regional, national, global and feedback: Several issues to be faced with constructing regional narratives', *Journal of Design History*, 18:4 (2005), 375.

15 G. Adamson, G. Riello and S. Teasley, 'Introduction: Towards global design history', in G. Adamson, G. Riello and S. Teasley (eds), *Global Design History* (London; New York: Routledge, 2011), p. 5.

16 G. Camuffo, M. Piazza and C. Vinti, 'TDM5. Un museo per una storia ancora da scrivere', in G. Camuffo, M. Piazza and C. Vinti (eds), *TDM5: Grafica Italiana* (Milan: Corraini Edizioni, 2012), p. 26.

17 T. Triggs, 'Graphic design history: Past, present, and future', *Design Issues*, 27:1 (2011), 3–6; Triggs, 'Designing graphic design history'; V. Margolin, 'Narrative problems of graphic design history', *Visible Language*, 28:3 (1994), 234–43.

18 R. Poynor, 'Out of the studio: Graphic design history and visual studies', *Design Observer* (1 October 2011), www.designobserver.com/feature/out-of-the-studio-graphic-design-history-and-visual-studies/24048, accessed 31 May 2023.

19 C. Vinti, 'Graphic designers, people with problems. Some thoughts from Italy', in G. Camuffo and M. Dalla Mura (eds), *Graphic Design World/Words* (Milan: Electa, 2011), p. 88.

20 D. Wang and A. O. Ilham, 'Holding creativity together: A sociological theory of the design professions', *Design Issues*, 25:1 (2009), 5–21; D. A. Guerin and C. S. Martin, 'The career cycle approach to defining the interior design profession's body of knowledge', *Journal of Interior Design*, 30:2 (2004), 1–22.

21 J. M. Woodham, *Twentieth Century Design* (Oxford; New York: Oxford University Press, 1997), p. 167.

22 See, for example, L. Armstrong and F. McDowell (eds), *Fashioning Professionals: Identity and Representation at Work in the Creative Industries* (London: Bloomsbury, 2018); G. Lees-Maffei, 'Introduction: Professionalization as a focus in interior design history', *Journal of Design History*, 21:1 (2008), 1–18; L. Armstrong, *The Industrialized Designer: Gender, Identity and Professionalisation in Britain and the US, 1930–1980* (Manchester: Manchester University Press, 2024).

23 L. Armstrong and F. McDowell, 'Introduction: Fashioning professionals: History, theory and methods', in Armstrong and McDowell (eds), *Fashioning Professionals*, p. 1.

24 M. Sarfatti Larson, *The Rise of Professionalism: A Sociological Analysis* (Berkeley; Los Angeles; London: University of California Press, 1977), p. 50; A. Abbott, *The System of Professions: An Essay on the Division of Expert Labour* (Chicago; London: University of Chicago Press, 1988).

25 V. Fournier, 'The appeal to "professionalism" as a disciplinary mechanism', *Social Review*, 47:2 (1999), 280–307.

26 E. Freidson, *Professionalism: The Third Logic* (Chicago: University of Chicago Press, 2001), p. 12.

27 L. Clarke and C. Winch, 'Introduction', in L. Clarke and C. Winch (eds), *Vocational Education: International Approaches, Developments and Systems* (London; New York: Routledge, 2007), pp. 1–17; Sarfatti Larson, *The Rise of Professionalism*, p. 42.

28 E. Wenger, *Communities of Practice: Learning, Meaning, and Identity* (Cambridge: Cambridge University Press, 1998), p. 95.

29 G. Millerson, *The Qualifying Associations: A Study in Professionalization* (London: Routledge & Kegan Paul, 1964), p. 12. On professional organisations, see also E. Freidson, *Professional Powers: A Study of the Institutionalization of Formal Knowledge* (Chicago; London: University of Chicago Press, 1986), pp. 196–9; Abbott, *The System of Professions*, pp. 79–83.

30 M. A. Hogg and D. J. Terry, 'Social identity and self-categorization processes in organizational contexts', *Academy of Management Review*, 25:1 (2000), 121.

31 S. Reicher, 'The context of social identity: Domination, resistance, and change', *Political Psychology*, 25:6 (2004), 929.

32 S. Worchel, J. Iuzzini, D. Coutant and M. Ivaldi, 'A multidimensional model of identity: Relating individual and group identities to intergroup behaviour', in D. Capozza and R. Brown (eds), *Social Identity Processes: Trends in Theory and Research* (London; Thousand Oaks; New Delhi: SAGE Publications, 2000), pp. 15–32.

33 C. Wilk, 'Introduction: What was Modernism?', in C. Wilk (ed.), *Modernism: Designing a New World, 1914–1939* (London: V&A Publications, 2006), pp. 12–21; K. Fallan, *Design History: Understanding Theory and Method* (Oxford; New York: Berg, 2010), pp. 105–12.

34 On modernism in the realm of graphic design, see R. Hollis, *Swiss Graphic Design: The Origins and Growth of an International Style, 1920–1965* (New Haven; London: Yale University Press, 2006), pp. 9–13; J. Aynsley, *Graphic Design in Germany 1890–1945* (London: Thames & Hudson, 2000), pp. 103–9 and 156–77; R. Hollis, *Graphic Design: A Concise History* (London: Thames & Hudson, 1996), pp. 37–75 and 130–78.

35 D. Ghirardo, 'Italian architects and fascist politics: An evaluation of the rationalist's role in regime building', *Journal of the Society of Architectural Historians*, 39:2 (1980), 109–27; S. Falasca-Zamponi, *Fascist Spectacle: The Aesthetics of Power in Mussolini's Italy* (Berkeley; Los Angeles; London: University of California Press, 1997). For a historiographical perspective, see M. Antliff, 'Fascism, modernism, and modernity', *The Art Bulletin*, 84:1 (2002), 148–69.

36 Exceptions to the mainstream discomfort of historians of Italian graphic design in dealing with the relationship between graphic design and Italian Fascism are still rare and include A. Colizzi, 'Bruno Munari and the Invention of Modern Graphic Design in Italy, 1928–1945' (PhD dissertation, University of Leiden, Leiden, 2011); C. Vinti, 'The New Typography in Fascist Italy. Between internationalism and the search for a national style', in M. Cortat and D. Fornari (eds), *Archigraphiæ: Rationalist Lettering and Architecture in Fascist Rome* (Renens: Ecal, 2020), pp. 49–66.

37 R. Ben-Ghiat, *Fascist Modernities: Italy, 1922–1945* (Berkeley; Los Angeles; London: University of California Press, 2001), p. 9.

38 J. Arthurs, M. Ebner and K. Ferris (eds), *The Politics of Everyday Life in Fascist Italy. Outside the State?* (New York: Palgrave, 2017); P. Corner, 'Collaboration, complicity, and evasion under Italian Fascism', in A. Lüdtke (ed.), *Everyday Life in Mass Dictatorship* (New York: Palgrave, 2016), pp. 75–93.

39 P. Corner, 'Italian Fascism: Whatever happened to dictatorship?', *Journal of Modern History*, 74:2 (2002), 349.

40 J. Aynsley and K. Forde (eds), *Design and the Modern Magazine* (Manchester; New York: Manchester University Press, 2007).

41 E. M. Thomson, *The Origins of Graphic Design in America: 1870–1920* (New Haven; London: Yale University Press, 1997), pp. 36–59.

1

Vocational education and the typographic roots of graphic design

In September 1923 the Milanese typography and graphic arts magazine *Risorgimento Grafico* launched the 'Referendum per l'insegnamento professionale' (Referendum for professional training).[1] Two contrasting models of vocational schools were up for consideration. On the one hand, the 'scuola-industria' (industry-school) produced goods for the market or collaborated with external companies. On the other hand, the 'scuola-officina' (workshop-school) operated outside market rules and supported the autonomy of education above commercial concerns. Nine months later, the final report concluded that thirteen of the twenty-two contributors favoured the workshop- over the industry-school. Only two pressed for a tight relationship between school and industry. The remaining seven opted for in-between positions.[2] The promoters of the referendum were pleased with what they considered the success of the initiative, not least because it had 'involved the entire group of bona fide experts and ... kept away the usual know-alls'.[3] Self-satisfaction aside, the involvement of vocational school educators and consultants, typographers, owners of printing firms and graphic industrialists, based in Milan, Turin, Florence and Rome, attests to the growing self-awareness of the graphic profession. Moreover, it suggests that vocational education was felt as a pressing issue that needed to be addressed in practice.

The relationship between professionalism and specialist training is at the core of this chapter. In it, I investigate the infancy of graphic design education in Italy and examine the changing role and meaning of graphic practice through the lens of vocational training. To this end, the experience of the Scuola del Libro in Milan from the mid-1920s to 1943, when an Allied air raid damaged the premises and forced the school to close temporarily, is analysed as a revealing case study of the interaction between practice and education. The school was an active part of the Milanese printing and typographic scene. It featured regularly in trade journals as a model for vocational training and good graphics. Prominent figures of Italian graphics worked in, studied in or collaborated with it. These included the editor of *Risorgimento Grafico*, Raffaello Bertieri, and the contributors to *Campo Grafico*, also known as 'campisti', whose personal involvement – as director and students/staff members, respectively – is here acknowledged when considering their critical stance. This chapter positions the Scuola del Libro at the centre of interwar debates on vocational education and modernisation of Italian graphics. As such, it does not simply chronicle its activity but argues that the school was used by different groups to promote conflicting agendas. More broadly, it roots graphic design in the lineage of typography and the printing trade by exploring the contribution that typographers, educators in vocational schools, editors of trade journals and workers of the printing industry made to the drafting of graphic design practice.

Educational ambitions

The dispute about vocational training published in *Risorgimento Grafico* between 1923 and 1924 provides a doorway to the historical background and socio-cultural framework of the Scuola del Libro. This debate offers valuable insights into internal disputes over training credentials. Professional schooling, sociologist Eliot Freidson observed, is key to professionalism as it is 'responsible for formalising the particular kind of knowledge and skill claimed by an occupation and for providing an intellectual basis for its jurisdictional claims and relation to other occupations'.[4] Discussions about training credentials are thus evidence that by the time of the referendum the transition from a spontaneous transmission of know-how through on-the-job learning to a standardised training under the control of the occupation was underway.

Supporters of the industry-school stressed the economic benefits of a market-oriented educational institution. Economic self-sufficiency enabled schools to avoid relying on uncertain public and private funding, and it was 'better to sacrifice a bit of *School* for the benefit of *Industry*, rather than shutting up shop due to the lack of adequate financial means'.[5] Yet schools were not to be run as profit-oriented businesses, but rather aimed at earning just enough to cover expenses and break even. Despite their closeness to the industry, schools were expected to be driven exclusively by pedagogical purposes. The goal was to provide pupils with industry-like work experience while testing their skills and knowledge in the safe environment of the school. By contrast, supporters of freeing vocational schools from commercial concerns believed in the far-reaching benefits of the workshop-school. Isolated from the market, workshop-schools promoted experimentation and pursued new knowledge. With their balance between technical training and workers' education, they raised the intellectual and moral level of workers in the printing industry. By fostering personal fulfilment and emancipation, they supported class and social advancement for the benefit of the graphic arts and printing trade as a whole. A shared concern among contributors to the referendum was that an industry-school might actually be detrimental to the printing industry itself. They feared such schools might exploit the unpaid and unskilled pupils to undersell products and be competitive in a market that was already suffering from unfair competition mostly blamed on amateurs. As professionalism was considered the antidote to unfair competition, for a vocational school to be the cause of unfair competition would be self-destructive.

When put in its historical context, the enquiry conducted by *Risorgimento Grafico* can be seen as the expression of a moment of self-reflection favoured by contemporary changes in the national educational system.[6] The need for vocational training had been felt in many industrial sectors in Italy since the mid-nineteenth century, as a consequence of production specialisation and technology advancement.[7] In the graphic and printing industries, the demand for specialised workers stemmed from the overall growth and mechanisation of the sector, whose industrialisation had sped up since the unification of Italy in 1861.[8] According to the 1859 Casati Law, vocational schools – that is, industrial schools, arts and crafts schools and vocational schools for women – fell under the jurisdiction of the Ministry of Agriculture, Industry and Commerce.[9] They had administrative autonomy and were supported by the municipalities, the local Chamber of Commerce and a number of local entities such as trade unions and industrialists' consortia. Their founding often depended on private initiatives and their activity responded to the needs of the local area. At the time of the referendum, the Italian system of education was being reformed according to the Gentile Reform of 1923.[10] With its elitist conception of education and focus on the humanities, the reform conceived by the fascist minister of education, Giovanni Gentile, had an overall marginal impact on vocational education, with the exception of the industrial arts sector.[11] This was moved in 1928 under the jurisdiction of the Ministry of Public Education – eventually renamed the Ministry of National Education in 1929 – and reorganised into art schools and institutes (secondary level) and higher institutes for the artistic industries (higher education).

If we read the results of the referendum through sociological lenses, the request for training to take place outside the market represented a critical step forward on the path to professionalisation. The autonomy of training can be seen as supporting the occupation as a whole, since 'the formal institutionalization of teaching … provides professions with a powerful resource by which to maintain and expand a defensible jurisdiction, a resource that encourages the systematic refinement, growth, and legitimation of their discipline'.[12] The preference for the workshop-school model was in line with the agenda of the Milanese printing trade unions, which had distinguished themselves as the most active in campaigning for workers' education. Concerning itself 'in teaching the social sciences to [those] who seek to use that knowledge for class, and possibly social, advancement', workers' education differed from mere vocational training.[13] While they championed continuous training in order to keep skills and knowledge up to date with the ever-changing printing technologies, Milanese trade unions also sought to nurture their members' intellectual and moral development, as well as their class awareness, with a view to social advancement.[14] But, as we have seen in this section, exactly how continuous training and intellectual, moral and social growth were to be attained through vocational education was up for debate.

Collective identities

Graphic practitioners' educational ambitions went hand in hand with the articulation of new forms of collective identity. From the perspective of social identity theory, collective or group identity is 'the image which a group has in the context of other groups'.[15] It entails a process of self-categorisation and the identification of a set of norms, values and beliefs that becomes associated with the in-group, and it is defined in comparative terms against relevant out-groups from which it seeks to differentiate itself.[16] As design historian Carlo Vinti argued, interwar internal debates were articulated through a 'dialectical confrontation between typographers and non-typographers, between the tradition of the art of printing and the numerous outsiders who were invading the field' of printed communication.[17] These outsiders were artists, architects, advertisers, writers and many other dilettantes with diverse backgrounds. The main concern arising from the confrontation was the need for a division of labour, that is, for 'the organization and coordination of the relations between workers performing different but interconnected specializations'.[18] In the typographic workshop, the boundaries of specialisation in question were those that demarcated the practitioners in charge of the design process from those responsible for its execution.

The issue was to decide in whose hands the design should be and what set of skills and knowledge this practitioner should have. But, first of all, what was this practitioner to be called? 'Operaio-artista' (labourer-artist), 'bozzettista' (layout expert), 'artista grafico' (graphic artist), 'regista della stampa' (printing director), 'architetto del libro' (book architect), 'tipografo artista' (typography artist) and 'progettista grafico' (graphic designer) are among the many terms that appeared in, and disappeared from, the pages of trade journals from the period. Each term corresponds to a somewhat different perspective on the ongoing articulation of graphic design practice. Nevertheless, whatever the specific differences of definition, they all include references to vocational education. In this section, I explain some of these terms by identifying their skillset and tools, the outcomes of their practice and their relationship with neighbouring fields of practice.

Typography and fine arts intersected in the professional profile of the graphic artist. This was a new professional figure who collaborated with the typographer. Raffaello Bertieri described the graphic artist as someone 'with a better training and wider competence than those acquirable in a workshop [who] could conceive new page layouts, fresher compositions and less mundane artefacts, and livelier and more effective arrangements of colour'.[19] The new type of practitioner described in *Risorgimento Grafico* was familiar with typography and possessed both technical skills and artistic sensibility. In contrast to the painter trained at the Beaux Arts academies who was 'utterly unfamiliar with any notion of graphic technology', the graphic artist was 'the perfect technician and the perfect aesthete'.[20] According to the campisti, the new aesthetic of Italian graphics was based on the alliance between graphic artists and typographers. A good understanding of modern art, and 'a truthful and deep "awareness of the craft"' were two prerequisites for a productive collaboration.[21] With their balance between technical and humanistic classes, vocational schools were held responsible for the success of this collaboration.

Within the pages of *Campo Grafico*, the definition of the graphic artist echoed back to the editors' call for collaborative efforts between graphics, avant-garde art and rationalist architecture. In support of this call, Attilio Rossi explained that geometric abstraction and modern typography shared similar concerns, as they both aimed 'to create aesthetic emotion on a surface through geometric elements': the abstract artist by arranging colours and geometric forms on the canvas; the modern typographer by balancing text, blank spaces and pictures on the page.[22] In a brief account of the most recent developments in Italian graphics, Rossi compared abstract paintings with examples of magazine page layouts (see figure 1.1). The featured exemplars were conceived by Guido Modiano and Edoardo Persico. Whereas the former was a typographer, type designer, printer and graphics critic, the latter came from outside the printing trade. Persico was a writer, art and architecture critic, and editor of the architecture magazine *Casabella*, who eventually became a prominent figure in the renovation of Italian graphics. The magazine page layouts selected by Rossi illustrate a significant innovation of Italian graphics, namely the two-page spread conceived as a single layout, also known as 'due pagine in una' (two pages in one).

The terms 'book architect' and 'typography artist' add more pieces to the mosaic of graphic practitioners' collective identity. They raise further questions concerning the tension between arts and graphics, between creativity and technique, and between insiders and outsiders of typography and the printing trade. Bertieri described the book architects as 'artists

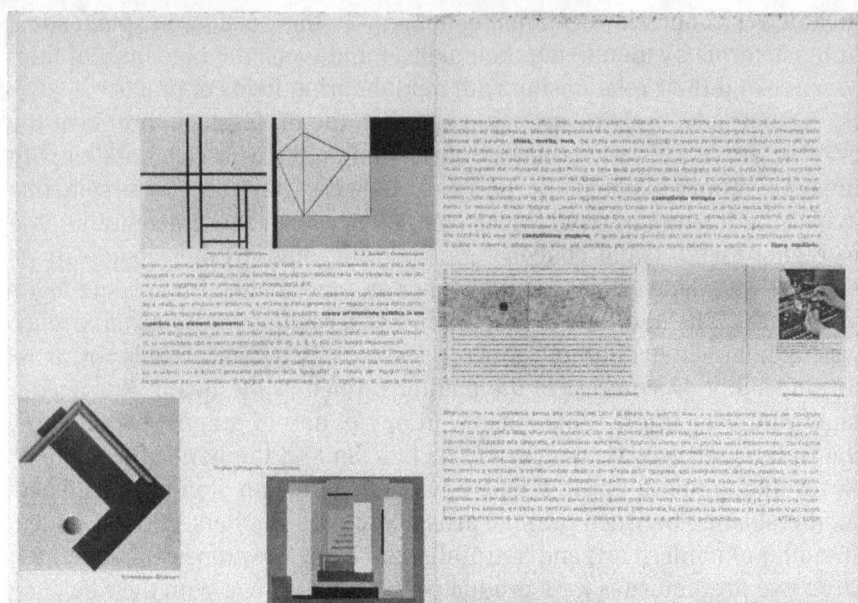

1.1 Double-page spread from Attilio Rossi's article 'L'evoluzione della tipografia in Italia', *Campo Grafico*, 5:9 (September 1937), 6–7. The article draws a parallel between Geometric Abstraction paintings (clockwise, works by Piet Mondrian, Atanasio Soldati, Virginio Ghiringhelli and Friedrich Vordemberge-Gildewart) and examples of two-pages-in-one layout by Edoardo Persico (left) and Guido Modiano (right).

who, for professional reasons, had the chance to acquire familiarity with the typographical workshop'.[23] The book architects were self-taught and in a privileged position – relieved of the burden of typographic tradition, they favoured experimentation and research. In contrast, the typography artists, who '[came] from the typography trade and [knew] all the tricks and necessities of their craft', were constrained by a technical background and their responsibility towards the reader.[24] In practice, the book architects and typography artists compensated one another. The former freely balanced text and pictures and focused on the overall effect of the new page to create experimental graphic exercises, while the latter adjusted the creative excesses of the book artists to the benefit of readability.

Bertieri's definition of book architects and typography artists triggered a polemical response from Modiano, who raised his voice in typographers' defence. He criticised Bertieri's misuse of the two-pages-in-one layout to illustrate the differences between the two figures. While Bertieri attributed the two-page spread to the book architects, Modiano claimed it for himself, a typography artist. The clarification was more than a mere authorship tussle. Indeed, it can be read as a jurisdictional dispute through 'direct negotiations or struggles with other occupational groups that may claim to be able to perform the same or contiguous and perhaps overlapping tasks in a division of labor'.[25] Modiano was 'reacting against the tendency to consider typographers ... as mere makers, more often than not clumsy and incompetent, of someone else's ideas and projects'.[26] Despite being one of the most vocal supporters of the positive contributions that outsiders could bring to typography and the printing trade, as his close collaboration with Persico attests, Modiano was arguing for a more prominent role for typographers during the design stage. He was against the idea that only book architects could conceive innovative graphic compositions, supposedly thanks to their free spirit. As a matter of fact, it was quite the opposite. The two-page spread stemmed from a thorough rethinking of typographic standards: thus only someone who was well aware of typographical principles and know-how could have conceived it. In other words, Modiano held that only someone who had learned the rules on-the-job, or even better at school, could break them.

The layout experts were a further configuration of the graphic practitioners' collective identity. The sketch was the most indicative tool and method in their hands. First, it was a creative device and an epistemological tool: a means of visualising and generating new ideas by putting down on paper an initial concept to then be adjusted and developed. In the first issue of *Campo Grafico*, in January 1933, Giovanni Peviani proposed some practical methods to convince his readership of the need to introduce design into the typographic process.[27] To support his claim, he argued that the sketch responded to the requirements of modern graphics. Having abandoned the constraints of the symmetrical layout, modern compositions were the outcome of a careful study of the contraposition of graphic units. The sketch enabled practitioners to seek the best balance between text, pictures and blank spaces and helped them to achieve the so-called 'libero equilibrio' (free equilibrium): an asymmetric layout in which text and pictures were freely arranged on the white page according to a dynamic layout that guided the reader's eye and was exemplified by the two-page spread. Secondly, the sketch was a communication device that fostered communication with both clients and makers.[28] By providing a preview of the end results without resorting to obscure jargon, it encouraged a more open-minded attitude on the part of clients and promoted their confidence in the typographers' competence, advice and creative role. It protected the typographer's interests and at the same time guaranteed the client's satisfaction. Moreover, the sketch was indispensable for conveying information to makers. In translating the drafted idea into printed matter, makers would passively improve their graphic taste, develop their understanding of modern graphics and thus be encouraged to achieve professional advancement. Finally, the sketch was the conceptual instrument on which the shift from maker to designer was based. It embodied a different step in the typographic process and a separate task in the printing workshop. If design and planning were a newly created, and still vacant, jurisdiction, the question was to whom the drawing of layouts should be entrusted. Peviani suggested it ought to be the layout expert trained in technical schools for workers of the printing trade to take over this vacant jurisdiction.

When in 1939 the editor of *Campo Grafico*, Enrico Bona, tried to sum up discussions surrounding the skills, knowledge and name of the fledgling practice, he concluded: 'One gets the general impression that definitions and cataloguing have begun to pile up without reaching, after much discussion, a concise formula.'[29] It was time to remedy this chaos, and the solution was for typography 'to rediscover itself [and] present itself to the public with its own means and men'.[30] The time was ripe for what Bona considered 'a modern definition, not pompous, and with a clear meaning', namely the 'progettista grafico'.[31] A synthesis of technique and aesthetics, the 'progettista grafico' was a multiskilled practitioner in charge of the 'progetto' (design) of all printed matter. Until trade schools were able to develop specific programmes for the training of this new figure, individual firms were to be in charge of the selection of talented workers who should be put in a position to study and specialise in the conception and planning of printed communication.

Literally, 'progettista grafico' corresponds to the English 'graphic designer', and over the years it has become the most common way to refer to the practice in Italian. However, the interwar and the twenty-first-century definitions of 'progettista grafico' do not coincide. Vinti elaborated on the differences and noted that the kind of practitioner described by Bona 'appears to be less an anticipation of the future professional graphic designers than a defensive reply to what was perceived as a siege against the printing trade'.[32] The clarification is correct. Yet, one should distinguish between outsiders to the trade whose intrusion into the printing workshop was perceived as harmful by the in-group, and outsiders whose entrance was, instead, welcomed. For example, whereas Bona recognised futurist artists and rationalist architects' contribution because they had pushed typographers to challenge tradition and break the rules of typography, he warned against the heterogeneous crowd of dilettantes that had followed them, for they had brought about confusion of competences both within the workshop and in the eyes of clients and the public.

The graphic practitioner described in the interwar trade journals attests to the division of labour in progress in the printing workshop during the period. Together with the graphic artist, the book architect, the typography artist and the layout expert, the 'progettista grafico' was the outcome of an open-ended negotiation on a shared collective identity. How the Scuola del Libro responded to the requests for specialised training coming from the field and adapted to the division of labour is explored in the following section.

The Scuola del Libro

The Scuola del Libro was founded in Milan in 1885 as the Scuola Professionale Tipografica (Typographic Professional School) and later renamed when it was partially absorbed by the Società Umanitaria (Humanitarian Society) in 1904. The Umanitaria was, and still is today, a non-profit, philanthropic institution formed around socialist-inspired welfare programmes.[33] Since its foundation in 1893, it had become a model for vocational schools in Italy, with deep roots in the area and leverage at the national level. Vocational education was one of the activities through which the Umanitaria attempted to promote the cultural and professional growth of the urban working classes and thus accomplish its mission 'to enable deprived people, without fear or favour, to rise again by themselves by providing assistance, work and education'.[34] Besides the Scuola del Libro, the Umanitaria also managed a school of applied arts, schools of electrotechnics, watchmaking and tailoring, a professional school for women and a specialised course for union officials.

The founding of the Scuola del Libro can be considered one of the outcomes of the educational agenda of the Milanese printing trade unions. As recalled in 1954 by the head of the vocational schools at the Umanitaria, Mario Melino, it operated 'in perfect harmony with the graphic arts trade unions, ... it [was] looked upon favourably by this sector which not only supported it, but also recognised it officially'.[35] Until the mid-1920s a wide range of trade organisations – such as the Sezione Milanese dei Combinatori e degli Impressori (Milanese Branch of Compositors and Printers), the Federazione del Libro (Book Federation), the Federazione dei Litografi (Lithographers Federation), the Unione Industriale Arti Grafiche (Graphic Arts Industrial Union) and the Associazione Tipografica-Libraria (Book-Typographic Association) – funded the school in partnership with state bodies. The certificate issued by the school was listed among the membership requirements in the 1907 regulations of the Milanese trade union. The regulations also recommended that industrialists allow apprentices to take up to three courses and expected them to promote apprentices to fully fledged workers upon provision of the school's certificate.[36] Industrialists were often the first to recommend that their apprentices and workforce enrol, and then monitored their attendance. The regular contributions in kind – from paper, ink and fonts, to printing presses, and paper cutting and linotype machines – further attest to the support of the graphics and printing community.

After a financially problematic period, the Umanitaria took over the management of the Scuola del Libro in 1933 in order to avoid its closure. Stakeholders, such as the Sindacato Poligrafico Fascista (Fascist Polygraph Trade Union), the Federazione Fascista dell'Industria Editoriale (Fascist Federation of the Publishing Industry) and the Unione Industriale

Arti Grafiche, had failed to fulfil their financial commitments towards the school. They had lost their administrative independence as a result of the regime's policy aimed at disciplining labour by destroying existing trade unions and replacing them with fascist ones under central control.[37] Together with the withdrawal of financial support from trade bodies, the Ministry of National Education, which had gained control over vocational education in 1928, had also cut down its annual contribution.[38]

The education on offer at the Scuola del Libro included three types of course: daily training, complementary and vocational. The daily training course was a two-year-long, full-time course – seven hours a day, Monday to Saturday – for pupils between twelve and fourteen years of age. The first year was common to all pupils, who acquired a basic understanding of techniques and media while being introduced to the different specialisations: hand composition, printing, bookbinding, lithography, electrotyping, stereotyping or photochemistry. In the second year, distribution among specialisations depended on pupils' own interests and aptitudes, but was also contingent upon the demand for apprentices coming from the industry. Former pupils often enrolled on the complementary and vocational courses, thereby showing awareness of the crucial role of technical training and liberal education in their professional advancement and personal fulfilment. Apprentices with two years' work experience were eligible to enrol onto the complementary evening courses. The enrolment prerequisite was reduced to one year when the candidate was a former pupil of the school. Eligible students had to be at least fifteen, or sixteen when applying for the complementary course in lithographic printing. On Sunday mornings, student-workers could attend the vocational courses and specialise in hand composition, typographic print, lithography, photogravure, bookbinding, and book gilding and decoration.

The composition of the student body in the interwar period was essentially determined exclusively on the basis of class and gender distinctions. This makeup mirrored the elitism and gender bias of the Italian educational system at the time. The Gentile Reform had hardened the class bias in schooling by downgrading technical instruction and using education as a means to promote social hierarchy, rather than facilitate upward mobility of motivated working-class youth.[39] Writing on gender distinctions in the education system during Fascism, historian Victoria de Grazia noted how girls' schooling was the expression of biases in the labour market and conformist social attitudes.[40] Female enrolment in secondary education in the mid-1930s broke down to under one-quarter of students at classical high schools, one-seventh at scientific schools, only one-tenth at industrial schools, and one-quarter at commercial and artistic institutes. Over the decade, the overall number of females enrolling in secondary education increased from 100,000 in 1930 to 350,000 in 1940, while their enrolment in university went up from 13 per cent of the overall student population during the 1920s to 21 per cent in 1940. Nevertheless, greater access to education was not followed by better work opportunities for women, due to the regime's bias towards male employment.[41]

Students at the Scuola de Libro were almost all male and often sons of people involved in the graphics, printing and publishing industries. They were otherwise likely to belong to the working class and the crafts-manship milieu. Students, all male, listed in the school register of the academic year 1935–36 were either sons of compositors, printers, typesetters, lithographers, graphic industrialists, bookbinders, stationers, newspaper distributors, warehouse workers in printing workshops and publishers, or sons of mechanics, railwaymen, public transport drivers, bricklayers, factory workers, tailors, upholsterers, waiters, packers, nurses and pedlars.[42] Evidence of female students is scant: from 1918 to 1921, promotional pamphlets included complementary classes for 'legatrici' (female book-binders); in the 1925–26 pamphlet, a special course for female paper sheet feeders on lithographic machines was advertised; according to the invitation card, the June 1937 exhibition featured graphic works by both 'allieve' and 'allievi' (female and male pupils).[43] A clause of the 1936 national contract for the regulation of apprenticeships in the graphics industry might explain the reduced presence of female students.[44] Whereas boys were obliged to attend the training courses before beginning an apprenticeship, a primary school diploma was the only requirement for girls, who could train exclusively as bookbinders, booksellers or paper sheet feeders. Thus, not only were girls able to access just a restricted list of occupations within the graphics industry, but they were also expected to learn directly on-the-job, for they were excluded from vocational training. This situation matches the typology of roles for women in graphic design described by design historian Martha Scotford. According to Scotford, the patriarchal construction of roles and a gendered perception of capabilities and expectations kept women practitioners out of certain areas of graphic design. This was the case with 'the typesetting and printing trades because these are mechanical, dirty and physically strenuous and, therefore, "not suitable"' for women.[45]

Within the tension between school and industry, the Scuola del Libro opted for the workshop-school model. Evening and weekend complementary and vocational classes allowed the educational activity to coexist with apprentices' and practitioners' everyday working routines. Pupils' technical training in the studio compensated for their lack of on-the-job learning. In order to foster a correct perception of practical work, they were put in charge of designing, composing, printing and binding the official publications and promotional material of the school. The visual output of the Scuola del Libro was the outcome of the collaboration between pupils of the different specialist departments. This detail adds an implicit pedagogical intent to the explicit promotional one. The curricula were regularly updated and modified in order to keep the syllabi up to date with current working practices. The changes mirrored technological advances and, as we shall see in the next section, the increased interest in everyday ephemera, in contrast to the previous focus on book design.

Following the merger with the Umanitaria in 1933, the school underwent a series of changes. The curricula were overhauled in an attempt to meet the requests for specialised training for the new figure of the graphic practitioner. The school was responsive to contemporary interest in promoting mutual understanding and cross-fertilisation with avant-garde art and architecture. It had been collaborating with avant-garde artists since the mid-1920s, when it had hired the painter Atanasio Soldati to lead the course on book and graphic arts decoration. Moreover, it acted occasionally as a public platform for *Campo Grafico* and its campaign for collaboration between typographers and graphic artists. In response to contemporary discussions about the importance of sketching, the role of drawing in the curriculum was strengthened, especially in the complementary classes in hand composition. After all, the school had been offering drawing classes since Bertieri's directorship between 1919 and 1925. Bertieri himself explained the school's 'essentially graphic' approach to the teaching of drawing: 'pupils learn how to draw neither a leaf nor a decoration, neither a vase nor a capital [of a column]; they rather get used to evaluating the masses and the structure of the alphabet, familiarise themselves with the page layout, and gain practice in the arrangement of blank spaces and the balance of a title ... on the empty page'.[46]

Due to the scarcity of archival documents and the lack of surviving student works, detailed reconstruction of the drawing classes is difficult. Nevertheless, the account of a former pupil on the applied arts courses at the Umanitaria provides insights into the teaching methods adopted. Students specialising in goldsmithing in the mid-1930s were asked to 'cut a 2 by 2 cm piece of black cardboard and a 1 by 4 cm grey one; paste [them] onto a 20 by 20 cm white background; arrange them so that they "look good" with one another and with respect to the background'.[47] By arranging and reordering geometrical shapes on a background and establishing rhythm and tensions between visual elements, students trained their relational seeing.[48] The assignment demanded a careful calculation of intervals, it showed how the slightest alteration affects the figure–ground relationship and nurtured the awareness of blank spaces. As such it was suitable for students of the Scuola del Libro, and it does not seem too far-fetched to assume that similar teaching methods might have been adopted there.

The school also adapted the curricula to the division of tasks in progress in the printing workshop. For instance, the focus of the hand-composition course moved from execution towards design. A note on the 1935 annual report attests to this shift: since it was felt that students did not have enough time to execute all the assignments they were given during their second year – a book, advertisements for newspapers and magazines, and a number of different commercial printed ephemera – it was suggested they should be trained 'in the execution of good, well designed and resolved sketches, featuring only approximate but explanatory elements', instead of actual printed artefacts.[49] Execution and design had become two different tasks.

Alongside the overhaul of the curricula, the workshop furniture and technical equipment were renewed to bring them up to date with current printing technologies. The typographic, bookbinding and photogravure workshops were equipped with a new paper-cutting machine and a Nebiolo D.G.B. rotary printing press. In addition to such adaptation to technological change, re-equipment also stemmed from the adoption of a visual vocabulary close to the modernist aesthetic. Let us consider the hand-composition workshop, for example. Since the use of 'old, worn-out, incomplete and old-fashioned fonts … *utterly inadequate* for the requirements of modern aesthetics' was deemed counterproductive, if not damaging, for the students' training, the equipment of the hand-composition workshop was renovated type by type.[50] First, in 1933 three series of what were considered to be the most modern typefaces were purchased in the regular, bold and light variants. Then, in 1936 sans-serif and elongated sans-serif wood and lead fonts were bought. Finally, in 1938 the Neon typeface was obtained and immediately put into use (see figure 1.2). Designed in 1935 by Giulio da Milano and produced by the Società Nebiolo in Turin, Neon is a sans-serif single-case typeface that combines both lower- and upper-case lettering.

Parallel to the vocational training, students attended complementary humanities classes: the goal of the balanced relationship between theory and practice being to train 'neither inept theorists, nor ordinary labourers', but to transform printing workers from passive makers into active collaborators with the graphic artists, if not into graphic artists themselves.[51] Classes included Italian grammar, general culture, applied mathematics, chemistry and physics – which were replaced by technology classes in 1926 – sport and drawing. The study of foreign languages – French, English and German – focused on the acquisition of specialist terminology, while history of art was taught in relation to graphic arts. Students also had access to a course library with its collection of assorted specialist literature, including magazines, handbooks, historical surveys and foreign trade journals.[52] The promotion of professional awareness – seen as taking pride in the profession, developing a spirit of association, being able to negotiate rights and duties with industrialists, and promoting professional improvement so as to achieve social advancement – was an additional aim of the humanities classes and was in line with the reform programmes undertaken by the Umanitaria.

1.2   Pamphlet advertising the complementary courses at the Scuola del Libro in Milan, academic year 1938–39.

Given its left-wing agenda, it was no surprise that Fascism opposed attempts towards workers' education undertaken at the school. The Umanitaria itself had been placed under compulsory receivership since 1924, for financial and political reasons. In 1929 Benito Mussolini's brother, Arnaldo, asked rhetorically about the Umanitaria: 'Is it possible that an Institution founded at the peak of the democratic era, raised in the shadow of that master of weakness and useless sentimentalism – namely reformist socialism – could turn into an efficient organisation, adequate for the requirements of the fascist civilisation?'[53] Alas, it was indeed possible. As recalled by Riccardo Bauer, antifascist director of the Umanitaria in the post-war period, 'Fascism impoverished the Umanitaria ... reducing it to just one professional institution among many ... it was distanced from its essential mission ... to animate, guide and spur the Italian labour move-ment, and to stimulate the search for new ways to organise the world of work, and the structure of Italian society.'[54] The activities of the institution were downsized and confined to vocational training.

The Scuola del Libro fell victim to the process of fascistisation of the Italian education system that had been underway since the late 1920s. A series of amendments to the Gentile Reform had turned the Italian school into an agency of indoctrination and a tool for the political formation of the fascist youth. The process entailed the politicisation of the curricula, the regimentation of teachers and the militarisation of education.[55] As a result of the fascistisation of the Scuola del Libro, 'Cultura Fascista' (Fascist Culture) was included in the curriculum, the Roman straight-armed salute was made compulsory, and the fascist dating system and symbols featured in all official publications as micro and macroscopic everyday incarna-tions of the regime.[56] Pupils were expected to be members of the fas-cist youth organisation, ONB, Opera Nazionale Balilla (National Balilla Organisation), while apprentices and workers had to be members of the fascist trade unions.

The submission to fascistisation by the Umanitaria and the Scuola del Libro can be read as a sign of how the regime conditioned people's attitudes and behaviour by using not only coercion but also control over access to social benefits such as the ability to work. However, opportunistic or pragmatic compliance with fascist institutions should not be confused with full adhesion to the PNF, Partito Nazionale Fascista (National Fascist Party). Rather, it falls into the grey area of 'consensus boundaries'.[57] Pragmatism was a common strategy towards the obligation to participate in fascist trade unions, as most people, and particularly the working class, could not afford the consequences of any alternative choice.[58] In ques-tioning the reasons for popular participation in Fascism, historian Paul Corner wrote that 'some kind of collaboration with the regime was implicit in these situations, even for those hostile to Fascism, and it was precisely collaboration of this type that generated the complicity that the regime was always trying to engineer'.[59] In the post-war period, as we shall see in chapter 4, exponents of the antifascist resistance movement were to reclaim the Umanitaria and resume the institute's commitment to political reform and progressive pedagogy, thereby playing an active role in the re-democratisation of Italian society.

Modern graphics at the Scuola del Libro

In a 1937 catalogue, Giuseppe Pagano, the architect and editor of *Casabella*, offered the following comment on the Umanitaria and its vocational schools: 'At the Umanitaria a very different wind is blowing: young and lively professors, up-to-date industrial technical equipment, order and clarity of ideas and, above all ... keen observation of contemporary needs and ideals.'[60] Perhaps even more passionate were his words of appreciation for the students' 'lively, fresh and current awareness of good and bad', as well as their 'unmistakable understanding of modern aesthetics [wherein] ornament and beauty lie first and foremost in the cleanliness, the honesty, the clarity, and in the elegant technical skills'.[61] Here, Pagano pointed to a favourable change in the school's organisation, methodologies and output in line with modern aesthetics. But what did this modern aesthetics look like?

After even the most cursory glance through the official publications and ephemera designed, composed, printed and bound by the pupils at the Scuola del Libro we are struck by just how much the visual language, aesthetics and techniques had changed in the early 1930s. Was such design change without its opponents? Was it just a coincidence limited to the school, or was there something more afoot? The design change in the visual output at the Scuola del Libro was, in fact, a key issue within the debate about the circulation of modern aesthetics that gripped graphic practitioners and critics in the interwar period, and in particular within the quarrel between the magazines *Risorgimento Grafico* and *Campo Grafico*. Here it is worth recalling that the editor of *Risorgimento Grafico*, Raffaello Bertieri, directed the school from 1919 to 1925, precisely when the campisti – Carlo Baldini, Eligio Bonelli, Pasquale Bressani, Carlo Dradi, Giuseppe Muggiani, Alfredo Pirondini, Giovanni Peviani and Attilio Rossi – were studying there.[62] As we shall see shortly below, it was the tension between Bertieri's approach and that of the campisti which lay at the root of the design changes noted above.

Let us briefly look at the situation before the changes were implemented. Compare the booklet for the academic year 1924–25 with that for the academic year 1930–31 (see figures 1.3 and 1.4). Both booklets feature engraved illustrations, ornaments, serif typefaces, centred and symmetrical page layouts, large margins and geometrical frames. In both cases, the book layout is the reference point. No attempt whatsoever is made to design a layout specific to advertising ephemera, whose purpose, use and audience are different from those of a book. The similar traditional approach to typography and layout in no way seems to reflect the fact that six years have passed, but rather demonstrates Bertieri's enduring influence within the school. Indeed, both exemplars draw on Bertieri's interest in the Italian typographic and printing tradition. They stem from

SCUOLA

~ DEL LIBRO ~

MILANO

LITOGRAFIA

Stampa litografica

(trasportatori)

Primo e Secondo corso. Sessantacinque lezioni di due ore per ogni corso. Due lezioni alla settimana

Stampa litografica

(avviamento a Macchinisti su macchina piana)

Corso unico riservato a Mettifoglio-aiutanti che lavorino come tali su macchina piana da almeno quattro anni. Settanta lezioni pratiche di due ore ognuna. Due lezioni alla settimana. Delle settanta lezioni almeno quindici saranno dedicate ad esercitazioni sul trattamento del trasporto

FOTO-TIPOGRAFIA

Fotografia

Due anni d'insegnamento. Settanta lezioni di due ore ognuna per ogni anno. Due lezioni alla settimana

(le lezioni sono aperte solamente per gli allievi del primo corso)

Incisione

Due anni d'insegnamento. Settanta lezioni di due ore ognuna per ogni anno. Due lezioni alla settimana

(la settimana sono aperte solamente per gli allievi del primo corso)

Tiraprove

Corso riservato ad operai fotoincisori, torcolieri litografi e/o pressori tipografi che percepiscano paga di lavorante effettivo. Settanta lezioni di due ore ognuna. Due lezioni alla settimana

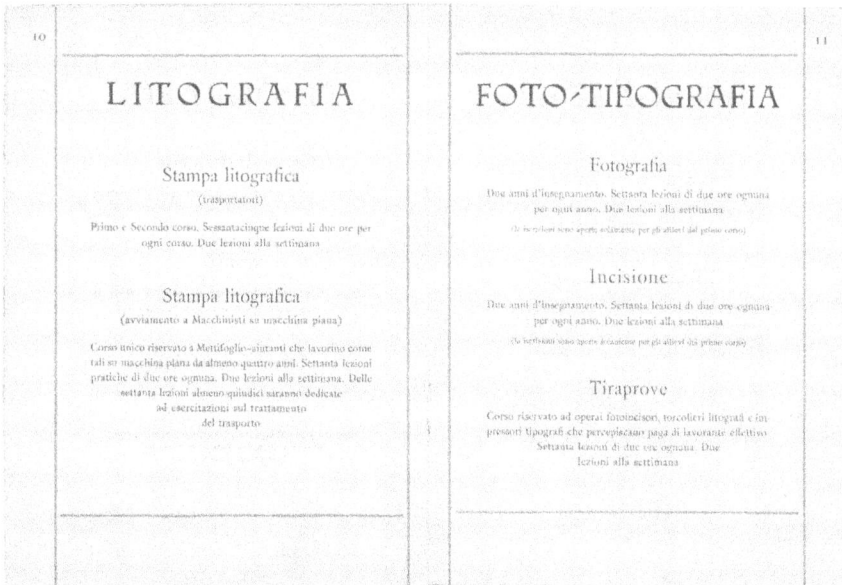

1.3   Booklet advertising the courses at the Scuola del Libro in Milan, academic year 1924–25.

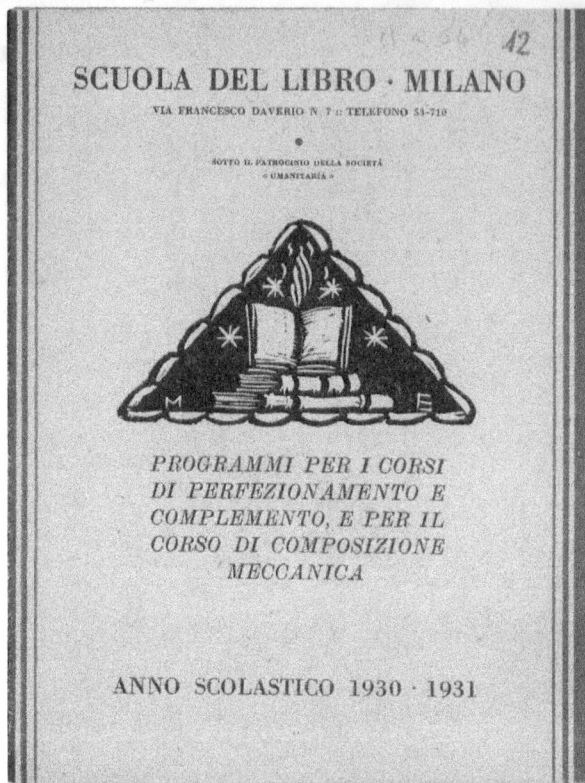

1.4   Booklet advertising the complementary courses at the Scuola del Libro in Milan, academic year 1930–31.

a conception of typography as Art with a capital A, that is, an autonomous and self-sufficient activity, and of book design as its highest expression. The school appears unaware of, or indifferent to, contemporary discussions that were challenging the idea of the book as a typographic artwork, as expressed, for instance, by Jan Tschichold in his landmark article against book art that was reviewed in the Italian trade journal *Graphicus* in 1927.[63]

The campisti took issue with Bertieri's approach to graphics and with his lasting influence on the output of the Scuola del Libro. Writing in 1966, Rossi stated that 'stretching the terms a bit, one could even assert that it was Bertieri himself who, as Director of the Scuola del Libro, awoke in many of [them] that combative impulse, which he then persistently failed to acknowledge'.[64] Their feeling of distance between the school and modern graphics was eloquently expressed by Dradi: 'While at Gropius' Bauhaus, in the Typography department, one taught a kind of graphics free from classical paradigms, asymmetrical and in line with the new principles of Rationalism; at the Scuola del Libro, under Bertieri's directorship, one taught the symmetrical page layout of the book that was the only model for the layout of any other kind of printed material.'[65] While Paul Renner was designing Futura, Bertieri was recasting sixteenth-century typefaces such as Sinibaldi and Incunabula that were, according to Dradi, 'more appropriate for a page [conceived by] William Morris than [for one] by a 1930s' typographer'.[66] The campisti blamed Bertieri for ignoring technological progress and disregarding changes in everyday printed ephemera. Conversely, they advocated simplicity and functionalism, and promoted an idea of typography as applied art whose sole aim was visual communication.

By the early 1930s Bertieri's influence was on the wane as the school moved towards more modernist-looking aesthetics. Take the pamphlets for the academic years 1932–33 and 1934–35 (see figures 1.5 and 1.6), for example. While the front page of the 1932–33 pamphlet is still modelled on the book frontispiece, the layout of the 1934–35 pamphlet abandons the rigidity of symmetry. The reading is enlivened and kept in rhythm by the steps-like arrangement and changes in the orientation of the text. Let us now open the pamphlets. The text printed on the left and right pages of the 1932–33 pamphlet is arranged symmetrically, as in previous exemplars. Yet, the sans-serif typeface and the functional use of colour are heralds of the design change in progress. By contrast, the two-page spread of the 1934–35 pamphlet is organised asymmetrically in a grid that facilitates a comparative reading of the text. With its flexible format and orientation, the two-pages-in-one layout is evidence of the attempt to abandon the book-inspired page layout and consider the specific use and manner of reading a pamphlet.

The asymmetrical composition and the grid layout, together with the lack of ornamentation and the use of sans-serif, exemplify the modern

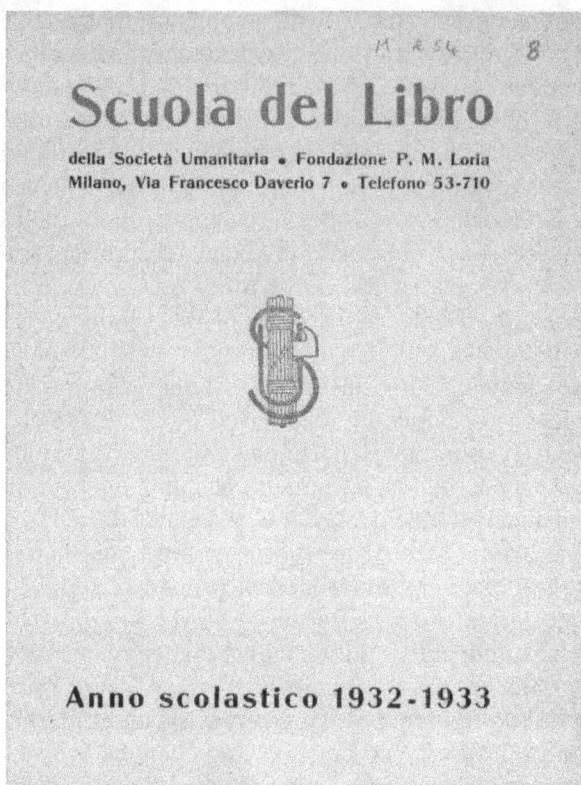

1.5   Pamphlet advertising the complementary courses at the Scuola del Libro in Milan, academic year 1932–33.

1.6 Pamphlet advertising the complementary courses at the Scuola del Libro in Milan, academic year 1934–35.

graphic taste that *Campo Grafico* had been promoting since its launch in 1933. This was the case with the pamphlet for the academic year 1936–37 that was included in the July 1936 issue (see figure 1.7). Devoted to the Scuola del Libro, the issue was itself designed by students who were commissioned to conceive both the page layout and the advertisements. Together with other exemplars of the school's output, the 1936–37 pamphlet was selected 'to give the reader a concrete demonstration of the merits of the technical training and, in particular, of the aesthetic improvement in line with the liveliest tendencies of modern taste attained by the school in recent times.'[67] It stands out from previous promotional ephemera by virtue of its square format. Folded twice, the pamphlet invites us to interact with it. It arouses our curiosity by anticipating some of the content hidden underneath the narrower front page. Inside, the horizontal bar replaces the vertical axis to produce a panoramic layout that ignores the physical separation of the three pages.

What is perhaps even more striking about the 1936–37 pamphlet is the use of typo-photo, namely the synthesis of photomontage and sans-serif. Not that photography had been absent in previous promotional ephemera. For example, the pamphlet for the academic year 1926–27 reveals, once unfolded, a picture of the printing workshop (see figure 1.8). Isolated from the rest with a geometric frame, the picture could be taken out with no need to rearrange the layout. The readability of the text would benefit from its absence since the double-page picture would not then interrupt the syllabication of the word 'allievo' (pupil) into 'al' and 'lievo'. The picture in figure 1.7 is a far cry from the use of the photographic medium we have just seen: first, it is a photomontage and as such it testifies to a changed photographic aesthetic; secondly, it is conceived as a formal element and used as a typographic tool in accordance with the principles of the New Typography.[68] The photomontage goes beyond the documentary intents of the two original photographs of the printing and the compositors' workshops. It uses the readability and communicative potential of the photographic medium to convey the idea of the Scuola del Libro as an inclusive institution that brings together all practices in the typographic trade and printing industry. The photomontage replaces the static and frontal perspective of the original pictures with a dynamic, diagonal perspective and an unusual point of view. The context of the studio is cut out and, owing to the omission of walls and other references to the environment, the compositors' cabinets appear to be floating above an abstract chessboard pattern. The close-up transforms drawers and stands into geometric forms to the benefit of the juxtaposition of image and text. By the same token, the decreasing sizes and the spiral-like arrangement of the text around the picture help mediate the contrast between the three-dimensionality of the photographic medium and the flat surface of the type.

1.7 Pamphlet advertising the complementary courses at the Scuola del Libro in Milan, academic year 1936–37.

1.8   Pamphlet advertising the daily training course at the Scuola del Libro in Milan, academic year 1926–27.

The move towards modernist aesthetics and away from a more traditional approach to typography also affected the public image of the
Umanitaria. Two exemplars of the Umanitaria official publications were
included as 'study material and for aesthetic enjoyment' in the series
'Documentari di Campo Grafico' (Campo Grafico's Documentaries).[69] The
first issue of 'Documentari' in February 1938 featured an invitation to
the students' chorale (see figure 1.9). As with figure 1.7, the half-width
left flap and the uncompleted text underneath invite us to interact with
and unfold the card. The shift between foreground and background and
reversal of positive and negative forms enliven the front-page design. The
enlarged dots of the halftone screen are treated as decorative elements
that create a dotted pattern in the background, thereby exposing the printing technology and process of mechanical production for aesthetic purposes. The June 1938 issue of 'Documentari' featured another exemplar of
ephemera advertising a series of events happening at the Umanitaria (see
figure 1.10). A series of parallel red segments of different lengths feature
in the double spread. These can be interpreted as three fasces. 'The new
typography's tendency towards abstraction', Vinti wrote, 'made it possible
to avoid any excessively direct references to the fascist iconography.'[70]
From today's perspective, the fascist symbol is not readily recognisable
unless one knows what one is looking at. Yet, considering the omnipres-
ence of the fasces in the daily imagery of the time, it would have been
easier for someone living in Italy under the Fascist regime to recognise
the symbol hidden behind the parallel lines.[71] Commenting on workers'
impassive reaction in the face of Mussolini's speech at the Turin plant of
automobile manufacturer Fiat in 1932, Corner argued that 'silence at key
(and obligatory) public demonstrations denot[ed] defiance and the main-
tenance of a certain autonomy of identity'.[72] Given that the Umanitaria
was originally formed around socialist-inspired welfare programmes, it is
tempting to read a political meaning into the radical simplification of the
fasces and their use as a geometric decorative element, rather than as a
straightforward propaganda tool.

Like a parent neglecting a wayward child, the more the Scuola del
Libro inclined towards *Campo Grafico*, the more Bertieri distanced himself
and his magazine from it. His editorial allegiance to the Scuola del Libro
waned in the 1930s: he included only one visual artefact and published
only two articles on the school in *Risorgimento Grafico* after 1933.[73] The
first of these articles was an overview of the history of the school, in
which the author, Mario Ferrigni, made no mention of the school's current activities.[74] The second was a review of the exhibition of the bookbinding and book decoration courses, in which Ferrigni commended the
revival of the binding of religious books, praising the balance between the
clear geometric decorations and asymmetrical layout, and the traditional
techniques and materials used, such as gilding, leather and parchment.[75]

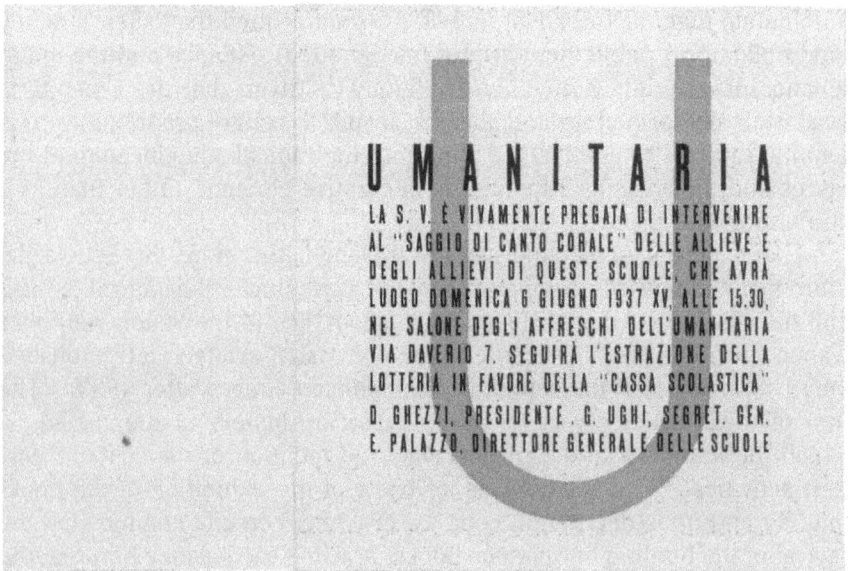

1.9 Invitation card to the students' chorale at the Società Umanitaria, 1938.

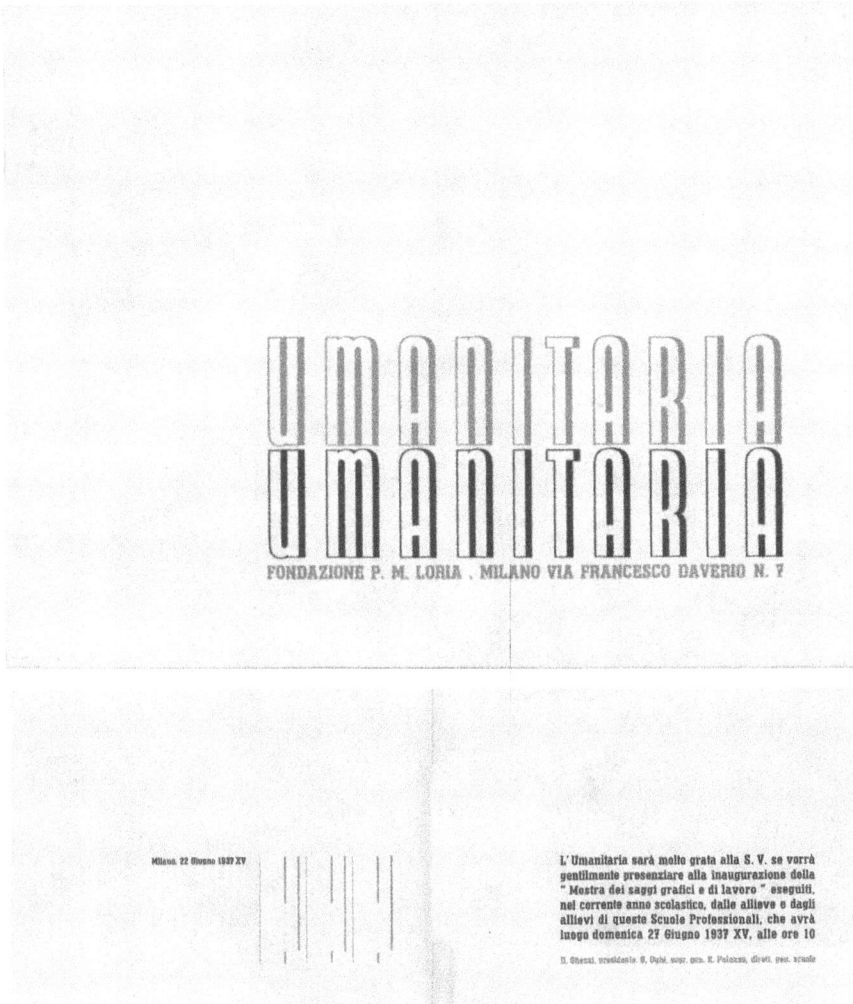

1.10   Invitation card to the students' exhibition at the Scuola del Libro in Milan, 1938.

Both articles were a safe compromise that enabled Ferrigni, and indirectly Bertieri, to comment upon the Scuola del Libro without making too many concessions to its modernisation.

The Scuola del Libro became a hotbed for the typographic renewal that had been promoted by the campisti. The similarities between the cover of the first issue of *Campo Grafico* and the front page of a pamphlet for the academic year 1940–41 visually attest to the like-minded dialogue between the magazine and the school (see figures 1.11 and 1.12). Both covers illustrate the variety of practices involved in the typographic and printing sectors: the focus is on practitioners and technical equipment,

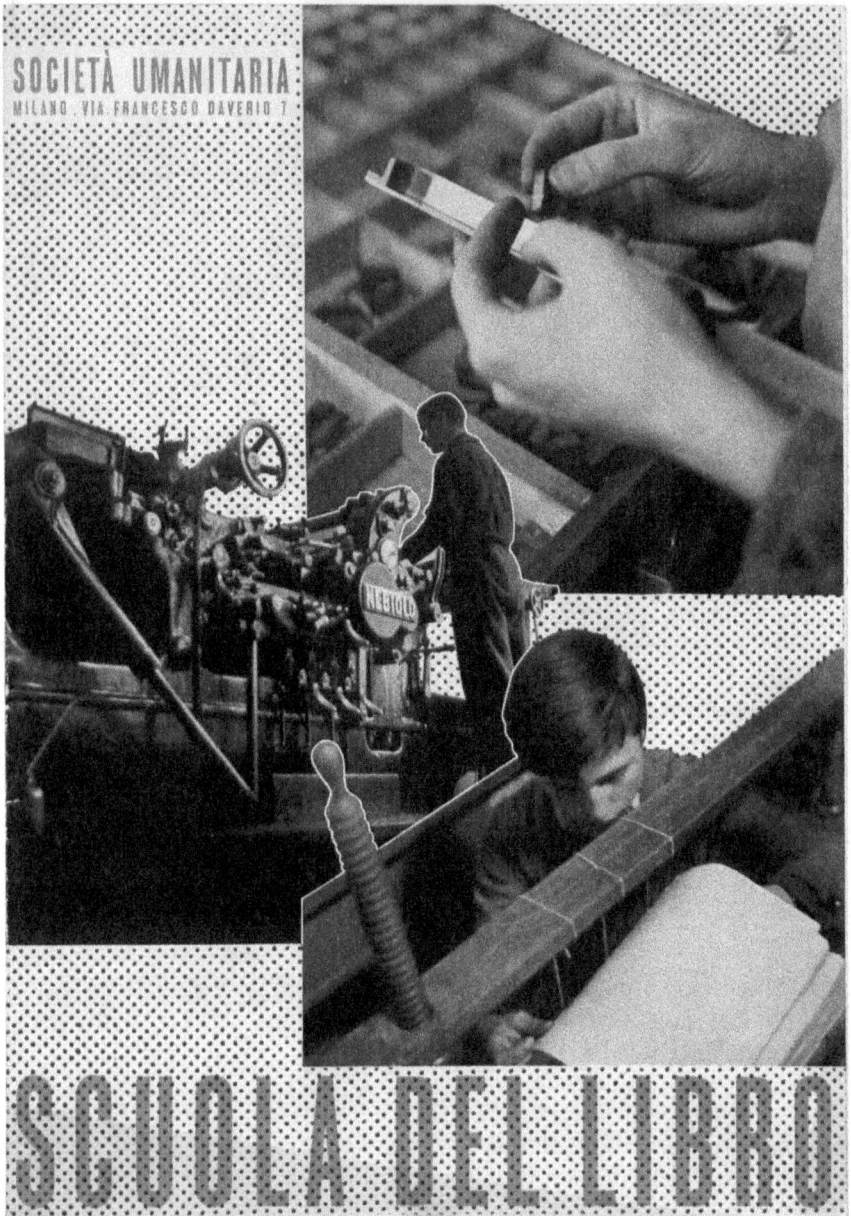

1.11   Pamphlet advertising the complementary courses at the Scuola del Libro in Milan, academic year 1940–41.

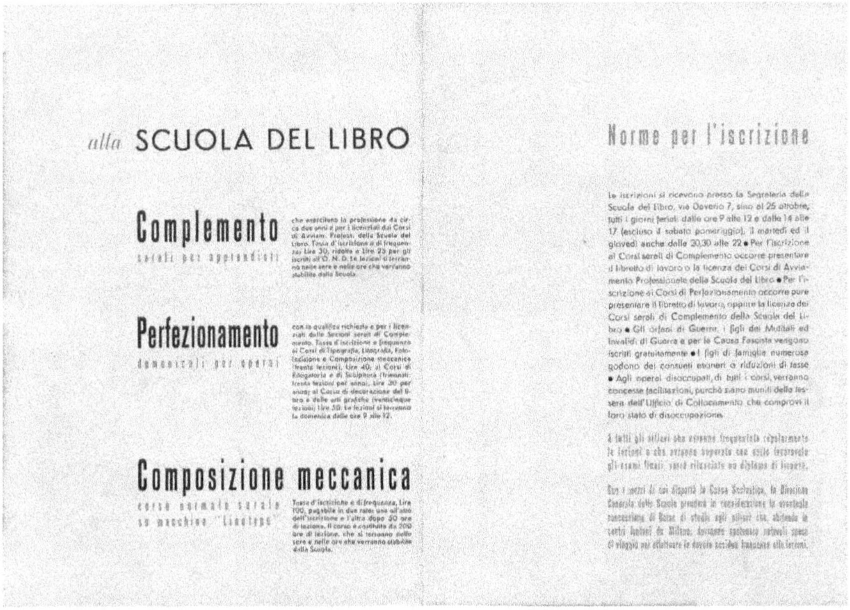

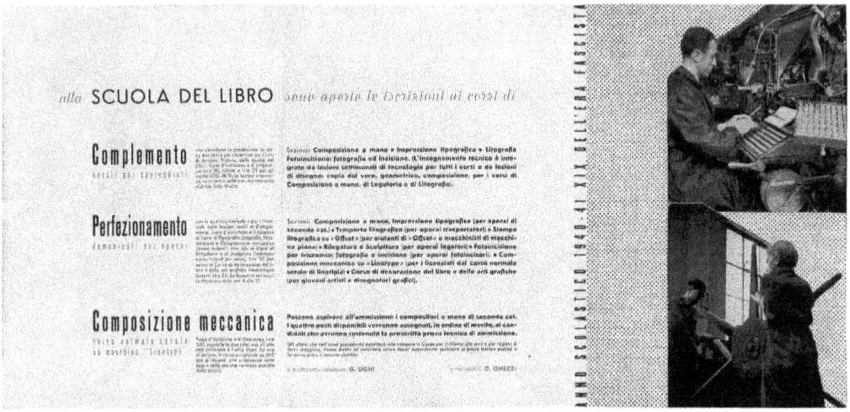

1.11 Continued

with an emphasis on daily work activities. Nevertheless, pictures are used for different purposes. The magazine's cover is a statement of intent: the blurry imagery conveys a general idea of studio practice and illustrates the tight relationship between the printing workforce and *Campo Grafico*, which was advertised as a magazine for practitioners, made by practitioners. By contrast, the sharp pictures in the 1940–41 pamphlet provide a detailed description of the diverse practices and technologies involved in typography and the printing process, hence they illustrate the school's educational offer. As with figure 1.9, the dots of the halftone screen

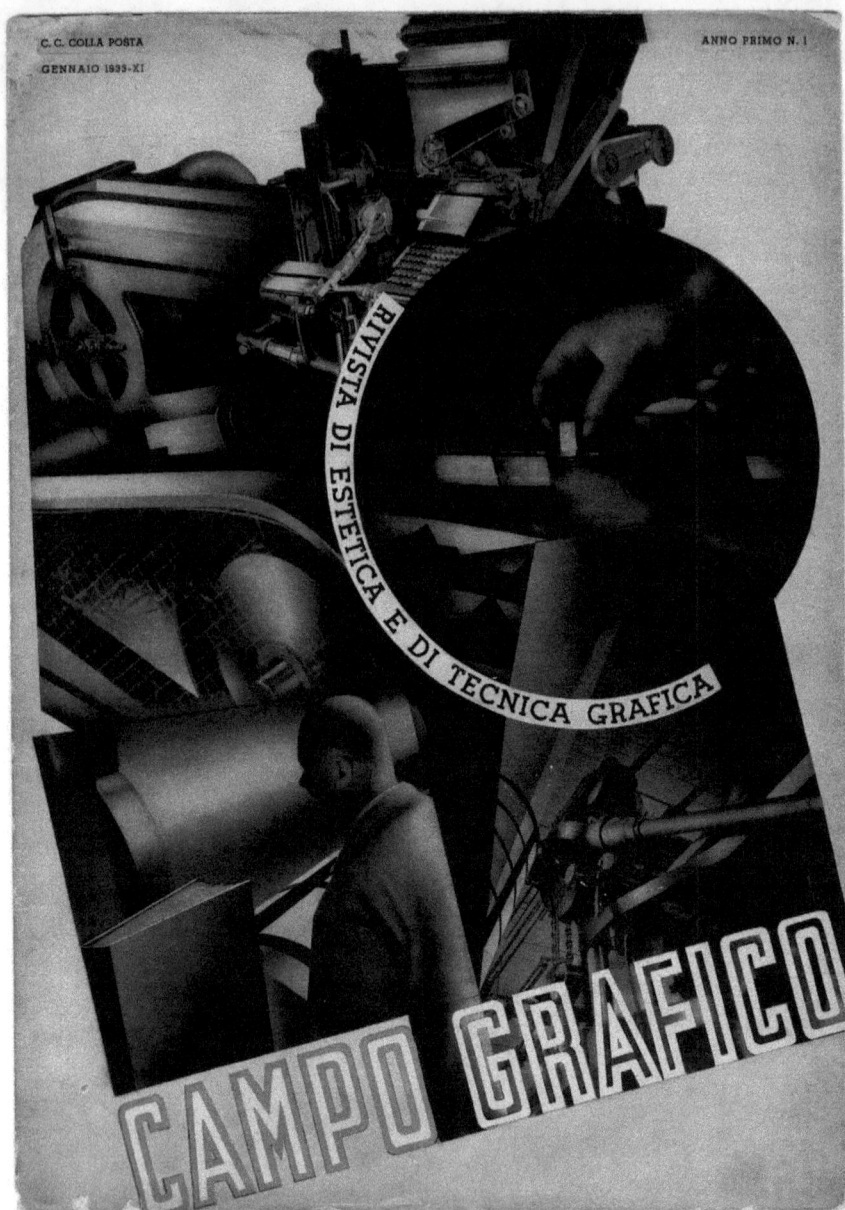

1.12   Cover of the first issue of the magazine *Campo Grafico* (January 1933).

create a decorative dotted background. By objectifying technology, they call attention to the reprographic technique. In doing so, the enlarged dots acquire an extra connotation: not only do they draw attention to the aesthetic character of mechanical reproduction, but they also appear to stand for the complementary photogravure courses that were advertised but not illustrated in the pamphlet.[76] The graphic language itself has changed. On the cover of *Campo Grafico*, diagonal and circular lines of force convey a dynamic rhythm, while the retouching of the borders makes the transition between pictures almost continuous and creates a crescendo that culminates in the enlargement of the compositor's hand. The layout of the pamphlet is, instead, based on a grid structure: a white outline frames the pictures, and the vortex movement is replaced by an intermittent cadence of juxtaposed planes. The emphasis on diagonal and circular lines of force, which in 1933 had echoed futurist art and graphics, has settled over the years into a grid structure closer to rationalist architecture.

The school's positive reputation in the field of typography and in the printing industry, and its past relationship with Bertieri, made the design change and the move towards a modernist aesthetic vital and instrumental for the campisti's campaign for the modernisation of Italian graphics. By featuring visual artefacts designed and produced at the Scuola del Libro, they were not only illustrating the spread of modernist graphics in Italy, but were also discrediting Bertieri's 'Dannunzian rhetoric of typography as art and poetry' that had been directing the school for over two decades.[77] On the one hand, the school's subscription to the guidelines promoted by *Campo Grafico* was capitalised upon by the campisti to legitimise their offensive against Bertieri, his magazine and the type of graphics they stood for. On the other hand, by changing its visual appearance, the Scuola del Libro was promoting a new self-image: changing from a restorer of Italian typographic tradition under Bertieri, into a modern school in line with experimental visual languages and modernist aesthetics.

The commercial art course at ISIA

Concurrently with the early 1930s changes in the management, curricula, technical equipment and the visual output of the Scuola del Libro, the director of the vocational schools at the Umanitaria, Elio Palazzo, promoted the reorganisation of ISIA, Istituto Superiore per le Industrie Artistiche (Higher Institute for the Artistic Industries). The reorganisation brought about the opening of the commercial art course in the academic year 1933–34. Design historians Elena Dellapiana and Daniela N. Prina argued that 'the Scuola del Libro was, along with ISIA, instrumental in securing the foundations of visual communication in Italy'.[78] True, the two institutions were among the first schools in Italy offering courses on proto-visual communication. But they represented two clashing approaches to graphic practice and training, as well as different dimensions of intra-group negotiation, which will now be compared.

ISIA was a school of decorative and applied arts founded in 1922 in Monza, a town 20 km northeast of Milan, by a consortium that included the municipalities of Milan and Monza in partnership with the Umanitaria.[79] It predated by one year the Gentile Reform that, as we saw above, was to reorganise the industrial arts education system. Courses included cabinetmaking, decorative painting and sculpture, ceramics, and gold- and silver-smithing. Central and Northern European educational models were brought to ISIA by many teachers who had trained or worked abroad.[80] The South Kensington Museum in London, with its annexed school, was a further reference model. Indeed, ISIA's statute established that parallel to the school a 'collection of art applied to the industry that would assist the students of the School, the makers, and the industrialists' should be created, together with a furniture museum.[81] In addition, the school took part in the international exhibitions in Monza. These exhibitions were the forerunners of the Milan Triennale, whose role in the articulation of graphic design practice in Italy will be addressed in chapter 3.

Responding to market demands for specialised practitioners, Palazzo suggested the opening of four new courses on window dressing, poster design, set design and graphic arts. The graphic arts course was to focus on book decoration and was intended as a direct continuation from the Scuola del Libro.[82] Notwithstanding the redevelopment proposal, the commercial art course was the only new course to open in 1933. As no sizeable evidence of graphic output other than propaganda and advertising posters has been found in the – admittedly heavily damaged and scattered – archive, it seems safe to infer that the commercial art course was conceived along the same lines as the poster design course. This was geared towards catering to the demand for trained poster artists coming from the regime in order to promote its propaganda policies. In the inventories of the school exhibitions, posters are described as sketched designs 'to be produced only in the event of someone placing an order that would have to be carried out off-site'.[83] The description suggests that since ISIA outsourced the production to external workshops, students of the commercial art course were not offered the same hands-on technical training as that available at the Scuola del Libro, where each step of the graphic production was dealt with in-house. Differences between the two schools did not stop there.

The commercial art course was assigned to Marcello Nizzoli and Edoardo Persico. Their recruitment fitted in with Palazzo's attempt to modernise ISIA by hiring prominent figures in contemporary cultural debates and promoters of Italian Rationalism, such as the art critic Agnolodomenico Pica, who taught art history, and the architects Giuseppe Pagano and Giovanni Romano, who were responsible for the art criticism class and the furniture workshop, respectively.[84] Nizzoli and Persico's involvement in the commercial art course, together with the attendance of prominent students, such as Giovanni Pintori and Costantino Nivola who are best known for their work at Olivetti in the post-war period, has attracted scholars' attention.[85] According to Dellapiana and Prina, by 'teaching graphic composition and advertising, [Nizzoli] brought to ISIA an intimate knowledge of different avant-garde conceptions and an experimental attitude to new visual languages'.[86] The underlying prejudice is that, with Nizzoli and Persico as educators, experimentation with modern visual languages and cutting-edge techniques is what one should expect to have occurred. However, both their direct involvement and their influence on the visual language adopted at ISIA need to be reassessed. No evidence of Nizzoli and Persico's collaboration with the commercial art course after 11 December 1934 was, in fact, found in the archive. On that date, Palazzo wrote a letter to the Monza mayor and the commissioner of the Milan–Monza–Umanitaria Consortium reporting the 'dismissal of two teachers of the commercial art course', and these are likely to have been Nizzoli and Persico.[87] Moreover, no archival evidence could be found to corroborate the substantial adoption of an experimental visual language. Posters designed by students present a rather figurative style, testifying to a pictorial approach to graphics that favours hand-drawn lettering and illustrations. In contrast to the Scuola del Libro, ISIA's graphic output appears barely to have been touched by visual and technological innovations promoted at the time.

The differences in approach to design education between the Scuola del Libro and ISIA mirrored the differences in approach to the graphics themselves. In contrast to the Scuola del Libro, the commercial art course at ISIA ignored any printed matter and graphic work other than posters. It remained closer to an idea of graphic arts as the commercial application of fine arts aesthetics and techniques, with an emphasis on an individual's creativity. While the Scuola del Libro adapted its curriculum in an attempt to train a practitioner in a way that could bridge the gap between the typographer's technique and an artist's creativity, the commercial art course at ISIA reiterated the divide that distinguished poster art – assigned to artists or practitioners with a fine arts background – from everyday printed matter – tasked to typographers, printers and a technical workforce. Scholars' interest in the commercial art course at ISIA, usually to the detriment of the Scuola del Libro, is symptomatic of a major bias afflicting Italian graphic design historiography, namely its focus on designers' originality and design celebrities.[88] Moreover, the highlighting of Nizzoli, Persico, Pintori and Nivola's involvement in ISIA conveys an idea of design education whose success depended on the individual brilliance of teachers and students, and which relied on personal intuition and creativity rather than formalised education and intra- and inter-professional negotiation about training credentials.[89]

The infancy of graphic design education in Italy

In a February 1940 letter to the Swiss graphic designer Max Huber, Antonio Boggeri offered the following comment on the state of Italian graphics: 'The Italian artists who devote themselves to the graphic arts are generally weak in *typography* and utterly ignorant of the theoretical fundamentals of modern *composition*. This is simply because here there are no specialist Schools for graphic arts.'[90] He then solicited Huber's involvement in Studio Boggeri in an attempt to position the Milanese graphics and advertising studio at the forefront of Italian graphics by hiring better-trained graphic practitioners coming from neighbouring Switzerland. In the first part of the passage, Boggeri's description of the graphic practitioner as someone who possesses technical skills and a good understanding of modern graphics chimes with aspects of the collective identity of graphic practitioners then under development. What is noteworthy about the second part is Boggeri's assumption of a cause-and-effect link between specialist training and professionalism.

To a certain extent Boggeri was right in complaining to Huber about the lack of specialist schools of graphic design in 1940s Italy, because the first graphic design courses at the Scuola del Libro did not appear until the mid-1950s, as we shall see in chapter 4. Yet, by looking into the infancy of graphic design education in Italy, this chapter has shown that graphic practitioners had been seeking to bridge the gap between design education and practice from the interwar period onwards. In 1943, when the school was forced to close temporarily until September 1946, attempts to agree a definition for the graphic practitioner were still ongoing. Even so, the articulation of a specialist language and agreement on a shared skillset and body of knowledge are evidence that a new professional identity was taking shape, while the transition from practice into vocational education attests to a greater self-confidence and awareness on the part of graphic practitioners. Sketching and an understanding of modern aesthetics were now recognised as tools in the hands of the new practitioner, whose identity was the result of a methodological shift from mere execution to conception.

The interwar history of the Scuola del Libro is significant as it gave a voice to typographers, educators in technical schools, owners of printing firms, editors of trade journals and workers involved in the everyday production of printed matter. This was a heterogeneous group of people whose role in the history of Italian graphic design has more often than not been neglected in favour of an emphasis on individual graphic designers and their isolated contributions. By adapting to the requests of graphic practitioners, typographers, printing industrialists and graphic arts critics, the school played an active part in the construction of the graphic designers' professional identity. It was at the centre of heated debates and became a breeding ground for the modernisation of graphic design in Italy.

Now it is to everyday practice, self-representation and the relationship between graphics and advertising that we turn our attention by looking at Studio Boggeri from its foundation in 1933 to the early post-war period.

Notes

1 Il Risorgimento Grafico, 'Per l'insegnamento professionale', *Risorgimento Grafico*, 20:9 (September 1923), 438.
2 Il Risorgimento Grafico, 'Per l'insegnamento professionale. Le conclusioni del referendum', *Risorgimento Grafico*, 21:7 (July 1924), 291–5.
3 'Aver interessato tutto il gruppo di veri competenti e … aver allontanato i soliti sapientoni'. Il Risorgimento Grafico, 'Per l'insegnamento professionale', *Risorgimento Grafico*, 21:5 (May 1924), 208.
4 Freidson, *Professionalism*, p. 84.
5 'Meglio sacrificare un po' di *Scuola* all'*Officina* piuttosto di dover chiuderne i battenti per mancanza di mezzi finanziari adeguati'. A. Recalcati in Il Risorgimento Grafico, 'Per l'insegnamento professionale', *Risorgimento Grafico*, 20:11 (November 1923), 535.
6 For an overview of the Italian educational system, see N. D'Amico, *Storia e storie della scuola italiana* (Bologna: Zanichelli, 2010).
7 C. G. Lacaita, 'Istruzione tecnico-professionale e modernizzazione fra Otto e Novecento', in C. G. Lacaita (ed.), *La leva della conoscenza: istruzione e formazione professionale in Lombardia fra Otto e Novecento* (Milan: Giampiero Casagrande Editore, 2009), p. 9.
8 A. Gigli Marchetti, 'Impresa e lavoro. L'industria tipografico-editoriale Milanese dalla fine dell'Ottocento al Fascismo', in Montecchi (ed.), *La città dell'editoria*, pp. 23–37; A. Scotto di Luzio, 'L'industria dell'informazione: periodici e quotidiani, giornalisti e imprenditori', in Bigazzi and Meriggi (eds), *Storia d'Italia*, pp. 341–2, 354–5.
9 A. Tonelli, *L'istruzione tecnica e professionale di Stato nelle strutture e nei programmi da Casati ai giorni nostri* (Milan: Giuffrè Editore, 1964), pp. 3–85.
10 G. Genovesi, *Storia della scuola in Italia dal Settecento a oggi* (Bari: Laterza, 2004), pp. 123–74; R. J. Wolff, 'Italian education during World War II: Remnant of failed fascist education, seeds of new schools', in R. Lowe (ed.), *Education and the Second World War: Studies in Schooling and Social Change* (London: The Falmer Press, 1992), pp. 73–83.
11 Tonelli, *L'istruzione tecnica e professionale di Stato*, pp. 89–127; A. Pansera, *La formazione del designer in Italia: una storia lunga più di un secolo* (Venice: Marsilio, 2015), pp. 20–2; M. Amari, *I musei delle aziende. La cultura della tecnica tra arte e storia* (Milan: Franco Angeli Editore, 1997), pp. 52–5.
12 Freidson, *Professionalism*, p. 98. On the relationship between professionalisation and standardised teaching, see also Sarfatti Larson, *The Rise of Professionalism*, pp. 40–52.
13 M. Hodgen, *Workers Education in England and in the United States* (London: Kegan Paul, 1925), p. 5.
14 A. Gigli Marchetti, *I tre anelli: mutualità, resistenza, cooperazione dei tipografi milanesi (1860–1925)* (Milan: Franco Angeli Editore, 1983), p. 203.
15 R. Brown and D. Capozza, 'Social identity theory in retrospect and prospect', in Capozza and Brown (eds), *Social Identity Processes*, p. x.
16 Reicher, 'The context of social identity'.
17 C. Vinti, 'Design & craft in the definition of the graphic designer: The debate in Italian graphic arts magazines', in J. Gimeno-Martinez and F. Floré (eds), *Design and*

Craft: A History of Convergences and Divergences. 7ᵗʰ Conference of the International Committee of Design History and Design Studies (ICDHS) 20–22 September 2010 (Brussels: VWK, 2010), p. 446.

18 Freidson, *Professionalism*, p. 41.

19 'Con maggiore competenza e miglior preparazione di quanto possa farsi in officina, può immaginare costruzioni nuove di pagine, formazioni più fresche e meno banali lavori, combinazioni più vivaci ed efficaci di colore'. R. Bertieri, 'Orientamenti nuovi della tipografia italiana', *Risorgimento Grafico*, 30:2 (February 1933), 86.

20 'Digiuno completamente di ogni nozione di tecnologia grafica ... il perfetto tecnico e il perfetto esteta'. M. Soresina, 'Per una estetica grafica italiana', *Risorgimento Grafico*, 30:3 (March 1933), 146.

21 'Una vera e profonda "conoscenza del mestiere"'. Campo Grafico, 'Presupposti alla collaborazione con l'artista', *Campo Grafico*, 2:3 (March 1934), 54.

22 'Creare un'emozione estetica in una superficie con elementi grafici'. A. Rossi, 'L'evoluzione della tipografia in Italia', *Campo Grafico*, 5:9 (September 1937), 6.

23 'Artisti che per ragioni di professione ebbero la possibilità di acquistare dimestichezza con le officine tipografiche'. R. Bertieri, 'Architetti del libro e tipografi artisti in Italia', *Risorgimento Grafico*, 35:4 (April 1938), 145.

24 'Dalla tipografia provengono e della loro arte conoscono tutte le malizie ed anche tutte le esigenze'. *Ibid.*, 147.

25 Freidson, *Professionalism*, p. 73. See also, Abbott, *The System of Professions*, pp. 2–3.

26 'Reagire contro la tendenza che considera noi tipografi ... soltanto degli esecutori, troppo spesso maldestri, o incapaci, delle idee e dei programmi altrui'. G. Modiano, 'Lettera aperta a Raffaello Bertieri', *Risorgimento Grafico*, 35:8 (August 1938), 340.

27 G. Peviani, 'La necessità dello schizzo', *Campo Grafico*, 1:1 (January 1933), 4–5.

28 C. Frassinelli, 'Utilità dello schizzo nel lavoro tipografico', *Graphicus*, 18:230 (August 1928), 11–12.

29 'Si ricava in generale l'impressione che le definizioni e le catalogazioni comincino a far mucchio senza arrivare, dopo tante discussioni, alla formula sintetica.' E. Bona, 'Del progettista grafico', *Campo Grafico*, 8:1 (January 1939), 3.

30 'Ritrovare se stessa, ... ripresentarsi al pubblico completa di mezzi e di uomini'. *Ibid.*, 5.

31 'Definizione moderna, senza pompa, e di preciso significato'. *Ibid.*

32 Vinti, 'Design & craft in the definition of the graphic designer', pp. 448–9.

33 S. Monno (ed.), *Umanitaria: cento anni di solidarietà* (Milan; Florence: Edizioni Charta, 1993); E. Decleva, *Etica del lavoro, socialismo, cultura popolare: Augusto Osimo e la Società Umanitaria* (Milan: Franco Angeli Editore, 1985); C. A. Colombo, '"Sapere, fare e sapere fare": la Società Umanitaria, un modello laico per la formazione e l'orientamento al lavoro', in A. Bovo, N. Pietro, M. Palmaro, V. Parisi, H. M. Polidoro and A. Santucci (eds), *L'alchimia del lavoro: i generosi che primi in Milano fecondarono le arti e le scienze* (Milan: Raccolto Edizioni, 2008), pp. 93–145.

34 'Mettere i diseredati, senza distinzioni, in condizione di rilevarsi da sé medesimi, procurando loro assistenza, lavoro, istruzione'. 'Statuto Organico della Società Umanitaria', in R. Bauer (ed.), *La Società Umanitaria. Fondazione P.M. Loria Milano, 1893/1963* (Milan: Società Umanitaria, 1964), p. 18.

35 'Perfetto accordo con le rappresentanze operaie delle arti grafiche ... la scuola è sentita con viva simpatia da questa classe, la quale non solo l'appoggia, ma la riconosce ufficialmente'. M. Melino, *La Scuola del Libro di Milano: documenti e fatti* (Milan: Società Umanitaria, 1954), p. 34.

36 Gigli Marchetti, *I tre anelli*, pp. 194–5.

37 M. Clark, *Modern Italy: 1871 to the Present*, 3ʳᵈ ed. (London: Routledge, 2014 (1984)), pp. 296–301.

38 Archivio Storico Società Umanitaria, Milan, Italy (hereafter ASSU), 1932–227–53, annual report, 'Note sulla Scuola del Libro della Società Umanitaria, Milano', 1932, pp. 3–4.
39 T. H. Koon, *Believe, Obey, Fight: Political Socialization of Youth in Fascist Italy, 1922–1943* (Chapel Hill: University of North Carolina Press, 1985), pp. 55–6.
40 V. de Grazia, *How Fascism Ruled Women: Italy 1922–1945* (Berkeley: University of California Press, 1992), pp. 149–57.
41 J. Dunnage, *Twentieth-Century Italy: A Social History* (London; New York: Routledge, 2002), p. 83; M. De Giorgio, 'Donne e professioni', in M. Malatesta (ed.), *Storia d'Italia. I professionisti* (Turin: Einaudi, 1996), pp. 476–84.
42 ASSU, school register for the academic year 1935–36.
43 ASSU, pamphlet, 'Scuola del Libro, Milano, anno scolastico 1918–19: corsi serali di completamento e di perfezionamento', 1918; ASSU, prospectus, 'Scuola del Libro, Milano: programma della Sezione di completamento, anno accademico 1925–26', 1925, p. 14; the invitation card featured in Anon., 'Documentari di Campo Grafico', *Campo Grafico* 6:6 (June 1938), 171.
44 Anon., 'La regolamentazione dell'apprendistato grafico', *Graphicus*, 23:6 (January 1936), 15–16.
45 M. Scotford, 'Messy history vs neat history: Toward an expanded view of women in graphic design', *Visible Language*, 28:4 (1994), 374.
46 'Essenzialmente grafico … l'allievo … impari non a disegnare una foglia od un fregio, un vaso od un capitello, ma si abitui a giudicare il valore delle masse e della struttura dell'alfabeto, prenda pratica nella suddivisione dei bianchi, nella proporzione di una pagina, nell'equilibrare un titolo … su di una pagina vuota'. R. Bertieri, 'La Scuola del Libro in Milano: la "Vita Nova"', *Risorgimento Grafico*, 21:8 (August 1924), 332.
47 'Ritagliare un cartoncino nero di cm 2x2 e uno grigio 1x4; incollare … su un fondo bianco di cm 20x20 posizionandoli in modo che "stessero bene" l'uno rispetto all'altro e rispetto allo sfondo'. F. R. Gambarelli, *Monza anni Trenta dall'Umanitaria all'ISIA* (Monza: Musei Civici Monza, 2001), p. 26.
48 The assignment recalls Josef Albers's basic design exercises for the preliminary course at the Bauhaus. See F. A. Horowitz, 'Albers the teacher: Design', in F. A. Horowitz and B. Danilowitz (eds), *Josef Albers: To Open Eyes. The Bauhaus, Black Mountain College and Yale* (London; New York: Phaidon, 2006), pp. 98–124.
49 'Eseguire degli ottimi schizzi, ben condotti, completi, con disegnati soltanto gli elementi di carattere indicativo'. ASSU, 1935–227–53, annual report, 'Scuola del Libro: note sul funzionamento della sezione serale di completamento e della sezione festiva di perfezionamento, 1935–36', pp. 1–2.
50 'Serie di caratteri vecchi, stanchi, incompleti e fuori ormai dai tempi attuali … *non rispondono più in modo assoluto* alle esigenze dell'estetica moderna'. ASSU, 1932–227–53, annual report, 'Note sulla Scuola del Libro della Società Umanitaria, Milano', 1933, p. 10. See also ASSU, 1937–227–53, annual report, 'Scuola del Libro: funzionamento dell'anno scolastico 1936–37 XV', 1937, pp. 3–4; ASSU, 1938–227–53, annual report, 'Scuola del Libro: funzionamento durante l'anno scolastico 1937–38 XVI E. F.', 1938, p. 3.
51 'Teorici inetti, o operai qualunque'. M. Ferrigni, 'L'insegnamento grafico in Italia', *Risorgimento Grafico*, 32:1 (January 1935), 28.
52 In the early 1930s, about thirty foreign specialist publications were available for consultation. These included: *Anales Graficos* (Buenos Aires), *Archiv für Buchgewerbe* (Leipzig), *Archiv für Buchbinderei* (Dresden), *Art et Decoration* (Paris), *Art et Métiers Graphiques* (Paris), *Bulletin Officiel des Maîtres Imprimeurs de France* (Paris), *Coreo Tipografico* (Barcelona), *Deutsche Buch und Steindrucker* (Berlin), *Freie Künste* (Leipzig), *Grafika* (Warsaw), *Grafika Polska* (Warsaw), *Graphische Revue* (Vienna), *L'Imprimerie* (Paris), *Linotype & Machinery* (Paris and London), *Magyar Grafika*

(Budapest), *Offset Buch und Werbekunst* (Leipzig), *Paginas Graficas* (Buenos Aires), *Papyrus* (Paris), *Photographische Cronik* (Halle), *Plastika* (Warsaw), *The American Printer* (New York), *The British Printer* (London), *The Inland Printer* (Chicago), *The Printing Art* (Cambridge, MA), *The Studio* (London), *Trabajo* (Montevideo), *Typographische Jahrbücher* (Berlin) and *Zeitschrift für Reproduktionstechnik* (Halle). For the complete list of books and periodicals held in the course library in 1931, see L. Ladelli (ed.), *Catalogo della biblioteca della Scuola del Libro in Milano* (Milan: Umanitaria, 1931).

53 'È possibile che un Ente sorto in pieno periodo democratico, allevato all'ombra del socialismo riformista che è stato maestro ... di debolezze, di inutili sentimentalismi, possa trasformarsi in un organismo efficiente, adatto alle esigenze della civiltà fascista?' A. Mussolini, 'L'Umanitaria fascista inizia la sua nuova vita', 1929, in E. Scarpellini, *Il teatro del popolo: la stagione artistica dell'Umanitaria fra cultura e società* (Milan: Franco Angeli Editore, 2003), p. 199.

54 'Il fascismo ha depauperato l'Umanitaria ... riducendola a una scuola professionale tra le tante ... l'ha allontanata ... da quella essenziale missione, che l'istituzione aveva sposato sin dall'origine, di animatrice, di guida, di sollecitatrice di vie nuove pel mondo del lavoro, per la struttura sociale italiana.' Bauer, *La Società Umanitaria*, p. 8.

55 Dunnage, *Twentieth-Century Italy*, pp. 91–5; D. Thompson, *State Control in Fascist Italy: Culture and Conformity* (Manchester: Manchester University Press, 1991), pp. 98–114; Koon, *Believe, Obey, Fight*, pp. 60–89.

56 Falasca-Zamponi, *Fascist Spectacle*, pp. 95–9 and 110–13.

57 G. Turi, *Il Fascismo e il consenso degli intellettuali* (Bologna: Il Mulino, 1980), p. 195.

58 P. Corner, *The Fascist Party and Popular Opinion in Mussolini's Italy* (Oxford: Oxford University Press, 2012), pp. 179–80; Corner, 'Italian Fascism', 325–51; M. Ebner, 'Coercion', in Arthurs, Ebner and Ferris (eds), *The Politics of Everyday Life in Fascist Italy*, pp. 77–98.

59 Corner, 'Collaboration, complicity, and evasion under Italian Fascism', p. 78.

60 'All'Umanitaria soffia un vento molto diverso. Professori giovani e vivi, attrezzatura industriale aggiornata, ordine e chiarezza di cose e di idee e soprattutto ... una attenta osservazione dei bisogni e degli ideali contemporanei.' G. Pagano, *Le scuole dell'Umanitaria anno XVI E.F.: Quaderno n. 1* (Milan: Società Umanitaria, 1937), n. p., also quoted in Bauer, *La Società Umanitaria*, p. 167.

61 'Senso vivo, fresco ed aggiornato del bello e del brutto ... inequivocabile comprensione dell'estetica moderna ... la decorazione e la bellezza sono innanzitutto nella pulizia, nell'onestà, nella chiarezza, nella elegante abilità tecnica'. *Ibid.*

62 M. Soresina, 'Raffaello Bertieri alla Scuola del Libro', in Anon., *Onoranze a Raffaello Bertieri nell'ambito del quinto centenario dell'introduzione della stampa in Italia* (Milan: Centro Studi Grafici, 1966), pp. 75–87; C. Vinti, 'Campisti a scuola. Come è nata l'avventura di *Campo Grafico*', in M. Della Campa and C. A. Colombo (eds), *Spazio ai caratteri. L'Umanitaria e la Scuola del Libro* (Milan: Silvana Editoriale, 2004), pp. 59–62.

63 G. P., 'Contro l'arte del libro?', *Graphicus*, 17:219 (September 1927), 17. This is a review of Jan Tschichold's article 'Die Opposition gegen Buchkunst und Buchkunstaustellung', *Die Literarische Welt*, 3:29 (1927), 3.

64 'Forzando un po' i termini, si potrebbe dire perfino che fu proprio Bertieri, quale Direttore della Scuola del Libro a destare in molti di noi quella forza combattiva che poi tenacemente non volle riconoscere.' A. Rossi, '*Campo Grafico* al tempo di Bertieri', in Anon., *Onoranze a Raffaello Bertieri*, p. 210.

65 'Mentre al Bauhaus di Gropius, nella sezione della Tipografia si insegnava una grafica libera da moduli classici, asimmetrica, allineata ai nuovi principi del razionalismo, alla Scuola del Libro di Milano diretta dal Bertieri si insegnava la pagina simmetrica del libro, matrice unica per l'impaginazione di qualsiasi altro stampato.' Dradi, *Millenovecentotrentatre*, p. 26.

66 'Più degni di una pagina di William Morris che di un tipografo degli anni "30"'. *Ibid.*

67 'Darà al lettore la dimostrazione reale del valore raggiunto dalla Scuola in questi ultimi tempi nell'insegnamento tecnico, e, in modo particolare, del miglioramento estetico secondo le correnti più vive del gusto moderno'. Anon., 'Editoriale', *Campo Grafico*, 4:7 (July 1936), 1.

68 J. Tschichold, *The New Typography* (Berkeley; Los Angeles; London: University of California Press, 2006 (1928)), pp. 87–95.

69 'Materiale di studio e di godimento estetico'. Anon., 'Documentari di Campo Grafico', *Campo Grafico*, 6:2 (February 1938), 36.

70 Vinti, 'The New Typography in Fascist Italy', p. 61.

71 On the schematic rendering of the fasces, see C. Lazzaro, 'Forging a visible fascist nation: Strategies for fusing past and present', in C. Lazzaro and R. J. Crum (eds), *Donatello Among the Blackshirts: History and Modernity in the Visual Culture of Fascism* (Ithaca; London: Cornell University Press, 2005), p. 18. On the incorporation of fasces into the everyday material culture, see D. P. Doordan, 'In the shadow of the fasces: Political design in Fascist Italy', *Design Issues*, 13:1 (1997), 42–3.

72 Corner, 'Collaboration, complicity, and evasion under Italian Fascism', p. 82.

73 The only visual artefact to feature in the *Risorgimento Grafico* during the 1930s and early 1940s was a pamphlet advertising an exhibition by students of the Scuola del Libro that was included in P. Trevisani, 'Piccoli stampati', *Risorgimento Grafico*, 34:2 (February 1937), 75. From 1922 to 1932, the Scuola del Libro appeared more than eighteen times in the pages of *Risorgimento Grafico*.

74 Ferrigni, 'L'insegnamento grafico', 23–31.

75 M. Ferrigni, 'Saggi di giovani rilegatori', *Risorgimento Grafico*, 33:10 (October 1936), 377–94.

76 On the treatment of enlarged halftone dots as expressive elements, see E. Lupton, 'Design and production in the mechanical age', in D. Rothschild, E. Lupton and D. Goldstein (eds), *Graphic Design in the Mechanical Age: Selections from the Merrill C. Berman Collection* (New Haven; London: Yale University Press, 1998), pp. 51–8.

77 'Retorica Dannunziana della tipografia come arte e poesia'. Rossi, '*Campo Grafico* al tempo di Bertieri', p. 216. 'Dannunzian rhetoric' refers to the Italian poet Gabriele D'Annunzio.

78 E. Dellapiana and D. N. Prina, 'Craft, industry and art: ISIA (1922–1943) and the roots of Italian design education', in Lees-Maffei and Fallan (eds), *Made in Italy*, p. 122.

79 For an overview of ISIA, see R. Bossaglia (ed.), *L'ISIA a Monza: una scuola d'arte europea* (Milan: Silvana Editoriale, 1986); A. Pansera, 'Gli ISIA. Da dove veniamo e chi siamo', in M. Bazzini and A. Pansera (eds), *ISIA design convivio. Sperimentazione didattica: progetti, scenari e società* (Milan: Edizioni Aiap, 2015), pp. 18–20; Pansera, *La formazione del designer in Italia*, pp. 15–20.

80 Bossaglia, *L'ISIA a Monza*, pp. 9–53.

81 'Raccolte di arte applicata all'industria a sussidio degli allievi delle Scuole, degli artefici, degli industriali'. Article 2.f and 2.g of the 'Statuto organico del Consorsio per l'Università delle Arti Decorative' (1922), in *Ibid.*, p. 177.

82 Archivio Storico della città di Monza, Monza, Italy (hereafter ASM), II.965.1, annual report and redevelopment proposal, E. Palazzo, 'Memoriale per il definitivo ed organico riordinamento finanziario e didattico dell'Istituto Superiore per le Industrie Artistiche della Villa Reale di Monza', 1933, pp. 12–15.

83 'Potrebbero essere realizzati soltanto con il verificarsi di qualche ordinazione che imporrebbe i loro sviluppi fuori sede'. ASM, AP.9/1, annual inventory of the students' works, 'Riepilogo generale della produzione delle diverse sezioni durante l'anno scolastico 1938–39 and 1940–41', 1938–41, n. p.

84 ASM, CAMMU 41.1, timetable, 'Notizie statistiche. Anno scolastico 1933–34', 1934; ASM, III.342.2, timetable, 'Elenco personale dell'ISIA. Anno 1936/37', 1937.

85 R. Cassanelli, U. Collu and O. Selvafolta (eds), *Nivola, Fancello, Pintori. Percorsi del moderno: dalle arti applicate all'industrial design* (Cagliari: Editoriale Wide, 2003).

86 Dellapiana and Prina, 'Craft, industry and art', p. 118.

87 ASM, II.695.1, letter from E. Palazzo to U. Cattaneo, 11 December 1934, p. 6. No mention was made as to the replacement. The painter, textile designer and book decorator, Ugo Zovetti, later became the commercial art teacher as his name appears in the staff list for the academic year 1936–37: ASM, III.342.2, timetable, 'Elenco personale dell'ISIA. Anno 1936/37', 1937, p. 2.

88 Dalla Mura and Vinti, 'A historiography of Italian design', p. 46; Camuffo, Piazza and Vinti, 'TDM5. Un museo per una storia ancora da scrivere', p. 28.

89 K. McCoy, 'Education in an adolescent profession', in S. Heller (ed.), *The Education of a Graphic Designer* (New York: Allworth Press, 2005), pp. 4–6.

90 'Gli artisti italiani che si dedicano all'arte grafica sono generalmente deficienti nella *tipografia* e ignorano completamente le teorie fondamentali della *composizione* moderna semplicemente perché qui non ci sono Scuole superiori di arte grafica.' Archivio Studio Boggeri, Meride, Switzerland (hereafter ASB), letter from A. Boggeri to M. Huber, 4 February 1940, p. 4.

2

Open Studio (Boggeri)

Writing in *Risorgimento Grafico* in 1931, Nino Caimi, founder of the Enneci advertising agency and former director of Erwa, the Milanese branch of the American advertising agency Erwin Wasey & Co., argued that, since the majority of graphic production consisted of commercial artefacts, it was crucial for the graphics industry to get involved in advertising.[1] To facilitate the crossover between practices, he recommended readers familiarise themselves with the principles of modern advertising: economy, rationality and effectiveness. A new generation of graphic practitioners answered Caimi's call for collaboration. In an attempt to extend their field of activity beyond book design and poster art, they turned their attention to everyday advertising-oriented printed material, as advertising offered them an alternative dimension to articulate their practice.

The interwar exchange between graphic practice and advertising was the foundation upon which Antonio Boggeri built and ran his studio, and it was the socio-cultural context within which he negotiated his own professional identity. Studio Boggeri opened its doors in 1933 in Via Borghetto 5, twenty minutes' walk from Milan Central Station (East) and the Duomo (West). It was 'a modern and simple-looking studio in an old patrician building', big windows, drawing desks, a small photographic studio with a darkroom and a 'permanently dripping palm tree' in the courtyard that stuck in the memory of one of the first foreign collaborators of the studio, the German graphic designer Käte Bernhardt.[2] Boggeri was a keen self-trained photographer with a background in music, and he had spent the eight years prior to the founding of Studio Boggeri in charge of the typo-lithography department at Alfieri&Lacroix. Here, he had familiarised himself with graphics and printing techniques, acquired expertise in the management of the whole production process and developed a network that proved to be instrumental once he opened a business on his own.

Among those interested in the history of Italian graphic design, Studio Boggeri garners unmatched attention.[3] It has been celebrated as the first full-service graphic design studio in Italy and one of the agents that transformed 1933 into the annus mirabilis of modern Italian graphics. However, despite its ubiquity in the literature, there has been surprisingly little interest in grounding the studio within its wider context. The list of three generations of Italian and Central European graphic designers who were attracted by what Boggeri himself described as 'an imaginary and yearned for Eden of enlightened clients who were flocking to Studio Boggeri [considering it] synonymous with the advertising avant-garde', is generally considered a self-explanatory reason for the prominent place it occupies in the larger narrative of twentieth-century Italian graphic design.[4]

By contrast, this chapter grounds Studio Boggeri within the larger socio-cultural context and historical and political circumstances, and provides new perspectives into working, commissioning and recruiting practices and strategies of self-representation from the studio's foundation to the early years of post-war reconstruction. By examining so far neglected or unpublished visual material, primary sources and archival documents, I examine how and why the studio promoted modernist techniques and aesthetics. In particular, I analyse self-promotional printed artefacts as evidence of Boggeri's professional confidence and expression of the studio's aesthetic principles and design practices. Overall, I employ Studio Boggeri as an iconic case study to advance understanding of the emergence of graphic design practice in Milan. Whereas chapter 1 rooted the origins of graphic design practice in the lineage of typography and the printing trade, this chapter introduces advertising as yet another factor in its articulation. By including advertising within the larger picture of Italian graphic design history, I seek to rectify a long-lasting prejudice that has tended to underplay, or deny outright, the kinship between graphic design and commercial art.

Advertising technicians and advertising artists

With a tradition of poster art that went back to the 1880s, advertising was no novelty in interwar Italy. However, it had undergone many significant changes over the years. Indeed, the build-up of a specialist literature and launch of trade journals; the founding of advertising agencies and development of complex promotional strategies; the organisation of national and international congresses and exhibitions; the teaching of courses on advertising and the founding of professional organisations, are all evidence of the relatively high level of modernisation and professionalisation the sector had reached by the mid-1930s.[5]

Economic and socio-cultural changes favoured the transformation of the Italian advertising sector. The acceleration of industrialisation, the growth of the middle-class market and changes in the distribution sector made more industrialists aware of, and interested in, advertising.[6] The economic policies undertaken by the regime accidentally affected manufacturers' approach towards, and reliance on, advertising. Previously export-oriented manufacturers turned to the home market due to the revaluation of the lira in 1927, and many of them had to reposition their products as 'Italian' following the proclamation of autarchy in 1936. In both cases, they resorted to advertising to sell their goods.[7] The regime itself had acquired 'a more proactive attitude towards the politicisation of commercial advertising'.[8] Whereas during the 1920s it had used advertising restrictions as a key agent for censorship, by the mid-1930s it had become 'actively involved in an increasingly entangled effort to transform the world of commercial advertising into the herald of a new fascist understanding of consumption and society'.[9] With the growth in demand for advertising, the supply of advertising space increased as well. Thanks also to technological progress and improved literacy levels of the population, the mass press – illustrated periodicals in particular – expanded circulation, diversified its target audiences and increased its reliance on advertising revenues.[10]

Changes in Italian advertising culture stemmed also from the circulation of US-inspired advertising methods that challenged the local tradition of poster art by promoting an idea of advertising as a science based on the principles of rationalisation and efficiency.[11] US advertising methods included market research, division and specialisation of tasks, consumer-oriented approaches and media planning. The Americanisation of European advertising was a transnational phenomenon of cultural transfer with an increasing impact in the post-war period, as we shall see in chapter 5.[12] Diverse channels promoted this transfer to and within Italy. Direct contact was facilitated by US advertising agencies J. Walter Thompson and Erwin Wasey & Co. opening branches in Milan in the late 1920s, and Italian advertising people working on the other side of the Atlantic. While the 1929 Great Crash and the autarchy policy of the Fascist regime cut short the Milanese business ventures of the US agencies, the Italians working in the US became the founders of the first Italian advertising agencies.[13] US advertising and marketing techniques had been documented in the specialist literature since the beginning of the twentieth century and they informed courses on advertising and business management taught at the Milan Polytechnic.[14] Trade journals, like the advertising, business administration and management magazine *L'Ufficio Moderno* and *La Pubblicità d'Italia*, also published articles on US approaches to marketing and advertising.[15]

The purported scientific methods of US advertising met the favour of a new profession that was seeking social legitimation: the 'tecnici pubblicitari' (advertising technicians). Lacking any artistic training, Italian advertising technicians were professionals who often came from fields like journalism or law. Similarly to their counterparts across the Atlantic, they considered advertising to be a new branch of business whose scientific legitimacy hinged upon the application of behavioural psychology, marketing research and statistics. They questioned the local Italian advertising system, which was based on direct contact between industrialists and commercial artists, and asserted their credentials as mediators. All the same, the methods of US advertising were not accepted unanimously, and some exponents of the old system began a 'strategy of resistance', defending the notion of advertising as an artistic expression.[16]

Debates within Italian advertising coincided with graphic practitioners' growing interest in commercial graphics. 'With the rationalist culture taking centre stage', advertising historian Giuseppe Priarone argued, 'the history of [Italian] advertising reached a crucial juncture [since] advertising was no longer entrusted to the *painter* but to the advertising *graphic practitioner*.'[17] The division and specialisation of tasks advocated by the advertising technicians was welcomed by a new generation of graphic practitioners who yearned to free themselves from the painterly dimension of poster art and the rigid schemes of the typographic tradition. Led by the editors of *Campo Grafico*, they demanded a shift of focus from book and poster design towards everyday printed matter. As we saw in chapter 1, they considered the so-called 'tipografia-arte' (typography as Art) as 'an anachronistic tendency' and deemed it to be 'detrimental and fatal to the advancement of [their] practice'.[18] Conversely, they expected typography to engage in real-life conditions of contemporary industrial society. As Guido Modiano put it, 'the characteristic products of our times [are] not books, but the magazine, the pamphlet, the catalogue'.[19]

Jobbing printing was the object of scrutiny in Italian specialised magazines of the time. Systematisation was a shared concern among contemporary European graphics movements. As design historian Jeremy Aynsley argued in his book on German graphic design, efforts to standardise typography and graphic design can be taken as a case study of how standardisation and modernism became synonymous.[20] Driven by an overriding concern with function and efficiency, Italian contributors to the standardisation of typography systematised techniques and visual languages in an attempt to codify principles and unify design standards. Different media required different aesthetics and it was 'illogical to force advertising matter into rhythms created for the book'.[21]

By setting standards of good design, articles were also an occasion for graphic practitioners or studios to showcase their works. This was the case with Studio Boggeri, whose promotional material for commerce and industry featured in the specialist press as an example of effective advertising. A pamphlet (see figure 2.1) and a poster promoting the coffee-roasting company Illy were selected by Modiano in a 1934 article on packaging.[22] Modiano used the advertising campaign, which was devised

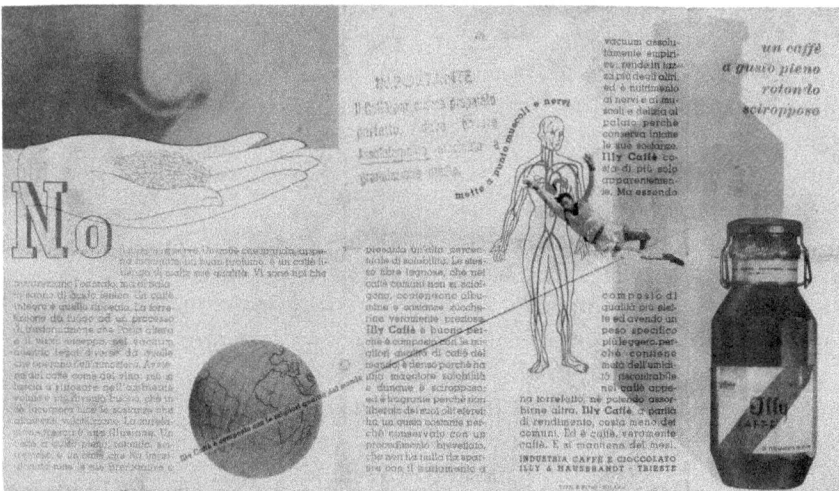

2.1 Advertisement for Illy Caffè by Xanti Schawinsky, 1934.

by Xanti Schawinsky for Studio Boggeri, to illustrate the concept of 'personalità aziendale' (business identity). In accordance with the technicians' scientific approach to advertising, this business identity consisted of an easily recognisable and coherent image that varied according to media and purpose. Firms were invited to follow the lead of Olivetti, which set up an in-house advertising office in 1931. Nothing was to be left to chance or improvisation because each aspect of a business, from the letterhead to the window display, contributed to its identity.

Articles promoting the collaboration between graphic practitioners and advertising technicians regularly appeared in trade journals of the period. A 1943 article in *L'Ufficio Moderno* described the advertising technician, the advertising artist and the typographer as the 'inseparable trinomial' of advertising work.[23] Knowledge of psychology, good organisational skills and a focus on commercial efficiency were the requirements of advertising technicians. Since they were expected to oversee the work of advertising artists and typographers, familiarity with graphic aesthetics and techniques was also recommended. The requirements of the advertising artists were creativity, good taste, expertise in graphic and printing techniques, and familiarity with modern advertising. The criterion for evaluating their work was how efficiently their design served the purpose of advertising. Execution was in the hands of the typographers. Collaboration implied specialisation and division of labour: typographers, advertising artists and technicians were cooperating occupations working together on distinct but related tasks that required negotiating their jurisdiction by articulating 'the content and character of [their] expertise and the functional relationship of that expertise to [the expertise] of the others'.[24]

It was against the background of the contemporary dialogue between typographic rationalism and the rationalisation of advertising that Boggeri articulated his professional identity. A closer look at the three editions of *Guida Ricciardi* provides evidence for this. Published between 1933 and 1942 by Giulio Cesare Ricciardi, co-founder of Balza-Ricc advertising agency, *Guida Ricciardi* was a directory and how-to handbook for people working in advertising and their clients. The preface to the first edition explained its aims in these terms: 'to facilitate the use of advertising means, remove or reduce the causes of the waste of time and money and prevent improvised intermediaries from stealing business illicitly, hence to contribute to the minimisation of costs and the greater efficiency of advertising through a simpler, more logical and more rational use of advertising means'.[25] The text goes on to clarify the importance of advertising in contemporary society, explain its principles and describe the different figures working in the industry.

Studio Boggeri featured in all three editions of *Guida Ricciardi*.[26] Each time, it was listed under a different category. In 1933 it was included among the studios of advertising photography; a hint at the paramount role played by photography in Boggeri's practice, to be explored later in this chapter. In 1936 it was labelled as both a specialised photography studio and an advertising technical agency. Then, in 1942, it was listed under the broad category of advertising agencies, companies, studios and consultancies. This ambiguity suggests there was difficulty in categorising Studio Boggeri. As a matter of fact, the studio did not entirely match any of the foregoing definitions. Similarly to an advertising technical agency, it selected the most suitable media, technique and visual language, and appointed the most appropriate graphic practitioner to fulfil a client's requests. However, it lacked the service of strategic consultancy that an advertising technical agency was expected to offer.

Looking at this categorisation in comparative terms, the definition of the studio as an advertising technical agency established a clear distance between it and the relevant out-group of advertising artists. Yet included among the latter would have been several practitioners who were working for the studio at the time: Bruno Munari, Marcello Nizzoli and Xanti Schawinsky.[27] In other words, the categorisation differentiated the services offered by the studio as a whole from those of its individual collaborators. Moreover, it is informative about the way in which Boggeri envisioned his own professional identity. If Studio Boggeri was an advertising technical agency, the most appropriate term to describe Boggeri's profession is probably 'advertising technician'. In this line, it is telling that when the alliance between advertising and graphic practitioners fell apart in the post-war period, as we shall see in chapter 4, Boggeri recognised himself as belonging to the technicians' rather than the artists' category.[28]

A red B between two black dots

From the very outset, Boggeri carried out a coherent strategy of self-promotion of the studio: logos, stationery, pamphlets and advertisements were all expressions of a carefully designed business identity. In addition to the explicit self-promotional function, these graphic artefacts connoted design methodologies and aesthetics adopted and advocated by Studio Boggeri. Whereas the current literature on the studio celebrates works commissioned by iconic clients, such as Olivetti and Pirelli, this and the following section shift the focus inward and present a group of little-known self-promotional ephemera. Examining self-promotional strategies from the perspective of self-image and representation reveals how Boggeri expressed his professional ambitions in visual terms, and used self-promotional material to fashion his own professional identity.[29] Cultural readings of identities see them as 'constructed within, not outside, discourse … [and] understands them as produced in specific historical and institutional sites within specific discursive formations and practices, by specific enunciative strategies'.[30] In the case of Boggeri and his studio, the professional and business identities were constructed, understood, valued and performed within the language and discourse of modernist design, the historical context of Fascist and post-war Italy, and the collaborative efforts between graphic and advertising practices.

For the launch of the studio, Boggeri commissioned the Parisian foundry Deberny et Peignot to design the first logo. The foundry had been at the forefront of European type design since the mid-eighteenth century. At the time of Boggeri's commission, it was well known for its experimental promotional publications that featured in international trade journals. By turning to Deberny et Peignot, Boggeri was commissioning a renowned foundry with the clear intention of positioning Studio Boggeri within both the typographic tradition and the modernist graphic vanguard at the same time. This strategy is implicit in the design of the logo itself, for it is reminiscent of the typographic tradition while also giving a discreet nod to modernist graphics (see figure 2.2). Set in Didot, the B is evocative of French neoclassical typography and reminiscent of the local Bodoni. Simple but original, the typo-symbol conceals a clever stratagem. The red B between two black dots is a fragment, a close-up of the brand name Studio Boggeri: the two black dots turn into the two 'o's of Studio Boggeri with the red B placed between twelve symmetrically arranged letters.

Seven years later, Boggeri commissioned Max Huber to redesign the red B between two black dots. The Swiss graphic designer simplified the original design by replacing the elegant serif and the two dots with a bold geometrical sans-serif and two circles. The new logo stands out in the heading of the redesigned A4 letterhead (see figure 2.3). As design historian Robin Kinross observed, the business letterhead was the item 'most thoroughly affected by standardisation'.[31] Huber's design is evidence of this: the asymmetrical layout, the larger left-hand margin for punch holes, the use of fine rules as means of inner organisation, the standard paper size and the meaningful use of colour to direct the viewer's eye comply with the design principles of typographic rationalism. Once the letterhead is used, additional aspects emerge. First, the bottom-right red B reinforces the signature 'Antonio Boggeri' by initialising the sender's surname. Secondly, the signature shows how Boggeri took the idea of business identity to the extreme, making no distinction between himself and his studio. Indeed, the small mark before the surname transforms Boggeri's signature into the logo: in combination with the dot of the i, the mark turns the signature into a handwritten version of the red B between two black dots.

Advertisements are yet another aspect of Studio Boggeri's business identity. Featuring in graphics, design and architecture magazines and advertising trade journals and publications, they targeted an audience that was familiar with discourses around the rationalisation of advertising and modernist graphics. Photography, drawing, advertising, propaganda and graphic works were the buzzwords of Boggeri's promotional vocabulary.

2.2 Frontispiece of the promotional booklet *L'uovo di Colombo*, 1937. The manicule indicates the red B between two black dots, the first logo of Studio Boggeri designed by the Parisian type foundry Deberny et Peignot in 1933.

Whereas nowadays the use of the word 'propaganda' might raise eyebrows, in interwar Italy the term was often used as a synonym for publicity, with no political implication. Palette, square ruler, paintbrush, halftone screen, camera lens, paint tubes, nibs, compass, pins and paper clips are recurring elements in the studio's advertisements. The advertisement

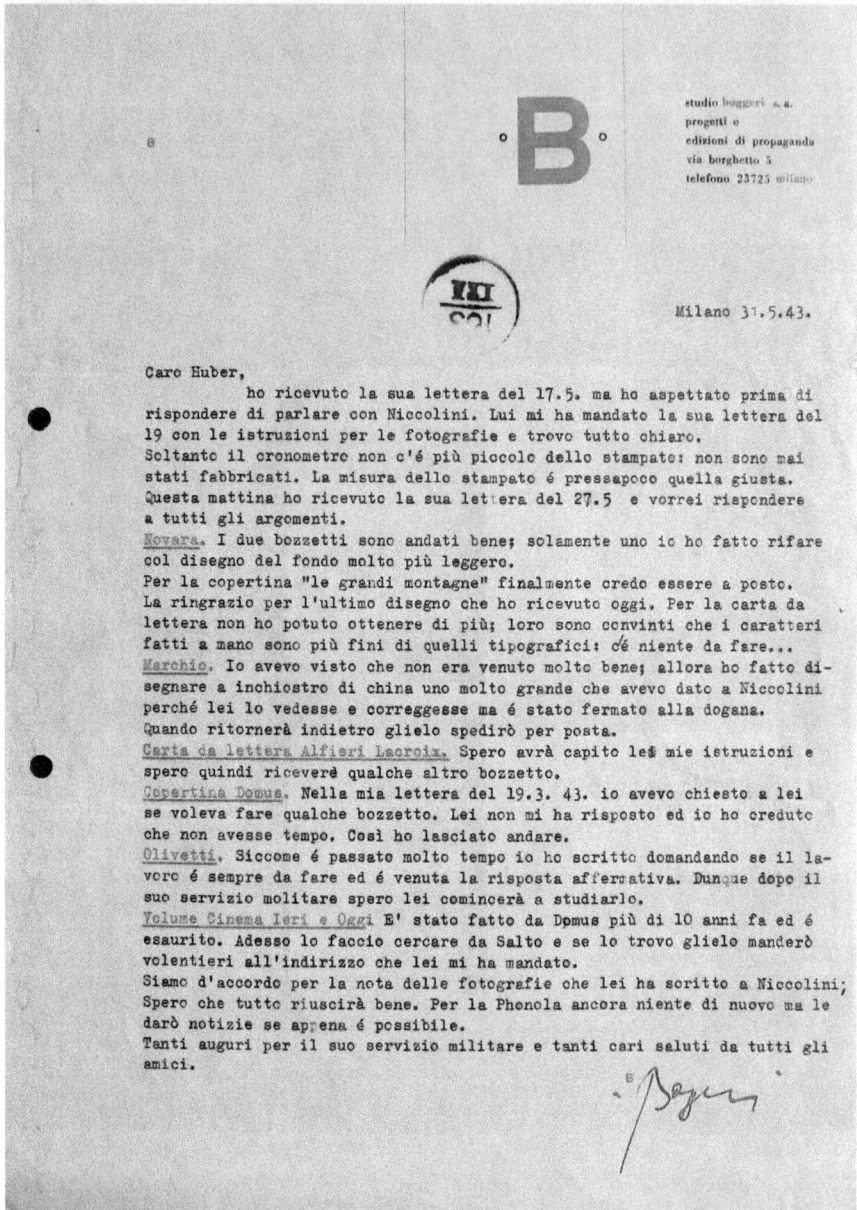

studio boggeri s. a.
progetti e
edizioni di propaganda
via borghetto 5
telefono 23725 milano

Milano 31.5.43.

Caro Huber,
        ho ricevuto la sua lettera del 17.5. ma ho aspettato prima di
rispondere di parlare con Niccolini. Lui mi ha mandato la sua lettera del
19 con le istruzioni per le fotografie e trovo tutto chiaro.
Soltanto il cronometro non c'é più piccolo dello stampato: non sono mai
stati fabbricati. La misura dello stampato é pressapoco quella giusta.
Questa mattina ho ricevuto la sua lettera del 27.5 e vorrei rispondere
a tutti gli argomenti.
Novara. I due bozzetti sono andati bene; solamente uno io ho fatto rifare
col disegno del fondo molto più leggero.
Per la copertina "le grandi montagne" finalmente credo essere a posto.
La ringrazio per l'ultimo disegno che ho ricevuto oggi. Per la carta da
lettera non ho potuto ottenere di più; loro sono convinti che i caratteri
fatti a mano sono più fini di quelli tipografici: cé niente da fare...
Marchio. Io avevo visto che non era venuto molto bene; allora ho fatto disegnare a inchiostro di china uno molto grande che avevo dato a Niccolini
perché lei lo vedesse e correggesse ma é stato fermato alla dogana.
Quando ritornerà indietro glielo spedirò per posta.
Carta da lettera Alfieri Lacroix. Spero avrà capito le mie istruzioni e
spero quindi riceverà qualche altro bozzetto.
Copertina Domus. Nella mia lettera del 19.3. 43. io avevo chiesto a lei
se voleva fare qualche bozzetto. Lei non mi ha risposto ed io ho creduto
che non avesse tempo. Così ho lasciato andare.
Olivetti. Siccome é passato molto tempo io ho scritto domandando se il lavoro é sempre da fare ed é venuta la risposta affermativa. Dunque dopo il
suo servizio molitare spero lei comincerà a studiarlo.
Volume Cinema Ieri e Oggi E' stato fatto da Domus più di 10 anni fa ed é
esaurito. Adesso lo faccio cercare da Salto e se lo trovo glielo manderò
volentieri all'indirizzo che lei mi ha mandato.
Siamo d'accordo per la nota delle fotografie che lei ha scritto a Niccolini;
Spero che tutto riuscirà bene. Per la Phonola ancora niente di nuovo ma le
darò notizie se appena é possibile.
Tanti auguri per il suo servizio militare e tanti cari saluti da tutti gli
amici.

2.3   Letterhead of Studio Boggeri, featuring the second version of the red B between two black dots logo designed by Max Huber in 1940.

devised by Munari in 1935 is no exception to this rhetoric (see figure 2.4). The caption 'photography – drawings – graphic works' corresponds to the pictures in the three circles: a photo shoot, the graphic practitioner's tools and a selection of graphic works by the studio.

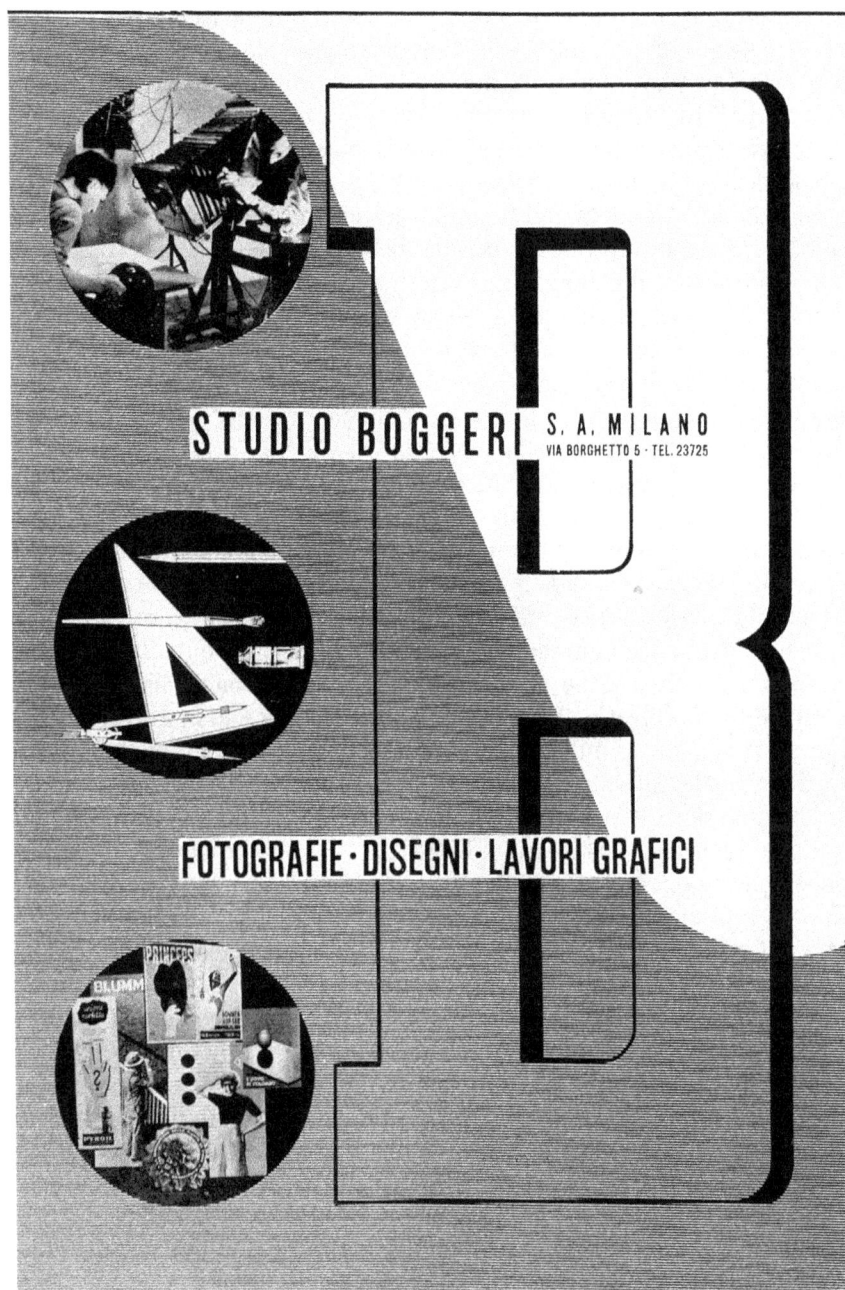

2.4 Advertisement for Studio Boggeri, designed by Bruno Munari in the mid-1930s and published in *Guida Ricciardi: pubblicità e propaganda in Italia* (1936), p. 387. In the lower circle one can identify (clockwise) Xanti Schawinsky's posters for Cervo and Cosulich, the front cover of the promotional booklet *L'uovo di Colombo*, Erberto Carboni's pamphlet for Montecatini and Antonio Boggeri's advertising photograph for a hat manufacturer.

Reiteration contributes to a narrative carefully constructed by Boggeri over the years through the application of tropes that were borrowed from modernist imagery. The instruments of the engineer rather than the tools of the artist, the square ruler, the compass and the camera, shifted the focus away from the final product towards design, technology and production process. Contemporary viewers were no strangers to this rhetoric, and so were likely to understand its implications and acknowledge Boggeri's intentions in using it. Similar images were published in magazines and trade journals of the time. This was the case with the cover of Franz Roh and Jan Tschichold's book *FotoAuge* (1929) featuring El Lissitzky's self-portrait *The Constructor* (1920) in the May 1931 issue of *Casabella*, or with Luigi Veronesi's and Erberto Carboni's advertisements featuring compass and square ruler that were published in the second and third editions, respectively, of *Guida Ricciardi*.[32]

Means of representing Studio Boggeri also included promotional publications. The booklet *L'uovo di Colombo* celebrated four years of activity (see figure 2.5). Here the studio is described as 'the latest expression of advertising techniques and art', and clients are assured that 'its specialised Italian and foreign artists, and its technical organisation, provide [their] ideas with the safest guarantee of effective and brilliant outcomes'.[33] After four years of activity the studio could boast an enviable list of clients: among others, Olivetti, the porcelain manufacturer Richard-Ginori, the chemical company Montecatini, the cosmetic company Helena Rubinstein, Illy and Nestlé. Private companies apart, Studio Boggeri also worked for the insurance institute, INA, Istituto Nazionale delle Assicurazioni (National Insurance Institute) and for Italy's largest broker of advertising spaces and agency of choice for autarchic and collective campaigns for national products, UPI, Unione Pubblicitaria Italiana (Italian Advertising Union). Finally, it also produced graphic works tied to the regime, such as the advertisement for a 1934 propaganda exhibition.

The advertisement for the Esposizione dell'Aeronautica Italiana (Italian Aeronautical Exposition) is part of a body of work done by Studio Boggeri that carried fascist connotations, including its regular contributions to *La Rivista Illustrata del Popolo d'Italia* and the highly politicised organ of the fascist union of advertising agencies, *La Pubblicità d'Italia*. In his investigation of mass participation in the regime's public events, historian Paul Corner distinguished 'true believers' from those 'asking the question, "What does the regime offer me?" and others asking, more cautiously, "What happens if I don't collaborate?"'[34] A passage from Xanti Schawinsky's autobiography provides some insight into Boggeri's endorsement. 'Among my friends', he writes, 'I was assured that they are liberal-thinking citizens of the world who, however, had to surrender their consent to the outside world through forced incorporation into the party associations.'[35] If we take Schawinsky at his word and count Boggeri

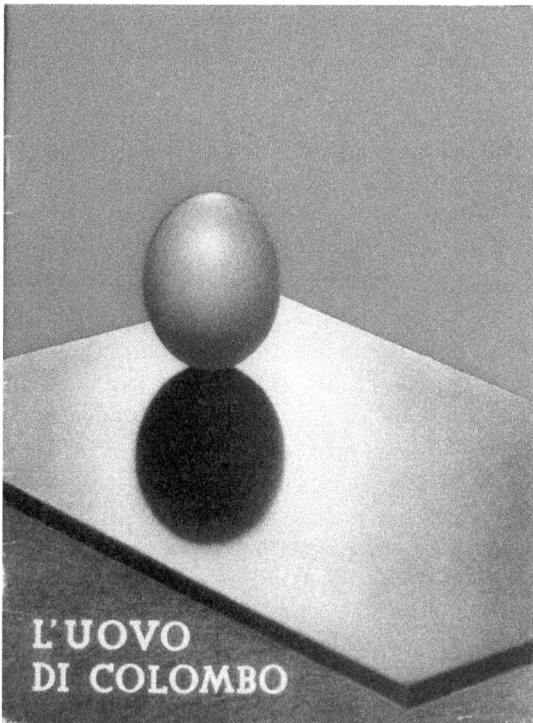

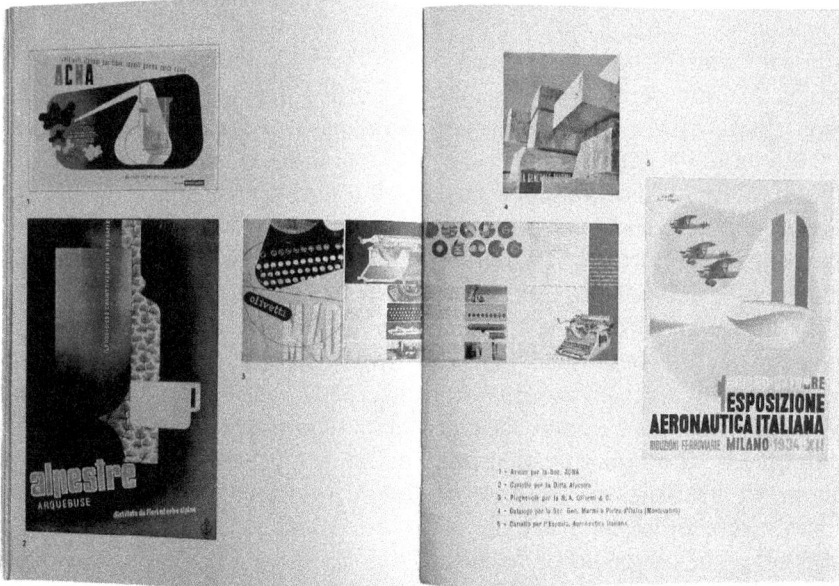

2.5 Cover and double-page spread from *L'uovo di Colombo*, 1937. The advertisements for the typewriter Olivetti M40 and the Esposizione dell'Aeronautica Italiana were designed by Xanti Schawinsky in 1934.

among his friends, then we can perhaps rule out genuine enthusiasm as a reason Boggeri might have designed works that carried fascist connotations. However, the question as to whether Boggeri's endorsement falls under the category of opportunistic support, pragmatic acceptance or constrained choice remains without a clear answer. For sure, in the post-war period he was aware that this body of work put him and the studio in an awkward position.

As discussed in chapter 1, practitioners' accommodation to the regime cannot be approached in oppositional terms – that is, fascist vs antifascist, consensus vs resistance – as 'for many Italians, employment and social standing depended upon accommodating one's values, appearance, family, and everyday ritual to the political and social codes of Fascism'.[36] For fine and commercial artists the Confederazione nazionale dei sindacati professionisti e artisti (National Confederation of Artists and Professionals' Syndicates) had represented since its foundation in 1928 the main control system. The Confederation – renamed Corporazione professionisti e artisti (Corporation of Professionals and Artists) in 1934 – was an umbrella organisation that also included trade unions for architects, writers and journalists. Membership was virtually obligatory for anyone who wanted to work and access the regime's patronage and monopoly over exhibition and distribution.[37] Similar conditions and requirements applied to the advertising agencies and space brokers who had been organised under the Sindacato nazionale fascista agenzie e case di pubblicità (National Fascist Union of Advertising Agencies and Firms) since the late 1930s.[38] Photographers, manufacturers of illuminated advertising or advertising objects – for example, promotional giveaways – were, instead, assigned to the Federazione autonoma delle comunità artigiane (Autonomous Federation of Artisan Communities). The implementation of the corporatist model within the advertising sector reflected the plurality of people involved and showed the regime's efforts to discipline labour, in general, and monitor the activity of Italian advertisers, in particular.[39]

Whereas in 1937 showing off a relation with fascist institutions might have furthered promotional goals, the involvement of the studio with propaganda activities and events was discreetly omitted in the post-war period. The printing dummy of a pamphlet designed by Huber after 1945 has a deliberate omission that demonstrates a pragmatic adjustment of Boggeri's strategies of self-representation (see figure 2.6). Pencil or ink marks sketch the page layout, while handwritten annotations indicate whether pictures should be reframed, repositioned or replaced. An underlined 'no' and a cross, which is drawn twice to reinforce the imperative message, warn that the cover of a publication on architecture must be taken out. Strikingly enough, the editing affects only the cover and not the two-page spread. Whereas the former features the fascist dating

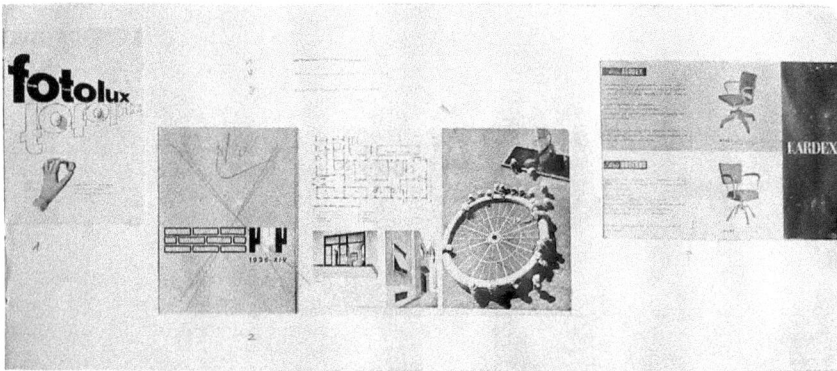

2.6 Printing dummy for a pamphlet advertising Studio Boggeri, designed by Max Huber, c. 1945.

system and three fasces, the architectural drawings, pictures and floor plans on the latter do not contain any reference to Fascism and could therefore stay. Thus, the dummy shows how Boggeri adjusted the studio's identity to align with the changed political situation of post-war Italy.

Similarly, a bilingual – Italian and French – pamphlet designed by Huber in 1945 indicates Boggeri's prompt response to the reopening of the international market and his desire to keep the studio at the vanguard of national and international graphics scenes. The text echoes interwar discussions over the rationalisation of advertising, as it reminds prospective clients that 'the design and execution of an advertising printed artefact based on modern ideas and style should be entrusted to specialists and technicians of the complex graphic field'.[40] Advertising was to be put in the hands of professionals and Studio Boggeri was able to supply clients with effective, clear, modern looking and technically faultless advertisements.

Advertising photography

In between the two versions of the red B between two black dots, Studio Boggeri used a different logo devised by Bruno Munari (see figure 2.7). Rather than 'subtly recalling the printing tradition', as design historian Alessandro Colizzi suggested, I would argue that Munari's logo explicitly recalls the very origins of photography, for it can be read as a schematic representation of a camera obscura.[41] The black square signifies the camera itself: an optical device usually in the shape of a box or a room with a small opening on one side. Intersecting at the median in the left side of the black square, the two straight lines delimit the field of view. The light cone passes from the external scene – the red rectangle – through the opening. Once inside, it projects onto the opposite surface

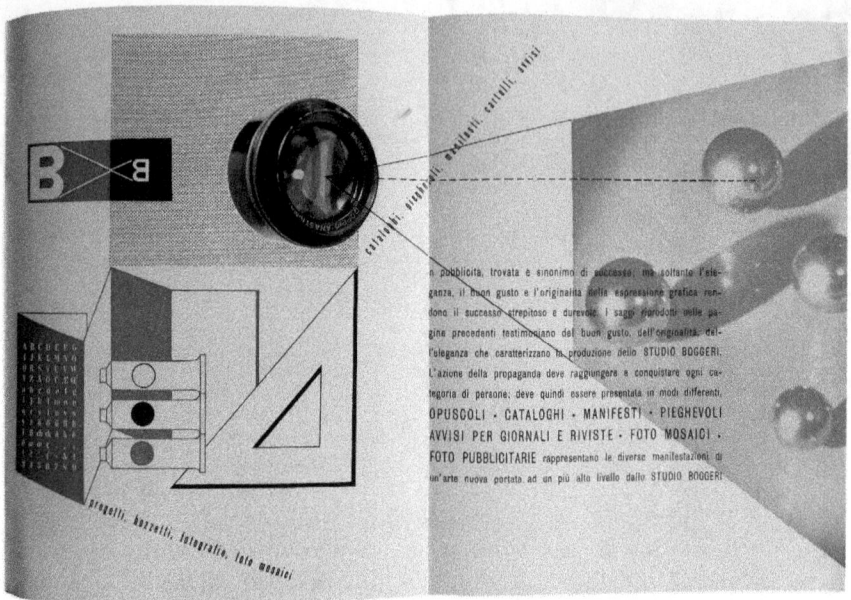

2.7 Foldout from the booklet *L'uovo di Colombo*, featuring Bruno Munari's logo for Studio Boggeri, 1937.

a smaller and flipped upside down and from left to right version − the small and inverted B − of the image outside the black square − the big B. Two pages from *L'uovo di Colombo* remove potential doubts about this interpretation. Here, the black square is arranged on a photographic camera that is made from juxtaposing a square cut out of a halftone screen and a lens from which two red diverging lines depart. Contained in the field of view of the camera, the foreshortened red picture chromatically echoes the red rectangle of the logo, thereby creating a direct dialogue between this and the montage. Thus, Munari's logo connotes Studio Boggeri and the photography technique. Pushing this reading further, it also embodies one of the main features of the studio: the use of photography.

If photography was a distinctive feature of Studio Boggeri, what was the photographic aesthetic it championed? An advertisement designed by the Swiss, Hungarian-born, graphic designer Imre Reiner answers the question (see figure 2.8). Here the allusion to modernist photography is straightforward. Arranged on top of a palette, a set square, a paint brush and a dotted halftone screen, the eye on the lens literally illustrates the main principle of the New Vision, a 1920s photography movement directly related to the Bauhaus. In the mid-1920s László Moholy-Nagy wrote that 'the photographic camera can either complete or supplement our optical instrument − the eye'.[42] It follows that the lens was considered a second

2.8 Advertisement for Studio Boggeri, designed by Imre Reiner in 1934 and published in *Campo Grafico*, 2:12 (December 1934), 267.

eye for looking anew at the world and discovering hitherto unseen aspects. This new way of seeing was based on the use of unusual and sharply angled viewpoints, bird's eye perspectives, radical cropping, extreme close-ups, strong figure–ground contrasts, dramatic plays of light and shade, and experimental techniques such as photomontages and photograms. The reference to the New Vision in Reiner's advertisement would have been hard to miss, as the advertisement was included in a special issue of *Campo Grafico* devoted to photography.[43]

Boggeri had been writing about modernist photography and its use in advertising and graphic arts since the late 1920s.[44] A cursory look at photography, graphic arts, advertising and architecture journals of the period demonstrates that modernist photography was widely discussed, energetically advocated and amply illustrated through articles, book reviews, recurring columns and translations of theoretical texts by members of the New Vision movement.[45] Paraphrasing Moholy-Nagy, Boggeri argued that whereas artistic photography – also known as Pictorialism – turned to painting as a source for its subject matter and technique, modern photography 'turned to the qualities of the medium itself [in order to reach] a new way of seeing the world and its objects, and reveal their hidden photogenic character through original images'.[46] Theory was put into practice: photographs by Boggeri and collaborators were published in illustrated magazines and specialist publications or included in the studio's own graphic output.

Boggeri's interest in photography was specific to its application to typography and advertising. Speaking in defence of advertising photography from the pages of *La Pubblicità d'Italia* in 1937, he complained about the persistent sceptical attitude of some clients. The article began with a 'meaningful anecdote [about] a client who insisted he should pay only half [of the agreed payment] for a sketch presented by a painter, because the artist had pasted on a pair of photographic legs rather than drawing them. The client protested loudly that he had been played with and that he felt swindled – he too, he said, was capable of a similar witticism.'[47] The anecdote voiced Boggeri's frustration. Despite his efforts, photography was still misconceived.

The campisti backed up Boggeri's efforts to promote photography as graphic practitioners' 'favourite working tool, ultimate medium and nearly main collaborator'.[48] In their opinion, it was by then 'undisputed that photography had revolutionised graphics aesthetics and undeniably enriched its potential'.[49] To be sure, these views were in line with the principles of the New Typography that adopted photography as 'the obvious means of visual representation' and 'an essential typographic tool of the present'.[50] Advocates of advertising photography based their argument upon a number of factors. To begin with, they considered the immediacy and purported accordance of photography with reality to be what made this technique particularly suitable for advertising purposes. Advertising photography promoted consumers' confidence by relying on viewers' belief that photography corresponds to reality and that an advertisement featuring photographs cannot lie.[51]

Likewise, advertising photography was considered the most appropriate field for the application of photomontage.[52] First, photomontage was regarded as a suitable advertising tool because, like most advertisements, it includes both figurative elements and lettering. Secondly, it was suited to advertising thanks to its fragmented quality and dynamism that made it 'the one and only manifestation of modern illustration'.[53] Thirdly, it provided a manipulated version of the claimed unmediated representation of reality of the photographic medium. Juxtaposition favoured non-linear narratives and created visually compelling and emotionally persuasive images that lent a degree of plausibility that made an advertisement more effective, thanks to the viewer's tendency to read the photographic fragment as indexical.

Well before the opening of the studio, Boggeri had experienced the increasing prominence of photography within mass media while working at Alfieri&Lacroix. The printing house specialised in illustrated periodicals featuring extensive use of photography and an innovative graphic look, such as *La Rivista Illustrata del Popolo d'Italia* and the popular science magazine *Natura*. Illustrated press had emerged in Italy in the late nineteenth century, but it was only in the 1930s that rotogravure printing techniques allowed a high-quality reproduction of photographs. Contemporary commentators were quick to point out how the use of photography as a typographic tool initiated a deconstruction of the traditional page layout. Attilio Rossi's article 'L'evoluzione della tipografia in Italia' (The evolution of typography in Italy) in the September 1937 issue of *Campo Grafico* summarises how the 'functional demands of the use of photography' required the rejection of the symmetrical page layout and eventually led to the elaboration of a new graphic aesthetic based on the 'unified vision of the two pages' that ignored the physical separation of the central binding and replaced the vertical axis with the horizontal bar (see figure 2.9).[54] Modiano's brochure *25 Anni Olivetti* and Persico's redesign of the magazine *Casabella* in 1933 are usually identified among the early examples of a mature application of the two-pages-in-one model. But it is in the illustrated magazines of the 1930s that Vinti suggested looking for its origins.[55]

The entrance of photography into the fields of advertising and graphics initiated a rethinking of the traditional typographic rules and page layout, paving the way to what eventually was to become modern graphics. This section has acknowledged Boggeri's contribution to this process, focusing on the use of photography in advertising (noun) and on the advertising (verb) of photography as tools in the hands of graphic practitioners.

Signed advertisements

The name 'Studio Boggeri' features in peripheral yet visible positions in posters and advertisements. This 'signature' is a small detail that might

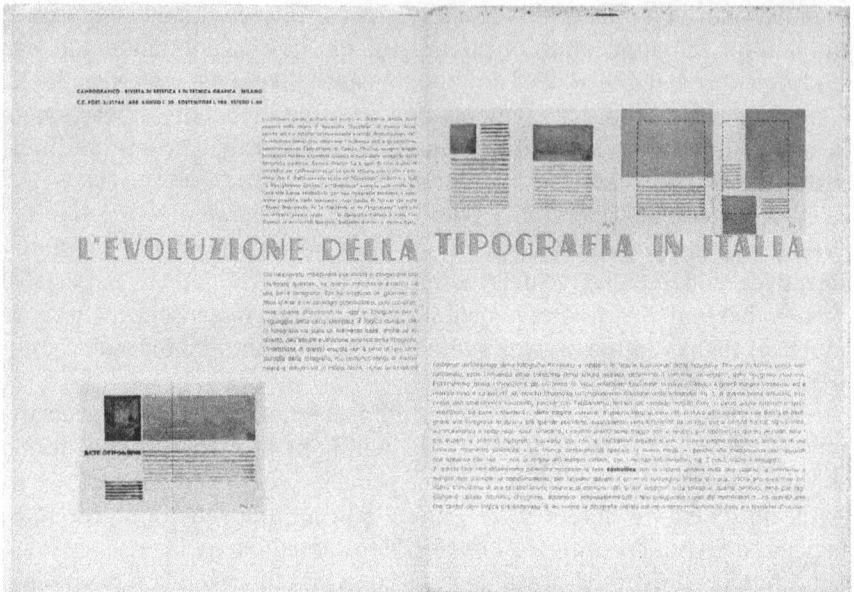

2.9 Double-page spread showing the impact of photography on the page layout of illustrated magazines, from Attilio Rossi's article 'L'evoluzione della tipografia in Italia', *Campo Grafico*, 5:9 (September 1937), 5–6.

pass unnoticed. However, it is an additional aspect of Boggeri's strategies of self-representation that provides a clue for investigating power dynamics within the studio. Signing graphic works was a common, but seldom talked about, practice at the time. The few discussions on the subject demonstrate contemporaries' awareness of its connotative potential. From the point of view of the graphic practitioners, the signature was a double-edged sword: a strategic form of self-publicity that could turn into a self-defeating pitfall when mismanaged. Writing in *Risorgimento Grafico* in 1928, Armando Mazzanti warned readers to avoid signing works that corresponded to the bad taste of the client: 'signing the printed material' could in fact jeopardise graphic practitioners' reputation, since the signature 'would make [them] known to the public not for what [they were], but rather for what [they] were forced to be'.[56] From the clients' perspective, concerns were raised as the signature was suspected to be counterproductive to the promotional purposes of the advertisements. In her book on US advertising in the first half of the twentieth century, art historian Michele H. Bogart observed similar discussions. She argued that the signature 'lessens the effectiveness and strength of advertising [and] augments the name recognition of the artist, his reputation and hence his price' by drawing attention away from the advertised product.[57] Yet, disadvantages could turn into advantages. If the audience were familiar with the named commercial artist or agency, the signature commodified the advertisement: it attracted viewers to the image itself and made them more likely to give attention to the advertised product. It connoted the good taste of the client who commissioned the renowned commercial artist or agency. Good taste was consequently reflected in the advertised product and transferred to the buyer.

The signature was a vehicle of self-representation and promotion used by the different actors involved in the design process: the studio, the individual graphic practitioner and the client. A closer look at the advertisements of Richard-Ginori confirms this practice. During the 1930s the porcelain manufacturer ran an advertising campaign in the architecture and design magazine *Domus*. The advertisements featured modernist aesthetics and were signed by key names of Italian graphics, such as Franco Grignani, Erberto Carboni and Studio Boggeri. The promotional strategy was consistent with Richard-Ginori's attempt to associate the company's name with design excellence: a strategy that had begun in the early 1920s with the hiring of architect and industrial designer Gio Ponti as art director. The effectiveness of the advertisements hinged upon the fact that readers of *Domus* were already familiar with, and appreciated, modern design, and were likely to recognise names and associate them with cutting-edge graphics. As such, they were able to understand and evaluate the company's strategy of self-representation. Viewed from the other side, to be associated with Richard-Ginori was also beneficial for those who signed the advertisements. On the mutually advantageous relationship between professionals and clients, sociologist Andrew Abbott suggested that those 'who serve high-status clients receive some reflected glory' and that 'high-status clients [tend to] pick high-status professionals to the extent that they can'.[58] By signing Richard-Ginori's advertisements, Grignani, Carboni and Studio Boggeri were capitalising on the high-status commission in order to forge their professional reputation and attract new clients. The signature was thus a form of self-publicity for the studio and the individual practitioner alike: it allowed them to mark their presence in the market, thereby functioning as a sort of business card for prospective clients.

At times, advertisements displayed two signatures, as was the case with Richard-Ginori's advertisement featuring the double signature 'Studio Boggeri – Erberto Carboni' (see figure 2.10). The double signature provides insight into the dialectical relationship between Boggeri and the graphic practitioners working under him. Visual culture historian Gennifer Weisenfeld related the practice of signing to the emergence of the new figure of the commercial artist in interwar Japan. According to Weisenfeld, advertising works, 'which were labelled with the artists' names, made a strong statement about the important role of the designers', since they allowed designers 'to be pulled out from behind the scenes and given the social recognition they deserved'.[59] The double signature in figure 2.10 pulled out from behind the scenes not only the graphic practitioner, but also the hierarchy within the studio. In particular, it tipped the scales between individual authorship and teamwork. For Boggeri, the inclusion of the designer's name was a subliminal way to assert his supervision, claim

RICHARD·GINORI

negozi principali: milano, corso littorio, 1 · via dante, 13 · torino, via roma, 15 · genova, via xx settembre, 3 · trieste, via carducci, 20 · firenze, via rondinelli, 7 · bologna, via rizzoli,10 pisa, via vittorio emanuele, 18 · roma, via del tritone, 177 · napoli, via roma, 213 · cagliari, largo c. felice · sassari, piazza azuni · s. giovanni a teduccio (napoli) · littoria (roma)

XIII

2.10   Advertisement for Richard-Ginori, designed (and signed) by Studio Boggeri – Erberto Carboni and published in *Domus*, 8:96 (December 1935), XIII.

credibility for the studio by showing off its extended team and suggest the idea, or arouse the suspicion, that what designers did when working alone was different from what they could do when collaborating with Studio Boggeri. For external consultants, to have their name alongside Studio Boggeri was a way to claim authorship and assert at the same time both their independence from, and belonging to, Boggeri's team. Depending on the viewer's perception of Studio Boggeri, to be identified as members of the team could connote professionalism and modern graphics, and hence act as an effective tool of self-representation and promotion in view of future commissions.

For his part, Boggeri was well aware of what was at stake when allowing designers to sign their works, and how this could reflect on the studio's image. In February 1942, he wrote a letter to Huber: the Swiss magazine *Typographische Monatsblätter* was going to publish a special edition on Italian graphics and Boggeri asked Huber, who was spending the war years in Switzerland, to provide the editors with exemplars of his works for the studio. In his letter, he specified that 'it [was] essential that he presented his works as STUDIO BOGGERI – HUBER'.[60] Other graphic studios of the period used the signature to find a balance between individual and team authorship. The designers Ricas (Riccardo Castagnedi) and Munari, for instance, conveyed their flexible attitude towards working both in tandem and individually by signing their works, 'R+M', 'ricas+M' or 'R+munari'.[61] A similar strategy was adopted by the duo composed of the campisti Carlo Dradi and Attilio Rossi, who reversed the order of their surnames – that is, 'Dradi–Rossi' or 'Rossi–Dradi' – to signal the main contributor.

xanti – studio boggeri

From the early days of the studio, Boggeri carried out a steady search for foreign graphic designers. The outcome of this recruiting policy was the transit of a succession of Central European, mainly Swiss, graphic designers, many of whom used their work experience at Studio Boggeri as a springboard for their career in Italy. Why Boggeri was so keen on collaborating with foreign graphic designers and associating his studio with Swiss graphic design in particular, and how this recruiting policy related to strategies of self-representation, are the main questions of the last two sections of this chapter.

Imre Reiner and Käte Bernhardt were the first foreigner designers to join the studio in 1933, but the event that established Studio Boggeri as the focal point of progressive graphic design in Italy was the arrival of Xanti Schawinsky later that same year. The Swiss photographer, visual artist, graphic and set designer of Polish Jewish descent had enrolled at the Bauhaus in 1924. With Adolf Hitler's rise to power in 1933 he escaped from

Germany and sought refuge in Milan until 1936, when the Italian political situation and professional considerations led him to flee once more. This time, he moved to the US, where he re-joined with fellow Bauhauslers at the Black Mountain College in North Carolina.

Schawinsky's decision to leave Nazi Germany for Fascist Italy might appear, from today's perspective, at the very least unfortunate. However, although proving ill-fated in the long term, his stay in Milan was, in fact, well timed. Up until the promulgation of the racial laws in 1938, victims of racial discrimination or people whose career was hindered under Nazi rules found Italy a rather appealing destination.[62] Without denying the authoritarian nature of Italian Fascism, nor downplaying the atrocity of its oppression, one could argue that the country offered a viable alternative to Germany. This appears especially to have been the case within the cultural sector. Writing about Schawinsky's experience in Milan, art historian Torsten Blume defined Italy as '*the* place for European graphic designers seeking refuge where creative and artistic modernism was not persecuted'.[63] As historian Jonathan Petropoulos argued, Mussolini's more pluralistic cultural policy appeared to be 'a model for reconciling modernism with Fascism'.[64] For those who were left worrying about their fate in Nazi Germany after the closure of the Bauhaus in 1933, 'Fascist Italy … provided [a] reason for … hopefulness'.[65] Writing in a letter to Marcel Breuer in April 1934 that 'xandi [blew] the pipe in italy and promise[d] to lead [them] all … to paradise', Ise Gropius confirmed that Schawinsky was persuaded that early 1930s Milan was not only a safe place, but also a place where his career and those of fellow Bauhauslers could thrive.[66] In an August 1936 letter to his wife, Tut, Oskar Schlemmer reported that Schawinsky had suggested he should move either to the US, or to Italy, for, 'there [was] a founder's year atmosphere over there, a lot of enthusiasm, and they want[ed] the latest and newest'.[67] Although he had already transferred to the US by then, the passage shows that Schawinsky's decision to leave Italy had not affected his positive perception of the country. In fact, it suggests his departure might have been a deliberate career choice, rather than a desperate flight. Whatever his precise reasons for leaving may have been, his departure was well timed, as his life and working conditions would have changed dramatically had he stayed a bit longer.

Arriving in Milan in the late autumn of 1933, Schawinsky was welcomed by a community of artists, architects and graphic practitioners who were eager to hear about his first-hand experience of the Bauhaus. The rationalist architect Luciano Baldessari was his point of contact in town, but it was Gino Ghiringhelli, co-founder of Galleria Il Milione, who introduced him to Boggeri. Upon his arrival at Studio Boggeri, Schawinsky devised its New Year's greetings card: a photomontage that represented Boggeri and Schawinsky as dandies wearing military decorations on lacy

waistcoats (see figure 2.11). The card is reminiscent of the Bauhaus culture of gift giving for it mocks conventional masculinity, offers an alternative to militarised manhood and puts contradictions in gender roles on
display.[68] It implies an audience that could understand the visual joke and
its references to the European avant-garde. Overall, it announced that
Studio Boggeri and Schawinsky were going to change the rules of the
game in Italian graphics in the coming year.

Despite what was to be a relatively short stay, the years Schawinsky
spent in Milan were very productive and he received commissions from the
most prestigious clients of the time: Olivetti, Illy and Motta among others.
Olivetti was Schawinsky's major client. Besides posters, advertisements

2.11   New Year's greetings card for Studio Boggeri, designed by Xanti Schawinsky, 1933.

and other graphic works, he redesigned the logotype, took care of the interior design of the Turin showroom (1934) and co-designed the typewriter Studio 42 (1935) with the architects Luigi Figini and Gino Pollini.[69] For Illy, Schawinsky designed the first advertising campaign and the prototype of an espresso machine. For the confectionery company Motta, he took care of the window dressing of the flagship bar located at the entrance of the Galleria Vittorio Emanuele II on the side towards the Duomo. The double signature, 'xanti – studio boggeri', featured in most works, thereby attesting to Boggeri's key intermediary role.

But there is an aspect of Schawinsky's work at Studio Boggeri with which it can be difficult to come to terms. How was it that someone fleeing Nazi Germany was eventually to go on to design works that served as vehicles for fascist propaganda? Most such works featured in *La Rivista Illustrata del Popolo d'Italia* and were also signed 'xanti – studio boggeri'. This was the case, for example, with a propaganda poster celebrating the 99.84 per cent majority obtained by the PNF at the plebiscitary elections held on 26 March 1934 that was included as a loose-leaf in the April 1934 issue of the magazine. Featuring a photomontage that portrays an acclaiming crowd from which Mussolini emerges as the literal head of the Italian people, '1934-XII SI' has attracted the interest of scholars addressing the use of modernist techniques and aesthetics to further fascist ideology.[70] The myopic focus on form of most of the literature to date denies the possibility of both a complex insight into Schawinsky's accommodating attitude towards Fascism and a better understanding of the poster in context.

On the one hand, when considering the choices Schawinsky made during his stay in Milan between 1933 and 1936 one needs to consider, as we did earlier for Boggeri, the regime's use of coercion and control over access to social benefits as underlying conditions. Once in Italy, historian Klaus Voigt argued, 'émigrés could not escape in their daily life and work the fascist environment around them and had to somehow adapt to it'.[71] Schawinsky operated within the limits and opportunities set by the regime, and it is tempting to dismiss his accommodation as individual opportunism or a misunderstanding of what Italian Fascism really was. His belated political awakening is implied in a passage from his autobiography, where he says, 'for the time being, there was no sign that things would be different five years later. … It was inconceivable to me how quickly a mood could change; for nationalism was not only incomprehensible to me but appeared as a spiritually limited manifestation of misguided people who follow their shepherd like sheep to their doom.'[72] Still, one is left wondering how disengaged and naive he could have been at the time of his stay. For sure, the regime's mechanisms of surveillance and repression did not pass unnoticed by him, as he received regular visits from an officer who would 'inquire about my well-being and whether I liked Italy', and he was also aware of another guest in his guesthouse spying on political conversations and blackmailing people.[73]

On the other hand, a reading of the poster within the socio-cultural situation and professional environment of early 1930s Italy is revealing of just how much fascist rhetoric was ingrained in everyday life and practice.[74] Figures 2.12 and 2.13 show two different versions of '1934-XII SI' and provide information about uses and mediation of the poster. In figure 2.12, the original photomontage without any typographic element hangs above the doorway of Motta flagship bar. The shot is undated, but it does not seem too far-fetched to date it to the time of the fascist plebiscite. On that occasion, the propaganda display would have contributed to the overall rhetoric of the Galleria Vittorio Emanuele II. As we shall see in chapter 3, the double arcade hosted at its centre a temporary installation designed by Edoardo Persico and Marcello Nizzoli, which also invested modernist aesthetics and techniques with fascist meanings (see figure 3.5). Figure 2.13 features yet another version of the poster that differs from the previous two in respect of the caption '1936–XV'. The modified caption dates the shot to the last two months of 1936 and shows how the poster was reused after Schawinsky's departure. The picture records the visit to the Motta factory by the federal secretary of the PNF for Milan, Rino Parenti. Visits to everyday venues by members of the PNF, or even better by Mussolini himself, were expressions of the regime's efforts to capture public places and influence the everyday life of Italian people.[75] Both pictures link Schawinsky's poster to Motta and are evidence of the company's attempt to cash in on the popularity of Mussolini. This commercial strategy by Motta was not an isolated stance, as at the time the Duce was at the centre of Italian consumer culture.[76]

Given the growing isolation of Fascist Italy, Schawinsky's time working in Milan represented an unmatched opportunity for design exchange. It enabled Milan's graphic practitioners to check out in person and at first hand methods, languages and techniques they had read about in the specialist press. The October 1935 issue of *L'Ufficio Moderno* was devoted to the Bauhausler. The editorial introduced Schawinsky as an expert in modern advertising whose work was the outcome of a careful analysis of product, service and audience, rather than personal creative whim.[77] His approach was encapsulated in the concept of 'functional advertising'. Schawinsky himself explained that functional advertising 'turns to technique rather than mysticism – to rigor rather than monumentality – to realism rather than symbolism – to logic rather than depiction – to functionalism rather than decoration – to documentary rather than theatrical'.[78] In promoting professionalism and specialisation, it replayed contemporary exchanges between the advertising sector and graphic practice.

Schawinsky was the link between the Milanese and the European avant-garde. On two different occasions in the autumn of 1934, he was

2.12   Display window of the bar Motta in the Galleria Vittorio Emanuele II, Milan, published in *La Rivista Illustrata del Popolo d'Italia*, 14:11 (November 1935), 178.

2.13   Member of the PNF visiting the Motta factory in Milan, November–December 1936.

briefly reunited in Milan with fellow Bauhauslers Lazlo Moholy-Nagy and Walter Gropius. In mid-September, Schawinsky wrote to Gropius about Moholy-Nagy's visit and recalled the evening they had spent talking about colour photography together with Boggeri and the editor of *La Rivista Illustrata del Popolo d'Italia*, Marco Luigi Poli.[79] In the same letter, he tried to organise an exhibition of Gropius's work to be held at Galleria Il Milione. This was in view of the architect's stopover in town the following month on his way to Zurich from Rome, where he was to attend an international theatre conference as an official delegate from Germany.[80] The exhibition never took place, but one can assume Schawinsky's influence behind the publication of an article by Gropius in the April 1935 issue of the architecture magazine *Quadrante*.[81] At Galleria Il Milione, he curated an exhibition of Josef Albers's wood engravings, whereas he did not succeed in staging Oskar Schlemmer's Triadic Ballet at the 6th Milan Triennale of 1936.[82] Outside the Bauhaus circle, Schawinsky also accompanied Boggeri to Zurich in 1935 and introduced him to the photographer and teacher at the Kunstgewerbeschule (School of Applied Arts), Hans Finsler.[83]

The collaboration with the Bauhausler Schawinsky was, for Boggeri, a chance to overcome what he saw as Italian provincialism. It was, moreover, part of his wider strategy to position the studio at the forefront of European graphics by basking in the reflected glory of the Bauhaus. All in all, Schawinsky's help was vital to the making of Studio Boggeri's reputation, and he attracted other promising Swiss graphic designers who followed his example in the ensuing years.

The Swiss do it better

Whereas Schawinsky was already an established artist and designer when he arrived in Milan, the Swiss graphic designers who followed him across the Alps to work at Studio Boggeri were often young graduates. Despite having little work experience, their training in Switzerland was a guarantee, as in Boggeri's opinion Swiss design schools provided students with 'a foundation of fundamental rules in order to deal with the main assignments of typography without any hesitation'.[84] As we saw in chapter 1, education and professional training were a major concern in interwar Milan. Still in its infancy in Italy, design education created a favourable environment for the highly trained graphic designers coming from neighbouring Switzerland. Boggeri's position was in line with the historiographical canon according to which better-trained Swiss designers arrived in Milan and taught the profession to their Italian counterparts. Until the mid-2010s most of the literature on the community of Swiss graphic designers in Milan reiterated the same stereotypical narrative celebrating the fruitful encounter between Swiss formal severity and precision and Italian poetic vein and experimental curiosity.[85] More recent attempts have questioned this oversimplified narrative by looking at everyday design practice, networks and national design canons.[86]

When he arrived in Milan in February 1940, Max Huber was only twenty-one. In the previous five years, he had attended the foundation year at the Kunstgewerbeschule in Zurich, had done an apprenticeship at Althaus Studio and had worked for Conzett&Huber. Upon his arrival, he visited Studio Boggeri and left behind a business card that appeared to have been printed but had actually been executed by hand. Once he spotted the visual deceit Boggeri instantly hired Huber, or at least this is how the event has been passed down in the literature.[87] However, the correspondence between Boggeri and Huber tells us a different story. It was, in fact, the graphic designer Gérard Miedinger who recommended Huber. Boggeri had gotten in touch with Miedinger in the autumn of 1939 asking for a 'young Swiss artist' who would be willing to join the studio.[88] Huber was asked to provide references and a portfolio, advised to learn some Italian or French, and questioned about his work practice, sketching skills and familiarity with the photographic medium. The terms of the collaboration were also discussed in advance. Huber complained about the lack of independence that had prevented him from demonstrating his talent during previous work experiences. In response, Boggeri promised a working relationship based on mutual respect and creative autonomy.[89] Rather than a serendipitous encounter, the hiring of Huber was the outcome of Boggeri's programmatic recruiting campaign. Notwithstanding its doubtful veracity, the anecdote of the business card yields evidence as to the way in which designers tend to portray themselves and their history by drawing on the rhetoric of the creative individual.

Soon after Italy's entrance into the war in June 1940, Huber returned to Zurich. But he continued working long distance for Studio Boggeri until 1945, when he moved back to Milan. During wartime, Boggeri continued to receive commissions from diverse clients. Some commissions were one-offs, like that for the design of the logo for a dried fruit and vegetables company in March 1942, and the packaging and labelling for a new line of nail varnish in January 1943.[90] The timing of these commissions is noteworthy. Italy's engagement in World War II turned out to be an economic disaster. From the beginning of the conflict the gross domestic product had decreased on average by almost 10 per cent every year, until in 1945 it dropped back to the level of 1906.[91] The black market was blooming in 1942 and most products were subject to strict rationing. Advertising for foodstuffs, in particular preserved and canned food and cosmetics, had increased in number and variety since the 1920s, but shortage of raw materials and the war effort drastically restricted both production and consumption.[92] Other commissions came from long-term clients, such as the publisher De Agostini, which commissioned the rebranding of the company's visual identity in the summer of 1942.[93]

The long-distance collaboration with Huber was conducted by post and facilitated by a business associate of the studio who travelled for work from Milan to Zurich on a regular basis. The war and the political situation were barely mentioned in the correspondence, possibly to avoid censorship. Two letters written in the summer of 1943 stand out: in these Huber congratulated Boggeri for the beginning of the Italian Campaign in July and asked about the consequences of the Allies' bombing raid over Milan in August.[94] Due to difficulties moving cash across borders, Huber was often paid in kind in the form of books, magazines and work tools. At times, though, even the exchange of goods was prevented by export bans, as was the case with the radio Phonola 547 designed by the brothers Castiglioni that Huber requested repeatedly, without success.

The collaboration followed a pattern: Boggeri briefed Huber, passed on clients' requests and suggested possible solutions; Huber sent sketches and a description; then an exchange of ideas about appropriate modifications followed. In the winter of 1941, the studio was commissioned by the magazine *La Pubblicità d'Italia* for the layout of an article on advertising for pharmaceutical products that had been written by Boggeri himself. Only four days passed between Boggeri's briefing letter and Huber's first sketch. In his reply, Huber specified that the background of the first page was going to be either light grey or bright green with a horizontal window framing the sloping title, that the pictures were to be freely arranged in the following pages and that the text was to be set in Bodoni. The proposed design did not satisfy Boggeri, who would have preferred a more geometric feeling to it. The final layout corresponded to Huber's original idea, thereby suggesting Boggeri's openness to dialogue.[95] In February 1942, Olivetti commissioned two advertisements promoting the typewriter, Studio 42, to feature in the magazine *Illustrazione Italiana*. The theme was free, but Boggeri recommended that at least one of the advertisements should refer to the modern house. This time, Huber followed Boggeri's advice to the letter by including an architectural plan of a two-storey building and a picture of an office interior.[96] In some other cases, the briefing was illustrated by Boggeri with a sketch. The sketched logo for the dried fruit and vegetables company, Vitam was the departure point for Huber's final version in which he replaced the original apple with what he considered to be the 'more characteristic shape' of a pear (see figures 2.14 and 2.15).[97] By positioning the brand name in correspondence with the core of the fruit and by using dynamic lettering, Huber fulfilled the client's request for a logo that conveyed the idea that the dried food conserved all the vitality and vitamins of the fresh product.

The above design projects for a magazine layout, an advertisement and a logo provide new insight into the studio's everyday work practice and relationships. By revealing the actual choices made by Huber and Boggeri at different stages, the three projects shift the focus from the

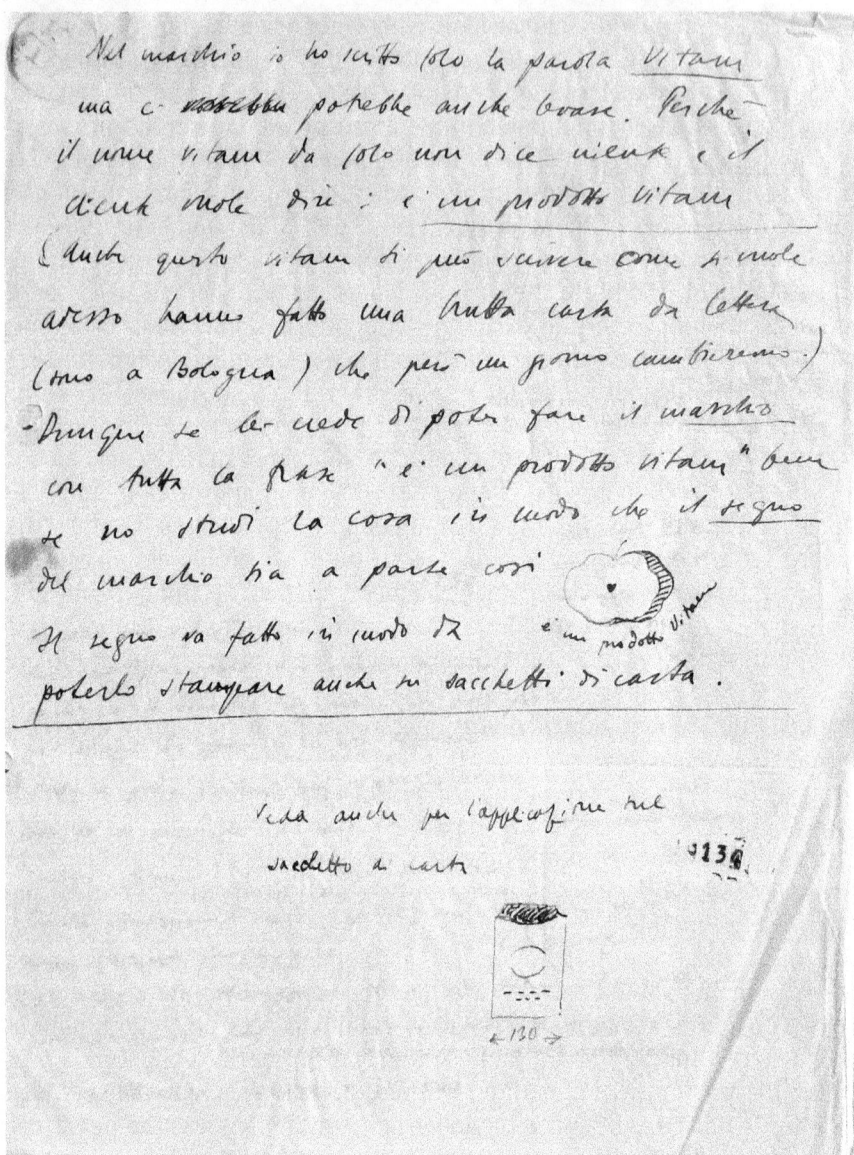

2.14   Letter from Antonio Boggeri to Max Huber, 7 March 1942.

final product to the design process and show this to have been a collab-orative venture. They also characterise and substantiate the romanticised and hagiographic descriptions of Boggeri as a charismatic leader who 'acted as a manager and a catalyst, inspired and stimulated ... his pupils who presented different tastes and inclinations as well as diverse cultures and sensibilities, ... understood their talents and promoted their personal

2.15 Logo for Vitam, designed by Max Huber – Studio Boggeri, 1942.

skills'.[98] And they do so by showing how his technical know-how enabled Boggeri to conduct a peer dialogue with his collaborators based on mutual trust; to discuss methodologies, provide valuable feedback and heed advice during both the conception and production process.

Despite the fact that the collaboration by correspondence was working effectively, Boggeri turned tirelessly to Huber and other acquaintances on the other side of the Alps for advice in finding another Swiss graphic designer who could work in person in Milan. This is not to say that Studio Boggeri was left without any graphic practitioner on site during Huber's absence. It could, in fact, count on Remo Muratore and, at least up to the end of 1943 when he joined the Italian resistance movement, Albe Steiner. In June 1942, Boggeri wrote to Huber: 'I want at least one "graphic practitioner" who always stays in Milan.'[99] A few weeks later Boggeri informed Huber that he had written also 'to [Emil] Schulthess for advice about the "graphic practitioner"'.[100] In both letters the inverted commas enclose the word 'grafico'. By highlighting the word, the punctuation marks signal a non-straightforward meaning but, at the same time, seem to hint at an untold understanding and shared agreement on the required professional skills and knowledge.

Boggeri's persistence in looking for a graphic designer outside the national borders may downplay the professionalism of Italian practitioners. Yet, what made Swiss graphic designers so attractive in Boggeri's eyes was not only their professional know-how, but also their international network of designers, photographers, publishers and clients to which the network of no Italian graphic designer of the time was likely to compare. Moreover, Swiss graphic designers carried an added connotative value due to the celebrated international reputation of the so-called Swiss Style.[101] Indeed, the preference in Swiss graphic design for asymmetrical and geometrical compositions, grid layout, standardised design systems and long-term planning, together with the exclusive use of sans-serif typefaces and photographic images, was linked with ideas such as 'professionalism', 'precision', 'internationalism', 'objectivity', 'seriousness' and 'trustworthiness'. As was the case with Schawinsky and his relationship to the Bauhaus, Boggeri's recruiting strategy was aimed at using these tacit connotative values as a sales tool. But his interest in Swiss graphic design and designers was not unconditional. On the contrary, he was aware of both their qualities and deficiencies. He criticised the risk of sterile and rigid repetition of aesthetic principles and technical rules, advocating that designers should refrain from intolerant formalism and base their work on the cultural context and specificity of the task.[102]

Swiss graphic designers were a business card to access and claim a position in the international graphic design circle, and indeed Boggeri's hunt for associates across the Alps carried on during the post-war period. In November 1954, he addressed the members of the VSG, Verband Schweizerischer Grafiker (Association of Swiss Graphic Designers) with a direct call for interest in the association house organ *Chamäleon*: 'Studio Boggeri … is looking for a young Swiss graphic designer'.[103] The number of Swiss graphic designers active in Milan grew along with the boom of the Italian post-war economy. In 1946, Carlo Vivarelli was in Milan briefly and collaborated with Boggeri. A year later Walter Ballmer moved to town and worked for Studio Boggeri until 1955, when he was hired by Adriano Olivetti. In 1953, it was the turn of Aldo Calabresi, who became Boggeri's chief consultant over the following ten years and was replaced by Bruno Monguzzi, who started working at the studio in 1961. Other Swiss graphic designers who worked at Studio Boggeri over the years included Lora Lamm, Max Schneider, Warja Honegger-Lavater, René Martinelli and Hans-Ulrich Osterwalder.

All graphics lead to Boggeri

Given both its prominent clients and star-studded roster of designers, Studio Boggeri was no ordinary studio. For this reason, it has been celebrated in the literature as the first full-service graphic design studio in

Italy, a game changer in the panorama of interwar Italian graphics. But without grounding this experience within the wider context, the definition is nothing more than an unsatisfactory historiographical label. Likewise, the list of the many Italian and foreign graphic designers who worked at Studio Boggeri over the years is not self-explanatory evidence for the prominent position it occupies in the larger history of twentieth-century graphic design, but rather reduces the studio to an empty space through which prominent figures of graphic design happened to pass. Setting aright this misleading image has been the main aim of this chapter.

By opening the doors of Studio Boggeri, this chapter has provided a more complex understanding of the hitherto unquestioned contribution of the studio to the drafting of graphic design practice in Milan. The focus on working, commissioning and recruiting practices and changing strategies of self-representation has offered new perspectives into the complexities of the studio. The acknowledgement of the multifaceted nature of Boggeri's role has corrected the hagiographic tendency of most of the current literature: he was not only the founder of Studio Boggeri and the careful coordinator of its identity, but also a vocal advocate of the use of photography as a graphic tool and a contributor to contemporary debates on modernist graphics and advertising. More broadly, a more subjective side of Fascism and its impact on everyday life and practices has emerged here, as we explored the realm of individual experiences and understood practitioners' choices as depending on the social-cultural situation and professional context, and their own interest and needs. Finally, we have looked at how advertising allowed graphic practitioners to differentiate their practice from poster art and the typographic tradition of book design by offering them a vacant jurisdiction in which to stake their claim.

The Milan Triennale is the subject of the next chapter, which examines graphic practitioners' strategic use of mediating channels to improve public understanding, acquire a status, and create a market for both graphic products and practice.

Notes

1 N. Caimi, 'La pubblicità e l'industria grafica', *Risorgimento Grafico*, 28:5 (May 1931), 237–40.
2 'Dentro il vecchio palazzo patrizio, lo studio era moderno e semplice ... la palma perennemente gocciolante'. K. Bernhardt, quoted in P. Fossati and R. Sambonet (eds), *Lo Studio Boggeri: 1933–1973. Comunicazione visuale e grafica applicata* (Cinisello Balsamo: Pizzi Editore, 1974), n. p.
3 B. Monguzzi (ed.), *Lo Studio Boggeri: 1933–1981* (Milan: Electa, 1981); G. Fioravanti, L. Passarelli and S. Sfligiotti (eds), *La grafica in Italia* (Milan: Leonardo Arte, 1997), pp. 8–10 and 76–9; D. Baroni and M. Vitta (eds), *Storia del design grafico* (Milan: Longanesi & Co., 2003), pp. 135–9; G. Anceschi, 'Il campo della grafica italiana: storia e problemi', *Rassegna*, 6 (1981), 8–12; J. Aynsley, *A Century of Graphic Design* (London: Mitchell Beazley, 2001), pp. 84–5; Hollis, *Graphic Design*, pp. 138–46.

4 'Un immaginario e sognato Eden di illuminati committenti affluiti allo Studio Boggeri, sinonimo di avanguardia pubblicitaria'. A. Boggeri, 'Una B rossa fra due punti', *Rassegna*, 6 (1981), 20.

5 B. Gaudenzi, 'Il fascismo in vetrina', in F. Fasce, E. Bini and B. Gaudenzi, *Comprare per credere. La pubblicità in Italia dalla Belle Époque a oggi* (Rome: Carocci, 2016), pp. 41–83; I. Di Jorio, 'Pubblicità e propaganda durante il fascismo. Saperi e transfer di competenze fra mercato e politica', *Italia Contemporanea – Sezione Open Access*, 3:291 (2020), 209–36.

6 A. Arvidsson, *Marketing Modernity: Italian Advertising from Fascism to Postmodernity* (London; New York: Routledge, 2003), pp. 44–64; G. L. Falabrino, *Effimera e bella: storia della pubblicità italiana, Venezia 1691–Roma 2001* (Turin: Gutenberg, 2001), pp. 215–39.

7 A. Arvidsson, 'Between Fascism and the American dream: Advertising in interwar Italy', *Social Science History*, 25:2 (2001), 169; Gaudenzi, 'Il fascismo in vetrina', pp. 66–7; E. Scarpellini, *L'Italia dei consumi. Dalla Belle Époque al nuovo millennio* (Rome; Bari: Laterza, 2008), pp. 91–2.

8 B. Gaudenzi, 'Press advertising and fascist dictates: Showcasing the female consumer in Fascist Italy and Nazi Germany', *Journalism Studies*, 14:5 (2013), 665.

9 *Ibid*.

10 D. Forgacs, *L'industrializzazione della cultura italiana (1880–1990)* (Bologna: Il Mulino, 1990), p. 113.

11 E. M. Thomson, '"The science of publicity": An American advertising theory, 1900–1920', *Journal of Design History*, 9:4 (1996), 253–72.

12 V. De Grazia, *Irresistible Empire: America's Advance through Twentieth-Century Europe* (Cambridge, MA; London: The Belknap Press of Harvard University Press, 2005).

13 F. Fasce and E. Bini, 'Irresistible empire or innocents abroad? American advertising agencies in post-war Italy, 1950s–1970s', *Journal of Historical Research in Marketing*, 7:1 (2015), 9–11.

14 G. Prezzolini, *L'arte di persuadere* (Milan: Lumachi, 1907); A. Lancelotti, *Storia aneddotica della réclame* (Milan: Riccardo Quintieri Editore, 1912); E. Roggero, *Come si riesce con la pubblicità* (Milan: Hoepli, 1920); R. Pomé, *Concezione moderna della pubblicità: lezioni tenute al Politecnico di Milano per il Corso di Dirigenti di Aziende Industriali (Aprile–Maggio 1936–XIV)* (Rome: Edizioni della Federazione Nazionale Fascista Dirigenti Aziende Industriali, 1936).

15 C. Carotti, '"L'Ufficio Moderno" di Guido Mazzali e il G.A.R.: una presenza culturale democratico-socialista nella Milano degli anni Trenta', *Storia in Lombardia*, 2 (2001), 67–92.

16 De Grazia, *Irresistible Empire*, pp. 256–8.

17 'Con l'imporsi della cultura razionalista, matura una scelta decisiva nella storia della pubblicità: la pubblicità non è più affidata al *pittore* ma al *grafico* pubblicitario.' G. Priarone, *Grafica pubblicitaria in Italia negli anni Trenta* (Florence: Cantini, 1989), p. 13.

18 'Anacronistica tendenza … dannoso e esiziale ai fini del progresso del nostro mestiere'. Anon., 'Ostacoli', *Campo Grafico*, 2:5 (May 1934), 101.

19 'I prodotti caratteristici del nostro tempo … non i libri ma la rivista, l'opuscolo, il catalogo'. G. Modiano, 'Situazione grafica', *Quadrante*, 11 (May 1933), 21.

20 Aynsley, *Graphic Design in Germany*, p. 103.

21 'È illogico voler costringere la materia propagandistica dentro ritmi creati per il libro'. G. Modiano, 'Sulle tendenze costruttive grafiche in Italia', *Graphicus*, 27:4–5 (April–May 1937), 31.

22 G. Modiano, 'Necessità pubblicitaria della confezione e dell'imballaggio', *L'Ufficio Moderno*, 9:7–8 (July–August 1934), 361–5.

23 A. Marzagalli, 'Pubblicitario, artista, tipografo: un trinomio inscindibile', *L'Ufficio Moderno*, 28:5–6 (May–June 1943), 84–6.

24 Freidson, *Professionalism*, p. 56.

25 'Facilitare l'impiego dei mezzi di pubblicità, … eliminare o … ridurre al minimo le cause di sciupio di tempo e di denaro, di porre un freno all'illecito accaparramento di affari da parte di intermediari improvvisati, … contribuire insomma al minor costo e al maggior rendimento della pubblicità attraverso un più facile, logico e razionale impego dei mezzi pubblicitari'. G. C. Ricciardi (ed.), *Guida Ricciardi: la pubblicità in Italia* (Milan: Edizioni L'Ufficio Moderno, 1933), p. 8.

26 *Ibid.*, p. 179; G. C. Ricciardi (ed.), *Guida Ricciardi: pubblicità e propaganda in Italia* (Milan: Edizione Pubblicità Ricciardi, 1936), p. 378 and 393; G. C. Ricciardi (ed.), *Guida Ricciardi: pubblicità e propaganda* (Milan: Edizione Pubblicità Ricciardi, 1942), p. 301.

27 Ricciardi (ed.), *Guida Ricciardi* (1936), p. 371.

28 Anon., 'I consigli direttivi della FIP e delle otto associazioni nazionali aderenti', *La Pubblicità: Bollettino Mensile della FIP e Associazioni Aderenti*, 9:12 (December 1955), 8.

29 Armstrong and McDowell, 'Introduction', pp. 12–14. See also, L. Armstrong, 'A new image for a new profession: Self-image and representation in the professionalization of design in Britain, 1945–1960', *Journal of Consumer Culture*, 19:1 (2017), 104–24.

30 S. Hall, 'Introduction: Who needs "identity"', in S. Hall and P. du Gay (eds), *Questions of Cultural Identity* (London: Sage Publications, 1996), p. 4.

31 R. Kinross, 'Introduction to the English-language edition', in Tschichold, *The New Typography*, p. xxviii.

32 Anon., 'Il libro bello: occhio e fotografia', *Casabella*, 41 (May 1931), 57; Ricciardi (ed.), *Guida Ricciardi* (1936), p. 376; Ricciardi (ed.), *Guida Ricciardi* (1942), p. 308.

33 'L'espressione ultima della tecnica e dell'arte pubblicitaria … i suoi artisti specializzati, italiani e stranieri, e la sua organizzazione tecnica, offrono alle vostre idee le più sicure garanzie di realizzazione efficace e geniale'. ASB, promotional booklet by Studio Boggeri, *L'uovo di Colombo*, 1937, n. p.

34 Corner, 'Collaboration, complicity, and evasion under Italian Fascism', p. 78.

35 'Unter meinen Freuden wurde mir beteuert, dass sie liberal-denkende Weltbürger sind, die jedoch durch die erzwungene Eingliederung in die Parteiverbände nach außen hin ihre Zustimmung haben abgeben müssen.' Bauhaus-Archiv, Berlin, Germany (hereafter BA), Xanti Schawinsky, folder 1–5, *Autobiographie 'Fragment'*, typewritten autobiographical account by X. Schawinsky, 1968–71, p. 178 of the transcription.

36 Ebner, 'Coercion', p. 90.

37 M. Carli, *Vedere il fascismo. Arte e politica nelle esposizioni del regime (1928–1942)* (Rome: Carocci, 2020), pp. 25–7; M. Stone, *The Patron State: Culture and Politics in Fascist Italy* (Princeton: Princeton University Press, 1998), pp. 21–8; G. Turi, *Lo Stato educatore. Politica e intellettuali nell'Italia fascista* (Bari: Laterza, 2002), pp. 76–103.

38 Gaudenzi, 'Il fascismo in vetrina', pp. 50 and 67–8.

39 Di Jorio, 'Pubblicità e propaganda durante il fascismo', p. 220.

40 'La progettazione e la realizzazione di uno stampato pubblicitario di concezione e gusto moderni dovrebbero essere affidate a specialisti e tecnici del complesso settore grafico'. ASB, promotional pamphlet by Studio Boggeri, design by M. Huber – Studio Boggeri, 1945, n. p.

41 Colizzi, 'Bruno Munari', p. 157.

42 L. Moholy-Nagy, *Painting, Photography, Film* (Cambridge, MA: MIT Press, 1969 (1925)), p. 28.

43 *Campo Grafico*, 2:12 (December 1934).

44 A. Bianchi, 'Antonio Boggeri, fotografia modernista e pubblicità', *L'Uomo Nero*, 8:7–8 (2011), 275–91; C. Chiappini, 'Antonio Boggeri: considerazioni su un protagonista della grafica italiana', *Ricerche di S/Confine*, 3:1 (2012), 138–48.

45 In the early 1930s *Casabella* devoted a regular column to German photography. This featured reviews of pivotal publications such as Frank Roh and Jan Tschichold's book *Foto Auge* (1929) and László Moholy-Nagy's monograph *60 Fotos* (1930), as well as reproductions of works by El Lissitzky and Man Ray: Anon., 'Fotografia tedesca', *Casabella*, 39 (March 1931), 48–9; Anon., 'Fotografia tedesca', *Casabella*, 40 (April 1931), 52–3; Anon., 'Fotografia tedesca', *Casabella*, 41 (May 1931), 57–8; Anon., 'Fotografia tedesca', *Casabella*, 49 (January 1932), 60. Modernist photographers, such as Eli Lotar, Germaine Krull, Martin Munkácsy, László Moholy-Nagy, Marx Ernst, Max Burchartz and E. L. T. Mesens, were featured in advertising trade journal and graphics magazines of the time, while the magazine *Note Fotografiche* published an article by Moholy-Nagy in 1932: L. Moholy-Nagy, 'Su l'avvenire della fotografia', *Note Fotografiche*, 9:2 (August 1932), 59–60.

46 'Affida alle qualità proprie del mezzo i risultati di un modo diverso di vedere il mondo e i suoi oggetti svelandone il riposto carattere fotogenico in immagini inedite'. A. Boggeri, 'Commento', *Luci ed Ombre: Annuario della Fotografia Artistica Italiana* (Turin: Il Corriere Fotografico, 1929), p. 14.

47 'Storiella piena di significato: quella del cliente che pretendeva pagare la metà un bozzetto presentatogli da un pittore perché questi vi aveva incollato un paio di gambe fotografiche invece di disegnarle. Il cliente strillava di essere stato giocato, si sentiva defraudato, era capace, diceva, lui pure di simili spiritosità.' A. Boggeri, 'La fotografia nella pubblicità', *La Pubblicità d'Italia*, 1:5–6 (November–December 1937), 16.

48 'Strumento di lavoro favorito, il mezzo risolutivo, il collaboratore quasi principale'. A. Boggeri, letter to A. Rossi, *Campo Grafico*, 2:12 (December 1934), 271.

49 'Che la fotografia … ha rivoluzionato l'estetica grafica e ne abbia arricchito in modo grandioso le possibilità è ormai pacifico'. Campo Grafico, 'Fotografia e tipografia', *Campo Grafico*, 2:12 (December 1934), 269.

50 Tschichold, *The New Typography*, pp. 88 and 92.

51 R. Marchand, *Advertising the American Dream: Making Way for Modernity, 1920–1940* (Berkeley: University of California Press, 1986), pp. 149–53; M. H. Bogart, *Artists, Advertising, and the Borders of Art* (Chicago: University of Chicago Press, 1995), pp. 171–204.

52 G. Modiano, 'La tecnica dell'annuncio VI: l'illustrazione', *L'Ufficio Moderno*, 10:3 (March 1935), 129–30; M. Ferrigni, 'Fotografia pubblicitaria', *Risorgimento Grafico*, 31:2 (February 1934), 88–126.

53 'L'unica espressione dell'illustrazione moderna'. L. Veronesi and B. Pallavera, 'Del fotomontaggio', *Campo Grafico*, 2:12 (December 1934), 278.

54 'Le esigenze funzionali dell'impiego della fotografia … perché imponeva un'irragionevole riduzione della fotografia … la visione unitaria della due pagine'. Rossi, 'L'evoluzione della tipografia in Italia', 4–5.

55 C. Vinti, 'L'estetica grafica della "nuova tipografia" in Italia', *Disegno Industriale Industrial Design*, 2: 2 (2002), 18–19.

56 'Firmando lo stampato che ci farà conoscere al pubblico, non per quello che siamo, ma per quello che ci fu imposto di essere'. A. Mazzanti, 'Tipografi e clientela', *Risorgimento Grafico*, 25:5 (May 1928), 218.

57 Bogart, *Artists, Advertising, and the Borders of Art*, p. 144.

58 Abbott, *The System of Professions*, p. 122.

59 G. Weisenfeld, 'Japanese modernism and consumerism: Forging the new artistic field of "shôgyô bijutsu" (commercial art)', in E. K. Tipton and J. Clark (eds), *Being Modern in Japan: Culture and Society from the 1910s to the 1930s* (Honolulu: University of Hawaii Press, 1994), p. 79.

60 'Bisogna che lei presenti i lavori come STUDIO BOGGERI – HUBER'. ASB, letter from A. Boggeri to M. Huber, 6 February 1942.

61 Colizzi, 'Bruno Munari', pp. 123–75.

62 K. Voigt, *Il rifugio precario: gli esuli in Italia dal 1933 al 1945* (Florence: La Nuova Italia Editrice, 1993), pp. 202–3 and 497–8.

63 T. Blume, *Xanti Schawinsky: Album* (Zurich: Jrp Ringier, 2016), p. 19, italics added.

64 J. Petropoulos, *Artists Under Hitler: Collaboration and Survival in Nazi Germany* (New Haven; London: Yale University Press, 2014), p. 72.

65 *Ibid.*, p. 7. See also W. Nerdinger, 'Bauhaus architecture in the Third Reich', in K. James-Chakraborty (ed.), *Bauhaus Culture: From Weimar to the Cold War* (Minneapolis; London: University of Minnesota Press, 2006), p. 140.

66 'xandi bläst die lockpfeife in italien und verspricht uns dort alle … ins paradise zu führen'. Smithsonian Institute, Archives of American Art, Washington, USA (hereafter AAA), Marcel Breuer Papers, box 1, reel 5709, frames 479–584, letter from I. Gropius to M. Breuer, 18 April 1934, p. 2.

67 'Dort herrsche Gründerjahrestimmung, viel Elan, und man wolle das Letzte und Neueste'. Letter from O. Schlemmer to T. Schlemmer, La Sarraz, 23 August 1936, in T. Schlemmer (ed.), *Oskar Schlemmer: Briefe und Tagebücher* (Stuttgart: Gerd Hatje, 1977), pp. 6–7.

68 E. Otto, 'Designing men: New vision of masculinity in the photomontages of Herbert Bayer, Marcel Breuer, and László Moholy-Nagy', in J. Saletnik and R. Schuldenfrei (eds), *Bauhaus Construct: Fashioning Identity, Discourse and Modernism* (London; New York: Routledge, 2009), pp. 183–204.

69 D. Fornari and C. Barbieri, 'The Olivetti showroom in Turin: A fragment of the Bauhaus in Italy', in D. Fornari and D. Turrini (eds), *Olivetti Identities: Spaces and Languages 1933–1983* (Zurich: Triest Verlag, 2022), pp. 60–73; C. Barbieri and D. Fornari, 'The lost typefaces of Xanti Schawinsky: From the Bauhaus to Italy', in O. Moret (ed.), *Back to the Future; The Future in the Past. ICDHS 10th+1 Barcelona 2018* (Barcelona: Edicions de la Universitat de Barcelona, 2018), pp. 296–9.

70 D. Crowley, 'National Modernism', in Wilk (ed.), *Modernism*, pp. 34–60.

71 'Nella vita quotidiana e nel lavoro gli emigranti non potevano sottrarsi all'ambiente fascista che li circondava e dovevano in qualche modo adattarvisi'. Voigt, *Il rifugio precario*, pp. 201–2.

72 'Dass es nach fünf Jahren anders werden soll, davon war vorläufig noch nichts zu merken. … Es war mir unfasslich, wie rasch eine Stimmung umschlagen konnte; denn Nationalismus war mir nicht nur unbegreiflich, sondern erschien mir als geistig begrenzte Manifestation irregeführter Menschen, die wie Schafe ihrem Hirten ins Verderben folgen.' BA, Xanti Schawinsky, folder 1–5, *Autobiographie 'Fragment'*, typewritten autobiographical account by X. Schawinsky, 1968–1971, pp. 176 and 179 of the transcription.

73 'Erkundigte sich über mein Wohlergehen und ob mir Italien gefallen'. *Ibid.*, p. 178.

74 C. Barbieri and D. Fornari, 'Xanti Schawinsky and the fascist plebiscitary elections of 1934: Everyday design practice and visual culture in early-1930's Italy', *Journal of Design History*, 2023; epad026, https://doi.org/10.1093/jdh/epad026.

75 M. Berezin, *Making the Fascist Self: The Political Culture of Interwar Italy* (Ithaca: Cornell University Press, 1997), pp. 99 and 138–9.

76 S. Gundle, 'Un Martini per il Duce: l'immaginario del consumismo nell'Italia degli anni Venti e Trenta', in A. Villari (ed.), *L'arte della pubblicità: il manifesto italiano e le avanguardie* (Milan: Silvana Editoriale, 2008), pp. 38–62; S. Gundle, 'Mass culture and the culture of personality', in S. Gundle, C. Duggan and G. Pieri (eds), *The Cult of the Duce: Mussolini and the Italians* (Manchester: Manchester University Press, 2013), pp. 84–5. For a comparative perspective on the commercialisation of the dictators and political symbols in Italy and Germany, see B. Gaudenzi, 'Dictators for sale: The commercialization of the Duce and the Führer in Fascist Italy and Nazi Germany', in J. Rüger and N. Wachsmann (eds), *Rewriting German History: New Perspectives on Modern Germany* (London: Palgrave Macmillan, 2015), pp. 267–87.

77 Noi, 'Presentazione', *L'Ufficio Moderno*, 10:10 (October 1935), 437–8.
78 'Si rivolge alla tecnica anziché al misticismo – alla precisione anziché alla mon-umentalità – al realismo anziché al simbolismo – alla logica anziché alla rappre-sentazione – al funzionalismo anziché all'ornamento – al documentario anziché al teatrale'. X. Schawinsky, 'Pubblicità funzionale', *L'Ufficio Moderno*, 10:10 (October 1935), 467.
79 BA, Inv. Nr. 657978, GS 19 Private Korresp., letter from X. Schawinsky to W. Gropius, Milan, 16 September 1934.
80 F. McCarthy, *Gropius: The Man Who Built the Bauhaus* (Cambridge, MA: The Belknap Press of Harvard University Press, 2019), pp. 285–91.
81 W. Gropius, 'Razionalizzazione nella economia edile', *Quadrante*, 24 (April 1935), 7, 10–13, 15, 19 and 25.
82 *Il Milione*, 34 (December 1934–January 1935); Staatsgalerie Stuttgart, Stuttgart, Germany, Archiv Oskar Schlemmer, Inv. Nr. AOS 2015/1816, letter from O. Schlemmer to X. Schawinsky, 20 April 1936.
83 Hollis, *Swiss Graphic Design*, p. 22.
84 'Una base di regole fondamentali per affrontare senza incertezze i compiti princi-pali della tipografia'. Boggeri, 'Una B rossa fra due punti', 20.
85 B. Richter, 'Zurich–Milan', in C. Brändle, K. Gimmi, B. Junod, C. Reble and B. Richter (eds), *100 Years of Swiss Graphic Design* (Zurich: Lars Müller, 2014), pp. 137–43; B. Richter (ed.), *Zürich–Milan* (Baden: Lars Müller Publishers, 2007); W. Georgi and T. Minetti (eds), *Italian Design Is Coming Home. To Switzerland* (Amsterdam: Polyedra, 2011); Hollis, *Swiss Graphic Design*, pp. 135–7.
86 D. Fornari, 'Swiss style made in Italy: Graphic design across the border', in R. Lzicar and D. Fornari (eds), *Mapping Graphic Design History in Switzerland* (Zurich: Triest Verlag, 2016), pp. 152–89; C. Barbieri and D. Fornari, 'Speaking Italian with a Swiss-German accent: Walter Ballmer and Swiss Graphic Design in Milan', *Design Issues*, 37:1 (2020), 26–41.
87 G. Bosoni, M. Campana and S. von Moos (eds), *Max Huber* (London; New York: Phaidon, 2006), p. 8.
88 'Jeune artist suisse'. ASB, letter from A. Boggeri to G. Miedinger, 1 September 1939.
89 ASB, letter from A. Boggeri to M. Huber, 1 January 1940; ASB, letter from M. Huber to A. Boggeri, 21 January 1940; ASB, letter from A. Boggeri to M. Huber, 4 February 1940.
90 ASB, letter from A. Boggeri to M. Huber, 7 March 1942; ASB, letter from A. Boggeri to M. Huber, 20 January 1943.
91 G. Toniolo, 'An overview of Italy's economic growth', in G. Toniolo (ed.), *The Oxford Handbook of the Italian Economy Since Unification* (Oxford; New York: Oxford University Press, 2013), p. 20; Dunnage, *Twentieth-Century Italy*, pp. 118–19; Scarpellini, *L'Italia dei consumi*, p. 90.
92 Gaudenzi, 'Il fascismo in vetrina', p. 73.
93 ASB, letter from A. Boggeri to M. Huber, 20 January 1943; ASB, letter from A. Boggeri to M. Huber, 13 August 1942.
94 ASB, letter from M. Huber to A. Boggeri, 13 August 1943; ASB, letter from M. Huber to A. Boggeri, 6 September 1943.
95 A. Boggeri, 'Stampati pubblicitari per i medici', *La Pubblicità d'Italia*, 5:50–4 (August–December 1941), 28–35. ASB, letter from A. Boggeri to M. Huber, 24 November 1941; ASB, letter from M. Huber to A. Boggeri, 28 November 1941; ASB, letter from A. Boggeri to M. Huber, 7 December 1941; ASB, letter from M. Huber to A. Boggeri, 11 December 1941.
96 ASB, letter from A. Boggeri to M. Huber, Milan, 1 February 1942; ASB, letter from M. Huber to A. Boggeri, 9 February 1942; ASB, letter from A. Boggeri to M. Huber, 23 February 1942.

97 'Forma più caratteristica'. ASB, letter from M. Huber to A. Boggeri, 14 March 1942.

98 'Ha fatto da manager e da catalizzatore, ha ispirato, ha sollecitato ... I suoi pupilli hanno gusti e inclinazioni diverse, hanno diversa cultura e sensibilità, ... ne ha capito il genio e ne ha sviluppato le capacità personali'. L. Sinisgalli, 'Boggeri regista grafico', *Linea Grafica*, 5:3–4 (March–April 1952), 67.

99 'Io voglio che almeno un "grafico" resti sempre a Milano.' ASB, letter from A. Boggeri to M. Huber, 10 June 1942.

100 'Per il "grafico" ho scritto anche a Schulthess per un consiglio'. ASB, letter from A. Boggeri to M. Huber, 5 September 1942.

101 Hollis, *Swiss Graphic Design*; Brändle, Gimmi, Junod, Reble and Richter (eds), *100 Years of Swiss Graphic Design*; Lzicar and Fornari (eds), *Mapping Graphic Design History in Switzerland*; D. Fornari, R. Lzicar, S. Owens, M. Renner, A. Scheuermann and P. J. Schneemann (eds), *Swiss Graphic Design Histories* (Zurich: Scheidegger & Spiess, 2021).

102 Boggeri, 'Una B rossa fra due punti', 21.

103 'Studio Boggeri ... sucht einen jungen Schweizer Grafiker'. Anon., 'Offene Stellen', *Chamäleon*, 25 (November 1954), 6.

3

Graphic design and good taste at the Milan Triennale

Ever since its beginnings in 1923, the Milan Triennale has been a prestigious international exhibition of architecture, design and applied arts. From the outset it became a key arena for the mediation of national and international design discourses, 'the place to see and be seen' for those seeking to shape their reputation in the design world.[1] With the opening of the 6th Triennale approaching, the typographer Ezio D'Errico urged readers of the May 1936 issue of *Graphicus* to capitalise on the public platform for the practice's own good. He advised they ought to 'put before the eyes of the public "what should be done" next to "what should not be done"; demonstrate that what was done yesterday is wrong and why it is wrong; demonstrate that what we want is right and why it is right'.[2] He then added emphatically: 'The Milan Triennale provides us with a good opportunity to proclaim a crusade that will shape the new mentality of Italian typography. Let us try not to miss this opportunity'![3] Ironically, graphic design was omitted from the 6th Triennale. But D'Errico's appeal was not in vain. His was, in fact, one of the many contemporary voices that were calling for the Triennale to be used as a public arena for visibility and design exchange: a platform to claim professional validation, set standards, promote graphic design discourses and showcase criteria of good taste.

After having explored education and everyday practice, and introduced typography, advertising and photography as neighbouring fields of practice, we now turn our attention to strategies of self-representation and mediation and to exhibition design. By exploring the presence of graphic design at the Triennale, this chapter traces the mediation of graphic designers' public image from the early 1930s to the late 1950s. Scholars have recognised the 'key function' that the Triennale played 'in the birth of design and the development of graphics' in Italy.[4] How and to what extent it helped graphic designers to articulate their collective identity, negotiate strategies of self-representation and shape public understanding of the practice are the central concerns here. Switching focus from the design on display to the design of the display, I also suggest that exhibition design offered graphic practitioners a means of experimenting and extending their field of action into the third dimension. The last section of the chapter will show how the significance of the Triennale was not limited to its key role as an agent of mediation through the exhibition of graphic design. Equally revealing was, in fact, its role as a commissioning body. The Triennale was itself an institutional client that commissioned graphic practitioners to design its visual identity. As such, it recognised their specialist knowledge and sanctioned their definition of good taste.

Educating the client

In June 1934, the editors of *Campo Grafico* wondered why the same client who was still asking for outdated floral decorations and ornamental fonts was also sitting behind a 'perfectly rational desk'.[5] To explain this contradictory behaviour, they suggested that architects and product designers had stopped considering the client's opinion and were designing interiors and furniture according to their own taste. Once shown the benefits of the new design, the clients could do nothing but accept it. The campisti recommended readers to follow architects and product designers' example. They could use self-promotional material as an example of good taste: font specimens, for instance, could be sent to clients together with a selection of graphic compositions illustrating the correct use of each font. Their 'clear superiority in practice' was expected to convince even the most reluctant and unwilling client to relegate authority over all printed matter to the graphic design expert.[6] The client's alleged bad taste was nothing more than a 'dishonest excuse'; responsibility was placed back in the hands of graphic practitioners who had the right and the duty 'to stimulate modern good taste' in their clients and the general public.[7] The campisti's recommendation complied with the modernist project to elevate the designers' role to a 'didactic relationship with clients, printers and consumers'.[8] Their morally charged approach to design was nothing new: it had originated in the nineteenth-century design reform movement and had gone on to characterise the ideological dimension and moral connotations of modernism.[9] But their didactic agenda was not merely a question of aesthetics; there was more to it than met the eye.

A rhetoric of 'good design' and 'good taste' resonated through graphic practitioners' and critics' discussions about what was to be represented and who was to control the means of representation. If we understand taste as socially defined, then we need to address the social function that statements about, and demonstrations of, good taste perform. As sociologist Pierre Bourdieu wrote, 'taste classifies, and it classifies the classifier'.[10] Taste is a class marker, an identity-building element that legitimises social differences, orders the relationships between social groups and distinguishes social subjects. Graphic practitioners' request for the exclusive privilege to define – and modify if required – the criteria that differentiate 'good' from 'bad' taste can be interpreted as a means of articulating their affiliation to a specific social group, as well as a way of creating, expanding and maintaining the practice's area of exclusivity. From this perspective, it is also possible to regard graphic practitioners' efforts to educate their clients' tastes in terms of an exercise of power.[11]

An occupation gaining authority over its clients – and then maintaining it over time – is one of the steps it takes in achieving professionalisation. It must negotiate its jurisdiction not only with respect to other occupational groups, as we have seen in the previous two chapters with typography and advertising, but also with 'consumers of labour', that is, the clients and the general public.[12] As sociologist Valérie Fournier put it, occupations 'seek to govern in the name of something outside of themselves' in order to 'establish their legitimacy in the eyes of those in the name of whom they govern'.[13] In Italy, as will become clearer in the following pages, the 'good taste' discourse was used by graphic practitioners as a legitimation

3.1   Exterior of the Padiglione della Stampa at the 5th Milan Triennale, 1933: view of the Mostra delle Arti Grafiche and the Mostra Internazionale della Fotografia.

device, a means of claiming the exclusive right to determine and evaluate the way a work should be performed, thereby creating clients' dependence and attaining their trust.

But how did graphic practitioners intend to construct and mediate a self-conscious public image, educate public taste, attain authority over the client, have their expertise recognised and establish a market both for themselves and for their products? Writing in *Campo Grafico* in 1938, Enrico Bona suggested that 'all the experimental means of the modern technique of propaganda' should be used to promote greater understanding of the practice.[14] But first and foremost, he identified exhibitions as the most appropriate public platform to illustrate 'the concept of good and bad in the graphic arts'.[15] In Bona's view, not only were visitors to exhibitions expected to grasp the criteria of good taste, but also to gain an understanding of printing techniques and production costs. In other words, exhibitions were to be used as arenas to reveal to the public some 'professional terminology and insights' into the practice in an attempt to attract 'public sympathy to [the practice's] own definition of tasks and its own approach to solving them'.[16] As such, they were to correct general misconceptions and misunderstandings that were causing the devaluation of the printed work and the poor consideration shown for the practice. According to Bona, graphic practitioners should take the German Pavilion at the 5th Milan Triennale in 1933 and the 1932–34 MRF, Mostra della Rivoluzione Fascista (Exhibition of the Fascist Revolution) in Rome, as examples.[17]

A humiliating comparison

Everyday printed ephemera made their entrance into the Milan Triennale for the first time at the Mostra delle Arti Grafiche of the 5th Triennale. The presence of the graphic arts in the previous events – three Biennale (1923, 1925 and 1927) and one Triennale (1930) which had taken place in Monza – had been restricted to book design.[18] In 1933, by contrast, all kinds of printed matter and techniques were accepted. For contemporary critics, 'the acknowledgement that the graphic arts [had] their own distinctiveness within the bigger picture of the decorative arts and artistic industries deserved to be welcomed by graphic artists with a sense of self-conscious pride and ... honour'.[19] Pages from trade magazines, illustrated periodicals and books, advertisements and business stationery were pinned onto the wall panels and arranged in the vitrines along the gallery space (see figure 3.1). The Chiattone typographic workshop caught the attention of some reviewers who praised the way in which it had effectively turned invoices, letterheads, business cards, return receipts and wrapping paper into self-promotional material and offered hints at how to improve clients' tastes.[20]

3.2   Installation shot of the German Pavilion at the 5th Milan Triennale, 1933.

Although the majority of commentators agreed on the significance of the event, they also had criticisms to make that stirred up heated discussions in specialist magazines and trade journals over the following two years. First, reviewers denounced the lack of an effective curatorial agenda. They found that the exhibition conveyed a fragmented and heterogeneous message and resembled a trade fair. Secondly, commentators disputed the decision to build a separate pavilion specifically for the exhibition of printed artefacts without consulting any graphic practitioner. They criticised the wrong lighting and complained about the marginal positioning of the pavilion, which was ironically dubbed the 'farm tool shed'.[21] Thirdly, the inclusion of press media and graphic arts within the same pavilion was considered misleading. Besides the Mostra delle Arti Grafiche, the Padiglione della Stampa also hosted the Mostra Storica del Giornalismo (Historical Exhibition of Journalism), the Mostra della Stampa Contemporanea (Exhibition of Contemporary Press) and the Mostra Internazionale della Fotografia (International Exhibition of Photography). Reviewers considered the joint exhibition a dangerous mistake that reinforced misunderstandings due to the ambiguity of the Italian term 'stampa', which can indicate either the printing process and the resulting printed artefact, or the print media. To present the printing industry and the press as synonymous corroborated the confusion of the general public and damaged the ongoing articulation and mediation of graphic design practice.

Guido Modiano became the most hard-edged critic of the Mostra delle Arti Grafiche and got into an argument with Raffaello Bertieri, who disapproved of Modiano's decision to boycott the exhibition. According to Bertieri, 'there [were] too few [graphic practitioners] in Italy [who were] struggling for the recognition of [their] art to take the liberty of such no-show protests'.[22] Instead of boycotting, graphic practitioners should have been uniting in a collective effort to demand social and economic status. Viewed through the lens of social identity and self-categorisation theory, Bertieri's reproach can be regarded as a call for in-group coop-eration and cohesion, and hence a request to put individual differences aside in the interests of the practice as a whole.[23] The crossfire went on for almost a year. Modiano lamented the missed opportunity to promote the modernisation of Italian graphics by showing, both to practitioners and clients, examples of good design in accordance with the principles of the New Typography. As we shall see, Modiano took the mediation of graphic design practice into his own hands seven years later when he realised his curatorial vision at the 7th Triennale of 1940.

Criticism was heightened by the inevitable comparison with the German Pavilion curated by Paul Renner on behalf of the Deutscher Werkbund (see figure 3.2). Like the Mostra d'Arte Grafica, the pavilion was devoted to the graphic arts and printing industries. But, according to Italian reviewers, to compare the two exhibitions was humiliating.[24] Unlike the Mostra d'Arte Grafica, the German Pavilion was a comprehensive exhi-bition that conveyed a coherent message. Exhibits were arranged by kind: advertisements, pamphlets, magazines, posters and packaging. A special section was devoted to type design, with a slideshow illustrating the his-torical development of style in type design and comparing letterforms with contemporary architecture and figurative arts. Italian commentators appreciated the dialogue between disciplines that presented typography as a product of its time subjected to technological and aesthetic changes. Works by exponents of the New Typography were included in the pavil-ion: Herbert Bayer, Max Burchartz, Willy Baumeister and Heinrich Jost, among others. The exhibition also featured works by Imre Reiner and Xanti Schawinsky, who, as discussed in chapter 2, were the first of a number of foreign designers hired by Antonio Boggeri in order to posi-tion his studio at the forefront of the Milanese design scene. The German Pavilion became the reference point for future exhibitions, and its reso-nance was still to be heard more than three years later when, in a review of the 6th Triennale of 1936, Modiano declared that Italian graphic practi-tioners were 'indebted to Paul Renner'.[25]

As noted in chapter 2 when discussing Schawinsky's stay and work in Milan, Italy in the early 1930s, and Milan in particular, was seen as a viable alternative to Nazi Germany thanks, among other things, to Mussolini's more pluralistic cultural policy.[26] The 5th Triennale occurred at the beginning of what historian Ruth Ben-Ghiat identified as the first phase of the German-Italian collaboration, namely the period between Hitler's 1933 takeover in Germany and the 1936 Rome–Berlin Axis which strengthened the relationship between the two dictatorships. During this period, Ben-Ghiat argued, 'culture emerged as [a] main arena for Italians to assert the primacy of their own brand of fascism'.[27] A review of Renner's pavilion published in the July 1933 issue of the German graphic design magazine *Gebrauchsgraphik* gives a sense of how the cultural policy of Fascist Italy was being seen through German eyes. The reviewer drew attention to a detail of the pavilion, namely 'a particularly beautiful bit of Futura reproducing Mussolini's saying: "We dare not plunder the inheritance of our fathers, we must create a new art"'.[28] The contributor then added: 'This warning deserves to be heard in Germany too.'[29]

The first of these two phrases from *Gebrauchsgraphik* suggests that contemporaries did not view printing Mussolini's words in Futura as inherently contradictory. The political connotation of the ultra-modernist typeface devised by Renner in 1927 was not so clear-cut, nor was that of modernist techniques and aesthetics being deployed in the service of fascist rhetoric.[30] The second phrase corroborates the argument that the greater tolerance shown towards modernists by Italian fascists as compared to that shown by National Socialists became a factor in the articulation of ideological differences between Italy and Germany. However, this perception of Nazi culture as monolithic and incompatible with modernism is biased and does not consider 'the ample evidence that the National Socialists – despite their own propaganda – often openly appropriated modernism for their own ends'.[31] This was especially true with graphic design. As exemplified by the work of Herbert Bayer, 'the [Nazi] regime allowed and even encouraged the usage of Bauhaus graphics in various venues so as to project a modernist self-image'.[32]

As for Fascist Italy, temporary propaganda displays and commemorative exhibitions exemplify how the Fascist regime openly appropriated modernism for its own ends, and how modernist techniques and aesthetics were often invested with fascist meanings during the 1930s. Together with the Milan Triennale and the Biennale festivals in Venice, they contributed to 'a comprehensive politics of Fascist spectacle that showcased the latest works of international modernism alongside the fruits of Fascist culture'.[33] Whereas in the previous two chapters we addressed the relationship between fascism and modernism from the perspective of everyday design practice, it is now to top-down events that we turn our attention.

From the page to the wall and back again

After the 5th Triennale, advocates for the renewal and professionalisation of Italian graphics began looking for alternative ways to articulate the public image of graphic design practice, and to correct the misleading message conveyed by the 1933 Mostra d'Arte Grafica. In addition to the German Pavilion, graphic practitioners showed interest in temporary propaganda displays and commemorative exhibitions. These events were remarkable for 'the treatment of the subject matter (historical, political, cultural, economic, social, in any case linked to the ideological horizon of Fascism) and for the modernity of the exhibition design'.[34] Focusing on the role played by graphic design as a crucial component of the exhibition apparatus, commentators formulated a more comprehensive understanding of the practice that included exhibition design as one of its expressions. Debates implicitly tackled graphic designers' concern about the exhibition context. Then, as it still is today, exhibiting graphic design was a contested practice likely to provoke complaints from those who found it a potential source of distortion and misrepresentation.[35] The criticism stems from the assumption that graphic design is misunderstood in the gallery space, as graphic objects are stripped of their function and lose meaning when out of context. But unlike graphics exhibitions, interwar propaganda displays offered practitioners an alternative venue for self-representation, one in which graphic design could be perceived in action as exhibition graphics.

In a June 1933 article entitled 'Alcuni aspetti grafici della Mostra della Rivoluzione Fascista' (Some graphic aspects of the Exhibition of the Fascist Revolution), Bertieri urged his colleagues 'to visit [the exhibition] as Italians first and then to analyse it as graphic practitioners'.[36] The MRF had opened in Rome at the Palazzo delle Esposizioni (Palace of Expositions) in October 1932 to celebrate the tenth anniversary of the March on Rome by which Benito Mussolini had come to power in Italy in late October 1922.[37] It was a mass event, closing after two years with over 3,700,000 visitors coming from every part of Italy and abroad. According to Bertieri, the MRF was far more influential for the fate of the practice than any other graphics exhibition of the period, because it was 'living and dynamic graphics' caught while performing 'its true expressive and propagandistic function'.[38] In his opinion, both the taste and the understanding of the general public had been deeply affected. Therefore, he exhorted colleagues to study the event and consider the consequences of the changed attitude towards graphics. In other words, if the MRF could be said to have affected public expectations, the public image of graphics should be renegotiated.

On the one hand, by urging his colleagues to visit the MRF 'as Italians first', Bertieri can be seen as supporting the regime's agenda, according to which all Italians were expected to make a patriotic pilgrimage to Rome.[39] On the other hand, however, by inviting readers to analyse the exhibition as graphic practitioners, he was recommending colleagues to take a critical stance during their visit. This distinction between visiting practices carried an underlying assumption that practitioners' cultural capital provided them with a different modality of looking and an interpretative framework that surpassed the limits of the general observer's ability to comprehend.[40] Furthermore, the recommended critical stance was at odds with the curators' attempt to create an immersive experience that would appeal to the emotions and affect the viewers on a subconscious level, thereby leading them to passively accept the propaganda message. It would be speculative to imply a political intent behind Bertieri's distinction between visiting practices. Nevertheless, his appeal to critical analysis suggests a certain degree of awareness of the manipulative use of media by the regime.

Bertieri described the MRF as the '"graphic" representation' of eighteen years of Italian history and the 'greatest, most original and most important "layout" that [he] had ever had the chance to see'.[41] The use of the expression 'impaginazione' (layout) suggests that exhibition and graphic design were perceived as part of a designed whole. In the same vein, Modiano defined the MRF as 'one of the most extended and heroic "layouts" of the time', thereby demonstrating that to approach exhibition design from a graphic design perspective was a common practice.[42] Looking at the MRF through the eyes of a graphic practitioner, Bertieri drew attention to the way graphic elements and technique had been translated onto a larger and three-dimensional scale, moving from the typographic page to the walls of the exhibition. He pointed out that the typographic characters were transformed into three-dimensional oversized letters. The thirty 1.60-metre-tall letters of the title standing above the entrance and the twin 6-metre-tall Xs – the Roman number 10 – framing the temporary façade were a case in point (see figure 3.3). The systematic repetition of the same word also exalted the physicality of the letterforms. This was the case with the word 'PRESENTE!' (HERE!) repeated around the circular walls of the Sacrario dei Martiri (Chapel of the Martyrs). Bertieri also remarked on the structural function performed by the graphic elements. Typographic and photographic compositions, and the technique of photomontage in particular, played a decisive role in framing together the heterogeneous selection of objects and documents on display.

Switching point of view, from the wall to the page, Bertieri wrote: 'If one were to detach some of the elements from the arrangement in which they are found on individual walls, one would notice that they can be effortlessly translated into various different page compositions: it could be said that they arrange themselves onto the page all by themselves.'[43] The exhibition catalogue had, therefore, the potential to be a 'graphic masterpiece'.[44] Alas, it lacked any kind of experimental use of typography and was criticised for the poor use of photography. The graphic compositions that featured in Bertieri's review can be regarded as an attempt at fixing the dullness of the official catalogue. In the graphic interpretation of the Sacrario dei Martiri (see figure 3.4), picture, text and coloured and white areas work together to reiterate the cross motif. The colours of the

Roma - La Mostra della Rivoluzione.

3.3   Postcard advertising the Mostra della Rivoluzione Fascista, featuring the façade of the Palazzo delle Esposizioni, designed by Mario De Renzi and Adalberto Libera, Rome, 1932.

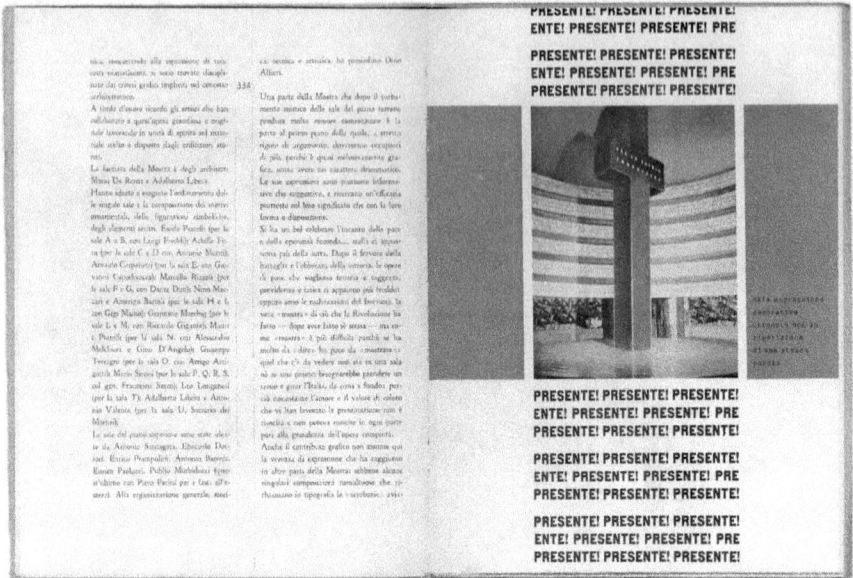

3.4   Double-page spread from Raffaello Bertieri's review of the Mostra della Rivoluzione Fascista, 'Alcuni Aspetti Grafici della Mostra della Rivoluzione Fascista', *Risorgimento Grafico*, 30:6 (June 1933), 334–5.

graphic composition mirror the black of the walls and the cross, and the blood-red pedestal in the actual room. The halved line of text that breaks the upper edge of the page conveys the impression of a text scrolling on a loop behind the central picture. Here, as in the actual room, the word 'PRESENTE!' refers to the living memory of the fallen for the fascist cause. Its seemingly endless repetition conveys the impression of a shouting crowd that is willing to sacrifice itself in answer to the call 'Per la Patria Immortale' (For the Immortal Fatherland) inscribed on the cross.

Bertieri's review of the MRF demonstrates his ability to switch graphic registers: a more conservative approach to the magazine page layout, with its two centred columns of justified text and serif font, coexists with experimental graphic compositions, whose expressive use of sans-serif font, photography, coloured forms and blank areas follows the principles of the New Typography. Architecture historian, Brian McLaren, in his analysis of the representation of the MRF in the illustrated architectural magazines of the period, distinguished between the pages of *Casabella* in which 'the process of translation from the three dimensions to the two was recognized' and those of *Architettura* 'attempting simply to document the exhibition'.[45] Similarly to the article in *Casabella*, Bertieri's review provided a series of fragmentary representations. In both cases, the MRF 'existed in this way only in the images that [the two magazines] presented'.[46] In the pages of *Casabella*, McLaren argued, 'the reproduction of architecture became a new kind of production [and] the source for architectural ideas independent of the original exhibition'.[47] As a source for graphic ideas, Bertieri's graphic interpretation of the Sacrario dei Martiri conveys an impression of him that is in contradiction with the one given in chapter 1. This contradiction offers a chance to examine the historiographical dichotomy that sees Bertieri and *Risorgimento Grafico* as die-hard guardians of the Italian typographic tradition, over and against the more experimental attitude of *Campo Grafico* and the campisti. As such it portrays a different version of Bertieri, one where he is receptive to change and understands the potential of modernist visual language.

Exhibition design and typography away from the page

The relationship between graphic and exhibition design grew stronger in the mid-1930s, to such an extent that graphic practitioners claimed jurisdiction over exhibition design, considered as a typographic grid in three dimensions. In 1934, two temporary displays caught graphic practitioners' attention: the propaganda display in the Galleria Vittorio Emanuele II in Milan for the occasion of the plebiscitary general elections held on 26 March, and the Sala delle Medaglie d'Oro (Gold Medals Hall) at the EAI, Esposizione dell'Aeronautica Italiana (Italian Aeronautics Exhibition). Both displays were co-designed by the industrial and graphic designer, Marcello Nizzoli, and the graphic designer and editor of *Casabella*, Edoardo Persico. In both cases, the exhibition space was conceived graphically and structured using modular elements to build a three-dimensional typographic grid.

The temporary display at the Galleria Vittorio Emanuele II consisted of a gridded structure of white and orange scaffolding whose colour and material contrasted with the neoclassical interior of the two glass-vaulted intersecting arcades (see figure 3.5). Relying on the brainwash potential of incessant repetition, a picture of Mussolini appeared multiple times and was distributed along the metal grid next to excerpts from his speeches, signs praising the Duce and the fascist revolution, and other photographic panels. Four loudspeakers complemented the visually overwhelming structure and turned the temporary display into a multisensory experience. The poster with the silhouette of Mussolini that hung from the scaffolding was also pasted onto the pillars and scattered along the arcades next to five other posters. These were conceived by Persico in collaboration with Nizzoli, Bramante Buffoni and Umberto Zimelli, and featured photographs with extreme close-ups, dramatic silhouettes, aerial perspectives and unexpected changes of scale, combined with a condensed sans-serif lettering in an asymmetrical layout.

Once more, Persico's propaganda posters illustrate the use of modernist imagery and techniques to convey content attributable to fascist

3.5 View of the propaganda display in the Galleria Vittorio Emanuele II, designed by Marcello Nizzoli and Edoardo Persico on the occasion of the fascist plebiscite on 26 March 1934.

rhetoric. As such, Carlo Vinti noted, they have been 'virtually banned from the history of Italian graphic design, probably precisely because they document the close connection between the new typography and fascist propaganda'.[48] Co-founders of *Campo Grafico*, Attilio Rossi and Carlo Dradi, retrospectively wrote that they refused to publish Persico's posters in their magazine in opposition to the fact that 'modern graphics – the most effective communication media – was being used to spread lies'.[49] This anecdote has frequently been cited in the literature as an example of an early stance against Fascism by Italian graphic designers, in an attempt to provide democratic legitimation for the protagonists of the modern movement in Italy.[50] Indeed, the campisti neither published nor commented on the posters at the time of the plebiscitary elections. However, they reprinted an article by Modiano that featured four of the five posters in the November–December 1935 issue of *Campo Grafico* (see figure 3.6).[51] Ignoring the content to focus on form and technique, Modiano identified Persico's posters as a model for the application of the principle of the New Typography, and typo-photographic montage in particular, and praised the use of a modular layout as a means to give a sense of unity to the five variations within the series.

The reprint of Modiano's article featuring Persico's propaganda posters was neither the first, nor the last, time that *Campo Grafico* featured graphic artefacts combining modernist graphics with fascist rhetoric.[52] It is not my intention here to cast doubt on the antifascism of the campisti, but rather to complicate simplistic equations between politics and style in line with Vinti's critical analysis of the New Typography in Fascist Italy. 'In Italy', Vinti argued, 'the battle for the modern took place in a cultural and

3.6 Double-page spread featuring four propaganda posters designed by Edoardo Persico for the fascist plebiscite in 1934, from Guido Modiano's article 'Manifesti', *Campo Grafico*, 4:1 (January 1936), 244–5.

ideological framework strongly dominated by fascism and its willingness to politicise all forms of expression. ... Fascism influenced the debate on typography ..., providing ideological reasons supporting not only the defenders of the tradition but also a substantial part of the modernist front.'[53] To contemporary eyes, to invest modernist techniques and aesthetics with fascist meaning was not as outrageous and unacceptable as Rossi and Dradi's anecdote suggested.

A couple of months after the fascist plebiscite, Nizzoli and Persico collaborated once again at the EAI. In the Sala delle Medaglie d'Oro, they used a modular structure of threadlike squares to create a white three-dimensional typographic grid that hung between the two black areas of the floor and ceiling (see figure 3.7). Lines of text and photographic documentation of the heroic gestures of World War I pilots were arranged soberly in a rhythmic, asymmetrical layout that made little concession to the bombastic rhetoric of the regime's propaganda.[54] In his analysis of Nazi exhibition design and modernism, art historian Michael Tymkiw suggested it would be better to avoid talking about spectatorship in binary terms – that is, active vs passive audiences – and instead to use the term 'engaged spectatorship' to indicate disparate efforts 'to provoke complex modes of viewing

3.7   View of the Sala delle Medaglie d'Oro at the Esposizione dell'Aeronautica Italiana, exhibition design by Marcello Nizzoli and Edoardo Persico, Milan, 1934.

and thereby inspire visitors to think about the relationship between their own bodies, the objects they saw, and the exhibition environments in which they moved and stood while viewing'.[55] Tymkiw's definition resonates with Nizzoli and Persico's modes of addressing their spectators. Visitors were granted a certain freedom of movement: while they could only walk around the scaffolding in the Galleria Vittorio Emanuele II, they were put inside the exhibition space at the Sala delle Medaglie d'Oro where the transparency and overlapping of the modular structures created an immersive gridded space. In both cases, the exhibition layout encouraged 'variations in sensory perceptions based on a spectator' position and movement in space'.[56]

Held from June until October 1934 at the Palazzo dell'Arte in Milan – that is, the location of the Triennale – the EAI was described as 'a festival of the trends in European architecture and of their resonance in Italy'.[57] After visiting it with Schawinsky, Walter Gropius gave enthusiastic feedback in a postcard to Luigi Figini and Gino Pollini and congratulated the architects on their design for the Sala dei Precursori (Pioneers' Room).[58] In Rome, the Gropiuses had already visited the MRF whose 'strongly Russian-influenced presentation' had attracted Ise's curiosity.[59] Indeed, the exhibition in Rome contained many references to Russian Constructivism that contemporary critics were quick to notice.[60] According to Ise, the architects of the EAI had learned from the Werkbund exhibition in Paris (1930) and the Deutsche Bauausstellung (German building exhibition) in Berlin (1931). Writing to Marcel Breuer, she expressed her disappointment in the current state of exhibition design in their country: 'it is a pity to see how germany is now simply failing to continue working on these things'.[61] However, Ise's complaint ignored what Tymkiw considered as the 'possibility for formal experimentation that existed for artists, architects, graphic designers, and others involved in designing exhibition spaces meant to promote the ideas and policies of National Socialism to members of the general public'.[62] Indeed, as Tymkiw went on to point out, exhibitions beyond the fine arts served as sites of formal experimentation in the field of exhibition design in Nazi Germany. This was the case with the exhibition, Deutsches Volk – Deutsche Arbeit (German People – German Work), held in Berlin in April 1934. Ise's forgetfulness regarding this exhibition is rather curious. She could easily have drawn comparisons between her husband and Joost Schmidt's design of the nonferrous metals exhibit and aspects of the EAI, namely between the tower and the modular structure of overlapping cubes from the nonferrous display, and Giuseppe Pagano's spiral from Icaro's Room and Nizzoli and Persico's gridded display in the Sala delle Medaglie d'Oro.

The paths of graphic and exhibition design merged at the Triennale in 1936. Much to graphic practitioners' dismay, the committee of the 6th Triennale had decided to keep the graphic arts out of the event. The official reason for this exclusion is unknown: an article in *Campo Grafico* pointed to Italy's military effort in the colonial war in Ethiopia (October 1935–May 1936), whereas Vinti identified the unexpected death of Persico in January that year and Pagano's resignation from the Triennale committee as potential causes.[63] Practitioners had been waiting for a second chance to promote the practice's public image ever since the disappointment of the Padiglione della Stampa in 1933. In June 1935, a group of graphic practitioners had made a formal request to the organising committee, in which they exhorted members 'to avoid wasting for a second time the opportunity to shape the conscience of modern typography in Italy'.[64] The document provides evidence of the desire to make use of the Triennale as a public arena to claim aesthetic and social legitimacy for graphic design practice. Alas, the requests fell on deaf ears and the exclusion marked yet another defeat.

However, the absence of a dedicated graphic design exhibition did not mean that graphic design itself was absent. Quite the contrary: graphic design was ubiquitous; despite not being represented as content, it participated in the 6th Triennale by way of the exhibition design. As the campisti put it, 'the graphic arts, left outside the door, enter[ed] through the window'.[65] Reviewers observed that 'the entire Triennale [was] arranged according to a graphic layout with a marked tendency towards abstraction'.[66] In particular, commentators drew attention to Giuseppe Pagano's design for the exhibition, Architettura rurale italiana (Rural Italian Architecture), and to the Salone della Vittoria (Victory Hall) in honour of the occupation of Addis Ababa and the annexation of the territory of Ethiopia in early May that year. With its use of standardised and modular elements and arrangement of the visual material in a chart-like layout, Pagano's exhibition design recalled the above-mentioned Sala delle Medaglie d'Oro. Persico and Nizzoli conceived the design of the Salone della Vittoria together with the artist Lucio Fontana and the architect Giancarlo Palatini (see figure 3.8).[67] The portraits of ancient Roman Consuls and Emperors – Scipio, Caesar, Augustus, Trajan and Constantine – caught the attention of reviewers. The reference to the Roman Empire was a propaganda device aimed at legitimising the regime's imperialist policies.[68] Made of cement inlay, the pictures mimicked grainy photographs. The likeness to enlarged halftone dots provided the historical figures with a modern appeal through the connotative value of the reprographic technique.

In his review, Modiano argued that the exhibition design of the 6th Triennale was, together with the MRF and the EAI, 'evidence for the existence of the authority of "grafismo"'.[69] By 'grafismo' (graphism) he meant the presence of graphic elements, materials and techniques outside the typographic page. His definition for this rather difficult to pinpoint concept was 'typography for non-typographers'.[70] However, graphism, he

3.8 Detail of the Salone della Vittoria at the 6th Milan Triennale, exhibition design by Edoardo Persico, Marcello Nizzoli and Giancarlo Palatini, 1936.

warned, should not be confused with amateurism. It was, rather, a move away from the typographic tradition and the idea of typography as Art towards a cross-fertilisation between graphics, rationalist architecture and visual arts, all of which shared, in his view, a tendency towards abstraction and geometric and elementary design. The interdisciplinarity of exhibition design made it the perfect field for exploring collaboration with outsiders to the typographers' milieu: architects, artists and photographers. The cross-fertilisation found expression in the exhibition design at the 6th Triennale, where 'modern architecture had found in the *typographic* taste an opportunity and a reason for new forms of expression'.[71]

Modiano and Italian graphic practitioners were not alone in their enthusiasm for exhibition design. It is interesting to note that during the same period Bayer said he 'began to feel that design in two dimensions only [was] confining and limited' and discovered 'exhibition design ... to be a new medium of communication, which [went] beyond the use of graphics in two dimensions. It embrace[d] all possible visual media, all dimensions of space, and include[d] oral–aural techniques.'[72] Bayer's words recall Modiano's concept of graphism and exhibition design as 'typography's greatest expression, ... a projection into the third dimension of the graphic form'.[73] By opening the door of the typographic workshop to the mutual influences of different scenes that were not strictly connected to the graphics industry and printing trade, the concept of graphism contributed to the broader understanding of graphic design practice as it emerged at the intersection with the closely related fields of typography, commercial art, visual art, architecture and exhibition design.

Ten years of modernist debate

Officially absent in 1936, graphic design re-entered the Triennale in 1940. The 7th Triennale was the last under fascist rule: it opened on 6 April, 'in the midst of a European crisis, a political, economic, social crisis', and closed only two months later, on 9 June, when Italy ended its neutrality by entering World War II, which had broken out in September 1939.[74] By 1940 the possibility for political and ideological debate had been closed. The chosen theme, 'Order – Tradition', set the tone of the overall event, which turned its back on the more pluralistic approach to culture of previous years, in favour of nationalistic choices, as exemplified by architect Marcello Piacentini's design for the E42 district in Rome.

Putting the imminent war aside, the Mostra Grafica (Graphics Exhibition) set out finally to meet practitioners' expectations. Curated by Modiano, the exhibition was intended as an 'evaluation of ten years of modernist debate' and aimed to convey 'a persuasive documentation of "Graphism"'.[75] According to Modiano, 'neither the deepest and most interesting characteristics of the graphic arts, nor a clear explanation of [their] requirements and purposes [had] ever been provided to the public in Italy before'.[76] In an attempt to improve public understanding of the practice and officially associate modernist graphics with the notion of good taste, he curated a comprehensive exhibition with a coherent and didactic message. Modiano's agenda distinguished the Mostra Grafica from the

1933 Mostra delle Arti Grafiche. This latter had been heavily criticised by Modiano himself for its weak curatorial agenda, which he said had reinforced public misunderstanding. In contrast to the 5th Triennale, all members of the exhibition committee, co-curators and exhibition designers of the Mostra Grafica were either graphic practitioners themselves or worked in close contact with them. In this instance at least, graphic practitioners had gained exclusive control over who and what should represent their practice, how the graphic works should be displayed and who should control the means of representation.

The Mostra Grafica was carefully structured in seven sections that were 'aim[ed] at familiarising the public with the intimate aspect of graphics: its techniques, the sources of a lively typography, the artists who [had] been able to translate the modern taste into graphic terms and, finally, a noble page of typography and Italian publishing: i.e., the limited editions'.[77] Curated by Luigi Veronesi, the first section explained the graphic techniques and clarified the role of the printing industry in the Italian economy. The panel 'La grafica nella coerenza del gusto' (Graphics and its coherency with taste) illustrated the history of Italian graphics while drawing a comparison with architecture and figurative arts. The panel featured works by Herbert Bayer, Jan Tschichold and El Lissitzky as exemplars of good taste. The sources of modern graphics were further clarified in the second section, which was curated by Bruno Munari. Reproductions of futurist, abstract and constructivist artworks were displayed, together with rationalist architecture and photographic compositions, around a tree trunk that metaphorically represented the family tree of modern graphics. The third section was curated by Modiano himself and was intended as a 'triumph of the modernist idea'.[78] As such, it included a selection of what he saw as the most significant examples of the modern graphic taste that had been designed in Italy since 1933.

Commercial advertising and political propaganda were the focus of the fourth section (see figure 3.9). As we saw in chapter 2, the boundaries between advertising and propaganda were flexible. At the time, the two terms were used as synonymous, and the two practices were understood as intertwined. 'What is called advertising in the bourgeois regime', graphics and architecture critic Giulia Veronesi explained in 1937 in *Campo Grafico*, 'goes under the name of propaganda under the fascist regime.'[79] Since the 1930s, commercial advertising had undergone a process of politicisation, with corporative and collective advertisements playing a key role in the implementation of autarchic policies.[80] Small advertisements were displayed in a suspended structure, a succession of three-dimensional white frames enclosing a series of white panels in an accordion bookbinding-like arrangement. Posters were hung in a display case against the wall and included works by Carboni, Veronesi, Nizzoli and Schawinsky. Three exemplars of Persico's propaganda posters for the fascist plebiscite of 1934 were

3.9 View of the fourth section of the Mostra Grafica at the 7th Milan Triennale, exhibition design by Leonardo Sinisgalli and Giovanni Pintori, 1940. Two posters designed by Xanti Schawinsky for Illy and Cervo (1934), Erberto Carboni's poster for the summer cruises Italia (1937) and three propaganda posters for the fascist plebiscite conceived by Edoardo Persico (1934) are hanging on the wall in the background.

also on display. The fifth section consisted of a number of monographic displays. In the sixth section, which was curated by Ezio D'Errico, pages and covers of magazines were displayed on a suspended, curved structure reminiscent of the impression roll of a rotary printing press (see figure 3.10).

Finally, the seventh section showed Modiano's awareness of the strengths and weaknesses of modernist vocabulary. Curated by Bertieri and devoted to book design, this section was the expression of a compromise position, having a more conservative approach to graphics. This inclusion of a traditionalist approach might seem to have been at odds with Modiano's celebration of the victory of modernism. On the contrary, however, it can be interpreted as the implicit acknowledgement that the application of modernist techniques and aesthetics to all and every type of printed matter was inappropriate. As declared by Modiano in 1937, 'the layout of the literary and pure typographic book [was] the outcome of a centuries-old selection and its form [was], possibly, definitive'.[81] This more cautious attitude towards modern graphics is all the more meaningful if we consider that by the late 1930s Tschichold himself had turned against what he perceived as the intolerant formalism of the New Typography.

3.10 View of the sixth section of the Mostra Grafica at the 7th Milan Triennale, curated by Ezio D'Errico, exhibition design by Leonardo Sinisgalli and Giovanni Pintori, 1940.

He objected to the fact that the application of its principles was limited to publicity work and modern subject matter, and hence inappropriate for many other purposes, book design above all.[82] As already argued by Vinti, the inclusion of this section suggests that by the time of the 7th Triennale the quarrel between exponents of a more traditionalist approach to book design and advocates for the modern graphic taste had been mitigated, thereby enabling in-between positions to be held.[83]

The seventh section was not the only aspect of the Mostra Grafica at odds with Modiano's endeavour to use the Milan Triennale as a showcase for the modern graphic taste. The catalogue could not have been further removed from what might have been expected after reading the exhibition agenda: a letterpress and hand-sewn booklet with the text composed in an italicised serif font and arranged in a symmetrical and justified layout (see figure 3.11). The titles are the only exception to an otherwise conservative look. By ignoring the central fold, the capitalised red titles link the double-page spread and create a moderate version of the two-pages-in-one layout.

The Mostra Grafica featured in two special issues of the German magazines *Deutscher Drucker* and *Druck und Werbekunst* devoted to Italian graphics that were printed in July 1941 and early 1942, respectively. Writing in *Deutscher Drucker*, the former director of the advertising department of Olivetti, Renato Zveteremich, described the exhibition as a 'fundamental point' that had provided an overview of a decade of Italian graphic production.[84] Giovanni Pizzuto held a similar position in *Druck und Werbekunst*. Ex-collaborator of *Campo Grafico*, Pizzuto argued that the exhibition demonstrated the way in which 'the new aesthetics had penetrated the Italian production'. He then pointed out that, 'as foreseen by Modiano, the graphic practice [had become] the field of specialist artists rather than of typographers pure and simple'.[85] Featuring bilingual German-Italian articles, the special issues are evidence of a new phase in the cultural relationship between Nazi Germany and Fascist Italy. Following the 1936 Rome–Berlin Axis and the signature of the Italian-German Cultural Accord in November 1938, exchange, cooperation and competition marked the partnership between the two allied countries.[86] This dynamic also characterised the relations of the two regimes in the field of advertising, with effects both on the local and the transnational scenes. Locally, Italian specialist publications such as *La Pubblicità d'Italia* and *Guida Ricciardi* (1941) became bilingual after the outbreak of war and included long articles on German advertising. Transnationally, exchanges and cross-visits intensified until representatives of the Werberat der deutschen Wirtschaft (Advertising Board of the German Economy) and the Federazione nazionale fascista degli ausiliari del commercio (National Fascist Federation of Trade Auxiliaries) established the Italo-Germanic Committee for Advertising and Economic Propaganda at the end of 1941.[87]

After almost a decade of lively argumentation, the Mostra Grafica signalled the greater self-awareness and professional confidence that had been attained by Italian graphic practitioners by the early 1940s. Italian graphic design was gradually taking shape at the convergence between typography, visual arts and rationalist architecture, and it had become the field of a new professional figure who was not strictly linked to the printing and advertising industry, or the typographic workshop. Modernist

VII TRIENNALE DI MILANO
APRILE-GIUGNO 1940 - A. XVIII
PRESIDENTE GIUSEPPE BIANCHINI —
COMITATO ESECUTIVO RAFFAELE CALZINI · PIETRO   CHIESA · MARCELLO PIACENTINI · GIO PONTI · C A FELICE

Il Comitato esecutivo della Triennale ha incaricato della preparazione della Mostra grafica una Commissione della quale fan parte:

Raffaello Bertieri, Aldo Borletti, Osvaldo Cappelli, Franco Ciarlantini, Ezio D'Errico, Leo Longanesi, Edoardo Malusardi, Giovanni Mazzocchi, Guido Modiano, Marcello Nizzoli, Elio Palazzo, Luigi Poli, Giovanni Scheiwiller,

Leonardo Sinisgalli e Giovanni Treccani degli Alfieri: Guido Modiano e Leonardo Sinisgalli, membri esecutivi. Il programma della Mostra è stato particolarmente disposto da Guido Modiano; Leonardo Sinisgalli ha progettato l'allestimento ambientale della Mostra stessa, in collaborazione con Giovanni Pintori.

Di questo opuscolo, sono stati tirati 1000 esemplari.

ESEMPLARE 671

3.11   Exhibition catalogue for the Mostra Grafica at the 7th Milan Triennale, designed by Guido Modiano, 1940.

aesthetics and techniques were, moreover, officially associated with the notion of good taste.

Let us now investigate whether graphic designers' use of the Triennale as an arena for the mediation of the practice succeeded in adapting to the political, cultural and economic context of post-war Italy, by looking at two graphic design exhibitions that were included in the Triennale in the 1950s.

The rhetoric of good taste and the post-war agenda

The Mostra d'Arti Grafiche e Pubblicità (Graphic Arts and Advertising Exhibition) at the 9th Triennale in 1951 was the first graphic design exhibition to be included in the Triennale in the post-war period.[88] Curated by Dino Villani, advertising technician and first chair of ATAP, Associazione Italiana Tecnici e Artisti Pubblicitari (Italian Association of Advertising Technicians and Artists), and Erberto Carboni, the exhibition demonstrated the resilience of the 'good taste' discourse as a legitimation device. A selection of the most recent advertisements from the US, France, the UK, Switzerland, the Netherlands, Denmark, Spain and Japan welcomed visitors to the exhibition space. At the time, the Italian advertising industry still lagged behind most Western countries in terms of expenditure, but its turnover grew by 150 per cent over the decade.[89] The exhibition continued with a retrospective of about fifty years of graphics and advertising in Italy and ended with the section 'advertising of tomorrow'. Curators had invited fifteen graphic designers and poster artists to design the 'advertising that the artist and technician will be able to make once they are no longer dependent upon the arbitrary requests of inexperienced clients'.[90] The initiative maintained the interwar rhetoric about the need to educate clients and the general public.

The Mostra d'Arti Grafiche e Pubblicità was a historical overview with a focus on advertising and poster art. Its major goal was to show how advertising used experimental visual languages as a means to attract viewers' attention and to introduce the general public to a certain type of cutting-edge aesthetics that they would not otherwise come across.[91] Centre stage was taken by a semi-floating structure conceived by Carboni in honour of the poster artist Leonetto Cappiello (see figure 3.12). Its spiral form recalled the orange peel in Cappiello's iconic poster for the spirit, Campari Bitter (1921), that was printed multiple times in both original and close-up, cropped versions. Writing in the trade journal *Bollettino Centro Studi Grafici*, an anonymous commentator criticised Carboni for having designed 'scenery in which printed artefacts [were] used to fill up spaces, rather than rational supports that would have allowed [visitors] to see the printed artefacts in the best possible way'.[92] The reviewer compared the spiral structure to the Tower of Babel, spreading the lies and sins of advertising. This acidic comparison forewarned of internal arguments that, as

3.12   View of the Mostra d'Arti Grafiche e Pubblicità at the 9ᵗʰ Milan Triennale, curated by Dino Villani, exhibition design by Erberto Carboni, 1951.

will be discussed later in chapter 5, were to unsettle the relationship between advertising and graphic design in the years to come.

By the time of the Mostra di Arte Grafica (Graphic Arts Exhibition) at the 11ᵗʰ Triennale of 1957, curators' priorities had changed to include a far-reaching agenda. In addition to illustrating once again the criteria of good design 'against a slapdash attitude and unpreparedness, in defence of a frail profession', curators – Egidio Bonfante, Aldo Colombo, Franco Grignani, Attilio Rossi, Leonardo Sinisgalli and Ignazio Weiss – focused on the economic and cultural impact of graphic design and on the resulting responsibility of graphic designers towards society.[93] The overt political agenda was clearly expressed in the introductory text that greeted visitors on the wall in the exhibition space and appeared in the catalogue with the unambiguous title, 'Responsabilità della grafica' (The responsibility of graphics):

> No other medium has proved to be more persuasive, more subverting, more dangerous or more edifying [than printed paper]. Some pieces of paper are more offensive than an insult, more unpleasant than a purge. We will show you some uses of printed paper as a tool of control, persuasion, information, culture and amusement. … Among the resources available to our civilisation, [visual communication] is the most corruptible, the most vulnerable, but certainly … the liveliest and least suppressible. … Printed pages look for

proselytes, accomplices and clients among people who are often unprepared and naive. It is best if the general public learns to recognise its invisible inter-locutor at a glance.[94]

Addressing a public that was 'more and more threatened by the prolifera-tion of printed paper', curators were committed to nurturing alert, critical and informed viewers/readers.[95] As such, they aligned with contemporary discussions and efforts aimed at producing active citizens in the terms of post-war humanism.[96] As I shall discuss in detail in chapter 4, promoters of the professionalisation of graphic design in Milan in the post-war period, especially those involved in education, gained in awareness and assumed responsibility for their socio-cultural role, thereby taking a political and ideological stance on their practice.

Despite it not being mentioned explicitly in the introductory text, the reference to the recent past of the fascist dictatorship was difficult to miss, as was also the implicit mistrust of propaganda, be it either political or com-mercial. Such tacit left-wing indictment of advertising was in line with public criticism of the advertising industry and the disputes on the moral issues of consumer culture which emerged during this period, incited by crusading writings such as Vance Packard's book, *The Hidden Persuaders* (1957).[97] In his analysis of post-war British consumer society, business historian Stefan Schwarzkopf showed how the ideological climate of the Cold War, with 'its anxieties about mass suggestion, as well as its partisan battles over the issues of individualism, freedom and consumer choice', was mirrored in the 'political challenges and cultural anxieties' encountered by British advertisers from the 1940s to the early 1960s.[98] In Italy, too, advertising became a politically and culturally sensitive matter and mass consumption formed an important part of political debates between the centrist party DC, Democrazia Cristiana (Christian Democrats) and the PCI, Partito Comunista Italiano (Italian Communist Party). The attitude to mass consumption on the part of both parties had its ambivalences: the DC had trouble juggling its Catholic-inspired values with those of consumerism, while the PCI reacted against what was seen as an imposition of the American model of life yet recognised the potential of modern consumer goods.[99]

The patronising tone and condescending attitude of the curators of the Mostra di Arte Grafica irritated the journalist, former partisan and prominent PCI member, Rossana Rossanda. Writing in the Marxist cultural and political weekly magazine *Il Contemporaneo*, Rossanda sarcastically defined Sinisgalli as a 'hater of the written word ... who describes the circulation of the press around the world as one would speak about an invasion by a swarm of locusts, and alerts "the simple and naive people" to the evil power of suggestion of the printed page'.[100] The critique does not necessarily reflect general public opinion, but it does raise the question of the visitors' response to the exhibition.

The curators of the Mostra di Arte Grafica had sought to engage different kinds of audience and to provide both the general and the specialist public with a clear, easy to understand, yet precise and challenging, content, together with the instruments to understand and evaluate the technicalities, outcomes and broader impact of graphic design.[101] However, feedback provided by visitors suggests that the curators' efforts to reach a broader audience were not fulfilled. Thirty-eight days after the opening, only 8.8 per cent of the visitors who had filled in the feedback forms selected the Mostra di Arte Grafica as their favourite exhibition. The most successful exhibition was the Mostra Internazionale dell'Abitazione (International Exhibition of the Dwelling), with 56.2 per cent of the vote, followed by the exhibition of glass and pottery with 40.6 per cent. The industrial design exhibition was ranked eleventh, with 15.2 per cent of the vote. These statistics were based on a sample of 13,649 respondents, representing about 30 per cent of the total visitors. Although arguably biased and scientifically inadmissible, the statistics call into question the popularity of the Mostra di Arte Grafica and thus the curators' success in expanding its outreach.[102]

A further aspect of the 11th Triennale casts doubt on graphic designers' strategies of self-representation. In 1957, graphic design was also included in the exhibition that followed the Mostra di Arte Grafica, namely the Mostra Internazionale dell'Industrial Design (International Exhibition of Industrial Design). Devoted to 'grafica industriale' (industrial graphics), showcase no. 17 featured the June 1957 issue of the industrial design magazine and house organ of the ADI, *Stile Industria*, with a cover design by Michele Provinciali, along with issues of the French publication *Esthétique Industrielle* and the American periodicals *Industrial Design* and *Design*. By limiting the understanding of industrial graphics to industrial design magazines, the showcase presented graphic design as a mere messenger, rather than as a design form in its own right.

The concurrent presence of graphic design in the Mostra di Arte Grafica and the Mostra Internazionale dell'Industrial Design introduced industrial designers as an additional neighbouring practice over and against which graphic designers struggled to negotiate their own collective identity in post-war Italy. The issue of how to portray a practice that now had a footing in both the world of advertising and that of design will be discussed at length in chapter 5 by looking at the foundation and early years of professional design associations in Milan.

An educated client

So far in this chapter, we have focused primarily on the exhibition of graphic design at the Triennale. However, another highly significant aspect was the direct involvement of graphic designers in the promotion and visual communication of the event itself. As graphic designer Italo Lupi put it, 'the influence of the Triennale on graphics was not through exhibited objects, but through its institutional graphics production. That is, by making graphics, not by showing graphics. Graphic design is self-demonstrating.'[103] As a commissioning body the Triennale turned from being a mediating channel, by means of which graphic designers were attempting to educate the taste of clients and articulate their social identity, into an educated client itself, and one that sanctioned graphic designers' own definition of good taste. To explore the relationship between graphic design and the Triennale from a designer/client perspective is also revealing of the amount of authority in the eyes of the client that the practice had attained, since this relies largely on whether 'the customer/clients themselves feel that they can leave important judgements relating to them in the hands of the individual'.[104] In this case, the client was entrusting its very visual identity to the hands of individual graphics professionals.

The 7th Triennale in 1940 was the first to present a consistent proto-visual identity. Earlier in this chapter I pointed out that the catalogue of the Mostra Grafica was at odds with Modiano's vision of the exhibition as a triumph of modernism. Yet attention should be drawn to the logo on the cover that was designed by Enrico Ciuti. As design historian Mario Piazza observed, Ciuti's design demonstrates 'the attempt to design a logo and express a visual synthesis that includes a combination of aspects: the regime's rhetoric, the centrality of Milan, the year of the event, but also a refined decorative feeling'.[105] Indeed, the logo includes the regime's symbol of the fasces, the heraldic emblem of the House of Visconti – the so-called 'Biscione' (big snake) – and the Roman numeral seven. Featured across different printed matter – from the cover of the catalogue to the letterhead, from the poster (see figure 3.13) to the admission ticket – it was the key recurring element around which the identity of the 7th Triennale was articulated.

Seven years later at the first post-war Triennale graphic design was officially absent with no exhibition specifically devoted to it. In the emergency climate of reconstruction, graphics was put aside to focus all efforts on the urgent question of 'dwelling'.[106] Nevertheless, it embedded itself in the event by articulating and mediating the very image of the Triennale. Featuring an elongated and bold sans-serif font of even width, in which the angular rigidity of the T is counterbalanced by the roundness of the 8, Albe Steiner's logo became the foundation upon which Max Huber built the visual identity of the 8th Triennale of 1947. Huber's visual communication system was more consistent and pervasive than ever before in the history of the Triennale. On the larger scale, the logo T8 invaded the cityscape: it assailed commuters travelling on public transport, guided visitors through road signage and tried to pique pedestrians' curiosity stencilled on the pavements in the environs of the Palazzo dell'Arte (see

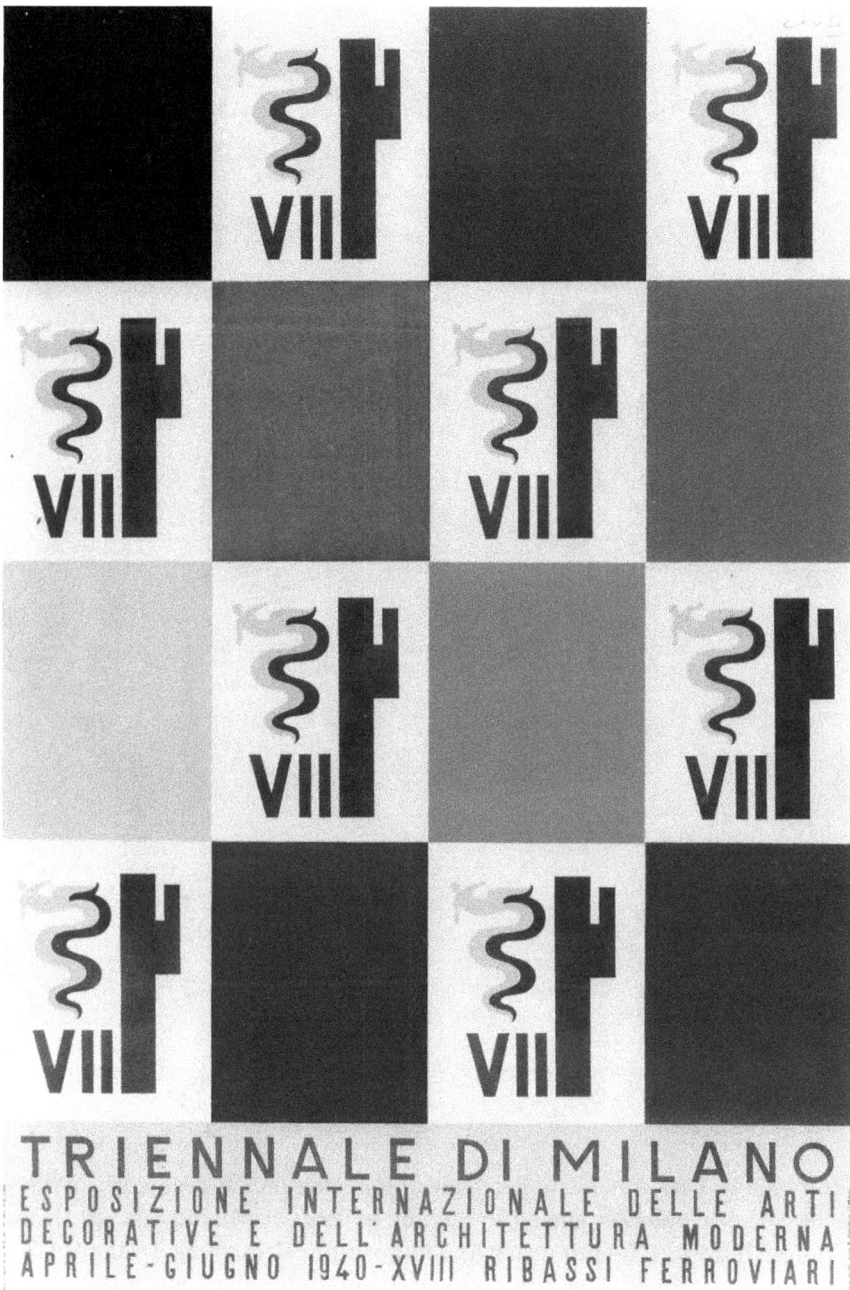

3.13   Poster and logo for the 7th Milan Triennale, designed by Enrico Ciuti, 1940.

3.14 Signage stencilled on the pavement in Viale Alemagna advertising the 8th Milan Triennale, designed by Max Huber, 1947.

figure 3.14). On a much smaller scale, it featured on the keyboards of type-writers that were customised to include as 'an advertising prompt … the gigantic letters: T 8 Q in order to compose the acronyms: T8 [and] QT8' (see figure 3.15).[107] The strategy was so effective that the 8th Triennale was rebranded and indeed became known as 'T8'. The acronym QT8 referred to an experimental housing quarter conceived by the architect Piero Bottoni and intended as a testing-ground for prefabricated building methods that were expected to respond promptly to the reconstruction agenda.

ottava Triennale di Milano 1947

uffici: palazzo dell'arte al parco
Milano
telefoni: 12850 153069 153081
telegrammi: triennale milano

Uno spunto pubblicitario, usato per la
" Ottava Triennale 1947 ", è stato quel
lo di inserire, nella tastiera delle mac
chine per scrivere, i caratteri giganti:

T   8   Q

per formare le sigle:

T8   T8   T8   T8   T8   T8   T8

QT8   QT8   QT8   QT8   QT8   QT8

Esempio:
" La Ottava Triennale di Milano - T8 -
" si è fatta promotrice della creazione
" del QT8 - Quartiere Sperimentale Model
" lo della Triennale di Milano. "

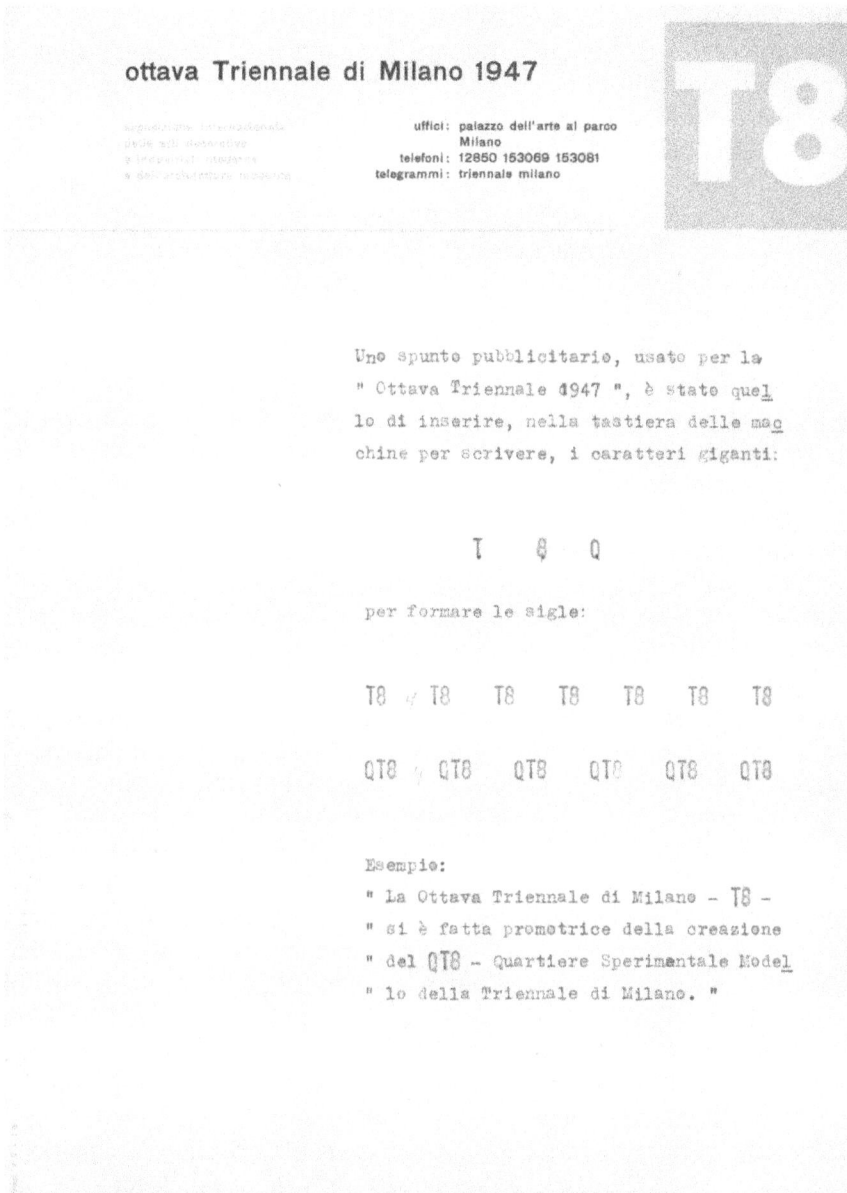

3.15   Archival document explaining the use of the customised keyboard keys T, 8 and Q for the 8th Milan Triennale, 1947.

Bright and bold colours add a touch of playfulness to an otherwise austere design based on a limited set of visual elements whose sources are reduced to typography alone. Not yet a strict colour-coded system, they add to the connotative reading of the visual artefacts. On the cover of the catalogue a yellow and a blue line enclose a bright red T8 (see figure 3.16). While the even width of lines and text highlights the geometric quality of the letterforms, the three primary colours refer to colour reproduction. The enlarged halftone screen in the background reiterates the reference to the reproduction techniques. Like the catalogue, the bronze medal certificate presents a symbolic use of colours while exemplifying the ideological function of abstract compositions in the post-war period (see figure 3.17).[108] The abstract picture recalls the strict geometry and rhythmical compositions typical of Concrete Art paintings.[109] The areas of plain colour refer to the seven countries that took part in the T8. Green, red, white, black, yellow and blue triangles are combined to suggest the Italian, Belgian, Czechoslovakian, Swedish, Swiss, Austrian and Argentinian flags. So, what at first glance may have appeared as an abstract composition of colourful triangles turns out to be a poetic graphic composition on the renewed dialogue and mutual exchange between countries. Indeed, 'to strengthen ... the basis of a new and humane civilisation' after the trauma of World War II was the goal of the T8.[110]

The visual vocabulary of Huber's communication system for the T8 was rooted in modernist aesthetics: it features the Akzidenz Grotesk font, lowercase writing, asymmetrical layout, grid compositions, active use of the white page, and variation of type sizes and weights to emphasise content and rhythm in the typographic composition. All elements aligned the T8 visual identity with the guidelines of Swiss Style, also known as International Typographic Style or simply International Style, which was to gain an excellent reputation worldwide over the course of the 1950s. The association of International Style with positive connotations, such as internationalism, clarity, neutrality, precision and functionality, also wedded this aesthetic to professionalism.[111] The visual identities of the Triennales which followed diverged from orthodox interpretations of mainstream modernist aesthetics. As such they presented the different definitions of good taste in visual communication endorsed by each Triennale. Within the Italian context, the director of the Ufficio Pubblicità (Advertising Department) at Olivetti, Leonardo Sinisgalli, stood out as spokesperson for a versatile approach to visual communication. He acknowledged the effectiveness of modernist graphics without disdaining a pictorial approach that made use of illustrations, expressive drawings and decorative elements inspired by organic and biological forms, in order to counterbalance contemporary anxieties concerning technology and industry.[112]

Nizzoli's pictorial logo of the 9th Triennale of 1951 appears at odds with a design whose sources were otherwise drawn largely from typography (see figure 3.18). As explained in the catalogue, it was 'a free interpretation of Egyptian ideograms' that was intended 'to suggest quite evidently one of the oldest and best-known decorative traditions: that of the lapidary inscription, which is ... truly the origin of any decorative expression, from

3.16　Cover of the exhibition catalogue for the 8th Milan Triennale, designed by Max Huber, 1947.

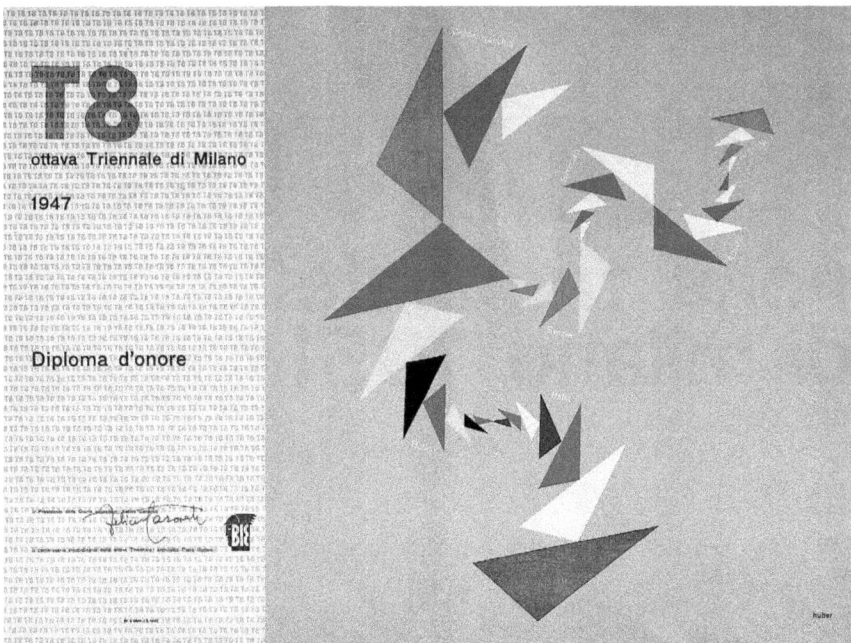

3.17　Bronze medal certificate designed by Max Huber, 8th Milan Triennale, 1947.

3.18   Poster for the 9th Milan Triennale designed by Ernst Scheidegger, featuring Marcello Nizzoli's logo, 1951.

the most ancient to the most recent'.[113] When contextualised within post-war humanism, the reference to ancient Egypt might be interpreted as an attempt to rediscover a common cultural heritage beyond time and space; an attempt to erase differences and propose a universal language embedded in the history of humankind.[114] But the eclecticism of Nizzoli's hieroglyph was not without its detractors. Writing in the graphics magazine *Linea Grafica*, a reviewer disparaged the 'wrinkled coldness' of the logo, criticising Nizzoli for having substituted 'the ugly logo of the fasces with an unappealing Assyrian or Egyptian one' and recommending a return to simpler forms of visual expression that eschewed allegory and symbolism.[115] Bearing in mind the use of the symbolism of ancient Rome during Fascism, the critique suggests a sense of diffidence towards the rhetorical use of ancient emblems.

Munari's logo for the 10th Triennale in 1954 features a typographic approach to trademark design similar to Steiner's T8 (see figure 3.19).

3.19 Badges featuring Bruno Munari's logo for the 10th Milan Triennale, 1954.

However, letterforms are smoothed and edges rounded; forms have moved away from geometry towards organic shapes so as to convey a sense of cosy gentleness with a hint of playful irony. This smooth-edged interpretation of modernist vocabulary rediscovers the appeal of ornament as approachable interface. Whereas Nizzoli turned to history and culture, Munari favoured smooth and sinuous forms inspired by nature. Modernist aesthetics was also absent from the visual communication of the 11th Triennale in 1957. Both the logo and the poster, which were designed by the architect and product designer, Ettore Sottsass Jnr, and graphic designer and painter, Eugenio Carmi, respectively, featured a pictorial approach rooted in the Arte Informale movement with its focus on expressive and spontaneous gesture (see figures 3.20 and 3.21). At the time, the adoption of forms derived from abstract expressionist visual vocabulary had become a common feature of a certain kind of Western design that rejected the functionalist stance in favour of freedom of expression and individuality.[116]

Archival documents provide insights into the client/designer relationship. The back-and-forth dialogue between the secretary general of the 9th Triennale in 1951, Giuseppe Gorgerino, and Nizzoli shows Gorgerino's awareness of the importance of a consistent visual communication system and his confidence in Nizzoli's expertise. 'It is essential', Gorgerino wrote, 'for the official publications of the 9th Triennale to share a unique and consistent style.'[117] And he invited Nizzoli to 'keep an eye on' the design of all items of printed matter in order to ensure they shared a 'certain family likeness'.[118] Object labels and wall graphics were also under Nizzoli's supervision, so as to create a 'unique system'.[119] As had been the case with

Undicesima Triennale di Milano
esposizione internazionale
delle arti decorative e industriali moderne
e dell'architettura moderna

TESSERA
SERVIZIO

Il Presidente

3.20   Conference badge featuring Ettore Sottsass Jnr's logo for the 11th Milan Triennale, 1957.

3.21 Poster for the 11th Milan Triennale, designed by Eugenio Carmi, 1957.

Huber at the T8, Nizzoli conceived a coherent and coordinated image that was the outcome of a design approach to visual communication whose role in the professionalisation of graphic design in Italy will be explored later in chapter 5. Exchanges between Gorgerino and Nizzoli became more frequent with the approach of the opening date on 12 May 1951, and the designer's work did not terminate then. Quite the contrary, Gorgerino wrote again to Nizzoli at the end of May requesting the design of a sheet of paper to write restaurant orders on 'in tune with the characters and colours of the Triennale'.[120] What this internal communication tells us is that, whereas in the interwar period graphic practitioners had often been protesting against the Triennale and not being recognised as the only practice with jurisdiction over visual communication, in 1951 roles, ironically, were reversed. This time, it was Gorgerino who had to urge Nizzoli to come daily to the Palazzo dell'Arte to take care of last-minute issues. Graphic designers had managed to turn the Milan Triennale into an educated client, that is, a commissioning body which recognised and valued professional knowledge and insisted on a certain degree of professionalism.

All the same, the very fact that the design of the logo of the 11th Triennale in 1957 was entrusted to an architect and product designer, rather than to a bona fide graphic designer, would at first sight seem to bring into question my argument for the Milan Triennale having become an educated client over which graphic designers had gained authority. However, a closer look at the commissioning process shows that in January 1956 a select list of graphic designers was, in fact, invited to submit a design for the logo of the forthcoming Triennale, but that none of the submitted sketches was believed to 'encapsulate the aims and goals of the Milan Triennale'.[121] New sketches were submitted at the beginning of April. Was the second call for submissions extended to a heterogeneous group of professionals, since it then became Sottsass, and not a graphic designer, who eventually designed the logo? Regardless of its outcome, the commissioning process shows that the Milan Triennale actually consulted graphic designers first, thereby acknowledging their expertise. But, at the same time, it also demonstrates graphic designers' lack of success in obtaining exclusive jurisdiction over visual communication. In other words, graphic designers had convinced the organisers of the Triennale, and possibly the design community at large, that they were the most suitable, but not yet the only, profession entitled to deal with visual communication.

Mediation and commission

The Milan Triennale holds a special place within the larger history of Italian graphic design, both as a mediating channel and as a commissioning body.

Although sporadic, the participation of graphic design in the event from the interwar period to the late 1950s was instrumental in the articulation and promotion of graphic design practice in Italy. Bearing the burden of having to be representative of the entire practice, each exhibition can be seen as one assertion in an ongoing discussion; a snapshot taken at more or less regular intervals that captured a moment in the work-in-progress of construction and mediation of the practice's self-identity and public image.

Writing on the state of Italian graphics in 1947 in the Swiss magazine *Graphis*, Boggeri explained how 'the new Italian advertising art was ... born out on the walls of a few exhibitions. Nothing further was needed except to transfer it to paper.'[122] Although not as simple as Boggeri suggested, exhibition design and exhibitions did contribute significantly to the 'birth' of graphic design in Italy. The intersection of graphic and exhibition design promoted experimental approaches and multidisciplinary exchange between insiders and outsiders to the typographic workshop, to the benefit of graphic design practice as a whole. Over two decades, a rhetoric of good taste and good design served graphic practitioners as a legitimation device to claim, obtain and possibly maintain, authority over the client and the broader public. The Triennale offered a public stage to turn this strategy of self-representation into action and seek aesthetic as well as social legitimacy for the profession. The use of good taste as a key discursive strategy to further professionalisation reveals it clearly to have been a cultural process and social construction underpinned by an aesthetic as well as a system of behaviours and a set of rules.

Covering about twenty-five years, this chapter has shown that there was continuity between the interwar and post-war debates surrounding graphic design, and has addressed the issue of the adaptation of design discourses to changing political circumstances. The chapter has also introduced topics that will be further developed later in this book: the problematic position of the practice caught between advertising and design will be explored in chapter 5; meanwhile, graphic designers' responsibility towards society will now be investigated in chapter 4.

Notes

1 K. Fallan, 'Milanese mediations: Crafting Scandinavian design at the Triennali di Milano', *Konsthistorisk Tidskrift*, 83 (2014), 1.

2 'Mettere praticamente davanti agli occhi del pubblico "quello che si deve fare" vicino a quello "che non si deve fare". Dimostrare che quello che si è fatto ieri è sbagliato e perché è sbagliato. Dimostrare che quello che vogliamo noi è giusto e perché è giusto'. E. D'Errico, 'Lo spirito moderno e la tipografia italiana', *Graphicus*, 26:5 (May 1936), 9.

3 'La Triennale di Milano, ci offre una buona occasione per bandire la crociata che formerà la nuova mentalità tipografica italiana; cerchiamo di non perdere questa occasione'. *Ibid.*

4 'Funzione cardine per la nascita del design e lo sviluppo della grafica'. R. Riccini, 'Disegno industriale italiano. La costruzione di una cultura fra istituzioni e territorio', in A. Bassi, R. Riccini and C. Colombo (eds), *Design in Triennale 1947–68: percorsi fra Milano e Brianza* (Milan: Silvana Editoriale, 2004), p. 17.

5 'Perfette scrivanie razionali'. Campo Grafico, 'Il gusto del cliente', *Campo Grafico*, 2:4 (April 1934), 77.

6 'Evidente superiorità pratica'. *Ibid.*, 78.

7 'Disonesta scusa ... stimolare nel cliente quel buon gusto moderno'. Campo Grafico, 'Come si suscita il gusto grafico', *Campo Grafico*, 2:6 (June 1934), 124–5.

8 P. Jobling and D. Crowley, *Graphic Design: Reproduction and Representation since 1800* (Manchester; New York: Manchester University Press, 1996), p. 144.

9 S. Yasuko, 'Designing the morality of consumption: "Chamber of Horrors" at the Museum of Ornamental Art, 1852–53', *Design Issues*, 20:4 (2004), 43–56; Woodham, *Twentieth Century Design*, pp. 154–60.

10 P. Bourdieu, *Distinction: A Social Critique of the Judgement of Taste* (Cambridge, MA: Harvard University Press, 1984), p. 6.

11 S. Hayward, '"Good design is largely a matter of common sense": Questioning the meaning and ownership of a twentieth-century orthodoxy', *Journal of Design History*, 11:3 (1998), 217–33.

12 Freidson, *Professionalism*, p. 73.

13 Fournier, 'The appeal to "professionalism"', 285.

14 'Tutti i mezzi sperimentali della tecnica propagandistica moderna'. E. Bona, 'Pubblico e grafici', *Campo Grafico*, 6:10–12 (October–December 1938), 245–6.

15 'Il concetto del bello e del brutto in arte grafica'. *Ibid.*

16 Abbott, *The System of Professions*, p. 60.

17 Bona, 'Pubblico e grafici', 245–6.

18 On the Mostra del Libro (Book Exhibition) at the 1st Monza Biennale, see Anon., *Prima esposizione internazionale delle arti decorative: Consorzio Milano-Monza Umanitaria* (Milan: Casa Editrice Bestetti & Tumminelli, 1923), pp. 61–3; A. Pansera, *Storia e cronaca della Triennale* (Milan: Longanesi & Co., 1974), pp. 139–41. On the 2nd Monza Biennale, see Anon., *Seconda mostra internazionale delle arti decorative: catalogo* (Milan: Case Editrici Alpes e F. de Rio, 1925). On the Galleria delle Arti Grafiche (Gallery of the Graphic Arts) at the 4th Monza Triennale, see Anon., *IV Esposizione triennale internazionale delle arti decorative ed industriali moderne: catalogo ufficiale* (Milan: Casa Editrice Ceschina, 1930), pp. 171–5; E. Braun, *Mario Sironi and Italian Modernism: Art and Politics under Fascism* (Cambridge: Cambridge University Press, 2000), p. 105; M. Pigozzi, 'Grafica industriale', in Anon., *Gli annitrenta. Arte e cultura in Italia* (Milan: Mazzotta, 1982), p. 472. On the Monza 1st, 2nd and 3rd Biennale of 1923, 1925 and 1927, and the 4th Triennale of 1930, see A. Pansera (ed.), *1923–1930 Monza verso l'unità delle arti* (Milan: Silvana Editoriale, 2004).

19 'Il riconoscimento di una individualità propria alle arti grafiche nel gran quadro delle arti decorative e delle industrie artistiche, meritasse di essere considerate dagli artisti grafici con lo spirito di consapevole orgoglio e ... onore'. M. Ferrigni, 'Gli artisti grafici alla V Triennale di Milano', *Risorgimento Grafico*, 31:1 (January 1934), 41. For the complete list of exhibitors, see Anon., *V Triennale di Milano: catalogo ufficiale* (Milan: 1933), pp. 525–7; Anon., *V Triennale di Milano: Padiglione della Stampa* (Milan: Casa Editrice Ceschina, 1933), pp. 61–3.

20 Ferrigni, 'Gli artisti grafici alla V Triennale di Milano', 29–31.

21 'Rimessa per gli attrezzi agricoli'. G. Modiano (Un Astensionista), 'Parole, parole, parole', *Risorgimento Grafico*, 31:4 (April 1934), 165.

22 'Siamo troppo pochi in Italia a faticare per il riconoscimento del valore dell'arte nostra per permetterci il lusso di certe proteste assenteiste'. R. Bertieri, 'Ad un collega che si astiene', *Risorgimento Grafico*, 30:3 (March 1933), 141.

23 Reicher, 'The context of social identity'.
24 G. Modiano, 'Padiglione della Stampa', *Campo Grafico*, 1:7 (July 1933), 122; Il Risorgimento Grafico, 'Le arti grafiche alla Triennale', *Risorgimento Grafico*, 30:9 (September 1933), 521; Anon., 'Arti grafiche alla Triennale', *Campo Grafico*, 1:10 (October 1933), 171–2; Modiano, 'Parole, parole, parole', 165; Anon., 'Ancora sulla Triennale: onestà e responsabilità', *Campo Grafico*, 2:9 (September 1934), 197.
25 'Debitori di Paul Renner'. G. Modiano, 'Triennale 1936', *Risorgimento Grafico*, 34:1 (January 1937), 22.
26 M. Stone, 'The State as patron: Making official culture in Fascist Italy', in M. Affrom and M. Antliff (eds), *Fascist Visions: Art and Ideology in France and Italy* (Princeton: Princeton University Press, 1997), pp. 205–38; Ben-Ghiat, *Fascist-Modernities*, pp. 20–9; L. Malvano, *Fascismo e politica dell'immagine* (Turin: Bollati e Boringhieri, 1988).
27 R. Ben-Ghiat, 'Italian Fascists and National Socialists: The dynamics of an uneasy relationship', in R. A. Etlin (ed.), *Art, Culture, and the Media under the Third Reich* (Chicago: University of Chicago Press, 2002), p. 260.
28 Anon., 'Das deutsche Buchgewerbe auf dem V. Triennale in Mailand', *Gebrauchs-graphik*, 10:7 (July 1933), 11. The quote is an excerpt of Benito Mussolini's speech at the Accademia di Belle Arti in Perugia on 26 September 1926.
29 *Ibid*.
30 P. Shaw and P. Bain, 'Introduction. Blackletter vs. Roman: Type as ideological surrogate', in P. Shaw and P. Bain (eds), *Blackletter: Type and National Identity* (New York: Princeton Architectural Press, 1998), pp. 10–15.
31 P. Betts, 'The Bauhaus and National Socialism: A dark chapter of modernism', in J. Fiedler and P. Feierabend (eds), *Bauhaus* (Cologne: Könemann, 1999), p. 34. See also, P. Betts, *The Authority of Everyday Objects: A Cultural History of West German Industrial Design* (Berkeley; Los Angeles; London: University of California Press, 2004), pp. 23–72; W. Nerdinger, *Bauhaus-Moderne im Nationalsozialismus: Zwischen Anbiederung und Verfolgung* (Munich: Prestel, 1993).
32 *Ibid*., p. 36. For a critical analysis of Herbert Bayer's work for the National Socialists, see U. Brünning, 'Herbert Bayer – Universal design for the National Socialist economy and state', in Fiedler and Fierabend (eds), *Bauhaus*, pp. 332–45; P. Rössler, *Herbert Bayer: Die Berliner Jahre – Werbegrafik 1928–1938* (Berlin: Bauhaus-Archiv, 2013).
33 Ben-Ghiat, 'Italian Fascists and National Socialists', p. 260.
34 'Per la trattazione del tema (storico, politico, culturale, economico, sociale, in ogni caso legato all'orizzonte ideologico del fascismo) e per la modernità degli allestimenti'. Carli, *Vedere il fascismo*, p. 35.
35 L. Brosseau, M. Dalla Mura, C. Imbert and J. Sueda, *Graphisme en France 2018: Exhibiting Graphic Design* (Paris: Centre National des Arts Plastiques Graphisme en France, 2018); G. Camuffo and M. Dalla Mura (eds), *Graphic Design, Exhibiting, Curating* (Bolzano: Bozen-Bolzano University Press, 2013); R. Poynor, 'We need more galleries that exhibit graphic design', *Print*, 64:2 (April 2010), www.print mag.com/featured/observer-we-need-more-galleries-that-exhibit-graphic-design/, accessed 31 May 2023.
36 'A visitarla come italiani prima e ad analizzarla come grafici poi'. R. Bertieri, 'Alcuni aspetti grafici della Mostra della Rivoluzione Fascista', *Risorgimento Grafico*, 30:6 (June 1933), 338.
37 Carli, *Vedere il fascismo*, pp. 59–120; Braun, *Mario Sironi and Italian Modernism*, pp. 145–57; D. Ghirardo, 'Architects, exhibitions, and the politics of culture in Fascist Italy', *Journal of Architectural Education*, 45:2 (1992), 67–75; J. T. Schnapp, *Anno XX: la Mostra della Rivoluzione Fascista del 1932* (Pisa; Rome: Istituto Editoriali e Poligrafici Internazionali, 2003); J. T. Schnapp, 'Fascism's museum in motion', *Journal of Architectural Education*, 45:2 (1992), 87–97; M. Stone, 'Staging Fascism:

The Exhibition of the Fascist Revolution', *Journal of Contemporary History*, 28:2 (1993), 215–43; M. Stone, 'The anatomy of a propaganda event: The Mostra della Rivoluzione Fascista', *Carte Italiane*, 1:12 (1992), 30–40.

38 'Grafica viva, dinamica ... sua genuina funzione espressiva e propagandistica'. Bertieri, 'Alcuni aspetti grafici della Mostra della Rivoluzione Fascista', 321.

39 E. Gentile, *The Sacralization of Politics in Fascist Italy* (Cambridge, MA; London: Harvard University Press, 1996), pp. 117–21.

40 P. Bourdieu and A. Darbel, *The Love of Art: European Art Museums and their Public* (Cambridge: Polity Press, 1991), pp. 37–70; P. Bourdieu, *The Field of Cultural Production* (New York: Columbia University Press, 1993), p. 218.

41 'La rappresentazione "grafica" ... la più grandiosa e la più originale e la più importante "impaginazione" che ci sia capitato di vedere'. Bertieri, 'Alcuni aspetti grafici della Mostra della Rivoluzione Fascista', 321.

42 'Una delle più vaste ed eroiche "impaginazioni" di questo periodo'. G. Modiano, 'Cinque manifesti', *Graphicus*, 24:10 (October 1934), 21.

43 'Se si distaccano alcuni elementi dalla disposizione nella quale si trovano nella realtà delle singole pareti, ci si accorge di poterli tradurre senza sforzo in forme diverse di pagine: si direbbe che vadano da sé a disporsi in pagina.' Bertieri, 'Alcuni aspetti grafici della Mostra della Rivoluzione Fascista', 333.

44 'Capolavoro grafico'. *Ibid.*, 337. D. Alfieri and L. Freddi (eds), *Mostra della Rivoluzione Fascista* (Bergamo: Officine dell'Istituto Italiano delle Arti Grafiche, 1933).

45 B. McLaren, 'Under the sign of the reproduction', *Journal of Architectural Education*, 45:2 (1992), 103. The articles analysed by McLaren are M. Sarfatti, 'Architettura, arte e simbolo della Mostra del Fascismo', *Architettura*, 12:1 (January 1933), 1–17; E. Pifferi, 'Mostra della Rivoluzione', *Casabella*, 64 (April 1933), 38–41.

46 *Ibid.*

47 *Ibid.*

48 Vinti, 'The New Typography in Fascist Italy', p. 51.

49 'La grafica moderna, efficacissimo mezzo di comunicazione, servisse a diffondere le menzogne'. Dradi, *Millenovecentotrentatre*, p. 15.

50 G. Veronesi, *Difficoltà politiche dell'architettura in Italia: 1920–1940* (Milan: Christian Marinotti Editore, 2008 (1953)), pp. 110–12; A. Branzi, *Introduzione al design italiano: una modernità incompleta* (Milan: Baldini e Castoldi, 1999), p. 117.

51 G. Modiano, 'Manifesti', *Campo Grafico*, 3:11–12 (November–December 1935), 244–5. The article was a shorter version of a previous article: Modiano, 'Cinque manifesti'.

52 E. Bona, 'Stampati dello stato', *Campo Grafico*, 3:4 (April 1935), 78–9; G. Modiano, 'Quattro righe', *Campo Grafico*, 5:5–6 (May–June 1937), 14–15. From April to December 1933, Attilio Rossi and Carlo Dradi designed the covers of fascist sports illustrated monthly magazine, *Lo Sport Fascista*: C. Dradi, 'Appunti per una storia della comunicazione visiva', *Bollettino del Centro Studi Grafici*, 61:1–2 (March–June 2009), 18–19.

53 Vinti, 'The New Typography in Fascist Italy', p. 53.

54 Carli, *Vedere il fascismo*, p. 130.

55 M. Tymkiw, *Nazi Exhibition Design and Modernism* (Minneapolis; London: University of Minnesota Press, 2018), p. 70.

56 *Ibid.*, p. 68.

57 'Una rassegna delle tendenze dell'architettura europea, e della loro risonanza in Italia'. A. M. Mazzucchelli, 'Stile di una mostra', *Casabella*, 80 (August 1934), 6.

58 Museo di arte moderna e contemporanea di Trento e Rovereto, Rovereto, Italy, Fondo Figini e Pollini, Fig-Pol 5.1.4.1, postcard from W. Gropius and X. Schawinsky to L. Figini and G. Pollini, October 1934.

59 'Stark russisch beeinflusster darstellung'. AAA, Marcel Breuer Papers, box 1, reel 5709, frames 585–639, letter from I. Gropius to M. Breuer, 24 October 1934.

60 Vinti, 'L'estetica grafica della "nuova tipografia" in Italia', 22; Braun, *Mario Sironi and Italian Modernism*, pp. 152–4; Stone, 'Staging Fascism', 224.

61 'Es ist ein jammer zu sehen, wie deutschland jetzt bei der weiterarbeit an diesen dingen einfach ausfällt'. AAA, Marcel Breuer Papers, box 1, reel 5709, frames 585–639, letter from I. Gropius to M. Breuer, 24 October 1934.

62 Tymkiw, *Nazi Exhibition Design and Modernism*, p. 4.

63 Campo Grafico, 'Le arti grafiche alla VI Triennale di Milano 1936', *Campo Grafico*, 4:5 (May 1936), 85; C. Vinti, 'Modiano e la "Mostra Grafica" alla VII Triennale', *Progetto Grafico*, 4–5 (2005), pp. 50–63.

64 'Non si perda un'altra occasione per formare una coscienza tipografica moderna anche in Italia'. Campo Grafico, 'Tipografia e Triennale', *Campo Grafico*, 3:6 (June 1935), 127. Signatories were: De Arcangelis (Pescara), Guido Modiano (Milan), Edoardo Persico (Milan), Renzo Bianchi (Roma), Attilio Rossi (Milan), Giulio da Milano (Turin), Nino Strada (Milan), Antonio Boggeri (Milan) and Renato Zveteremich (Ivrea).

65 'L'arte grafica, lasciata fuori dalla porta, entra dalla finestra'. Campo Grafico, 'Le arti grafiche alla VI Triennale di Milano', 85.

66 'Tutta la Triennale è stata impaginata graficamente con spiccata tendenza verso l'astrattismo'. E. D'Errico, 'VI Triennale di Milano', *Graphicus*, 27:2 (February 1937), 14.

67 P. Curtis, *Patio and Pavilion: The Place of Sculpture in Modern Architecture* (London: Ridinghouse Editor, 2008), pp. 28–41; F. Mugnai, 'Il classico in una stanza. Il Salone della Vittoria alla VI Triennale di Milano', *Firenze Architettura*, 2 (2016), 50–7.

68 Malvano, *Fascismo e politica dell'immagine*, pp. 151–6; Lazzaro, 'Forging a visible fascist nation'; A. T. Wilkins, 'Augustus, Mussolini, and the parallel imagery of Empire', in Lazzaro and Crum (eds), *Donatello Among the Blackshirts*, pp. 53–65.

69 'Documentazioni dell'esistenza dell'autorità del "grafismo"'. Modiano, 'Triennale 1936', 30.

70 'La tipografia ai non tipografi'. Modiano, 'Cinque manifesti', 21.

71 'L'architettura moderna abbia trovato nel gusto *tipografico* occasioni e motivi per espressioni nuove'. Modiano, 'Triennale 1936', 28–31.

72 H. Bayer, *Herbert Bayer: Painter, Designer, Architect* (New York: Reinhold, 1967), quoted in Aynsley, *Graphic Design in Germany*, pp. 201–3.

73 'Manifestazione di tipografia superiore … una forma grafica proiettata nella terza dimensione'. G. Modiano, 'Un posteggio e una vetrina nel commento di un tipografo', *Campo Grafico*, 7:3–5 (March–May 1939), 103, 104.

74 'In piena crisi europea, crisi politica, economica, sociale'. Anon., *VII Triennale di Milano: guida* (Milan: S.A.M.E., 1940), p. 11.

75 'Bilancio di una decennale polemica modernista … convincente documentazione del "Grafismo"'. *Ibid.*, pp. 185–6.

76 'Mai in Italia il pubblico è stato messo a contatto con gli aspetti più intimi ed interessanti delle arti grafiche o con i risultati chiariti nei presupposti e nei fini'. G. Modiano (ed.), *La Mostra Grafica alla Triennale* (Milan: Società Grafica G. Modiano, 1940), n. p.

77 'Si propone di avvicinare il pubblico agli aspetti intimi della grafica: alle sue tecniche, alle fonti di una tipografia viva, agli artisti che hanno saputo tradurre in termini grafici il gusto moderno, e, infine, a una nobile pagina della tipografia ed editoria italiane: le edizioni a tiratura limitata'. Anon., *VII Triennale di Milano*, p. 185.

78 'Trionfo della tesi modernista'. G. Modiano, 'L'arte grafica alla VII Triennale di Milano', *Industria della Stampa*, 11:4–5 (July–August 1940), 194.

79 'Ciò che in regime Borghese si chiama pubblicità, in regime fascista ha nome propaganda.' G. Veronesi, 'Pubblicità', *Campo Grafico*, 5:5–6 (June 1937), 38.

80 Di Jorio, 'Pubblicità e propaganda durante il fascismo'; Gaudenzi, 'Il fascismo in vetrina', pp. 57–83.

81 'Il libro letterario o di tipografia pura ... è costruzione portata da una selezione di secoli alla forma, forse, definitiva'. Modiano, 'Triennale 1936', 25.

82 Kinross, 'Introduction to the English-language edition', p. xxxviii; Aynsley, *Graphic Design in Germany*, pp. 212–14.

83 Vinti, 'Modiano e la "Mostra Grafica" alla VII Triennale'.

84 'Punto fermo'. R. Zveteremich, 'Die italienische Werbekunst in der Gegenwart – Panorana attuale della pubblicità italiana', *Deutscher Drucker: Deutschland-Italien Heft* (July 1941), 387.

85 'Le nuove estetiche siano penetrate nella produzione italiana ... come prevedeva Modiano, la grafica è piuttosto un campo per gli artisti specializzati che per i puri tipografi'. G. Pizzuto, 'Guido Modiano, ein Italienischer Drucker – Evoluzione della tipografia in Italia attraverso l'opera di Guido Modiano', *Druck und Werbekunst: Italienische Werbegraphic*, 1 (1942), 7.

86 Ben-Ghiat, 'Italian Fascists and National Socialists', pp. 262–4.

87 Di Jorio, 'Pubblicità e propaganda durante il fascismo', pp. 234–5; Gaudenzi, 'Il fascismo in vetrina', pp. 77–9.

88 For an overview of the Milan Triennale in the post-war period, see Bassi, Riccini and Colombo (eds), *Design in Triennale 1947–68*, pp. 46–53; G. Bosoni, 'Le Triennali del design', in G. Petrillo and A. Scalpelli (eds), *Milano anni Cinquanta* (Milan: Franco Angeli Editore, 1986), pp. 758–78.

89 Fasce and Bini, 'Irresistible empire or innocents abroad?', 13.

90 'Pubblicità che si potrà realizzare quando l'artista ed il tecnico non subiranno più arbitrarie imposizioni da parte di committenti poco esperti'. Archivi della Triennale di Milano, Milan, Italy (hereafter ATM), TRN 09 DT 210 V, letter from D. Villani and E. Carboni to a list of fifteen graphic designers. See also, ATM, TRN 09 DT 210 V, 'La pubblicità di domani', 27 February 1951.

91 A. Pica (ed.), *Nona Triennale di Milano: catalogo* (Milan: S.A.M.E., 1951), pp. 86–8; ATM, TRN 09 DT 112.02 V, 'La sezione della grafica pubblicitaria', press release, pp. 1–3.

92 'Invece che dei supporti razionali per far vedere nel miglior modo possibile degli stampati, uno scenario in cui gli stampati gli servono per riempire gli spazi'. Anon., 'Le arti grafiche alla Triennale', *Bollettino Centro Studi Grafici*, 5:31 (June 1951), 1.

93 'Contro la faciloneria, l'improvvisazione, per la difesa di un mestiere delicato'. L. Sinisgalli, 'La responsabilità della grafica', in A. Pica (ed.), *Undicesima Triennale: catalogo* (Milan: Arti Grafiche Crespi, 1957), p. 121.

94 'Nessun altro mezzo si è dimostrato più persuasivo, più sconvolgente, più pericoloso più edificante. ... Ci sono pezzi di carta più offensivi di un insulto, più sgradevoli di una purga. Mostreremo alcune applicazioni della carta stampata come strumento di dominio, di persuasione, di informazione, di diletto. ... Tra i beni di cui dispone la nostra civiltà ... è il più corruttibile, il più vulnerabile, ma certamente ... il più vitale e insopprimibile. ... le pagine stampate cercano proseliti, complici, clienti tra gente spesso sprovveduta e innocente. È bene che il pubblico impari a distinguere con un colpo d'occhio il suo interlocutore invisibile'. *Ibid.*

95 'Pubblico ogni giorno più minacciato dalla inflazione della carta stampata'. *Ibid.*

96 On the impact of post-war humanism in international exhibition and design fairs, see D. Crowley, 'Humanity rearranged: The Polish and Czechoslovak Pavilions at Expo 58', *West 86th*, 19:1 (2012), 88–105.

97 V. Packard, *The Hidden Persuaders* (London: Longmans Green, 1957). Packard's book was published the following year in Italian: V. Packard, *I persuasori occulti* (Turin: Einaudi, 1958).

98 S. Schwarzkopf, 'They do it with mirrors: Advertising and British Cold War consumer politics', *Contemporary British History*, 19:2 (2005), 134.

99 Arvidsson, *Marketing Modernity*, pp. 84–9 and 94–5; S. Gundle, 'L'americanizzazione del quotidiano. Televisione e consumismo nell'Italia degli Anni Cinquanta',

Quaderni Storici, 21:62 (1986), 561–94; S. Gundle, *I comunisti italiani tra Hollywood e Mosca. La sfida della cultura di massa (1943–1991)* (Florence: Giunti, 1995).

100 'Odiatore della parola scritta ... che descrive la diffusione della stampa nel mondo come si parla di una invasione di cavallette, e mette in guardia "la gente semplice e innocente" dal malvagio potere di suggestione della pagina stampata'. R. Rossanda, 'I nodi vengono al pettine', *Il Contemporaneo*, 10 August 1947, quoted in Pansera, *Storia e cronaca della Triennale*, p. 440.

101 ATM, TRN 11 DT 058.01 V, 'Riunione della commissione della Mostra Grafica del 19 Settembre 1956', meeting minute, 19 September 1956.

102 Archivio Albe e Lica Steiner, Politecnico di Milano, Milan, Italy (hereafter AALS), D b.14 fasc.9, 'Il contatto con il pubblico', Autumn 1957. The same document also reports the feedback of visitors of the 9th Triennale. In 1954, 5,042 visitors responded on the feedback forms that were distributed only during the last sixty days of the event. The Mostra d'Arti Grafiche e Pubblicità was ranked twelfth with 27.6 per cent of the vote. The glass and pottery exhibitions were first and second with 52.5 and 47.1 per cent, respectively.

103 I. Lupi, 'Italo Lupi', in Bassi, Riccini and Colombo (eds), *Design in Triennale 1947–68*, p. 136.

104 G. Ritzer, 'Professionalism and the individual', in E. Freidson (ed.), *The Professions and their Prospects* (Beverly Hills; London: Sage Publications, 1971), p. 64.

105 'Il tentativo di progettare un marchio, formulare una sintesi visiva che contenga l'insieme degli aspetti: la retorica di regime, la centralità di Milano, l'annualità dell'evento, ma anche un fine senso decorativo'. M. Piazza, 'Le storie visive della triennale', in S. Annichiarico and M. Piazza (eds), *Come comete: annunci e messaggi nella grafica della Triennale* (Milan: Charta, 2004), p. 22.

106 P. Bottoni (ed.), *T8 catalogo–guida* (Milan: Meregalli, 1947), p. 8.

107 'Uno spunto pubblicitario ... i caratteri giganti: T 8 Q per formare le sigle T8 QT8'. ATM, TRN_08_RG_011, letterhead (A2 – T8), with typewritten proposal to include the giant characters T, 8, Q in the typewriter keyboard.

108 D. Crowley, 'Europe reconstructed, Europe divided', in D. Crowley and J. Pavitt (eds), *Cold War Modern: Design 1945–1970* (London: V&A Publishing, 2008), pp. 58–9.

109 H. R. Bosshard, 'Concrete art and typography', in C. Bignens, H. R. Bosshard and G. Fleischmann (eds), *Max Bill: Typography, Advertising, Book Design* (Zurich: Niggli, 1999), pp. 56–106.

110 'Risaldare ... le basi di una civiltà nuova ed umana'. Bottoni (ed.), *T8 catalogo–guida*, p. 12.

111 Hollis, *Swiss Graphic Design*; Brändle, Gimmi, Junod, Reble and Richter (eds), *100 Years of Swiss Graphic Design*; Lzicar and Fornari (eds), *Mapping Graphic Design History in Switzerland*; Fornari, Lzicar, Owens, Renner, Scheuermann and Schneemann (eds), *Swiss Graphic Design Histories*.

112 C. Vinti, *Gli anni dello stile industriale 1948–1965: immagine e politica culturale nella grande impresa italiana* (Venice: Marsilio, 2007), p. 185.

113 'Libera interpretazione di caratteri ideogrammatici egiziani ... postulare con molta evidenza una delle più antiche e illustri tradizioni decorative: quella della scrittura lapidaria, la quale ... è veramente matrice di ogni forma decorativa, dalle più antiche alle più recenti'. Pica (ed.), *Nona Triennale di Milano*, p. 5.

114 On post-war fascination for primitive cultures and human origins, see J. Pavitt, 'The bomb in the brain', in Crowley and Pavitt (eds), *Cold War Modern*, pp. 113–15.

115 'Freddezza rugosa ... al brutto marchio del fascio il non bello assiro o egiziano'. Anon., 'Un elogio e un rimprovero', *Linea Grafica*, 3:9–10 (September–October 1950), 276.

116 Betts, *The Authority of Everyday Objects*, pp. 122–8, see in particular Figure 28, p. 127.

117 'E necessario che ... pubblicazioni ufficiali della Nona Triennale abbiano uno stile unico e concorde.' ATM, TRN_09_DT_014_C, internal communication memorandum by G. Gorgerino for M. Nizzoli, 22 March 1951.

118 'Tenere d'occhio ... una certa aria di famiglia'. *Ibid.*

119 'Schema unico'. ATM, TRN_09_DT_014_C, internal communication memorandum by G. Gorgerino for M. Nizzoli, 29 March 1951.

120 'Intonato con i caratteri ed i colori della Triennale'. ATM, TRN_09_DT_014_C, internal communication memorandum by G. Gorgerino for M. Nizzoli, 31 May 1951.

121 'Sintetizza gli scopi e le finalità della Triennale di Milano'. AALS, D b.14 fasc.9, letter from U. Zanchetta to A. Steiner, 20 February 1956. Invited designers were Enrico Ciuti, Max Huber, Bruno Munari, Giovanni Pintori, Michele Provinciali, Marcello Nizzoli, Antonio Rossi and Albe Steiner.

122 A. Boggeri, 'Advertising art in post-war Italy', *Graphis*, 18 (1947), 149.

4

Education and practice, working hand in hand

In the aftermath of World War II, it was not just a question of rebuilding the bombed cities, but also a matter of rehabilitating Italian society at large after twenty years of fascist dictatorship. Education became a vehicle of political, social and economic reconstruction of the country: by nurturing political understanding and engagement, it was expected to contribute to the formation of democratic citizens and the promotion of a democratic culture.[1] Design education aligned with the prevailing spirit of social and democratic idealism and the sweeping reformist stance that character-ised the years of reconstruction. In the 1950s and through the 1960s, it emerged as a key concern of the local and international design commu-nity. Interest in education stemmed, as we shall see, from the growing awareness of the social impact and cultural meaning of design.

Building on approaches to design education sketched out in chapter 1, in this chapter I develop two lines of argument. First, I contend that in the post-war period design education became a political activity aimed at training practitioners who acknowledged the social impact of design and assumed responsibility for it. Secondly, I suggest that for Milan's graphic designers, teaching was a means of engaging inventively in the practice and helping it develop by exploring, refining and defining it collectively, while at the same time ensuring new generations of practitioners were prepared. By approaching design education and practice as equal partners engaged in a mutual relationship, I thus explore education not as a mere prerequisite for professionalisation, but as an active agent that affects pro-fessionalisation in return.[2]

The Scuola del Libro and the Convitto Scuola Rinascita in Milan were reform-oriented educational institutions that joined in with efforts at re-democratising the country and training a new generation of politically aware and socially minded practitioners. The practitioners teaching in these schools formed a like-minded community, and they furthered the ongoing articulation of graphic design practice in Italy by contributing to transnational exchanges on design pedagogy and practice taking place not only within the schools but also outside them in the pages of trade magazines and at national and international conferences. The schools' activities serve here as case studies in order to take a look at the experimental intermediate phase of graphic design education in Italy – between its infancy in the interwar period and the founding of the first graduate courses of graphic design in the 1960s – and for investigating the social values and political stance acquired by both design education and practice in post-war Milan.

Educating for democracy

Italians held their first free general elections for over twenty years on 2 June 1946. Voters, including women for the first time in Italian history, chose between the republic (54.2 per cent) and the monarchy (45.8 per cent), and they elected representatives to the Constituent Assembly.[3] The new democratic constitution came into force in January 1948. The first twelve articles list the 'Fundamental Principles' on which the Italian Republic is founded: they are of a programmatic nature rather than meant for immediate actuation. In particular, article 3 identifies 'the duty of the Republic to remove all economic and social obstacles that, by limiting the freedom and equality of citizens, prevent full individual development and the participation of all workers in the political, economic and social organisation of the country'.[4] Article 4 recognises the right of all citizens to work (paid employment) and tasks the Republic with providing suitable conditions to render this right effective. Despite it not being mentioned, education is implicit here.[5] On the one hand, it represented a key instrument for the fostering of individual fulfilment and the conscious exercise of civic and social rights and duties. On the other hand, education, and vocational schools in particular, could serve as a means for implementing the right to work through the acquisition of the appropriate knowledge and skills.

The Società Umanitaria in Milan embraced the post-war belief in education as the basis for a democratic society.[6] While, as discussed in chapter 1, the Fascist regime had taken a stand against its left-wing agenda, during the post-war period the Umanitaria was able to renew its commitment to radical political reform and progressive pedagogy. Writing in 1954, the director of the Umanitaria, Riccardo Bauer, explained that vocational schools 'neither create nor nurture a monster of mechanical skills but raise a *man*'.[7] In his opinion, 'vocational and technical education [were] driven by a distinct *educational* criterion and aimed at strengthening and enriching the intellectual and moral personality of the pupil and future worker'.[8] Under the motto 'educating for democracy', the Umanitaria took on responsibility for the re-education of a generation that had grown up under Fascism. Combining vocational training with political re-education it committed itself to nurturing politically conscious and socially responsible thinkers, thereby turning students into agents of democratic reform.

To be sure, the belief in education as a vehicle of social reconstruction was not unique to Italy. It was in fact a shared concern of the many countries that were striving to create the conditions to become genuinely democratic and peaceful.[9] Nowhere was this more visible than at the HfG, Hochschule für Gestaltung (Institute of Design) in Ulm, whose original aims were 'eradicating German nationalism and militarism by providing post-war youth with badly needed cultural ideals and moral direction'.[10] Co-founded in 1946 by Inge Scholl and the graphic designer Otl Aicher, the Volkshochschule (Community College) – as the HfG was originally named – was a school of democratic education. The project met the favour of the American occupation authorities, who became major stakeholders. Patronage was, however, contingent upon the dropping of explicitly socialist-oriented stances, and this turned the school into a key asset to the US Cold War cultural policy.[11] With the appointment of the Swiss designer Max Bill as director, the HfG shifted emphasis from political re-education to design instruction. The curriculum reflected this compromise: instruction in architecture and city planning, and visual and industrial design was supplemented with lectures on sociology, psychology, philosophy and contemporary history.

In Italy, the Umanitaria was just one of a cohort of reform-oriented educational initiatives engaging in the re-democratisation of the country. Another striking example of such initiatives is provided by the Convitti Scuola Rinascita. The Convitti were vocational schools set up in the immediate aftermath of War World II by a group of ex-partisans with the two-fold aim of preserving and cultivating the values of the Italian resistance movement and of allowing ex-partisans, war prisoners and orphans to return to school and complete their education.[12] In order to rehabilitate a generation that had grown up under the 'believe, obey, fight' rules of Fascism, the Convitti Scuola Rinascita promoted direct participation and self-management. In contrast to the Gentile Reform, vocational training was put on an equal level to the humanities, and the right to study irrespective of social class or economic background replaced the elitism of the fascist educational system.

The pedagogical experiment of the Convitti Scuola Rinascita was initiated in the summer of 1945 in Milan and soon expanded to the national level with the financial support of the Ministry of Post-war Support and the ANPI, Associazione Nazionale Partigiani d'Italia (National Association of Italian Partisans). By March 1946, eleven Convitti had been established in different cities of northern and central Italy: Bologna, Cremona, Genoa, Milan, Novara, Reggio Emilia, Rome, San Remo, Turin, Varese and Venice.

Each school was named after a partisan who had died fighting Fascism, and each one addressed a different professional field depending on the local traditional craft and industrial production. For example, workers in the agriculture sector and food industry trained in Bologna, naval workers in Genoa and mechanics in Turin.

In the late 1940s the Convitti Scuola Rinascita gradually lost official support as Italy entered a new political and social phase. The 1948 parliamentary election marked a clear shift from leftist politics towards the centre and 'changed the face of Italian life irrevocably'.[13] Voters were called upon to choose between two clashing ideologies: either a conservative, Catholic and capitalist vision of Italian society, as promoted by the DC, or a progressive, secular and socialist Italy, as envisaged by the FDP, Fronte Democratico Popolare (Popular Front), a leftist political coalition consisting of the Italian Communist and Socialist parties. The eventual victory of the DC ended the interparty coalition and antifascist unity that had characterised the early years of reconstruction. With the DC governing the country, the Convitti Scuola Rinascita became subject to frequent raids by police searching for evidence that could link the school with extremist wings of the PCI. The cutting of public funding led to the closure of the majority of the Convitti.

The Cooperativa Rinascita

A course for graphics and advertising was established, first in Rome in 1946 at the Convitto Giaime Pintor, and then moved to Milan in 1948 to the Convitto Amleto Livi. The relocation was motivated by economic factors. Since the advertising and printing sectors and publishing industry were more developed in the Milanese region, there were more work opportunities there than in Rome. Both the Convitto Giaime Pintor and Amleto Livi stand out by virtue of their star-studded staff and student bodies. To name just a few, Germano Facetti, best known as the art director at Penguin publishing house from 1960 to 1972, trained in Rome, while protagonists of Italian graphic design such as Albe Steiner and Max Huber taught in Milan. A critical analysis of the course is instructive as it offers valuable insights into the socio-political stances acquired by both graphic design education and practice in post-war Italy.

Educators and students subscribed to the antifascist and leftist agenda on which the Convitti Scuola Rinascita were built. Most teachers had contributed to the resistance movement: Steiner, Remo Muratore and Gabriele Mucchi had joined the Val d'Ossola partisans, while Sergio Rossi had fought with the Garibaldi brigade. Many students shared this militant background: Antonio Tubaro had fought with the Carlo Magno brigade, Gildo Moncada had lost a leg fighting to free the town of San Sepolcro in Tuscany, and Facetti had been arrested for antifascist propaganda and deported to Mauthausen concentration camp.[14] Political commitment also marked their future career choices. Muratore and Tubaro, for instance, took care of the visual communication of the PCI, while Albe Steiner and his wife and collaborator Lica Covo, who was also involved in the Convitti Scuola Rinascita dealing with administration and liaising with clients, constructed their professional image on antifascism.[15]

In line with the democratic ethos of the Convitti Scuola Rinascita, both educators and students partook in the organisation of the course. Meetings were arranged on a regular basis to discuss curricula, pedagogy and activities. In Rome and then in Milan, students attended classes in drawing, graphic layout, photography, type design, history of the graphic arts, advertising and propaganda, printing technology, Italian grammar and literature. Theory-based learning was put into practice in the workshop. In Rome, the course specialised in commercial art and training of the poster artist (see figure 4.1). With the move to Milan, the focus shifted towards everyday printed matter. The course adopted a different approach to graphics, seen as a social service rather than as a commercial application of fine arts for advertising purposes. Special emphasis was put on discussing the social duties and responsibilities of graphic design practice. The syllabus for a short course on the history of type design, advertising and propaganda ended with a

4.1 View of the type design class at the Convitto Scuola Rinascita Giaime Pintor in Rome, between 1945 and 1948.

discussion on 'the perspectives of the graphic artist – their social duties and responsibilities'.[16]

Teachers and students established the Cooperativa Rinascita (Rebirth Cooperative) in an attempt to attain financial autonomy. This was a studio for 'graphic design, execution and consultancy' in advertising, publishing, exhibition design and window dressing that supplemented the educational programme with paid, on-the-job training.[17] The cooperative was first founded in Rome in May 1948 and, in this case too, soon after relocated to Milan. Figure 4.2 captures the founding meeting of the Milanese Cooperativa Rinascita on 25 February 1949, at 11 p.m. Staging apart, the relaxed postures and easy-going demeanour of students and teachers suggest a rather informal and friendly environment. Steiner's archive, nevertheless, contains evidence of internal conflict.

Conflicts revolved around whether the cooperative should operate within or outside the school and this gave rise to fierce discussions. Two opposing pedagogical approaches were put forward.[18] On the one side, the so-called 'liberisti' (liberals) – Luigi Veronesi, Muratore and Huber – suggested outsourcing the students' work experience: educators would be expected to help students find job positions, while students would then

4.2 Photograph of the founding meeting of the Cooperativa Rinascita in Milan on 25 February 1949. Artemio Bin, Gildo Manacorda, Ettore Lazzarotto, Antonio Tubaro and Piero Ottinieri were students; Remo Muratore, Gabriele Mucchi, Albe Steiner, Claudio Conte and Max Huber were teachers. The picture was taken by students of Luigi Veronesi's photography course.

be required to give part of their income to the cooperative. On the other side, the so-called 'cooperativisti' (cooperativists) – Steiner and Mucchi – argued that the training and the work experience of students should happen within the Convitto and that teachers were to use their network of clients to provide commissions for the cooperative. The clash between the liberals and the cooperativists echoed the interwar controversy about vocational education, and in particular those arguments between supporters of the industry-school and the workshop-school explored in chapter 1. It is, moreover, evidence of internal disagreements within the graphic design community and of the enduring coexistence of conflicting approaches towards pedagogy. At issue was a recurring bone of contention in vocational schools, namely the balance between theoretical education and work experience.[19]

The conflict between liberals and cooperativists reached its apex in the summer of 1949, when the course of graphic arts and advertising was temporarily suspended due to students' dissent against the excessive workload. In order to self-finance the purchase of materials and technical equipment, students had been made to devote an increasing amount of time to paid work to the detriment of school hours.[20] Mucchi seized the opportunity to hold the liberal members of the Cooperativa Rinascita responsible for the situation. He declared himself 'firmly convinced … that the "liberal" stance had crucially damaged the way students were taught the discipline, and also their spiritual orientation'.[21] For their part, the liberals counterattacked. In Veronesi's opinion, it was the cooperatist attitude that was actually dangerous because 'students [were] treated like guinea pigs to test work methods and systems that [were] excellent in other social structures, but unfortunately utterly utopian (at least in the specific case of graphic/advertising work) within Italy's social structure' at the time.[22] He contested the cooperativists' good faith and accused Mucchi and Steiner of being driven by ideological and political purposes, rather than having the students' best interest at heart.

The graphics and advertising course reopened in the autumn of 1949 with the definitive adoption of the cooperativist approach. In response to students' requests and complaints, the working hours at the Cooperativa Rinascita were officially included in the course syllabus instead of being considered an extra-curricular activity. A preliminary period without on-the-job training was guaranteed. Finally, a set of rules regulating the distribution of profits was agreed upon: part of the profit was to be set aside for the school and the remainder was to be shared among students and educators according to billable hours and type of contribution to the collaborative work. We read in an undated document in Steiner's archive that the design practice was split into different tasks. These tasks fell into four categories to which points were assigned: design and execution – categories 1 and 2, respectively – were worth 5 points; category 3 was worth 4 points and included layout and exhibition design as well as client liaison; category 4 consisted of routine tasks and errands and was assigned 3 points.[23] Points were then multiplied by the work hours. The ranking of the tasks shows the definition of a scale of values that put design and execution at the very top of the design process.

Taking sides

The title of the aforementioned archival document, 'Proposta Hannes' (Hannes's suggestion), places the Cooperativa Rinascita within an unexpected international network of design exchange. Hannes who? To speculate that the 'Hannes' mentioned in the document might be none other than the Swiss architect Hannes Meyer does not seem too far-fetched. But what did the second director of the Bauhaus Dessau have to do with the Cooperativa Rinascita? Steiner is the link. The two had met in Mexico City, where Meyer had moved in 1939 and Steiner had lived from 1946 to 1948. They had been drawn together by their shared faith in and commitment to the communist cause. After his return to Milan, Steiner had kept in contact with Meyer and introduced him to his circle of friends and collaborators. Of greater relevance here is that they spent the summer of 1949 together in Val d'Ossola and that Meyer visited the Convitto Scuola Rinascita in the spring of 1950.[24] Thus, it seems safe to assume that Steiner had plenty of opportunity to discuss the cooperative with Meyer.

During a meeting of the Cooperativa Rinascita, Steiner pointed to the TGP, Taller de Grafica Popular (People's Print Workshop) in Mexico and the so-called Red Bauhaus as models of an ideologically committed and politically driven output.[25] The TGP was an artist collective that produced politically conscious prints.[26] These featured an expressive and realistic visual language and were designed to be accessible to a broad audience. Antifascism was the primary focus of TGP production, and artists turned to caricature, satire and heroic images to urge the viewer to action. In the words of Steiner, the artists of the TGP were 'very good communists whose honesty was undisputed and whose activity was devoted to the people'.[27] Despite acknowledging the many differences – different historical context, social environment and economic issues – Steiner was keen on drawing comparisons between the TGP and the Cooperativa Rinascita. Both projects attempted to advance social causes through visual communication: revolutionary goals in the case of the TGP, re-democratisation and preservation of the resistance spirit for the Convitti Scuola Rinascita.

In Steiner's admittedly biased interpretation, the TGP and the Bauhaus were closely linked: 'the Bauhaus moved ... to North America with Moholy-Nagy at the Institute of Design in Chicago, and to Central America with Hannes Meyer and in Mexico it was renamed Taller de Grafica Popular'.[28] Indeed, Steiner's proxy experience of the Bauhaus was communicated to him by Meyer. The second director of the Bauhaus was a controversial figure, responsible for radically reshaping the school by veering leftwards and bringing it into closer contact with trade unions and workers' movements. He had been demonised and almost forgotten in the post-war period and was only rehabilitated in the late 1950s by the Argentinian design theorist and educator Tomás Maldonado at the HfG in Ulm. Meyer's correspondence with Steiner and Mucchi reveals not only that Steiner and Mucchi were well aware of differences between Gropius's and Meyer's Bauhaus, but also that they were committed to helping Meyer make the legacy of the Red Bauhaus known in Italy through publications and exhibitions.[29]

By teaming up with Meyer and the Red Bauhaus, members of the Cooperativa Rinascita pitted their vision of design education and practice against the contemporary revision and celebration of the Bauhaus legacy undertaken by the United States Administration. As Paul Betts illustrated, the Bauhaus's success and canonisation after 1945 was the result of 'the occidental conversion of Bauhaus into ready Cold War cultural capital'.[30] The rebranding of Bauhaus modernism as expression of 'cultural liberalism with which all could sympathise and identify' was driven by the cultural imperatives of the Cold War.[31] It was shaped by a revisionist rewriting of its history and legacy, in particular the dismissal of any damaging leftist association and the suppression of all questions about its relationship with fascist regimes. Only in this manner could the Bauhaus satisfy the 'Cold War criteria of antifascism, anticommunism, and international modernism'.[32] Evidence concerning the relationship between modernism and Italian Fascism was provided in chapters 1, 2 and 3. This and Steiner and Mucchi's countertrend opposition to Western attempts to cleanse the historiography of the Bauhaus of any political orientation or leftist association reveal the constructed nature of the Cold War image of the Bauhaus and modernism more generally.

A vision of political reform and cultural regeneration shaped the output of the Cooperativa Rinascita. Work commissions were discussed together and selected according to their compliance with the leftist, reform-oriented aims of the cooperative. The trade union, CGIL, Confederazione Generale Italiana del Lavoro (Italian General Confederation of Labour), the partisans' association ANPI, the PCI, the cultural association Italy–USSR and the left-wing newspaper L'Unità were all loyal clients of the cooperative. The Cooperativa was keen on working on 'all those kinds of expressions that provide[d] the broadest category of people with a greater knowledge through clear and easily understandable language'.[33] Commissions featuring a cultural, political or social content were therefore most likely to be accepted. The design of the visual identity for the 2nd International Congress of the Syndicates that was held in Milan during the summer of 1949 and the anti-DC propaganda campaign for the 1951 council election checked all the boxes. The overlapping hemispheres, the seamless pattern of flags and the picture on the postcard of a bricklayer effortlessly carrying a heavy load visually conveyed the slogan of the congress: 'unity is the strength of the workers' (see figure 4.3). In marked contrast, the visual language of the poster could not have expressed things more differently (see figure 4.4). The words written on the fingers of the man warn voters what to expect in the case of a DC victory: war, unemployment, taxes and misery. Viewer-voters were urged to act and 'save Milan and Italy' from the claws of the DC and 'its accomplices', clearly identified as the US by the $ symbol on the ring.

The blunt pro-Soviet stance of both works positions the Cooperativa Rinascita within the political climate of the Cold War. By the late 1940s the Cold War had become firmly entrenched in Italy. The collapse of the wartime antifascist coalition among the three major parties – the Christian Democrats, the Communists and the Socialists – led to a clear-cut divide between pro-Western and pro-Eastern political forces.[34] The Cooperativa Rinascita stood by the PCI, thereby backing the party's alliance with the Soviet Union. Due to the Italian peninsula's key location in the Mediterranean region bordering the Soviet bloc, and the popularity of the PCI, which at the time was arguably the strongest Communist party in the western hemisphere, Italy was a privileged battlefield for Cold War politics and a strategic partner in US plans for the containment of the

4.3 Postcard advertising the 2nd International Congress of the Syndicates, designed by members of the Cooperativa Rinascita (Milan), 1949.

4.4 Anti-DC propaganda poster, designed by members of the Cooperativa Rinascita (Milan), 1951.

Soviet threat over Europe. The aforementioned victory of the DC in the 1948 general elections assured Italy's ties to Western powers. The country's placement under the American sphere of interest was furthered by its becoming a member of NATO in 1949. Then, the implementation of the Marshall Plan was set to seal American influence over Italy. The country stood to receive about $1.5 billion of the $13.3 billion to be distributed for European recovery between 1948 and 1952. This American aid would come at a cost, warned the PCI. But such hostility was bound to backfire as the majority of Italian voters perceived the US programme of investment to be positive for the reconstruction of the country.[35] In this light, the $ symbol in figure 4.4 acquires a specific political connotation standing for the external pressure the US was exerting through the Marshall Plan.

Yet, not all the commissions taken on by the Cooperativa Rinascita were politically laden. A member of the cooperative asked the following question during a meeting: 'Is it right or not to reject a capitalist work?'[36] Advertisements and promotional material for clients, such as the producer of household electrical appliances Fargas and white goods manufacturers Triplex and Ceramiche Pozzi, show that 'capitalist work' was not taboo and that designing commercial works was acceptable even to the more socialist-minded members of the cooperative. This commercial output shows a different side to the Cooperativa Rinascita: one that was less committed to the 'construction of a new world', closer to the market economy, and in interaction with consumerism and private consumption.[37] After all, Italy had undergone dramatic social and economic changes in the fifteen years that followed the end of World War II, turning from a rural to a mostly urban society, and from a production- to a consumption-driven economy.[38] The Fargas advertisement, in particular, speaks to the expansion – especially among the middle classes of centre-northern Italy – of the domestic electricity appliances industry between the early 1950s and the late 1960s.[39]

Despite many difficulties of both a financial and political nature, the Convitto Amleto Livi managed to stay open until the mid-1950s. Although relatively short-lived, this little-known educational initiative is crucial to understanding the later developments of graphic design education in Italy. Most of the teachers and students of the Convitto Amleto Livi migrated to the Scuola del Libro, moving from an experimental and militant venture to a more institutionalised and structured environment. However, before moving on to look at the Scuola del Libro in detail, graphic design education in Italy needs to be put into its broader context by considering contemporary design discourses and exchanges. It is to national debates about, and international models for, design education and practice that we now turn.

National debates and international models

Members of the Italian design community and leading personalities of the international design network convened at the 1st International Conference of Industrial Design at the 10th Milan Triennale in 1954.[40] 'Times [were] ripe for a thorough discussion on industrial design and its many-sided relationship with society,' the director of the Triennale, Ivan Matteo Lombardo, asserted in his opening speech.[41] Over the following days, debates addressed the meaning and definition of industrial design, questioned designers' role within, and responsibilities towards, society, and showed an awareness of the practice's involvement in wider cultural, social, political and economic orders. Attendance was extended to outsiders to the practice: key figures of the Italian cultural élite, such as art and architecture historian Giulio Carlo Argan, art and design critic Gillo Dorfles and philosophers Luciano Anceschi and Enzo Paci, joined the discussion. Their involvement suggests a widespread interest in the impact of design on society and, consequently, a shared concern for the education of designers. In his speech, Argan defined design as an agent of social integration and growth. He called for reform of the national educational system and for the founding in Italy of design schools with an international character. In the same vein, Max Bill argued that the social commitment and responsibilities of design practice pushed educational issues to the fore. In the closing remarks, the Triennale took it upon itself to 'promote and encourage the foundation of cultural organs aimed at advancing design practice and education in Italy'.[42] It committed to putting pressure on 'cultural institutions and productive organisations … in order that a School of industrial design should be established in Milan'.[43] All in all, education emerged as a key concern of the local and international design community.

Seven years later, another opportunity for transnational debate and information exchange around education presented itself at the 2nd Congress of ICSID, the International Council of Societies of Industrial Design. The conference was organised by the ADI and held in Venice in September 1961.[44] The initiative contributed to the ADI's efforts to foster the professional status of industrial design in Italy and was evidence of its commitment to the promotion of design education.[45] Indeed, as Giulio Castelli, co-founder of the plastic furniture manufacturer Kartell, put it at the first ADI meeting in 1956, only the establishment of schools of industrial design could enable 'the activity [of the industrial designer], which [was] still at an amateurish stage, to acquire the efficiency, the authority and the means of protection that are proper to a *licensed profession*'.[46] On a similar note, architect Enrico Peressutti, the ADI spokesman at the first ICSID meeting in 1957, suggested that the international council should accentuate its 'cultural and educational character' and encourage the exchange of educational experiences among members in order to 'improve the professional conditions of industrial designers in all countries'.[47]

Speeches at the 2nd ICSID Congress confirmed that awareness of the mutual relationship between professionalisation and education was now quite generalised.[48] According to the American designer, Peter Müller-Munk, who was professor at the Carnegie Institute of Technology in Pittsburgh and an ICSID co-founder, 'without an educational system that ensures the continuity of the professional practices, and without a body of knowledge that is indispensable for the professional work: there is no profession'.[49] On a more pessimistic note, Maldonado's speech problematised the role of education as an agent of professionalisation. 'If it is correct to say that the education of the industrial designer is generally confused and contradictory', he suggested, 'this is mainly because industrial design as a whole – as both a profession and a philosophy of a profession – is still confused and contradictory.'[50] Maldonado called upon designers to step back from everyday practice and think seriously about their profession:

> For a long time, the industrial designer has been busier 'making' than becoming aware of his 'making', more involved in extending his activity than in examining it in depth. ... But the new profession ... has already ceased for a good while to be in its 'infancy'. Thus, a careful self-reflection and a clarification of its goals and methods is today no longer a luxury but a necessity. And it is an urgent necessity.[51]

In other words, industrial designers were being urged to take time to explore their field of practice, to negotiate a shared body of skills and knowledge among themselves and with neighbouring practices and to define the boundaries of the discipline.

At the 12th Triennale in 1960, a year before the 2nd ICSID Congress, the ADI had curated an exhibition devoted to 'the illustration of the teaching of *Industrial Design* in two of the most important schools worldwide': the HfG in Ulm and the RCA, Royal College of Art, in London.[52] The exhibition provided the Italian audience with the opportunity to assess in person the achievements of design schools abroad. Prior to this occasion, information on international examples of design education had been available in print only. As the editor of the design magazine and ADI house organ *Stile Industria*, Alberto Rosselli, put it: 'The issue [of design education] is so urgent and as yet without an organic solution that any space devoted to what is currently happening outside the country, and to comments and suggestions from those who have specific experience on the topic, will never be excessive.'[53] International educational models were investigated in detail and commented upon in design magazines. Rosselli wrote: 'It is not easy to evaluate the interest to us of initiatives that are taking place in countries so different from ours, but it is certainly dangerous to think that it would be possible to transplant systems and methods of those countries into Italy.'[54] Thus, international educational models were to be adapted to the Italian cultural and social context and changed in order to respond to the requests and needs of the local industry.

From the mid-1950s onwards, both designers and the cultural élite in Italy had become interested in what was happening in Ulm.[55] They had heard about the HfG at international conferences. They had also read about it in a series of articles by Maldonado published between 1957 and 1959 in which the Argentinian educator had formulated his ideas regarding design education and had illustrated the scientific and technological core of the Ulmian approach and its roots in semiotics and information theory.[56] The Visual Communication Department in Ulm was the focus of two 1959 articles. In March, *Stile Industria* published a selection of images that documented the adoption of a boldly abstract vocabulary and the use and systematic variation of a limited set of geometric forms and graphic elements (see figure 4.5).[57] A couple of months later, the art historian and critic Pier Carlo Santini wrote in the cultural magazine *Comunità* that the Visual Communication Department 'train[ed] the whole of that category of specialists, usually referred to by the term graphics, that [was] conquering an ever-expanding field of action and involvement in modern life'.[58] To reach 'the clearest relationship possible between messages and public ... relying on ... perception theory and semiotics' was its primary goal.[59]

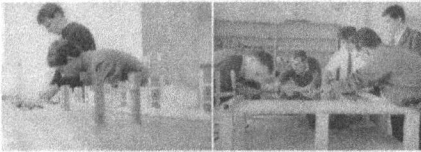

4.5 Double-page spread from Angelo Tito Anselmi's article 'Hochschule für Gestaltung, Ulm', *Stile Industria*, 6:21 (March 1959), 6–7.

Finally, some exponents of the Italian design community were able to gain direct experience of the institute as visiting professors or students. Invited as a guest scholar in May 1957, Dorfles was the first Italian visitor at Ulm. When I asked him about this experience, he described the HfG as a 'design fortress' where 'something completely new' was happening.[60] He then proffered an anecdote: when the philosopher Luciano Anceschi had asked for advice concerning his son, who was interested in design, Dorfles had told his friend to send him to the HfG in Ulm 'so that he [would] finally become a designer'.[61] Dorfles's words confirm design historian Raimonda Riccini's argument that in the late 1950s and through the 1960s, Italian 'architects, designers and artists considered an educational pilgrimage to the German city indispensable'.[62] The 'pilgrim' in Dorfles's anecdote was Giovanni Anceschi, who was to go on to study visual communication at the HfG between 1962 and 1966. Back in Italy, Anceschi brought this experience to the Corso Superiore di Disegno Industriale e Comunicazione Visiva (Graduate Course of Industrial Design and Visual Communication) in Rome, where he began teaching Basic Design in 1969.[63]

The coverage of the RCA in the Italian specialist press focused on the industrial design course; information about any other department was absent.[64] The School of Graphic Design finally attracted some attention in March 1964, when the graphic design magazine *Linea Grafica* reviewed the exhibition, 'GraphicsRCA'.[65] This was the first ever exhibition of graphic design to take place at the college, and it was held to mark the occasion of the fifteenth anniversary of the formation of the School of Graphic Design in 1948 (see figure 4.6).[66] According to the reviewer, 'GraphicsRCA' was

4.6   View of the exhibition 'GraphicsRCA' celebrating the fifteenth anniversary of the formation of the School of Graphic Design in 1948, London 1963.

a revelation. It showed not only the quality of graphic design education in Britain, but also the vitality and originality of British graphic design, which had reached an 'average level that was indeed among the best worldwide'.[67] A look inside the exhibition catalogue affords some insights into the state of graphic design practice in Britain at the time. We read in the introductory text by the head of the School of Graphic Design, Richard Guyatt, that the very term 'graphic design' was unknown before the war, and that when it was chosen 'with a certain sense of relief, but not conviction' to name the new department, 'no one was quite sure what it meant'.[68] Fifteen years later, the boundaries of graphic design were still vague and wide ranging, 'on the one side overlapping many other branches of design, on the other, becoming a medium of fine arts'.[69] Guyatt's judgement testifies to his awareness that the position of graphic design practice within the design community was still niche and ambiguous. Suspended between design and fine arts, graphic design's uneasy position was further jeopardised by its association with advertising. Indeed, as we shall see in chapter 5, British and Italian graphic designers were at the time dealing with similar problems and sharing related experiences.

Besides the HfG and the RCA, a third international example of design education attracted the attention of the Milanese graphic design circle, and this was the Institute of Design at the Illinois Institute of Technology in Chicago. Originally named New Bauhaus, the Institute of Design was founded by László Moholy-Nagy in 1937. Together with Josef Albers's experience at the Black Mountain College in North Carolina, the institute was responsible for the promotion of Bauhaus pedagogy in the US and contributed to the Cold War rewriting of the Bauhaus legacy.[70] The May 1953 issue of the graphic design journal *Bollettino del Centro Studi Grafici* featured an article by the graphic designer, Michele Provinciali, in which he reported on his experience as a student at the Institute of Design between 1951 and 1952.[71] Back in Milan, he began teaching from 1954 at the Scuola del Libro, where he adapted the model of the Institute of Design to the Italian context 'by making it more Mediterranean, and less Nordic'.[72] But Provinciali was not the only faculty member at the Scuola del Libro to have had first-hand experience with the Institute of Design. Graphic designer Massimo Vignelli joined the faculty in 1960 after a two-year teaching fellowship at the institute. In Chicago, Vignelli had had 'the opportunity to check out in person the effectiveness of the kind of training offered at the Bauhaus, even if in a milder American version'.[73]

Provinciali and Vignelli's involvement ensured a circulation of ideas regarding design education and practice from Chicago in the Italian design educational system. What is more, the impact of the Institute of Design on Italian graphic design did not stop at design education. In fact, the opening of the international graphic design firm Unimark International in 1965 can be linked to the institute.[74] Three founding partners of Unimark – Vignelli,

Jay Doblin and Ralph Eckerstrom – met through the network of professionals that gathered around the Institute of Design. A fourth co-founder, the Dutch-born, Milan-based graphic designer Bob Noorda, met Vignelli when they were both teaching at the Scuola del Libro. The case of Unimark shows how schools fostered professional networks and thereby created fertile ground for collaboration.

Up to this point in this chapter, we have seen how education was identified as an agent of re-democratisation of Italy during the years of reconstruction, and how domestic and transnational debates around the impact of design on society mirrored a growing interest in design education and in the key role it played in fostering social responsibility in a new generation of practitioners. It is from this perspective that we now turn our attention to the Scuola del Libro in Milan. The remaining three sections of the chapter will explore how the school responded to the democratic idealism and reformist stance of the reconstruction period, and how teaching there provided Milan's graphic designers with an opportunity to look at their own practice with some detachment, enabling them to clarify its goals and methods and articulate its profile.

Rebuilding the Scuola del Libro from its ruins

The premises of the Umanitaria were severely damaged during the Allies' bombing of Milan in 1943 and 1944 (see figure 4.7). The Scuola del Libro was reduced to dusty ruins, with few pieces of technical equipment and machinery capable of being salvaged. In September 1945, about five months after the end of the Italian Civil War and the Nazi occupation of the country on 25 April, a consortium was founded in order to finance the rebuilding and refurbishing of the school and to allow it to reopen its doors as soon as possible. Members of the Consorzio per la Scuola del Libro (Consortium for the School of the Book) included printing trade unions, associations of graphic industrialists and publishers, the Chamber of Commerce, the city of Milan, associations of partisans and war victims, the Centro Studi Grafici (Centre for Graphic Studies) and the Umanitaria itself. Piero Trevisani, teacher at the Scuola del Libro and member of the consortium, offered the following comment during a radio interview in January 1947: 'The fundraising challenge is open. Whoever can, should, contribute! The Scuola del Libro in Milan must rise again from its ruins ... more beautiful, more effective, more modern, livelier, and more Italian'![75] Detailed reports of both financial and in-kind contributions from publishers, printers, type foundries and paper manufacturers, and updates on the status of the reconstruction work, featured in specialist magazines and trade journals. Members of the Federazione Italiana Operai Poligrafici (Italian Federation of Polygraph Labourers) agreed to give one lira of their weekly salary towards the reconstruction of the school, amounting

4.7 The premises of the Società Umanitaria after the Allied bombing of Milan in 1943 and 1944.

to a grand total of approximately half a million liras per annum. In spite of this, minutes of meetings reveal there were continual struggles to pay off deficits and complaints about missed payments of the agreed financial contributions.[76]

The head of the vocational schools at the Umanitaria, Elio Palazzo, asked rhetorically in August 1945, 'What might be the situation of the Milanese graphics industry? Without a doubt it is difficult: an inadequately trained workforce, and no injection of new energies to face the multiple needs of the renewed industrial activity.'[77] Overall, the damage to the productive capacity of Italian industry by wartime destruction had been limited, with an 8 per cent loss of capital since 1938.[78] However, the Milanese publishing industry had been heavily compromised by the war. Many printing plants and publishing houses had been destroyed or damaged.

The wartime lack of imported cellulose and wood pulp, the loss of export market in France and the UK, and insufficient economic supply and support from the State had caused a 77 per cent drop in the book print run between 1940–41 and 1944.[79] The number of publications did not return to pre-war levels until the early 1950s.

Notwithstanding these setbacks, Milan maintained its role as capital of the Italian publishing industry.[80] An enthusiastic desire to restart and take part in the reconstruction of the country pervaded the publishing sector. The blossoming of the publishing industry in the immediate post-war years was not unique to Italy, and it has been interpreted by scholars as a reaction to censorship and suppression of free expression under dictatorial regimes. Writing about post-war Japan, historian John W. Dower observed that publishing was one of the first commercial sectors to recover, in response to a 'hunger for words in print'.[81] By the same token, Milanese publishers responded to the post-war urge to communicate and exchange ideas that provided the publishing industry with commercial opportunities and fostered its recovery.[82] Books and periodicals were the principal vehicles for spreading this post-war passion for participation in civic affairs and thirst for culture. In 1952, sales of weekly news magazines exceeded 20 million copies, which was about thirty times the number sold before the war.[83]

The recovering printing industry called for skilled and immediately employable workers. For the Scuola del Libro, responding to needs and requests from the industry and contributing to its recovery were a priority. Therefore, the retraining and re-education of current practitioners became the primary concern of the school. All its energies and limited finances were put into the evening and weekend courses for apprentices and practitioners. For the moment, the reactivation of the daily training courses for young pupils was put on hold. The first evening classes had begun in autumn 1946 in makeshift classrooms and workshops in the former gym. It was not until nine years later that they found an established venue.

In the autumn of 1955, the Scuola del Libro finally moved into a new purpose-built building designed by the architect Giovanni Romano (see figure 4.8).[84] In the summer of 1953, Romano and the school director, Enrico Gianni, had visited a number of graphic arts and printing schools in Germany and Switzerland to observe first hand the state of vocational school architecture abroad.[85] The resulting design responded to functionalist criteria and aligned with the ethos and pedagogy of the school. The glass façade dissolved differences between interior and exterior and allowed natural light to penetrate deep into the building. The framework of the curtain wall created a suggestive comparison with the typographical page layout. All departments were included in the four-storey building. Staircases on both sides facilitated movement from one department to another and conveyed the idea of a school in which there was no specialisation without understanding of the entire process: a harmonious organism in which all

4.8 Exterior of the Società Umanitaria in Milan, designed by Giovanni Romano, 1956.

parts worked together. Lavatories and service rooms were arranged on
the north side of the building, whereas classrooms and workshops were
located on the south side in order to benefit the most from natural light.
Workshops and classrooms communicated directly with each other, in line
with the school's ethos of practice and theory as two sides of the same coin.
Movable partitions allowed rooms to have flexible dimensions. The materials used for the flooring were selected according to the activities that would
take place in the room: rubber flooring for the hand composition workshop,
so as to avoid damaging the types in case they were to fall down; acid-
resistant tiles for the flooring of the photogravure workshop. In the words
of the director of the Umanitaria, Riccardo Bauer, Romano's building was
a 'true example of modern and rational school building: simultaneously a
workshop for technical training and a centre of moral and civic improvement'.[86] Here, from the late 1950s, students could attend the 'Corso per
Assistenti Grafici' (Course for Graphic Design Assistants).

The Course for Graphic Design Assistants and the sergeants of graphic design

The Course for Graphic Design Assistants was a three-year-long course for
pupils aged at least fifteen. The syllabus included technical and humanities classes: general culture, English, mathematics, visual and graphics
culture, type design, technical and free drawing, technology, design and

studio work. A major concern of the general culture classes was the development of a professional ethos in line with the socio-political agenda of the Umanitaria and the post-war belief that schools should produce responsible citizens aware of their civil and social rights and duties. The general culture classes familiarised students with 'key moments of the social, cultural and civic development' of contemporary society and provided them with 'the linguistic tools and critical attitude' that were necessary to act responsibly both as individuals and as professionals.[87] All in all, they made students aware of the impact of design on society and encouraged them to take responsibility for it.

Studio practice was at the core of the training of the graphic design assistant. The studio was 'the point of convergence of all theory-based classes and the point of departure for practice-based training; where students [were] expected to gradually acquire an effective, well-thought-out and rational graphic language, while expressing their own personal voice with ease'.[88] It fostered an objective and scientific approach to visual communication based 'neither on abstract schemes nor on personal preferences of the author, but rather [one that was] functional to the material, the product, the audience, etc.'.[89] During their first year, students tested out the limits and potential of tools and techniques by carrying out basic exercises with colour, form, negative–positive compositions, rhythm and layout. They cut, pasted and took apart examples of packaging and magazine or book layouts in order to understand the design process in reverse. Second-year students analysed and designed different types of printed material in collaboration with classmates. The accent was on acquiring a design methodology and students' attention was directed towards a careful analysis and thorough consideration of all the different aspects of an assignment: subject, content, purpose, costs, distributions, social and cultural issues, audience and technical aspects of the execution.[90] In the third year, the weekly hours spent by students in the studio increased from nine to twelve. During this final year, students designed and supervised the execution of a project that was realised across departments.

Third-year projects could be conceived by the students themselves, assigned by the teachers or commissioned by a third party outside the school. The Florentine publisher, Sansoni, for instance, commissioned the design of the paperback edition of its theatre series in 1959 (see figure 4.9).[91] The resulting covers lack any decoration besides the intrinsic beauty of the letterform in its regular, bold, italic, serif and sans-serif versions. The static centred layout is enlivened by the shifting of foreground and background and the reversal of positive and negative forms. Here it is worth pointing out that Vignelli worked for Sansoni from the early 1960s, and that the publisher became one of the clients of Unimark. This is no trivial coincidence, for it signals a direct connection between the school and the publishing industry and a mutual relationship between education

4.9 Book cover for the publisher Sansoni, designed by third-year students – Bollini, Brambilla, Comolli and De Roberto – of the studio practice at the Scuola del Libro in Milan, c. 1960.

and practice. As had been the case with the Cooperativa Rinascita, the Scuola del Libro benefited from the network of clients of its faculty, and vice versa. Students themselves took advantage of the situation, as some of them were given the opportunity to work for Vignelli and Noorda at the Milanese office of Unimark International.[92]

Students of the Course for Graphic Design Assistants were also put in charge of conceiving and supervising the execution of the official publications and promotional material of the Scuola del Libro, as well as ensuring their aesthetics were consistent and recognisable. They were thus given a voice in setting the criteria that differentiated 'good' from 'bad' design within the walls of the school. Official publications were the result of collaborative efforts among different departments and classes. This was the case with the brochure *Una lezione di storia 1922–1945* (A history lesson 1922–1945) that was the final output of a research project between the general culture class and the studio practice (see figure 4.10). The typographic grid on the cover becomes a metaphor for the authoritarianism of Fascism. The grid and the regime are ripped apart in 1945. The year of Italy's Liberation is written in red above the photograph of Mussolini's corpse hanging upside down in Piazzale Loreto, Milan, on 29 April 1945. The brochure was published in the early 1970s and hence lies outside the timespan covered in this book. It is nevertheless worth including, as it illustrates the commitment of the Scuola del Libro to carrying on with the

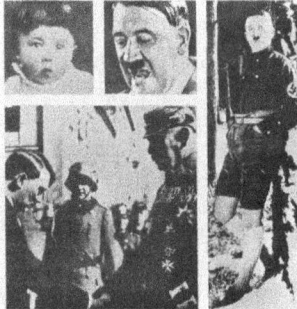

4.10   Booklet *Una lezione di storia 1922–1945*, collaborative project between students of the general culture class and the studio practice at the Scuola del Libro in Milan, under the supervision of Mario De Micheli and Albe Steiner, 1971–72.

mission of the Convitti Scuola Rinascita and to preserving the spirit of the Italian resistance movement in new generations of students.

Curricula, course syllabuses and content, as well as teaching methods, responded to the articulation of a transnational discourse around design education and practice that was emerging during the period. Information exchange with initiatives of design education abroad was promoted through a variety of channels. The Scuola del Libro had reacted promptly to the isolation of the war years by re-establishing connections with an international network of schools and specialist magazines from the late 1940s onwards. A number of letters were sent worldwide to announce the reopening of the school in 1948 and asking recipients 'to exchange technical and didactic informations [sic] and literature'.[93] Educators adopted and adapted ideas of education and practice formulated in design schools abroad. As Steiner clarified, it was not a case of 'following with pretentious laziness one experience or another (e.g., on the one hand the Bauhaus, and on the other the School of Chicago), but of deriving from our own economic, political, sociological, historic, cultural, etc. roots the typical elements that characterise *our own* way of living, thinking and working'.[94]

Steiner's pointing to the Bauhaus and the Institute of Design in Chicago as models for design education was not accidental, as both schools had links to the Scuola del Libro. On the one hand, Steiner had met and collaborated with Bauhaus director Hannes Meyer during his stay in Mexico City in the late 1940s, and Noorda had studied at the Instituut voor Kunstnijverheidsonderwijs (Institute for Education in the Applied Arts) in Amsterdam under the directorship of the Bauhausler Mart Stam. On the other hand, Provinciali and Vignelli had trained at the Institute of Design in Chicago. Provinciali had brought back with him from this experience an emphasis on problem-based learning and a focus on a design-led approach to visual communication. Vignelli was later to base his class at the Scuola del Libro on colour perception on the book *The Color Harmony Manual and How to Use It* (1942) by Egbert Jacobson, the art director of the Container Corporation of America.[95] This was a Chicago-based manufacturer of corrugated boxes whose founder, Walter Paepcke, had championed modern design and sponsored the Institute of Design. In Vignelli's class, students painted innumerable colour charts with different shades of the same colour, so that by the end of the year they ended up with a do-it-yourself version of Jacobson's manual.[96] The exercise trained students' manual skills and sharpened their colour perception. At the same time, it made up for the shortage of didactic material. Until the late 1960s, when there was a flourishing of how-to handbooks, teaching was based on the professional experience of the teachers and supplemented with self-published didactic materials, local and international graphic design and photography magazines, and actual graphic design artefacts.[97]

A cluster of Swiss designers was a further agent of exchange of international educational experiences. As graphic designer and teacher at the Scuola del Libro, Giancarlo Iliprandi put it, 'another key role in [the] Italy–Switzerland relationship was played by the graphic design course for assistants held at the Umanitaria'.[98] Indeed, the faculty could count the Swiss graphic designers Max Huber and Carlo Vivarelli and the photographer Serge Libiszewski among its members. By teaching at the Scuola del Libro, they introduced the Italian graphic design community to 'a method [and] a set of rules' that had been gaining international currency since the end of the war and that Iliprandi considered 'essential' for practitioners like himself who were self-taught.[99] The historiographical canon concerning Swiss graphic design in Milan, according to which better-trained Swiss designers arrived in town and taught the practice to their Italian counterparts, resonates in Iliprandi's words. As we saw in chapter 2 when looking into Antonio Boggeri's recruiting strategies, graphic design education in Switzerland had been deemed a guarantee of quality, precision, technical skills and formal perfection ever since the interwar period. This stereotypical narrative gained currency in the post-war period. Discussed and celebrated in design manuals and in specialist magazines of the time, graphic design education played a key role in establishing the international reputation of Swiss Style, with the Kunstgewerbeschule (School of Applied Arts) in Zurich and the Allgemeine Gewerbeschule (Vocational Trade School) in Basel acting as key players in the articulation of a national design discourse.[100]

Figures 4.11 and 4.12 bring us into the studio in the early 1960s. They portray the students of the Course for Graphic Design Assistants who at the time were referred to by the nickname, the 'sergeants' of graphic design. An article in *Pirelli*, the house organ of the homonymous tyre company for which various teachers at the Scuola del Libro worked, explains the curious nickname: the sergeant of graphic design was the 'studio assistant and not the actual *graphic designer*'.[101] As the author of the article and head of the vocational schools at the Umanitaria, Mario Melino, explained, the Course for Graphic Design Assistants aimed at training the design specialist rather than fuelling the 'megalomania' of the designer. Not all issues of visual communication needed the brilliance of the isolated genius, the 'general', but could equally be solved through a collaboration among 'semi-geniuses', the sergeants. In Melino's interpretation, the expression 'semi-genius' was not derogatory but indicated a hands-on approach to the practice. The sergeants were only the 'preliminary stage of the profession of the graphic designer'.[102] After the diploma, students were to complete their training on-the-job and work as studio assistants. Alternatively, they could continue studying at graduate level. This second option gradually gained currency with the setting up of graduate schools of design in Italy. Between 1960 and 1965, the first

4.11   Bob Noorda and students of the Course for Graphic Design Assistants at the Scuola del Libro in Milan, 1963–64.

4.12   Antonio Tubaro and students of the Course for Graphic Design Assistants at the Scuola del Libro in Milan, 1963–64.

graduate schools of industrial design – CSDI, Corso Superiore di Disegno Industriale (Graduate Course of Industrial Design) – opened in Venice (1960), Florence (1962) and Rome (1965). The Roman CSDI established a graphic design course during the academic year 1967–68 and was renamed Corso Superiore di Disegno Industriale e Comunicazione Visiva. Graphic design had also been taught in Urbino at the Corso Superiore di Arti Grafiche (Graduate Course of Graphic Arts) since 1962.[103]

In the photographs, the viewer's attention is naturally drawn to the female students in the foreground. Their prominent position in the possibly staged shots suggests that their very presence was remarkable. Whereas during the interwar period, as we saw in chapter 1, the student body had been composed almost exclusively of male students, by the late 1950s the daily courses for graphic assistants were also being attended by women. The makeup of the student body mirrored general advances in the levels of female education in post-war Italy. Since the late 1940s, the numbers of girls enrolled in secondary and higher education had increased, while the gender gap in the Italian educational system had been gradually narrowing. The percentage of girls in upper secondary education rose from 37.3 per cent in 1948–49, to 42.4 per cent by 1972–73. The proportion in higher education also grew from 26.3 per cent in 1951, to 27.6 and then 37.5 per cent over the following two decades.[104] The change in gender profile of students at the Scuola del Libro went hand in hand with a diversification in its social class profile: the student body was no longer confined to the sons of printing workers, but extended to also include the sons and daughters of middle-class graduate parents. If we read this demographic change through sociological lenses, it can be regarded as a by-product of the standardisation of professional knowledge. Formalised training, Magali Sarfatti Larson argued, commodifies a practice and encourages new members to access it by reducing the secrecy of the trade and making it more distinct and recognisable to the public.[105] In this view, the diverse student body at the Course for Graphic Design Assistants hints at a better general understanding of the practice and increased appeal to outsiders.

Learning by teaching

Let us now shift the focus away from the students towards the teachers. The Scuola del Libro attracted a number of outstanding local and foreign graphic designers. As such, it satisfied one of the requirements for the development of a specialised body of formal knowledge and skills. This was, as observed by Eliot Freidson, the presence of 'a group of like-minded people who learn and practice it, identify with it, distinguish it from other disciplines, recognise each other as colleagues by virtue of their common training and experience with a common set of tasks, techniques, concepts and working problems'.[106] Steiner, Iliprandi, Provinciali, Vignelli, Noorda, Huber and the other faculty members can be regarded as active members of a 'community of practice', as defined by educational theorist Etienne Wenger: a group of people who share a concern in what they do and who interact to learn how to do it better; practitioners who develop a shared repertoire of resources, engage in joint activities and discussions, share information and learn from each other.[107] As members of a community of practice, they participated in a jointly articulated and mutually understood discourse and negotiated their own identity through shared experiences of education and practice. They contributed to the continuous efforts to artic-ulate an 'uneven sketch' of what constitutes the practice: 'who is involved; what they do; what [their] everyday life is like; ... how people who are not part of the community of practice interact with it; ... and what learners need to learn to become full practitioners'.[108]

While training a new generation of 'sergeants' of graphic design, faculty members set the criteria of access to the practice, established the boundaries of the discipline, developed a shared discourse and outlined their collective identity. Teaching was a way of questioning and defining the requirements and aims of graphic design practice. A proposal for a new course in editorial design was covered with handwritten notes and comments by Steiner. These offer an example of how teachers mutually negotiated the criteria of inclusion or exclusion and delineated borders towards adjacent practices.[109] The twenty pages of detailed description of the editorial designer's profile were scribbled over by Steiner, who criticised the author of the syllabus, Ilio Negri, for confusing roles and tasks. As observed by architectural historians Mark Crinson and Jules Lubbock, 'debates over the content of the curriculum were debates over what the leaders of the profession believed that [they] should be and how their functions differed from those of other professions'.[110] By stress-ing the differences between editorial designers, editors, compositors and copywriters, Steiner was not only clarifying who the editorial designers were, but was also acknowledging a network of practices in an attempt to coordinate relationships between the different members of the publishing industry.

Teaching and learning within the community of practitioners that gath-ered at the Scuola del Libro was an experience of identity formation, 'an issue of refining [the] practice and ensuring new generations of members'.[111] During a lecture at the CSDI in Rome in 1967, Steiner introduced himself as a self-taught graphic designer who had learned the practice on the job. He then added that 'through this ... work experience, [he had] come to realise that it was impossible for the new generations to train for a profession which was involved in more and more areas of intervention in fields that [they] could never have even imagined might exist. And this is why [he had begun] to be interested in Schools.'[112] It was by getting involved in education that graphic designers could contribute to the ongoing articulation of their practice. The time spent with colleagues writing the course syllabi, outlining the professional profile and pinning down the students' requirements helped Iliprandi clarify requirements, aims, tools, tasks and status of a practice for which he, like Steiner, had not been trained. Iliprandi recalled that teachers at the Scuola del Libro 'studied the professional profile bearing in mind the tasks that those kids were expected to fulfil once they had graduated ... [the teachers] looked at the subjects, over and beyond design, that needed to be taught and tried to fill in the blanks'.[113] In sum, design education – seen both as learning and as teaching – was beneficial for the educators themselves, who 'learnt by teaching'.[114]

Post-war design education and graphic designers' responsibility towards society

The ongoing articulation of graphic design practice was the work-in-progress result of continuous negotiation, back and forth from day-to-day practice to the classroom. The analysis of debates around, and experiences of, design education from the reconstruction years to the 1960s I have carried out in this chapter has confirmed education as a key agent in the construction of graphic design practice in Italy. Moreover, I have confronted a common misunderstanding about design education, namely 'the belief that design education must follow behind design practice rather than work as an equal partner'.[115] The Convitti Scuola Rinascita and the Scuola del Libro proved to be crucial in establishing graphic design education in the country. While teaching basic skills and providing a new generation of graphic designers with broader liberal knowledge, social awareness and a sense of responsibility, educators were also engaged in investigating and understanding the nature of graphic design and then acting on this understanding in order to inform their own practice and collective identity. Thus, investigation of the Convitti Scuola Rinascita and the Scuola del Libro has shown that there was a reciprocal relationship between education and practice in design: practice shaped education and was in its turn shaped by education.

This chapter has also highlighted how education was a key factor in the broader quest to imbue design with social value and cultural meaning. By the mid-1950s, however, graphic design's close relationship with advertising and the commercial world was to emerge as a major obstacle to this quest. The next and final chapter of the book addresses the tension between advertising and design. To this end, it situates the changing organisational strategies of graphic designers in Italy within a network of national professional bodies and international design organisations, and contextualises them within transnational discourses around graphics, design and advertising.

Notes

1 R. Sani, 'La scuola e l'educazione alla democraia negli anni del secondo dopoguerra', in M. Corsi and R. Sani (eds), *L'educazione alla democrazia tra passato e presente* (Milan: Vita e Pensiero, 2004), pp. 43–62.

2 R. Buchanan, 'Education and professional practice in design', *Design Issues*, 14:2 (1998), 63–6.

3 P. Ginsborg, *A History of Contemporary Italy: Society and Politics, 1943–1988* (London: Penguin, 1990), pp. 98–101.

4 Anon., *Constitution of the Italian Republic* (Rome: Senato della Repubblica), www.senato.it/documenti/repository/istituzione/costituzione_inglese.pdf, accessed 31 May 2023.

5 D'Amico, *Storia e storie della scuola italiana*, pp. 433–6.

6 On the experience of the Umanitaria and similar organisations in the early postwar period in Milan, see G. Pisano, 'La difficile ripresa dell'associazionismo di massa dopo il Fascismo', in G. Bonini and A. Scalpelli (eds), *Milano fra guerra e dopoguerra* (Bari: De Donato, 1979), pp. 445–51; P. Panza, 'Le istituzioni culturali', in A. Gigli Marchetti (ed.), *L'età della speranza: Milano dalla ricostruzione al boom* (Milan: Skira, 2007), pp. 81–9.

7 'Non tanto si crea e si coltiva un mostro di abilità meccanica, quanto si allena un uomo'. R. Bauer, 'Problemi vivi della istruzione professionale', *Linea Grafica*, 7:1–2 (January–February 1954), 18. On Riccardo Bauer's views on vocational education and his commitment to the re-democratisation of Italy, see M. Melino (ed.), *Riccardo Bauer: la militanza politica, l'opera educativa e sociale, la difesa della pace e dei diritti umani* (Milan: Franco Angeli Editore, 1985).

8 'L'istruzione tecnica professionale deve essere orientata, con chiaro criterio *educativo*, nel senso di potenziare, arricchire la personalità intellettuale e morale dell'allievo, futuro lavoratore'. *Ibid.*

9 For international perspectives on the reform of the education system during the reconstruction years, with a focus on Germany and Japan, see B. M. Puaca, *Learning Democracy: Education Reform in West Germany, 1945–1965* (New York; Oxford: Berghahn Books, 2009); J. W. Dower, *Embracing Defeat: Japan in the Wake of World War II* (London: Allen Lane, 1999), pp. 244–51.

10 Betts, *The Authority of Everyday Objects*, p. 140. On the HfG, see R. Spitz, *HfG Ulm: The View Behind the Foreground. The Political History of the Ulm School of Design 1953–1968* (Stuttgart; London: Edition Axel Menges, 2002); H. Jacob, 'A personal view of an experiment in democracy and design education', *Journal of Design History*, 1:3–4 (1988), 221–34; H. Lindinger (ed.), *La scuola di Ulm: una nuova cultura del progetto* (Genoa: Costa & Nolan, 1988).

11 For discussions of the role played by the HfG in Ulm and the Bauhaus legacy within Cold War politics, see G. Castillo, *Cold War on the Home Front: The Soft Power of Midcentury Design* (Minneapolis: University of Minnesota Press, 2001), pp. 31–57; G. Castillo, 'The Bauhaus in Cold War Germany', in James-Chakraborty (ed.), *Bauhaus Culture*, pp. 171–93.

12 A. Becarelli (ed.), *A Scuola come in fabbrica: l'esperienza dei Convitti Scuola della Rinascita* (Milan: Vangelista Editore, 1978); A. Natta and L. Raimondi (eds), *Scuola e resistenza nei Convitti Rinascita* (Rome: ANPI, 1950); N. Augeri (ed.), *I Convitti della Rinascita* (Milan: Edizioni Aurora, 2016); A. Becarelli (ed.), *Diritto allo studio, dovere di studiare: cinquantennale dei Convitti-Scuola della Rinascita* (Novara: Istituto didattico pedagogico della Resistenza, 1994); F. Pruneri, *La politica scolastica del Partito Comunista Italiano dalle origini al 1955* (Brescia: Editrice La Scuola, 1999), pp. 115–24; F. Pruneri, 'The Convitti Scuola della Rinascita (The Boarding Schools of Rebirth): An innovative pedagogy for democracy in post-war Italy (1945–1955)', *Paedagogica Historica*, 52:1–2 (2016), 188–200.

13 R. A. Ventresca, *From Fascism to Democracy: Culture and Politics in the Italian Election of 1948* (Toronto; London: University of Toronto Press, 2004), p. 7. On the 1948 election, see also Ginsborg, *A History of Contemporary Italy*, pp. 112–20.

14 M. Zanantoni, *Albe Steiner: cambiare il libro per cambiare il mondo. Dalla Repubblica d'Ossola alle Edizioni Feltrinelli* (Milan: Unicopli, 2013), pp. 49–70; G. Mucchi, *Le occasioni perdute: memorie, 1899–1993* (Milan: Mazzotta, 2001); D. Muraca (ed.), *Germano Facetti dalla rappresentazione del lager alla storia del XX secolo* (Cinisello Balsamo: Silvana Editoriale, 2008), pp. 23–73.

15 A. Steiner (ed.), *Licalbe Steiner: grafici partigiani* (Milan: Edizioni Corraini, 2015).

16 'Le prospettive dell'artista grafico – i suoi doveri sociali e sue responsabilità'. AALS, D b. 2 fasc. 1, course syllabus, 'Proposta per un breve corso di storia del carattere, della pubblicità e della propaganda', A. Steiner, 1948.

17 'Progetti, esecuzione e consulenza grafica'. AALS, D b. 2 fasc. 1, promotional pamphlet.

18 AALS, D b. 2 fasc.1, meeting minutes, 'Verbale riunione dei tecnici corso di arti grafiche', 25 February 1949.

19 Lacaita, 'Istruzione tecnico-professionale e modernizzazione fra Otto e Novecento', pp. 16–17.

20 AALS, D b. 2 fasc.1, students' report, 'Corso di Arte Pubblicitaria: relazione degli allievi sull'andamento del corso', 14 October 1949.

21 'Fermamente convinto … che l'indirizzo "liberista" abbia nociuto in modo decisivo all'andamento dell'insegnamento alla disciplina, e anche all'indirizzo spirituale degli allievi'. AALS, D b. 2 fasc. 1, letter from G. Mucchi to the Convitti Scuola Rinascita directorship, 11 October 1949, p. 1.

22 'Gli allievi sono considerati cavie da esperimento per modi e sistemi di lavoro ottimi in altre strutture sociali, ma purtroppo assolutamente utopistici (almeno nel caso specifico del lavoro grafico/pubblicitario) nella struttura sociale dell'Italia d'oggi'. AALS, D b. 2 fasc. 1, letter from L. Veronesi to the Convitti Scuola Rinascita directorship, 18 October 1949, p. 1. See also, AALS, D b. 2 fasc. 1, letter from R. Muratore, M. Huber and C. Conte to the Convitti Scuola Rinascita directorship, 20 October 1949.

23 AALS, D b. 2 fasc. 1, handwritten undated document, 'Proposta Hannes'.

24 A. Maglio, *Hannes Meyer: un razionalista in esilio. Architettura, urbanistica e politica 1930–54* (Milan: Franco Angeli Editore, 2002), pp. 125–6.

25 AALS, D b. 2 fasc. 1, handwritten meeting minutes, 17 April 1950.

26 D. Miliotes, *What May Come: The Taller de Gráfica Popular and the Mexican Political Print* (New Haven; London: Yale University Press, 2014).

27 'Bravissimi comunisti di una onestà indiscussa, la loro attività è per il popolo'. Archivi della Parola, dell'Immagine e della Comunicazione Editoriale, Università degli Studi di Milano, Milan, Italy (hereafter APICE), Fondo Mucchi, b.46 UA1, letter from A. Steiner to G. Mucchi, 26 and 31 July and 1 August 1946.

28 'La Bauhaus si trasferisce … in America del Nord con Moholy-Nagy nella Scuola di Disegno Industriale di Chicago, in America Centrale con Hannes Meyer e in Messico si è chiamata Taller de Grafica Popular'. A. Steiner, *Il mestiere di grafico* (Turin: Einaudi, 1978), p. 9. On Hannes Meyer's contribution to the TGP, see Maglio, *Hannes Meyer*, pp. 42–6.

29 APICE, Fondo Mucchi, b.46 UA1, folder 'Messico – Albe, Lica, Hannes Meyer'.

30 P. Betts, 'The Bauhaus as Cold-War legend: West German modernism revised', *German Politics and Society*, 14:2 (1996), 87. For further discussions about the use of design education as instrument of cultural diplomacy during the Cold War, see G. Castillo, 'Design pedagogy enters the Cold War: The reeducation of eleven West German architects', *Journal of Architectural Education*, 57:4 (2004), 10–18.

31 *Ibid.*, 84.

32 *Ibid.*, 78.

33 'Tutte quelle manifestazioni che per il loro linguaggio chiaro e facilmente comprensibile alle più vaste categorie di persone contribuiscono a dare maggiore conoscenza'. AALS, D b. 2 fasc. 1, handwritten meeting minutes, 4 November 1950.

34 Ginsborg, *A History of Contemporary Italy*, pp. 98–118; Clark, *Modern Italy*, pp. 388–90.

35 M. del Pero, 'Containing containment: Rethinking Italy's experience during the Cold War', *Journal of Modern Italian Studies*, 8:4 (2003), 544.

36 'È giusto o no rifiutare lavoro di tipo capitalistico?'. AALS, D b. 2 fasc. 1, meeting minute, 26 June 1950, p. 2.

37 'Costruzione del nuovo mondo'. *Ibid.*

38 P. Scrivano, 'Signs of Americanization in Italian domestic life: Italy's postwar conversion to consumerism', *Journal of Contemporary History*, 40:2 (2005), 317–40; Scarpellini, *L'Italia dei consumi*, pp. 129–39.

39 Ginsborg, *A History of Contemporary Italy*, p. 215.

40 Fallan, 'Annus mirabilis', pp. 265–7.

41 'I tempi sono maturi per un dibattito approfondito sul tema dell'industrial design e i suoi multiformi rapporti con la società'. I. M. Lombardo, quoted in L. Molinari (ed.), *La memoria e il futuro: I Congresso Internazionale dell'Industrial Design, Triennale di Milano, 1954* (Milan; Geneva: Skira, 2001), p. 17.

42 'Promuovere e favorire l'istituzione di organi culturali atti a sviluppare in Italia l'esperienza e la preparazione dell'industrial designer'. *Ibid.*, p. 101.

43 'Gli enti culturali, gli organismi produttivi … affinché venga istituita a Milano una Scuola di industrial design'. *Ibid.*

44 See A. Grassi and A. Pansera (eds), *L'Italia del design: trent'anni di dibattito* (Casale Manferrato: Marietti, 1986), p. 53; R. De Fusco, *Una storia dell'ADI: 50* (Milan: Franco Angeli Editore, 2010), pp. 66–7; Pansera, *La formazione del designer in Italia*, pp. 48–9.

45 Pansera, *La formazione del designer in Italia*, pp. 38–44.

46 'Questa attività, che per ora da noi è ancora dilettantistica, acquisti l'efficienza, l'autorità e la possibilità di tutela di una *professione autorizzata*'. G. Castelli, 'La I riunione dell'A.D.I. a Milano', *Stile Industria*, 3:7 (June 1956), 3.

47 'Carattere educativo e culturale … per elevare le condizioni professionali dei disegnatori industraili in tutti i paesi'. E. Peressutti's speech at the first ICSID meeting, London, 29 June 1957, quoted in Grassi and Pansera (eds), *L'Italia del design*, p. 43.

48 Anon., 'Congresso dell'ICSID a Venezia', *Stile Industria*, 8:34 (October 1961), 1–28.

49 'Mancando un sistema didattico che dia continuità alla pratica di una professione, e senza un insieme di conoscenze indispensabili per l'esercizio professionale: non v'è professione'. P. Müller-Munk, 'Il design esiste come professione', *Stile Industria*, 8:34 (October 1961), 14.

50 'La formazione del disegnatore industriale è generalmente confusa e contraddittoria, la causa di ciò sta principalmente nel fatto che la totalità del disegno industriale, in quanto professione e filosofia di una professione, continua ad essere confusa e contraddittoria.' T. Maldonado, 'Formazione e alternative di una professione', *Stile Industria*, 8:34 (October 1961), 21.

51 'Per lungo tempo, il disegnatore industriale è stato più impegnato a "fare" che a prendere coscienza del suo "fare", più ad estendere la sua attività, che ad approfondirla. … Ma la nuova professione … ha già da tempo cessato di essere agli "inizi". Ne deriva che l'attenta riflessione su se stessa, la chiarificazione dei suoi propri fini e metodi, oggi non è più un lusso, ma una necessità. E una necessità urgente'. *Ibid.*

52 'Documentazione dell'insegnamento dell'*Industrial Design* in due delle maggiori scuole al mondo'. P. C. Santini (ed.), *12ª Triennale di Milano* (Milan: Arti Grafiche Crespi, 1960), p. 34.

53 'Il tema è talmente urgente ed ancora senza una risoluzione organica che non sarà mai eccessivo lo spazio dedicato a quanto viene oggi fatto anche fuori dal nostro paese, agli interventi ed al consiglio di quelle personalità che si sono formate una particolare esperienza in questo tema.' A. Rosselli, 'L'insegnamento del disegno industriale e la realtà produttiva', *Stile Industria*, 6:21 (March 1959), 1.

54 'Non è quindi facile valutare l'interesse di una esperienza effettuata in paesi così diversi dal nostro, ma è senz'altro pericoloso pensare di poter trapiantare sistemi e procedimenti di questi paesi in Italia.' A. Rosselli, 'Per una scuola di disegno industriale in Italia', *Stile Industria*, 5:17 (June 1958), 1.

55 G. Anceschi and P. G. Tanca, 'Ulm e l'Italia', in Lindinger (ed.), *La Scuola di Ulm*, p. 248; Pansera, *La formazione del designer in Italia*, pp. 51–3; R. Riccini, 'Tomás Maldonado and the impact of the Hochschule für Gestaltung Ulm in Italy', in Lees-Maffei and Fallan (eds), *Made in Italy*, pp. 89–105.

56 T. Maldonado, 'L'insegnamento superiore e la crisi dell'educazione', *Civiltà delle Macchine*, 5–6 (May–June 1957), 82–9; T. Maldonado, 'Scienza, tecnologia e forma', *Stile Industria*, 5:18 (August 1958), 44; T. Maldonado, 'Le nuove prospettive industriali e la formazione del designer', *Stile Industria*, 6:20 (January 1959), XIX–XXIV. On Tomás Maldonado and the Ulm model, see Betts, *The Authority of the Everyday Objects*, pp. 154–7 and 168–73; P. Betts, 'Science, semiotics and society: The Ulm Hochschule für Gestaltung in retrospect', *Design Issues*, 14:2 (1998), 67–82; Castillo, 'The Bauhaus in Cold War Germany', pp. 186–8. See also T. Maldonado, *Disegno industriale: un riesame* (Milan: Feltrinelli, 2008), pp. 45–69; T. Maldonado, *Arte e artefatti: intervista di Hans Ulrich Obrist* (Milan: Feltrinelli, 2010), pp. 28–34.

57 A. T. Anselmi, 'Hochschule für Gestaltung, Ulm: documenti di una scuola di disegno industriale', *Stile Industria*, 6:21 (March 1959), 3–20.

58 'Preparare tutta quella categoria di specialisti, che solitamente si designano col nome di grafici e che va conquistando un sempre più ampio campo d'azione e di impegno nella vita moderna'. P. C. Santini, 'La Scuola di Ulm: organizzazione e metodi di lavoro', *Comunità*, 72 (August–September 1959), reprinted in *Notizie AIAP*, 89 (May 1999), 16.

59 'Il più chiaro rapporto possibile fra i messaggi e il pubblico … appoggiandosi … alle cognizioni derivanti dalla teoria della percezione e dalla semiotica'. *Ibid.*

60 'Cittadella del design … qualcosa di completamente nuovo'. G. Dorfles, interview with the author, Milan, 11 March 2016.

61 'Così finalmente diventerà un designer'. *Ibid.*

62 Riccini, 'Tomás Maldonado and the impact of the Hochschule für Gestaltung Ulm in Italy', p. 91.

63 G. Anceschi, 'Design di base, fondamenta del design', *Ottagono*, 70 (September 1983), reprinted in *Notizie AIAP*, 10 (June 2000), 18–28.

64 G. Castelli, 'Le scuole di industrial design in Inghilterra', *Stile Industria*, 5:18 (August 1958), 37–8; M. Black, 'The Royal College of Art', *Stile Industria*, 8:32 (May 1961), 2–9.

65 R. Salvadori, 'La nuova grafica inglese e il Royal College of Art', *Linea Grafica*, 17:3–4 (March–April 1964), 105–8. Earlier information on the School of Graphic Design at RCA was published abroad in international graphic design magazines. See, for example, Meyer, 'Royal College of Art London', *Gebrauchsgraphik*, 30: 10 (October1959), 20–5; Meyer, 'ARK: The students' magazine of the Royal College of Art in London', *Gebrauchsgraphik*, 31:4 (April 1960), 36–43; R. Guyatt, 'The School of Graphic Design of the RCA, London', *Graphis*, 15:84 (July–August 1959), 290–307 and 398–9.

66 For a critical reading of the exhibition, see T. Triggs, A. Shaughnessy and A. Gerber (eds), *GraphicsRCA: Fifty Years and Beyond* (London, Royal College of Art, 2014); T. Triggs, 'Curating graphic design and its history', in Lzicar and Fornari

(eds), *Mapping Graphic Design History in Switzerland*, pp. 18–44. On the activity of the School of Graphic Design at the RCA, see also A. Seago, *Burning the Box of Beautiful Things: The Development of a Postmodern Sensibility* (Oxford: Oxford University Press, 1995), pp. 25–48; C. Frayling, *Art and Design: 100 Years at the Royal College of Art* (London: Collins & Brown, 1999), pp. 252–309.

67 'Livello medio che è certo tra i più alti del mondo'. Salvadori, 'La nuova grafica inglese e il Royal College of Art', 108.

68 R. Guyatt, 'Graphic Design at the Royal College of Art', in Anon., *GraphicsRCA: Fifteen Years' Work of the School of Graphic Design, Royal College of Art* (London: Lion & Unicorn Press, 1963), pp. 21–2.

69 *Ibid.*, p. 22.

70 H. Foster, 'The Bauhaus idea in America', in A. Borchardt-Hume (ed.), *Albers and Moholy-Nagy: From the Bauhaus to the New World* (London: Tate Publishing, 2006), pp. 92–102; A. Findeli, *Le Bauhaus de Chicago: l'œvre pédagogique de László Moholy-Nagy* (Sillery: Septentrion, 1995).

71 M. Provinciali, 'Institute of Design', *Bollettino del Centro Studi Grafici*, 8:53 (May 1953), n. p. See also M. Provinciali, 'I martedì del Centro: elementi per una sintassi della forma', *Bollettino del Centro Studi Grafici*, 8:65 (May 1964), n. p.; A. Mangiarotti, 'Institute of Design di Chicago: esperienze di insegnamento', *Stile Industria*, 2:4 (April 1955), 7–11; A. Rosselli, 'Design italiano a Chicago', *Stile Industria*, 6:23 (July 1959), 1; J. Doblin, 'Institute of Design Chicago', *Stile Industria*, 6:24 (September 1959), 1–5.

72 'Rendendole più mediterranee, meno nordiche'. M. Provinciali, 'Nel regno della sperimentazione', in Della Campa and Colombo (eds), *Spazio ai caratteri*, p. 126.

73 'L'opportunità di verificare sul posto la validità o meno del tipo di insegnamento fornito dalla Bauhaus, seppure nella blanda versione americana'. M. Vignelli, 'Umanitaria, anni '60. Un'aria nuova per la grafica', in Della Campa and Colombo (eds), *Spazio ai caratteri*, p. 134.

74 J. Conradi, *Unimark International: The Design of Business and the Business of Design* (Baden: Lars Müller, 2010).

75 'La gara di offerte è aperta. Dia chi può! La Scuola del Libro di Milano deve risorgere dalle rovine … più bella, più fattiva, più moderna, più viva, più italiana'. ASSU, script of a radio speech, P. Trevisani, 'Per la Scuola del Libro: radio conversazione', 31 January 1947, p. 2.

76 ASSU, 1945–66, letter from E. Palazzo and L. d'Aragona to the Federazione Italiana Operai Poligrafici, 22 September 1945; ASSU, 1948–35, meeting minutes, 'Consorzio della Scuola del Libro della Società Umanitaria: seduta del 15 Marzo 1948, ore 21', 15 March 1948, pp. 3–5.

77 'Quale sarà la situazione del campo grafico milanese? Senza dubbio grave, mano d'opera insufficientemente preparata, nessuna immissione di nuove energie per far fronte ai molti bisogni della risorgente attività industriale.' ASSU, 1945–66, untitled document by E. Palazzo, 28 August 1945, p. 1.

78 V. Zamagni, *The Economic History of Italy, 1860–1990* (Oxford: Clarendon Press, 1993), p. 321.

79 Forgacs, *L'industrializzazione della cultura italiana*, p. 143.

80 B. Pischedda, 'Editoria a Milano: 1945–1970. Gli anni dell'entusiasmo', in Montecchi (ed.), *La città dell'editoria*, pp. 125–39; L. Cavalli, 'Editoria: un'età d'oro dell'editoria italiana', in G. Aghina and A. Marangoni (eds), *Anni Cinquanta: la nascita della creatività italiana* (Milan: Skira, 2005), pp. 51–5; Ortoleva, 'A geography of the media since 1945', pp. 189–90. For a broader perspective on the economy of post-war Milan, see V. Castronovo, 'L'economia milanese alla fine della guerra e il confronto sugli obbiettivi della ricostruzione', in Bonini and Scalpelli (eds), *Milano fra guerra e dopoguerra*, pp. 7–34.

81 Dower, *Embracing Defeat*, p. 180.

82   A. L. Carlotti, 'Editori e giornali a Milano: continuità e cambiamento', in F. Colombo (ed.), *Libri, giornali e riviste a Milano. Storia delle innovazioni nell'editoria milanese dall'Ottocento ad oggi* (Milan: Editrice Abitare Segesta, 1998), pp. 179–90; A. Cardioli and G. Vigini, *Storia dell'editoria italiana: un profilo introduttivo* (Milan: Editrice Bibliografica, 2004), pp. 87–98.

83   A. Vittoria, *I luoghi della cultura. Istituzioni, riviste e circuiti intellettuali nell'Italia del Novecento* (Rome: Carocci, 2021), p. 143.

84   G. Barazzetta, 'Sede e scuole della Società Umanitaria', *Casabella*, 750–1 (December 2006–January 2007), 10–15; G. Romano, 'La ricostruzione dell'Umanitaria a Milano', *Casabella Continuità*, 214 (February–March 1957), 28.

85   Enrico Gianni's report featured the following schools: Höhere Fachschule für das Graphische Gewerbe (Stuttgart), Meisterschule für Deutschlands Buchdrucker (Munich), Druck und Verlagshaus (Frankfurt), Brönners Druckerei (Frankfurt), Druckerei Waisbecker (Frankfurt), Frankfürter Neue Presse (Frankfurt), Kust Gewerbe Schule der Stadt Zürich (Zurich). See ASSU, 1952–183, report by E. Gianni, 'Annotazioni: studi per la ricostruzione della Scuola del Libro di Milano della Società Umanitaria', 5 August 1953, p. 1.

86   'Vero esempio di moderna e razionale architettura scolastica: officina per l'addestramento tecnico e in pari tempo centro di elevazione morale e civile'. R. Bauer, *Scuola del Libro: programmi di insegnamento, anno scolastico 1954–1955* (Milan: Società Umanitaria, 1954), n. p.

87   'Punti nodali dello sviluppo sociale, e civile … fornirgli gli strumenti di linguaggio e l'atteggiamento critico'. ASSU, 'Corso serale per assistenti grafici: organizzazione e programmi', course outline, 22 October 1965, p. 3.

88   'È il punto a cui convergono gli insegnamenti teorici, e da cui si dipartono le esercitazioni pratiche; quello in cui l'allievo deve gradualmente giungere alla efficace, ragionata e razionale espressione grafica, avendo agio di manifestare il proprio linguaggio personale'. *Ibid.*, p. 11.

89   'Non secondo schemi astratti, o predilezioni personali dell'autore, ma in funzione del materiale, del prodotto, del pubblico a cui si rivolge, ecc.'. AALS, D b. 22 fasc. 1, report, 'Relazione sull'attività della Scuola del Libro nell'anno scolastico 1964–65', 1965.

90   AALS, D b. 22 fasc. 1, course syllabi by A. Steiner, 'Programma del II anno Corso Tecnico-Artistico per Grafici: paragrafo 9. progettazione, 1961/1962', 1961.

91   AALS, D b. 22 fasc. 1, correspondence between A. Steiner and the Casa Editrice Sansoni, 1959–60.

92   B. Noorda, 'Eravamo una squadra molto affiatata', in Della Campa and Colombo (eds), *Spazio ai Caratteri*, p. 143.

93   The letter was written in English, French and Italian and sent in July 1948. The London School of Printing, the New York School of Printing, the American Institute of Graphic Arts, the Carnegie Institute of Technology in Pittsburgh, the Grafiske Højskole in Copenhagen, the School of Printing in Bristol, Associacion Industriales Graficos in Buenos Aires and the Graphic School in Amsterdam responded to the request for information exchange. ASSU, 1948–35 and 1948–39, correspondence.

94   'Non si tratta di seguire con presuntuosa pigrizia una esperienza o un'altra (da un lato per esempio la Bauhaus e dall'altro la Scuola di Chicago) ma di trarre dalle nostre stesse radici economiche, politiche, sociali, storiche, culturali ecc. tutti gli elementi tipicamente caratteristici del *nostro* modo di vivere, di pensare e di operare'. A. Steiner, 'La mostra a fine anno alla Scuola del Libro della Società Umanitaria', *Linea Grafica*, 16:7–8 (July–August 1961), 239.

95   E. Jacobson, *The Color Harmony Manual and How to Use It* (Chicago: Container Corporation of America, 1942).

96   Vignelli, 'Umanitaria, anni '60', pp. 134–5.

97 ASSU, 1962–509, correspondence between the Scuola del Libro and Studio Repetto (Turin), October 1962–January 1963.

98 G. Iliprandi, 'An Interview with Giancarlo Iliprandi', in Georgi and Minetti (eds), *Italian Design Is Coming Home*, p. 19.

99 *Ibid.*, p. 18.

100 J. Müller-Brockmann, *Gestaltungsproboeme des Grafikers/The Graphic Artist and his Design Problems/Les problems d'un artiste graphique* (Teufen: Niggli, 1961); A. Hofmann, *Methodik der Form- und Bildgestaltung. Aufbau – Synthese – Anwendung//* Manuel de création graphique/*Graphic Design Manual. Principles and Practice* (Teufen: Niggli, 1965); E. Ruder, *Typographie* (Sulgen: Niggli, 1965).

101 'L'assistente di studio e non il *graphic designer* vero e propio'. M. Melino, 'I sergenti della grafica', *Pirelli*, 6 (December 1962), 104.

102 'Stadio preliminare alla professione del graphic designer'. Anon., *Società Umanitaria: relazione sull'attività sociale dal 1956 al 1960* (Milan: Società Umanitaria, 1960), p. 44.

103 S. Bastianelli and B. Fabbri, 'CSAG di Urbino: la prima scuola italiana di graphic design', *Progetto Grafico*, 24 (2013), 58–64; G. Trozzi, 'Quelli di via Conte Verde: per una storia del Corso di Disegno Industriale e Comunicazioni Visive di Roma', *Progetto Grafico*, 1 (2003), 102–5; M. Pastore, 'Il Corso Superiore di Design Industriale di Venezia 1960/1971: la comunicazione visiva nell'offerta didattica e il suo ruolo nella formazione di nuove figure professionali' (MA dissertation, IUAV, Venice, 2007).

104 P. Willson, *Women in Twentieth-Century Italy* (New York: Palgrave Macmillan, 2010), p. 117.

105 Sarfatti Larson, *The Rise of Professionalism*, pp. 42–6.

106 Freidson, *Professionalism*, p. 202.

107 Wenger, *Communities of Practice*, pp. 72–85.

108 J. Lave and E. Wenger, *Situated Learning: Legitimate Peripheral Participation* (Cambridge: Cambridge University Press, 1991), p. 95.

109 AALS, D b. 22 fasc. 1, undated course syllabus by I. Negri, 'Grafica editoriale'.

110 M. Crinson and J. Lubbock, *Architecture: Art or Profession? Three Hundred Years of Architectural Education in Britain* (Manchester: Manchester University Press, 1994), p. 2.

111 Wenger, *Communities of Practice*, p. 7.

112 'Attraverso quest'attività … mi sono reso conto che era impossibile che le nuove generazioni si preparassero ad una professione che aveva sempre più settori di intervento in zone che noi nemmeno si era pensato che potessero esistere. È per questo che ho cominciato ad interessarmi di Scuola.' Steiner, *Il mestiere di grafico*, p. 7.

113 'Abbiamo studiato il profilo professionale, tenendo in mente quello che poi si sarebbe richiesto a questi ragazzi una volta finita la scuola … vedevamo quali erano le materie che andavano insegnate, a parte progettazione, cercavamo di tappare tutti i buchi'. G. Iliprandi, interview with the author, Milan, 2 April 2014.

114 'E insegnando imparavo'. P. Tovaglia, in Anon., *Milano 70/70: un secolo d'arte, 1946–1970* (Milan: Museo Poldi-Pezzoli, 1971), p. 170.

115 Buchanan, 'Education and professional practice in design', 64.

5

The multiple identities of graphic design*

Ever since the mid-1950s, graphic designers in Italy have been members of one or other, or even both, of two distinct professional organisations: the Aiap and the ADI. Both associations were founded in Milan, in 1955 and 1956 respectively, and are still active today. But while the Aiap was the offspring of the interwar alliance between graphics and advertising, the ADI offered graphic designers the opportunity to renegotiate their professional identity in relation to industrial designers. The twofold choice of membership stems from the multiple collective identities of graphic designers and their flexible position at the intersection between two allegedly incompatible fields: advertising and design.

How and why the tension between advertising and design became a central and enduring feature in the professionalisation of graphic design practice is the main concern of this last chapter. In exploring how the organisational strategies of graphic designers in Italy changed from the mid-1950s and over the course of the 1960s, it focuses on internal and external conflicts, negotiations, alliances and compromise positions between and across groups.[1] Whereas in chapter 2 we saw that graphics and advertising were closely connected during the interwar period, this chapter shows how in the post-war period their relationship came to play a problematic role as it hindered graphic designers' claim to a place within the design community. This changed attitude can be contextualised within the contemporary emergence of a more systematic, socially committed and culturally sensitive approach to visual communication that was shared by a self-proclaimed international design community. At issue, then, is how graphic designers' collective identity was renegotiated with neighbouring practices and how local changes mirrored shifting transnational graphic design discourses.

The Aiap and the shaky alliance between graphics and advertising

In its very name – Associazione Italiana Artisti Pubblicitari (Italian Association of Advertising Artists) – the Aiap was evidence of the often-neglected relationship between graphic design and advertising, a relationship that was to play a problematic role in the ongoing definition of graphic design practice during the 1950s and 1960s.[2] The Aiap's foundation in 1955 followed the break-up of the ATAP into two separate organisations. The ATAP had united advertising technicians and artists under the same category since 1945. As we saw in chapter 2, advertising technicians and artists were actually two distinct figures that had slowly been emerging in the advertising industry from the interwar period onwards. The advertising technicians, for their part, considered advertising as a new branch of business administration and their work as science based. They followed the principles of rationalisation and efficiency, in line with a US-inspired approach to advertising that had gradually taken root in Italy during the post-war years. The advertising artists, on the other hand, were in charge of the conception of all types of promotional printed matter. Their category encompassed poster artists, illustrators, commercial artists and graphic practitioners. After a decade working together, the coexistence came to an end: advertising technicians and advertising artists went their separate ways and established the TP, Tecnici Pubblicitari (Advertising Technicians) and the Aiap.[3]

During its formative years, the Aiap functioned mainly as a social club for the Milanese graphics scene. Weekly dinners, parties and field trips provided occasions for informal networking, thus promoting comradeship and facilitating information exchange. However, simultaneously with this social agenda, the association formulated a more cogent political strategy in an attempt to carve out a professional status for its members. In line with sociologist Geoffrey Millerson's definition of 'qualifying association', the Aiap aimed at becoming a mediator and a guarantor of inter- and intra-professional, professional–client and professional–public relationships.[4] Its efforts at formulating and promoting a code of conduct and establishing a set of basic conditions of employment demonstrated its commitment to shaping the professional status and identity of its members, advancing and protecting their interests.

The Premio Giarrettiera Pubblicitaria (Advertising Garter Award) gives a sense of the rather light-hearted and irreverent atmosphere prevailing in the Aiap.[5] The peculiar name of the award referred to the restaurant just outside the Galleria Vittorio Emanuele II, the Taverna della Giarrettiera (Tavern of the Garter), where members used to meet weekly, and it was also an ironic take on the British Order of the Garter. The award itself consisted of an actual garter and a satirical drawing. This latter was made by a fellow member and signed by all attendees at the evening.

The campista, Carlo Dradi, was awarded the Premio Giarrettiera Pubblicitaria in 1956 (see figure 5.1).[6] The award plate features Dradi's logo for the Hotel Jolly with the caricatured profile of the graphic designer forming the top of the J. In 1962, Dradi returned the favour and made the award plate for the Turin-based type designer, Aldo Novarese (see figure 5.2). Pasted on the silhouette of a shank, the top of Novarese's head opens up and letters and numbers of varying colours and fonts spill out.

Although in the minority, women have been part of the Aiap since its foundation. Five of the seventy founding members were women: Umberta Barni and Brunetta Mateldi from Milan, Alda Sassi from Turin, Annaviva Traverso from Savona and Celeste Visigalli from Rome. Their number grew in the subsequent years. In 1963, thirteen of the 199 members were women.[7] If we look at these figures in percentage terms, however, the female contingent of the Aiap remained virtually unchanged, in fact it shrank slightly from 7 per cent in 1955 to 6.5 per cent in 1963. These figures mirror the situation described by gender historian Perry Willson in her study of women in twentieth-century Italy. The rates of women's employment, Willson pointed out, stagnated until the early 1970s. Only about a third of Italian women were employed during the 1950s and 1960s and, notwithstanding the modest increase in clerical and service jobs, 'overall numbers of "economically active women" remained stable at 4,913,853 in 1951 and 4,864,131 in 1961'.[8]

Membership of the Aiap encompassed both exponents of a more traditional approach to graphics and promoters of a different perspective on visual communication that was to gain increasing support in response to the shifting of graphic design discourses. Members included well-known figures of early-twentieth-century poster art, such as Marcello Dudovich, Sepo (Severo Pozzati) and Federico Seneca, and protagonists of the interwar update of Italian graphics in line with modernist aesthetics and techniques, such as Giovanni Pintori and Erberto Carboni. A younger generation of graphic designers, represented by Franco Grignani, Angelo G. Fronzoni and Pino Tovaglia, also subscribed. Perhaps inevitably, the coexistence of such a diversity of approaches to graphics was going to be challenged in the 1960s, when Aiap members began questioning the pertinence of both the term 'advertising' and 'artist' in the name of the association.

During the post-war period, the alliance between graphics and advertising was gradually undermined by the arrival, establishment and takeover of US-inspired full-service advertising agencies, such as CPV, Radar&Benson, J. Walter Thompson and McCann Erickson. As mass media scholar Simona De Iulio and Carlo Vinti observed – in a similar manner to what was happening to the advertising cultures of other European countries – the Americanisation of Italian advertising was a phenomenon of cultural transfer that took the form of cultural resistance, transformation and hybridisation.[9]

risolvere in concreto il problema; 15) il problema delle sensibilità, dell'equilibrio e dell'autodelimitazione si può definire un problema non particolarmente tecnico: è tuttavia indispensabile una formazione tecnica, specifica per l'impiego razionale dei mezzi idonei allo svolgimento delle relazioni pubbliche in ogni organismo e al di fuori di esso.

I premi per le P.R.

Durante la conferenza sono stati proclamati i vincitori dei premi istituiti dall'A.I.R.P. per i migliori programmi di relazioni pubbliche svolti da enti statali e privati nel corso del 1956. Questi premi consistenti in due targhe ed in una medaglia d'oro sono stati rispettivamente assegnati alla società Shell Italiana, alla Prefettura di Vicenza e alla società Esso Standard Italiana. Quattro diplomi al merito sono stati inoltre consegnati alla società Althea di Parma, all'Ispettorato Agrario Compartimentale per le Venezie, alla società Nebiolo di Torino e alla Rinascente di Milano. Un attestato è stato pure dato al dott. Vittorio Follini, direttore dell'Airworld Economics Information Service.

●

Comitato di Coordinamento tra l'A.I. Relazioni Pubbliche e l'Istituto Italiano P.R.

Si sono riuniti a Roma e a Milano i Consigli Direttivi dell'Associazione Italiana per le Relazioni Pubbliche e dell'Istituto per le Relazioni Pubbliche sotto la Presidenza del Cav. Gr. Cr. Umberto Baldini e dell'on. Roberto Tremelloni.

Preso atto del sempre maggiore sviluppo che le Relazioni Pubbliche stanno incontrando in Italia; considerata la necessità che i programmi di studio e di divulgazione e le attività e le iniziative attuate in questo settore dalle singole organizzazioni si uniformino a degli standards validi per l'Italia; riconosciuta la opportunità che l'inquadramento professionale e l'esame dei problemi relativi allo sviluppo della professione e dei servizi relativi trovino un organico inquadramento: i rispettivi Consigli Direttivi hanno formulato il voto che l'associazione Italiana per le Relazioni Pubbliche e l'Istituto Italiano per le Pubbliche Relazioni operino in piena unità di intenti e di programmi.

È stata perciò deliberata la formazione di un Comitato di Coordinamento composto dai due Presidenti e dai segretari: dott. Guido de Rossi del Lion Nero e dott. Lorenzo Manconi, che esamini e attui le iniziative indispensabili al raggiungimento degli scopi sopraddetti nell'ambito della Segreteria unica sul Fattore Umano affidata al dott. Cima Tonelli, segretario di presidenza dell'AIRP.

●

Un ufficio che legge migliaia di giornali

L'Eco della Stampa fondata nel 1901, vi rimette giorno per giorno articoli ritagliati da giornali e riviste a lui che riguardino una persona e sia un argomento, secondo l'ordinazione che avete dato. La sua sede è in Milano - Via Giuseppe Compagnoni, 28 - e potrebbe ricevere le condizioni di abbonamento, inviando un semplice biglietto da visita.

La "giarrettiera" pubblicitaria a Carlo Dradi

Un numeroso gruppo di artisti e di tecnici pubblicitari ha inaugurato, la sera di mercoledì 3 ottobre, alla Taverna della Giarrettiera di Milano, la ripresa degli «incontri» conviviali, così brillantemente iniziati nella decorsa primavera.

Intorno a Carlo Dradi, festeggiato dai colleghi, che si sono felicitati con lui per il conferimento del Premio Lorilleux, erano, fra gli altri, il prof. Ricas, vice-presidente della F.I.P., Franco Mosca, presidente e arch. Grignani vice-presidente dell'A.I.A.P., Dino Villani, le pittrici Umberta Barni ed Elda Mafalda Torreani, Attilio Rossi e il nostro direttore.

Al termine della simpatica riunione è stata consegnata a Carlo Dradi la «giarrettiera pubblicitaria», illustrata felicemente dall'arguto pennello di Gian Rossetti. Come di rito, nessun discorso, ma molto brio e molta cordialità.

●

Mercoledì, 7 novembre artisti, tecnici pubblicitari e tecnici della cinematografia pubblicitaria si sono riuniti alla "Giarrettiera" di Milano per festeggiare Nino Pagot. Ne daremo più ampia notizia nel prossimo numero.

Dradi ammira l'originale «menù» disegnato da Gian Rossetti.

Grafici e pubblicitari

Scrive Piero Castellenghi nell'«Italia Grafica»:

«I grafici siano presenti alle manifestazioni pubblicitarie e facciano sentire la loro voce in senso costruttivo: l'assenteismo e le pubbliche lamentele non contribuiscono a migliorare la situazione. E comunque utile e necessario che ai congressi organizzati dai pubblicitari partecipino anche alcuni grafici qualificati non soltanto come semplici osservatori, ma anche per intervenire ad esprimere il pensiero di una categoria che alla pubblicità dà un sostanziale ed insostituibile contributo».

Molto giusto. E i grafici saranno i benvenuti nei Congressi della Pubblicità. Arrivederci dunque a Trieste, nel prossimo maggio.

Artisti e tecnici pubblicitari festeggiano Carlo Dradi alla «Taverna della Giarrettiera» di Milano. Da sinistra: Franco Mosca, Umberta Barni, Gian Rossetti, Carmelo Cremonesi, Pino Tovaglia e in primo piano a destra Dino Villani.

7

5.1 Page from La Pubblicità: Bollettino Mensile della FIP e Associazioni Aderenti, 10:10 (October 1956), 7, featuring the campista Carlo Dradi receiving the Premio Giarrettiera Pubblicitaria, and a group photo with Aiap members at the Taverna della Giarrettiera (Milan).

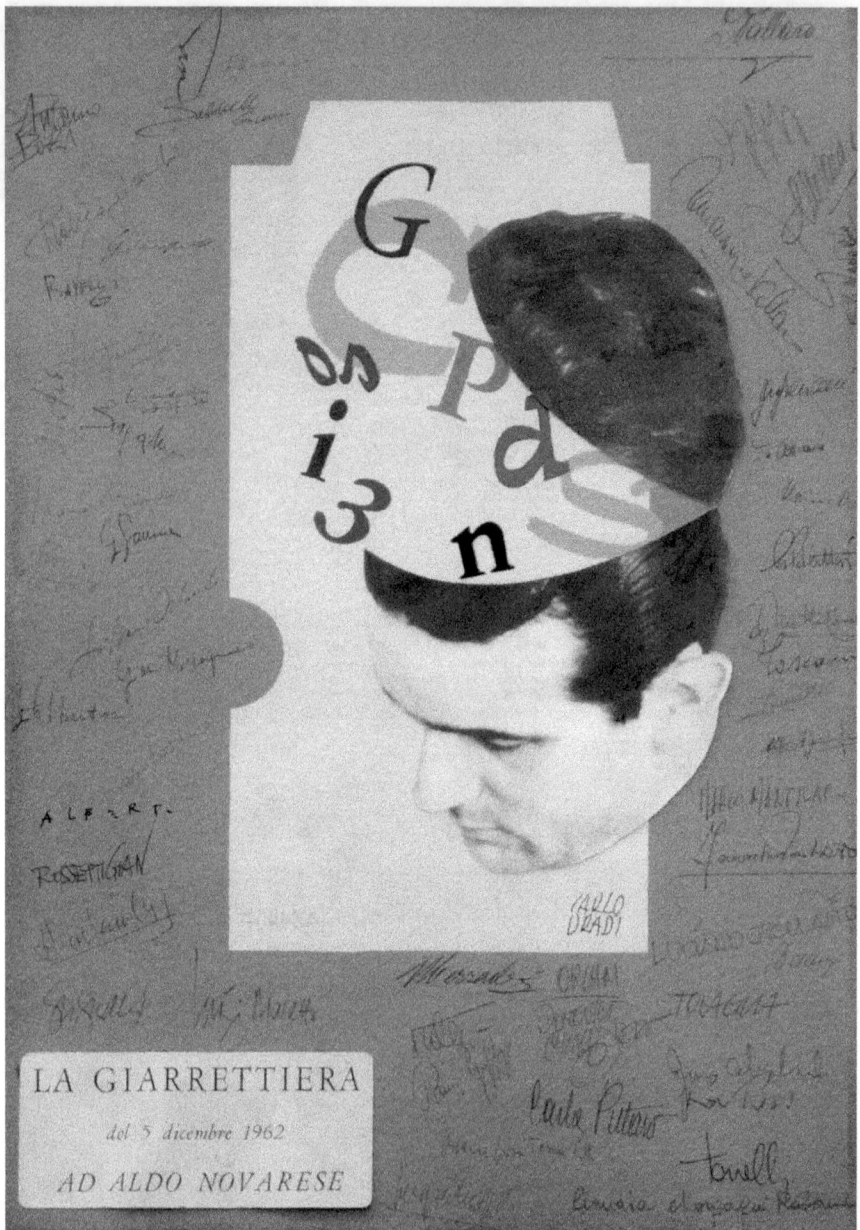

5.2   Premio Giarrettiera Pubblicitaria for Aldo Novarese, designed by Carlo Dradi, 1962.

US-inspired agencies found in Italy's main industries what they considered to be an inadequate advertising system, one often based on the close partnership between leading graphic designers and the in-house Advertising or Propaganda Departments. Italian advertising communication that pre-dated the dissemination of US-inspired practices privileged the representation of industry and production over commerce and consumption. It emphasised a company's identity rather than appealing to consumers' desires. By contrast, the US approach was marketing driven and consumer oriented. It was based on a division of labour and specialisation of tasks that downgraded the advertising artist from main character to one of the many actors involved in the process.[10] US-inspired advertising experts contested the effectiveness of local approaches: they considered graphic designers' visual experimentations detached from and unintelligible to the general public, and hence ineffective as advertising material. In their defence, their Italian counterparts accused the agencies of being more concerned with market research and media planning than with visual research and graphic invention. They criticised the mediocre standard of visual communication based on market surveys that was aimed at persuading and deceiving the consumer instead of upholding the cultural and aesthetic responsibilities towards the public that Italian graphics had previously taken upon itself.[11] Key figures from Italian culture and industry joined the discussions in defence of the pedagogical function of advertising and of its role in educating public taste.[12]

Despite attempts at mediation and compromise, by the early 1960s the gradual shift towards a more Americanised concept of advertising had put graphic designers' central role in advertising communication in jeopardy. However, while US-inspired full-service agencies were threatening to considerably reduce the field of action of graphic designers, or even to make them entirely redundant, Italian graphics for its part was leaning ever more decisively towards design. Ironically, graphic designers were asking permission to enter the design domain but were being looked down upon by industrial designers because of their compromising relationship with advertising.

The ADI and the poor relations of industrial design

The ADI, much like the Aiap, focused its activities primarily on securing the professional status of its members. This aim was pursued both internally – by building unity within the design community based on a shared set of professional knowledge, behaviour and goals – and externally – by promoting the practice and validating its social and economic status within society at large.[13] Locally, it teamed up with the Milan Triennale; internationally, it subscribed to ICSID.[14] As we saw in chapter 4, design education was one of the main concerns of the association. Commercial aims and professional goals were merged when it came to the criteria for the Compasso d'Oro (Golden Compass) award, that had been in the hands of the ADI since 1962.[15] But unlike the Aiap, ADI membership had been heterogeneous from the outset. Alongside industrial designers, the association welcomed architects, graphic designers, industrialists and intellectuals. Such heterogeneous membership suggests there was wide recognition of the ADI and broad support for its agenda. The involvement of industrialists and intellectuals ensured a tighter relationship between the realms of design, production and culture, as well as better political leverage at a governmental and institutional level. Yet, this diversity also made the association vulnerable to internal conflicts between in-groups with different access to power, status and prestige.[16]

Indeed, the membership of graphic designers in an industrial design association was not without its potential contradictions.[17] Practitioners like Marcello Nizzoli and Bruno Munari were active in both fields of graphic and product design. The crossover between design practices may explain why they were members of the ADI. However, a comment by the design critic Gillo Dorfles about Albe Steiner's involvement in the ADI hints at a rather different and more compelling explanation. According to Dorfles, an ADI member himself, Steiner was in fact driven by 'the opportunity to include graphics – that is *graphic design* – within the sphere of industrial design [and] confer the "status" of industrial design not only to graphic design applied in three dimensions, but also to that in two dimensions, as long as it was subsumed within a programmatic whole'.[18] Dorfles's words suggest that the ADI provided graphic designers with an institutional platform to stake claims for recognition as an independent practice that deserved to be re-categorised within the design domain. Graphic designers' involvement in the ADI was thus strategic. Whereas in the Aiap they could only compare themselves to, and negotiate their practice with, advertising technicians, within the organisational context of the ADI they were given the opportunity to articulate their professional identity in relation to the dominant in-group of industrial designers.[19]

Graphic designer and ADI member Giancarlo Iliprandi commented upon graphic designers' position in the ADI as follows: 'For a while, and by a while I mean for about twenty years, we felt like the poor relation. We were indeed part of the same family, but we were considered poorer!'[20] Despite being a minority group, key figures of Italian graphic design participated in the ADI from the beginning. Nizzoli, Pintori, Steiner and Huber attended the preliminary meeting in January 1956. Provinciali and Munari joined the association straight after.[21] Steiner was elected a member of the first executive committee alongside the architect, Enrico Peressutti, and the industrialists, Giulio Castelli and Antonio Pellizzari. Almost all of the subsequent executive committees included a graphic designer. Their involvement suggests a mindset existed within the association that made it likely to at least acknowledge, if not act upon, issues of visual communication.

Graphic designers left a mark of their presence in the ADI on the printed ephemera and publications they designed for the association over the years. As suggested with a good dose of sarcasm by Iliprandi, 'once a graphic designer was elected [ADI member] … there was always a chance that someone would ask for the design of a flyer and whatnot'.[22] In 1956, Steiner designed the visual identity of the ADI and then revamped it in 1964. In figure 5.3, the letters A, D and I are cut out from a dotted pattern that, as already seen in the previous chapters, is a recurring visual vocabulary of the modernist visual language: it explicates the printing medium while taking advantage of the decorative quality of the enlarged dots of the halftone screen. In this particular case, the halftone screen highlights the mechanical aspect, the series production and the reproducibility of graphic design. As such, it can be regarded as an expression of graphic designers' efforts to have their own practice included in the design domain. In 1964, Steiner opted for a simpler logotype (see figure 5.4). Similarities can be drawn between Steiner's design and the visual identity conceived for ICSID in 1968 by ADI member, Bob Noorda, on behalf of Unimark International (see figure 5.5). Both identities comply with the guidelines of the so-called Swiss or International Style: exclusive use of sans-serif typefaces, organisation of the text in an asymmetric grid layout and reduction of design resources to typography alone.

By putting their very visual identity in the hands of a graphic designer, the ADI and ICSID implicitly recognised the exclusive jurisdiction of the practice over visual artefacts. Both commissions are evidence of graphic designers' advancement towards professionalisation. However, as we saw in chapter 3 had been the case with the Milan Triennale, they did not gain authority over a generic client, but over someone ingrained in the local and international design culture. The ADI deputy director, Marco Zanuso, left any final decision regarding the design to Steiner, as his judgement was the most reliable.[23] The ICSID secretary, Josine de Cressonières, did not 'dare to lift a finger without [Noorda's] advice', and asked him on behalf of the council to act as their long-term graphic advisor.[24] As far as the ADI was concerned, however, the commission could also be seen as a mere sweetener. In other words, and as Iliprandi's sarcastic comment also seems to suggest, graphic designers' professional identity was not questioned so long as the ADI could directly benefit from their expertise. Indeed, on a more official level, their position within the association was still unsatisfactory.

In May 1962 the graphic designers in the ADI joined forces and established a graphic design division. The event was a reaction to internal power dynamics among the different in-groups that structured the industrial design association. As recalled by Iliprandi, whereas prior to the setting up of the division, graphic designers in the ADI would simply 'sit next to each other during the general assemblies', after it they showed up as a minority cluster that the dominant in-group of industrial designers could no longer ignore.[25] Something else was also afoot. In April 1962,

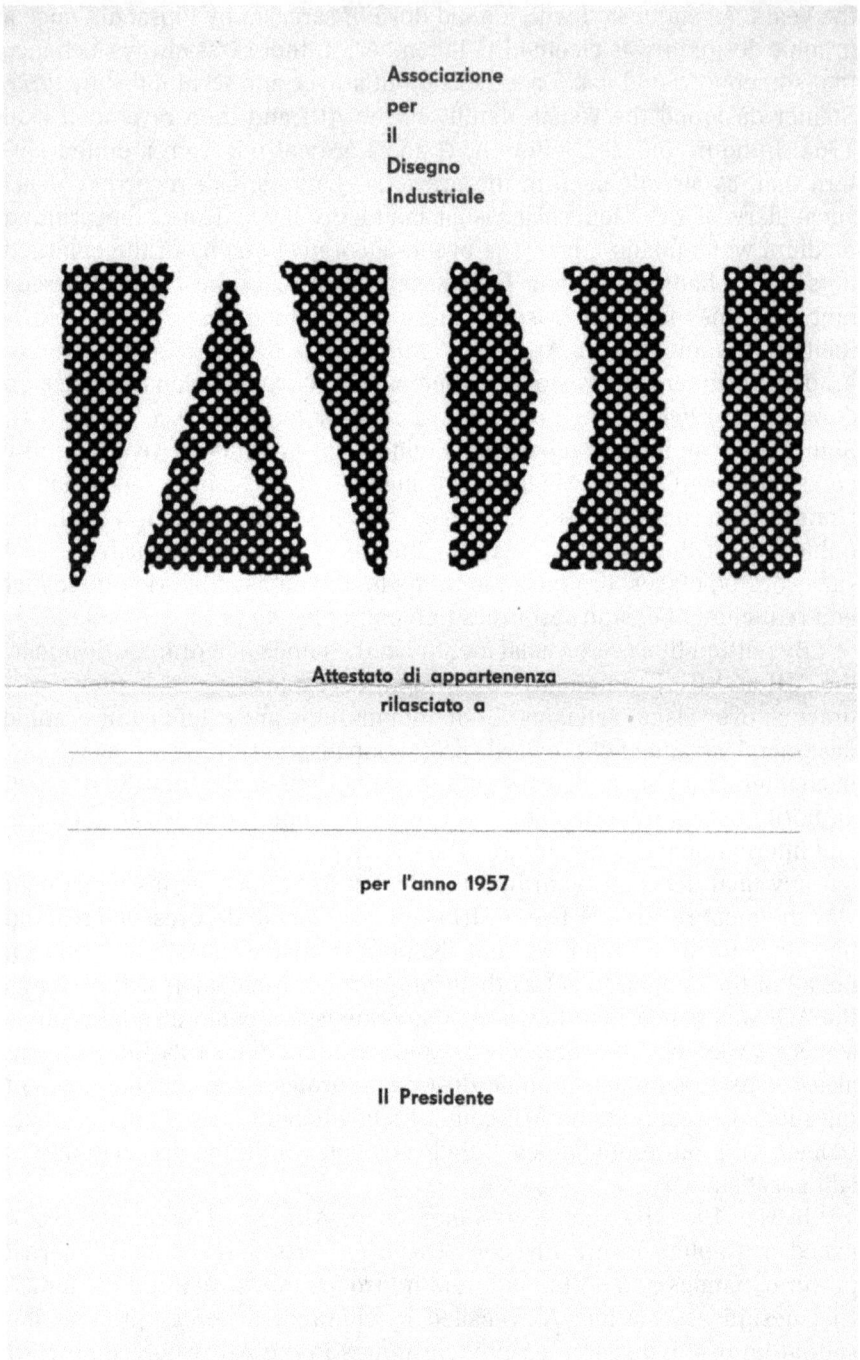

5.3 ADI membership certificate, designed by Albe Steiner, c. 1956.

ADI

Associazione   per   il   Disegno   Industriale

Milano

via   De   Togni   n. 29   telefono   89.73.53

5.4   Draft for the ADI letterhead, designed by Albe Steiner, 1964.

5.5   Draft for the ICSID letterhead, designed by Bob Noorda – Unimark International, 1968.

Alberto Rosselli disclosed news of the forthcoming graphic design division in the design magazine and association house organ *Stile Industria*, introducing 'a section of Italian graphics [that had] already expressed on several occasions, and recently again in the ADI, the desire to go beyond the conventional status of the profession and to develop their practice in a manner that made it more akin to industrial design'.[26] Members of the graphic design division aimed 'to put forward initiatives in this sector to be included in the ADI general agenda'.[27] Among the many proposals advanced were the following: the insertion of specific clauses concerning graphic designers into the statute; the request that a graphic designer member always be included on the management committee; the foundation of graduate schools specialising in visual communication; the organisation of an annual exhibition and conference; the publication of a catalogue; the launch of an award; the establishment of a professional register; and the drawing up of recommended rates for graphic design and packaging only. The overriding goal of the division was 'official (not merely formal or casual) recognition' of graphic design practice within the ADI and the design community at large.[28]

But before claiming official recognition, graphic designers in the ADI first had to clarify, define, negotiate and agree among themselves what their own collective identity indeed was. During the founding meeting, Giulio Confalonieri asked fellow members for the following clarification: 'I would really appreciate it if somebody could explain to me where the boundaries of our profession lie and clarify once and for all what a graphic designer is and what he actually does.'[29] This was an anything but simple task. There was disagreement even about the most appropriate terminology to use. What should they call themselves? Munari suggested using the term 'organizzatore delle comunicazioni visive' (visual communication organiser), whereas Iliprandi preferred the definition 'ordinatore delle comunicazioni visive' (visual communication coordinator). Despite the general uncertainty, members of the ADI graphic design division were able to agree on a vaguely common understanding of what their practice comprised. Drawing a distinction between their in-group and relevant outgroups, they defined it in comparative terms.[30] In particular, they made a distinction between graphic practitioners and graphic designers. A graphic designer was a graphic practitioner, but not all graphic practitioners were graphic designers; hence not all of them could be admitted to the ADI. The distinction was contingent upon the types of artefact produced and the kinds of methodology adopted. For instance, packaging was deemed more appropriate than advertising as it embedded the graphic practice within industrial production. Nevertheless, advertising was not completely out of the picture. It was, in fact, indicated as one of the expressions of graphic design, together with editorial design, signage design, infographics, exhibition design, moving image design, corporate image and many others.[31] Graphic designers were not identical to industrial designers. Graphic designers and industrial designers shared a similar approach and both were concerned with industrial production. As Provinciali put it, graphic designers '[had left] a phase based on sketches and [had entered] a phase based on methodology'.[32]

During the founding meeting, the idea of establishing a new professional body for graphic designers was taken into consideration, but it was concluded that it was actually in the interests of the practice to remain in the ADI together with the industrial designers. The ADI membership and the collaboration with fellow ADI members were deemed instrumental if graphic designers were to become an integral part of the design process. The Aiap was not suggested as an alternative professional body, nor even mentioned at all. This silence speaks volumes and indicates that members of the ADI graphic design division did not recognise themselves in the agenda of the Aiap. If the ADI membership were a means of distancing graphic design from advertising, then to be portrayed as advertising artists must have felt counterproductive to their demand for an official status in the design field. However, some members of the ADI graphic design division were actually members of both associations. Indeed, Erberto Carboni, Franco Grignani, Pino Tovaglia and Ezio Bonini had subscribed to the Aiap since its early years. On the one hand, their twofold membership reinforces the idea that the ADI and the Aiap represented different aspects of the same practice, whose boundaries, caught in between advertising and design, were still blurry. On the other hand, their multiple collective identities suggest that there must have been some similarities between the ADI graphic design division and the Aiap, thereby hinting at a certain flexibility of behaviours between the two groups.

In light of the still ambiguous perception of graphic design and the challenges that the practice faced in the fields of both advertising and industrial design in the early 1960s, the ADI graphic design division offers insight into more than the mere policy of the association. Its significance becomes evident once the organisational strategies of graphic designers in the ADI are set within contemporary debates around graphics, advertising and design, both within and beyond Italian national borders. These provided a backdrop for changes in the organisational strategies of graphic designers in Italy.

Graphics, advertising and design

Debates taking place in specialist periodicals of the time show the gradual distancing of graphics from the commercial sector and its shifting towards design. Take *Linea Grafica* and *Stile Industria*, for instance. The former was the house organ of the Milanese cultural association, Centro Studi Grafici (Centre for Graphics Studies), and it had taken over the legacy of *Campo Grafico*, which had been disbanded in 1939.[33] The latter was the mouthpiece for the ADI from 1954 to 1963, and it was dedicated entirely to industrial design. Design historian Kjetil Fallan suggested that '*Stile Industria* provides an excellent barometer for assessing significant changes in Italian design culture during the turbulent decade in which it operated'.[34] When compared with *Linea Grafica*, the magazine also provides a barometer for assessing the changing position of graphic design at the intersection of advertising and design.

Both *Linea Grafica* and *Stile Industria* felt the need in 1954 to justify to their readerships their interest in advertising. According to the editor of *Linea Grafica* and former campista, Attilio Rossi, it was impossible to document the work of practitioners like Erberto Carboni or Herbert Bayer without also taking into consideration their commercial output. Instead of adhering to a restrictive definition of graphics, he acknowledged the broadening field of action of graphic practices. In his opinion, at the end of the day 'the process of "visual conception" of a page, of an exhibition display or an advertisement [was] essentially the same'.[35] Meanwhile, the editor of *Stile Industria*, Alberto Rosselli, explained to his readership the reasons for presenting works by Pintori, Studio Boggeri, Grignani and Carboni in the very first issue of the magazine. As a sort of justification, he explained that this output was 'not considered in itself, but always contingent upon that unity between production and publicity that the magazine intend[ed] to assert'.[36] For Rosselli, advertising was of no interest in its own right, but only as means of mediation for industrial design.

In April 1955, Rosselli's article 'Grafica tecnica' (Technical Graphics) triggered a lively argument between the two magazines. In this, Rosselli identified the 'weaknesses' of Italian graphics in 'the prevalence of invention over analysis and research of the true aims of design'.[37] Technical graphics was the way forward. While advertising relied on the incessant search for the new and the surprising for its success, technical graphics concerned itself with informing, describing and conveying a message in the clearest and most effective way. Works by ADI members – Muratore, Steiner, Carboni, Pintori, Bonfante, Huber, Grignani, Tovaglia and Ciuti – illustrated Rosselli's concept of technical graphics. Under the title 'Grafica non grafica tecnica' (Graphics not Technical Graphics), Rossi's reply in *Linea Grafica* declared Rosselli's categorisation a nonsense. According to Rossi, it was 'a mistake to divide advertising into two categories: generic advertising and technical advertising'.[38] Responding to the charge of formalism, he blamed outsiders and amateurs who had taken advantage of the experimental path opened by the New Typography, but had engaged with the subject matter merely on a formal level. Finally, Rossi counterattacked and criticised *Stile Industria* for selecting graphic works solely for their formal aspect. In sum, Rossi and Rosselli were making the same accusation against each other. In his response, Rosselli clarified his understanding of technical graphics as a programmatic, consistent and comprehensive approach to industrial production that included both industrial design and advertising. The article ended with a statement of intent: the goal of *Stile Industria* was 'to cooperate with graphic practitioners in their research, to support them in affirming the necessity and esteem of their profession, and to establish a collaboration with architects and industrial designers'.[39] Graphic design was thus acknowledged as a new practice whose practitioners' demand for a place within the design community was to be supported. What the quarrel between *Linea Grafica* and *Stile Industria* tells us is that, notwithstanding their different vocabularies, audiences and perspectives, both magazines supported graphic designers' attempts to extend the boundaries of their field beyond one-off advertising commissions.

The underlying issue was the position of graphic designers in relation to industrial designers and whether graphics was part of design or not. From the pages of *Stile Industria*, Rosselli became a vocal advocate of the inclusion of graphic practice within the design domain. In an article entitled 'Grafici e industrial design' (Graphic Practitioners and Industrial Design) published in April 1962, he clarified the circumstances under which graphics could be part of design: 'In principle, graphic design can be considered part of industrial design, [but] the graphic expressions that mainly address advertising cannot be compared with, nor put on the same level as, the methodologies of industrial design. ... The basis for the development of the graphic design profession is therefore a new method of problem solving, ... an attitude proper to the "designer".'[40] To be re-categorised within design, graphic designers needed 'to release the focus of [their practice] from the field of mere advertising and increasingly insert [it] within the operative sector of modern industry'.[41] In other words, if the inclusion of graphics in the design domain was still on hold, its close association with advertising was to blame. To overcome this obstacle, graphic designers were expected to shift the focus of their practice towards a more systematic approach to visual communication, one that favoured the design of a comprehensive communication system over sporadic commissions.

Rosselli's welcoming attitude towards the entrance of graphics into the design domain found a supporter in Gillo Dorfles. In 1963, Dorfles published the book *Il disegno industriale e la sua estetica* (Industrial Design and Its Aesthetics) in which he formulated a definition of industrial design that included packaging as one of its many facets, albeit one with a close relationship to advertising.[42] The reasons for this inclusion were that packaging was three dimensional and that it featured both functional and aesthetic qualities, while simultaneously mediating the design product it contained. Indeed, packaging was the object of particular interest to graphic designers as its three-dimensional character was deemed a way to associate graphics with product design. Taking part in a roundtable on the relationship between graphics and design that was organised by *Linea Grafica* in the summer of 1969, Dorfles defined graphic design as a 'graphic work applied to an entire communication system' and clarified that 'when graphic design is not merely two-dimensional, but consists of a whole operational strategy that concerns visual communication within different sectors, we can definitely consider graphics as a design matter'.[43] Inclusion or exclusion from design was once again a question of methods. In 1972, a second, revised and extended edition of Dorfles's aforementioned book included the chapter, 'La grafica fa parte del design?' (Is Graphics Part of Design?).[44] The answer was that graphics was indeed part of design, so long as graphic designers adopted a systematic approach to visual communication. He then pointed to trademarks, logotypes and coordinated images as examples of visual output that could without any doubt be categorised as design.

Design coordination and corporate image were indicated as the most relevant and appropriate outcomes of design approaches applied to visual communication. Indeed, they provided graphic designers with a chance 'to be redeemed from the subordinate role of people in charge of decoration or cosmetics and to be actively assimilated into the production process'.[45] In other words, they allowed graphic designers to become an integral part of the industrial process, function as coordinators of a design programme and be recognised as worthy members of the design community. The design coordination programmes conceived by Pintori, Noorda, Carmi, Huber and Steiner – all members of the ADI graphic design division – for design-conscious companies such as Olivetti, Pirelli, Cornigliano, Barilla and La Rinascente, featured in specialist magazines as examples of systematic approaches to visual communication. With the exception of that for the department store, La Rinascente, all these programmes were included among a selection of European, North American and Japanese case studies in F. H. K. Henrion and Alan Parkin's *Design Coordination and Corporate Image* (1967).[46]

Together with design coordination and corporate image, the design of wayfinding systems and infographics was also indicated as antidotes that could redeem graphic design by distancing it from advertising. The 1964 Compasso d'Oro is evidence of a changed attitude towards graphic design practice. For the first time ever, the award was given to a graphic designer for a graphic design artefact: Bob Noorda was awarded the Compasso d'Oro, together with the architects Franco Albini and Franca Helg, for the design of the underground stations and signage system of the red line of the Milan underground, the MM1 (see figure 5.6).[47] For the MM1, Noorda took care of the entire visual aspect of the project: from nameplates to diagrammatic maps, from the logo to the colour-coding system. He committed to readability, clarity and functionality of the visual information and put the end user at the core of his design. For instance, he customised

5.6   Bob Noorda at the San Babila underground station in Milan, 1964.

the Helvetica typeface and selected matt surfaces that would not reflect artificial light in order to facilitate the readability of the white letters from a distance. Furthermore, he introduced the practice of repeating the name of an underground station at regular intervals along the walls of the platform, so that it could be easily read by passengers from the carriages of a train in transit.[48] The decision of awarding the Compasso d'Oro to Noorda was a sign that by the mid-1960s graphic designers had got their foot in the design door.

Transnational graphic design discourses

The shifting agenda of Italian graphic designers, and their changing organisational strategies, intersected with new ways of thinking about visual communication that had meanwhile been emerging within the international graphic design community. International design organisations and events offered Milan's graphic designers the opportunity to be part of, compare themselves with, and negotiate their collective identity with, an international community with common interests and problems.[49] They provided occasions for transnational encounters and promoted multidirectional exchanges between different local scenes. As such, they facilitated construction of networks, information exchange and articulation of collective discourses. Even more relevant here was that membership of international design organisations like the AGI, Alliance Graphique Internationale, and Icograda, International Council of Graphic Design Associations, provided Milan's graphic designers with a different institutional environment for negotiating their collective identity outside the local power dynamic between the Aiap and the ADI.

Physical evidence that graphic designers in the ADI looked abroad in an attempt to 'emancipate the practice from advertising and access the design domain can be found in the folder of the ADI graphic design division in Albe Steiner's archive that includes the statute of the AGI.[50] Founded in 1952, the AGI is an international association that unites world-leading graphic designers. By the end of the 1960s, Italian or Milan-based members included: Erberto Carboni, Franco Grignani, Bruno Munari, Giovanni Pintori (joined 1952), Albe Steiner (1955), Eugenio Carmi (1955), Max Huber (1958), Riccardo Manzi (1956), Massimo Vignelli (1965), Bob Noorda (1966), Giulio Confalonieri and Pino Tovaglia (1967).[51] All but Manzi were members of the ADI graphic design division as well. During its first two decades the AGI followed a pattern that closely mirrored changes in the Italian graphic design scene, as it slowly but steadily distanced itself from advertising and poster art.

AGI members met periodically at annual exhibitions and conferences. These acted as 'field-configuring events', that is, 'temporary social organizations such as tradeshows, professional gatherings, technology contests, and business ceremonies that encapsulate and shape the development of professions, technologies, markets, and industries'.[52] By providing a periodical setting to 'develop industry standards, construct social networks, recognize accomplishments, [and] share and interpret information', they contributed to the emergence and gradual articulation of graphic design practice.[53] The first AGI exhibition was held at the Louvre in Paris in 1955, and it stressed advertising in its very title: 'Art et publicité dans le monde' (Worldwide Art and Advertising). Poster art remained the focus of the following two exhibitions. The emphasis began to change at the fourth AGI annual exhibition, held at the Galleria d'Arte Moderna (Modern Art Gallery) in Milan in 1961 (see figure 5.7). Despite having a title that was similar to the Parisian exhibition, 'Grafica e pubblicità nel mondo' (Graphics and Advertising around the World) focused on design coordination programmes rather than individual commercial art posters and favoured informative over persuasive messages. A variety of printed materials encountered during an ordinary twenty-four-hour day was on display at the following year's exhibition, 'Graphic Design for the Community: Print Around the Clock', held at the Stedelijk Museum in Amsterdam in 1962, and this was done explicitly to demonstrate how engrained graphic design was in everyday life.

The AGI annual congresses provide further evidence for changes in the understanding of graphic design during the first half of the 1960s.

5.7 View of the AGI exhibition 'Grafica e pubblicità nel mondo' at the Galleria d'Arte Moderna, Milan, 1961.

In 1960 the AGI members met in St-Germain-en-Laye to debate 'whether [they] should be equated with the free artist or with the scientist, who is entrusted with finding the solution of a given problem'.[54] In answer to this question, Henrion described the graphic designer as 'an intermediary, a conveyor of information, who should in a very professional and competent way pass information on to the receiving masses', and added that it was more important to be 'anonymous but extremely professional and competent in the use of the visual syntax' than it was to develop a very personal style and concern oneself with aesthetics for its own sake.[55] On a similar note and four years later at the 1964 AGI congress in Alpbach, the Italian but London-based graphic designer, Germano Facetti, who – as mentioned in chapter 4 – had trained in Rome at the Convitto Scuola Rinascita, declared that visual communication had nothing to do with self-expression, persuasion or marketing, but rather was concerned with technology and information theory.[56] He set new tasks, priorities and standards for graphic design practice. Artistic skills and creativity were no longer enough: it was time for graphic designers to adopt a problem-solving approach to visual communication and learn new methods of research and analysis that would allow the efficient transmission of visual messages and achieve consistent long-term planning.

Similar discussions took place at the 1960 WoDeCo, World Design Conference, in Tokyo, which brought together exponents of the international design community to debate around issues of graphic design, among a variety of other topics.[57] One of the core questions discussed at WoDeCo under the general theme, 'Our Century: The Total Image – What Designers Can Contribute to the Human Environment of the Coming Age', was the idea of design as a social service, and hence of the designer's responsibility towards society. Tomás Maldonado opened the session on visual communication and explained how 'visual communication [had] become the object of scientific research ... but despite this the majority of designers still [thought] that the most important aspect of communication media [was] the artistic creativity and that the means of communication [were] mere secondary issues'.[58] He then directly criticised 'the bad habit of explaining communication by restricting it to the field of advertising' and identified this misunderstanding as the cause of graphic designers' undervalued cultural and professional status.[59] Representing Italy at WoDeCo, Max Huber spoke about the social responsibilities of design. In his presentation, he called for graphic designers' commitment to their public by offering informative and easily readable visual representations that would appeal to rationality rather than provoke emotional reactions. As he put it, 'only a coordinated and unified use ... of clear symbols, visually immediate and understandable by everyone, would significantly improve the relationship between people of different countries and languages, and between people who [were] already acquiring an international mentality'.[60] Emphasis was expected to shift away from designers' self-expression towards the clarity of design in communicating complex information to an ever more international audience. In line with the principles of International Style, this new thinking in visual communication was expressed visually through a preference for asymmetrical and geometrical compositions, grid layout, standardised design systems and the exclusive use of sans-serif typefaces and photographic images.

Icograda entered the transnational network of graphic design in 1963, bringing together graphic design associations, the AGI included. A look at the first decade of the activities of the international council provides further evidence for the estrangement of graphic design practice from commercial art and its shift towards design. According to Peter Kneebone, Icograda co-founder and first secretary, the early 1960s were 'exactly the right moment in the history of the profession, [when] "commercial artists" discovered that they were really "graphic designers"'.[61] But moving away from commercial art towards graphic design was not 'simply a matter of redesigning the label'.[62] On the contrary, it was the outcome of a process of negotiation and self-reflection on the identity and socio-cultural responsibilities of the practice. While participants at the first Icograda congress in Zurich in 1964 had yet again been asking themselves whether they were 'Commercial Artist or Graphic Designer', as set forth in its title, they were undoubtedly defining themselves as 'graphic designers' by the time it came to the 1966 congress in Bled. On this occasion, Henrion observed that 'just by calling [themselves] a different name [they did] not perform differently'.[63] In contrast to the commercial artists, graphic designers were problem solvers in the field of visual communication: they were expected to have an analytical approach to the understanding of communication issues and to adopt a methodological process in solving them. As had been the case with the AGI, the pattern of changes in Icograda's agenda shows that by the mid-1960s graphic design had become a matter of research, methodology, information handling, effective communication, long-term planning and design coordination.

The Aiap was among the first twenty-four subscribers, coming from eighteen different countries, to Icograda. By contrast, the ADI declined the invitation, but asked to be kept informed.[64] The graphic designers in the ADI were nevertheless represented in Icograda by virtue of their AGI and/or Aiap membership. Representatives of the Aiap took part in congresses and general assemblies of Icograda. Updates on the international council featured in the association's house organ, and vice versa. The Norwegian graphic designer and president of Icograda, Knut Yran, visited the Aiap in November 1966 and was celebrated, according to tradition, by a dinner at the Taverna della Giarrettiera.[65] Nevertheless, the Aiap resigned from Icograda in 1969 due to difficulties in meeting the membership fee. After this resignation, Icograda lacked an Italian member association until the mid-1980s, when both the Aiap and the ADI were granted membership.[66] By that time the ADI graphic design division had disbanded, but, even so, in 1991 one of its founding members, Giancarlo Iliprandi, was elected president of the international council.

Having (and keeping) a foot in both camps

Evidence presented so far in this chapter suggests that the foundation of the ADI graphic design division can be seen as a response to the articulation of a different approach to graphic design, both locally and internationally. But what about the Aiap? In fact, the association was not immune to contemporary changes. The emergence of new ways of thinking in visual communication, together with graphic designers' attempts to emancipate the practice from advertising, also had an effect on the Aiap. In 1964 the association changed name: it was retitled Associazione Italiana Artisti e Grafici Pubblicitari (Italian Association of Advertising Artists and Graphics), but it kept the original acronym. Although the term 'advertising' was still prominent in the new name, the addition of the term 'graphics' is evidence of a change in direction. The conjunction 'e' (and) is also revealing of that change. Indeed, Aiap members had chosen between Associazione Artisti Grafici Pubblicitari Italiani (Association of Italian Advertising Graphic Artists) and Associazione Italiana Artisti e Grafici Pubblicitari, and finally decided in favour of the latter. The difference is significant: the addition of the conjunction 'e', (and) turns 'grafici' from an adjective (graphic) that acts as a modifier of the noun 'artisti' (artists), into a noun (graphics). As such, the new name officially differentiated the Aiap membership by establishing a distinction between advertising artists and graphics.

A similar response to the tensions underlying the terms and definitions in graphic design can be detected in other countries at this time. Britain and the SIA, Society of Industrial Artists, are a case in point here.[67] In 1963, the society changed its name and become the SIAD, the Society of Industrial Artists and Designers. As design historian Jonathan M. Woodham has argued, the use of changeable terms such as 'advertising artist', 'commercial artist', 'graphic practitioner' or 'graphic designer' 'can lend insights into the changing politics of professional validation'.[68] Commenting on the name change of the SIA-D, he observed that the addition of the D was a reaction to the 'growing unease about the term "Artist" as an appropriate descriptor for a profession which sought recognition for itself on a par with engineers, lawyers, doctors and architects'.[69] The almost simultaneous name change of the SIA-D and the Aiap, with the addition of the words 'designers' and 'graphics', respectively, is evidence of an international shift in the identity and representation of design.

The flexible professional identities and multiple memberships of Milan's graphic designers came into play again in 1967, when the Aiap organised the exhibition 'Today's Italian Publicity and Graphic Design' at Reed House, in Piccadilly Circus, London. A picture of the entrance to the exhibition space appeared on the cover of the association's house organ, *Poliedro* (see figure 5.8). This features the exhibition poster conceived by Aiap and ADI member, Franco Grignani (see figure 5.9). The poster exemplifies Grignani's research on optical distortion: by activating and bringing to the fore the white background, the striped ribbon creates a three-dimensional distortion of the flat surface of the poster, while its colours recall the Italian green, white and red flag. When repeated and juxtaposed, as shown in the installation shot, the poster created a sort of string curtain that invited visitors into the exhibition space. Here, the works of about ninety advertising artists and graphic designers were on display (see figure 5.10).

A closer look at the participants in the London exhibition provides further information on the organisational strategies of graphic designers in Italy. These strategies reflect the ways in which relationships between and across groups, in particular between the Aiap and members of the ADI graphic design division, were changing. Although eligibility criteria restricted participation to Aiap members, the organisers decided to make an exception and invite a number of outsiders. Writing in *Poliedro*, Benca (Carlo Benedetti) remarked upon those graphic practitioners who were not members of the Aiap and observed that they were 'actually just a few' and that it was 'a shame that laziness, misinterpreted bohemian individualism

5.8   Cover of the Aiap house organ, *Poliedro*, no. 5 (January–April 1968), designed by Gino Sironi, with a photograph by Lelo Cremonesi.

or misunderstanding of the spirit of the statute of the association' were preventing them from joining in.[70] Enrico Ciuti, Giancarlo Iliprandi, Remo Muratore, Ilio Negri, Cecco (Francesco) Re and Albe Steiner were among the non-members included in the London exhibition. Together with Aiap members – Ezio Bonini, Erberto Carboni, Franco Grignani, Giovanni Pintori and Pino Tovaglia – they were representatives of the ADI graphic design division. As Benca explained, this exception that was being made to the rule was 'evidence of the generosity and maturity [of the association and] a nice demonstration of open-mindedness. ... On the occasion of being called upon to present an entire professional category abroad, the Aiap proved to be aware of its official national duties.'[71]

Today's
Italian
Publicity
and
Graphic
Design

from
november
3rd to 24th
1967

Reed House   82 Piccadilly Circus   London W.1

5.9   Poster for the exhibition 'Today's Italian Publicity and Graphic Design', designed by
Franco Grignani, 1967.

5.10   View of the exhibition 'Today's Italian Publicity and Graphic Design' at Reed House, London, 1967.

From the point of view of the Aiap, the public image of the practice as a whole benefited from the inclusion of ADI members. Through this, the exhibition could count on several AGI members, that is, on the so-called élite of international graphic design. However, why did members of the ADI graphic design division join in? Their personal interest in being exhibited abroad in an institutional context might have prevailed over their scepticism towards the Aiap and their reluctance to be compared with advertising artists. Yet, pragmatic personal interests offer only a partial explanation of the change of attitude of ADI graphic designers towards the Aiap. Once we take graphic designers' flexible professional identities and multiple memberships into account, alternative explanations come to the fore.

In fact, the ADI graphic designers' change of attitude towards the Aiap and their decision to join the London exhibition showed that there was a margin for mediation and that the international setting offered a neutral space for temporary alliances. By its very title, 'Today's Italian Publicity and Graphic Design' made a clear distinction between advertising and graphic design. At the same time, it also implied the possibility of coexistence and interaction between the two fields. As such, it can be regarded as the outcome of the contemporary reconciliation between graphics and advertising. The Italian advertising market had caught up since the early

1950s, when its expenditure of 543 liras per capita paled in comparison with the 3,240 and 25,683 liras of Britain and the US, respectively.[72] Its growth had been remarkable: the turnover grew by 150 per cent between 1949 and 1958 and grew by a further 60 per cent in the following decade. In 1962, advertising costs had reached circa 0.7 per cent of total consumer expenditure. 'With this catching up', sociologist Adam Arvidsson pointed out, 'there was also a significant restructuring of the industry.'[73]

By the second half of the 1960s graphic designers had found a new entry point into the advertising agency, as part of the creative team. In applying their experience as coordinators of complex systems of visual communication, they contributed to the team's efforts to articulate advertising as a coherent discourse and integral part of the coordinated image of a company. Here it is worth pointing out that the London exhibition was organised by the Aiap under the sponsorship of the D&AD, Design & Art Direction. This support was no trivial coincidence, for it signalled the reshaping of the relationship between graphics and advertising also outside Italy. The D&AD was founded in 1962 by a group of London-based advertising creatives and designers and its foundation has been interpreted as a signal of 'a profound shift in the cultural-economic orientation of actors that constituted the advertising industry' at the time.[74] This shift in the balance of power between different specialists working in the advertising agencies was a consequence of the impact of a new approach to advertising, one that championed creativity and effectiveness above market research and the science of selling as measures of good advertising.[75] During that period, advertising practices were being reshaped by the pairing of art directors and copywriters. This novel creative team was given greater authority in the development of a new kind of advertising, one that aimed at initiating a dialogue with the viewer/reader through witty and irreverent headlines, and smart and interactive advertisements. As such, this new approach to advertising turned the end user from a passive recipient into an active co-author of the advertising message.

Under the new guise of art direction, advertising gained a renewed appeal. This was in particular the case with a group of Milan's graphic designers and advertising creatives included in the 'Today's Italian Publicity and Graphic Design' exhibition, who in December 1966 had contributed to the foundation of a new professional body: the ADCM, Art Directors Club Milano. Like the D&AD in London, the ADCM brought together art directors, advertising creatives and graphic designers. Members of the ADCM considered art direction as a means for carving a new role for graphic practitioners in the advertising agency and reinventing the relationship between graphics and advertising on new bases distinct from commercial art and advertising artists. As Iliprandi, the first ADCM president, explained to readers of the March–April 1968 issue of the advertising magazine, *Sipradue*, design and art direction were two equally feasible career choices: 'Both paths entail combined research and investigation, interdisciplinary exchange, planning and teamwork, and thus, a precise operational methodology that is very similar for both creative processes. No wonder that the most important British association in this field is called Design & Art Direction.'[76] Art directors and graphic designers shared common ground in that they both supervised the coordination of complex and articulated systems of visual communication in multidisciplinary dialogue with different specialists.

Significantly, the ADCM was tightly intertwined with the ADI graphic design division and indirectly linked to the ADI itself.[77] Not only were three out of the five founding members – Giancarlo Iliprandi, Till Neuburg and Pino Tovaglia – also members of the ADI graphic design division, but many others joined soon after, and the first meetings of the newly founded club were held at the ADI headquarters. To a certain extent, the ADCM was the ADI equivalent in the field of advertising.[78] If the ADI offered graphic practitioners the chance to ground their practice in the design sector and negotiate their identity with industrial designers, the ADCM was a meeting point between graphics and advertising agencies and provided graphic practitioners with an organisational alternative to the Aiap in the field of advertising. Membership of the one organisation did not exclude membership of the other, but practitioners might have had a preference depending on the specific context and network in which their practice was set. In the context of 'Today's Italian Publicity and Graphic Design', the ADCM membership was more salient than that of the ADI. As members of the ADCM, the ADI graphic designers could then have their work exhibited in the same room as Aiap members without losing credibility or having their status threatened.

Graphic designers' inferiority complex and organisational strategies

So, the long-lasting struggle for graphic designers to be officially recognised went hand in hand with their own continuous calling into question of their professional identity and status. Indeed, whether graphic design was, or was not, part of design, remained an open question yet again at the end of a roundtable organised by *Linea Grafica* in collaboration with the ADI in the summer of 1969.[79] In the final remarks, the moderator and editor of *Linea Grafica*, Fabio Mataloni, pointed out that the actual issue at stake was not to decide once and for all whether graphic design belonged to the design domain, but rather whether the ADI was willing to accept graphic designers as equals with industrial designers. If this was not the case, then it was not a problem for the graphic design practice as a whole, but rather 'a problem for those graphic designers who wanted to stay in the ADI'.[80] He then added sarcastically that graphic designers were 'affected by some kind of inferiority complex', whereas 'design, if not the designers themselves, maybe suffer[ed] from another kind of illness: mythomania'![81]

By focusing on conflicts, exchanges and alliances between the different groups set within a network of national and international organisations, this chapter has explored a period of self-reflection and crisis that the practice of graphic design underwent from the mid-1950s and through the 1960s, both within and beyond Italy. Graphic designers' problematic sense of identity and their perceived inferior status to that of industrial design manifested themselves in their need to reaffirm, time and time again, that they belonged to the design community. Having a foot in two camps – advertising and design – meant the position of graphic design practice in Italy in the post-war period was ambiguous and uncertain. This was reflected in the fact that many graphic designers were, and sometimes still are, members of both the Aiap and the ADI. Others, instead, considered the two associations incompatible and representative of two separate practices: the one closer to advertising and the other rooted in design methodologies and at the service of communication rather than commerce.

The professionalisation of graphic design practice in Milan did not end in the 1960s. Nor was it actually limited to just Italy, as graphic designers from many countries were facing similar issues, sharing related experiences and adopting comparable solutions. As we have seen again and again in this book, design practices were in a constant state of formation, and local and international professional bodies played a part in this open-ended process.

Notes

* Excerpts from this chapter appeared previously in C. Barbieri, 'Negotiating graphic design between national and international design organisations: The case of the Associazione per il Design Industriale in Milan', in J. Aynsley, A. J. Clarke and T. Messell (eds), *International Design Organisations: Histories, Legacies, Values* (London: Bloomsbury, 2022), pp. 205–22.

1 Freidson, *Professional Powers*, pp. 185–208; W. R. Scott, *Institutions and Organisations* (London: Sage Publications, 2001), p. 50.

2 S. Heller, 'Advertising: Mother of graphic design', *Eye Magazine*, 5:17 (1995), 26–37; D. Crowley, 'Advertising and history: Admen plunder the past – with no history to call their own', *Eye Magazine*, 15:57 (2005), www.eyemagazine.com/opinion/article/advertising-and-history, accessed 31 May 2023.

3 A. Valeri, *Pubblicità italiana: storia, protagonisti e tendenze di cento anni di comunicazione* (Milan: Sole24Ore, 1986), pp. 81–93; L. Grazzani and F. E. Guida, *AIAP 70 × 70: eventi, personaggi e materiali di una storia associativa* (Milan: AIAP, 2015); M. Piazza, 'Grafica: creativi negli anni cinquanta', in G. Anghia and A. Marangoni (eds), *Milano anni cinquanta* (Milan: Franco Angeli Editore, 1986), pp. 163–9.

4 Millerson, *The Qualifying Associations*, pp. 148–80.

5 F. E. Guida, 'Giarrettiere, puntine e progettiste', in D. Piscitelli (ed.), *AWDA: Aiap Women in Design Award, premio internazionale design della comunicazione* (Milan: AIAP, 2015), pp. 34–6.

6 Anon., 'La "giarrettiera" pubblicitaria a Carlo Dradi', *La Pubblicità: Bollettino Mensile della FIP e Associazioni Aderenti*, 10:10 (October 1956), 7.

7 F. E. Guida, 'Donne della grafica italiana. Per una storiografia inclusiva', in Riccini (ed.), *Angelica e Bradamante*, p. 195.

8 Willson, *Women in Twentieth-Century Italy*, p. 118.

9 S. De Iulio and C. Vinti, 'The Americanisation of Italian advertising during the 1950s and the 1960s: Mediations, conflicts, and appropriations', *Journal of Historical Research in Marketing*, 1:2 (2009), 270–94; S. De Iulio and C. Vinti, 'La Publicité italienne et le modèle américain', *Vingtième Siècle. Revue d'Histoire*, 101 (2009), 61–80. On the impact of communication strategies and work models from across the Atlantic on the advertising cultures of other European countries, see De Grazia, *Irresistible Empire*; S. Schwarzkopf, 'From Fordist to creative economies: The de-Americanisation of European advertising cultures since the 1960s', *European Review of History*, 20:5 (2013), 859–79.

10 M. Galluzzo, 'I grafici sono sempre protagonisti? Pubblicità in Italia 1965–1985' (PhD dissertation, IUAV, Venice, 2018), pp. 53–96.

11 Vinti, *Gli anni dello stile industriale (1948–1965)*, p. 334.

12 G. Dorfles, *Le oscillazioni del gusto* (Milan: Lerici, 1958), pp. 160–3; I. Weiss, 'Il bello non è inefficace', *Pirelli*, 2 (April 1954), 55; I. Weiss, 'Panorama della pubblicità italiana', *L'Ufficio Moderno*, 31:3 (March 1957), 437–41.

13 De Fusco, *Una storia dell'ADI*; Grassi and Pansera (eds), *L'Italia del design*, pp. 38–67.

14 Grassi and Pansera (eds), *L'Italia del design*, pp. 41–3.

15 R. Rizzi, A. Steiner and F. Origoni (eds), *Design italiano: Compasso d'Oro ADI* (Cantù: Clac, 1998); Grassi and Pansera (eds), *L'Italia del design*, pp. 46–7; R. De Fusco, *Made in Italy: storia del design italiano. Nuova edizione* (Florence: Altralinea Edizioni, 2014), pp. 171–8; Fallan, 'Annus mirabilis', pp. 256–61.

16 Hogg and Terry, 'Social identity and self-categorization processes in organizational contexts'; M. A. Hogg and D. J. Terry, 'Social identity and organisational processes', in M. A. Hogg and D. J. Terry (eds), *Social Identity Processes in Organisational Contexts* (London: Taylor and Francis Group, 2001), pp. 1–12.

17 Grassi and Pansera (eds), *L'Italia del design*, p. 58; G. Iliprandi, A. Marangoni, F. Origoni and A. Pansera (eds), *Visual design: 50 anni di produzione in Italia* (Milan: Idea Libri, 1984), pp. 19–21; Vinti, 'Graphic designers, people with problems', p. 89.

18 'Opportunità di inserire la grafica – il *graphic design* – nell'ambito dell'industrial design ... riconoscere la "dignità" di disegno industriale a quel disegno grafico che fosse tridimensionale, ma anche a quello che – seppur bidimensionale – sottostasse ad una globalità programmativa'. G. Dorfles, in Anon., *Albe Steiner: comunicazione visiva* (Milan: Fratelli Alinari, 1977), p. 11.

19 Reicher, 'The context of social identity'; Worchel, Iuzzini, Coutant and Ivaldi, 'A multidimensional model of identity'.

20 'Noi ci siamo sentiti dei cugini poveri per un po' di tempo, e per un po' di tempo intendo dire quasi venti anni. Cioè eravamo parenti, però venivamo considerati più poveri!' G. Iliprandi, interview with the author, Milan, 7 January 2016.

21 AALS, D b. 14 fasc. 7, meeting minutes, 'Riunione del 7 Febbraio 1956, per l'Associazione del Disegno Industriale'.

22 'Se un grafico veniva eletto ... c'era sempre la possibilità che qualcuno gli chiedesse di disegnare un volantino o una cosa simile'. G. Iliprandi, interview with the author, Milan, 7 January 2016.

23 AALS, D b. 14 fasc. 7, letter from M. Zanuso to A. Steiner, 17 March 1964.

24 University of Brighton Design Archives, Brighton, UK (hereafter UBDA), ICSID Archive, 08-6-3 Noorda, Bob (1968–71), letter from J. des Cressonières to B. Noorda, 6 November 1968.

25 'Ci sedevamo vicini durante le assemblee generali'. G. Iliprandi, interview with the author, Milan, 7 January 2016.

26 'Un settore dei grafici Italiani, già in diverse occasioni e ancora recentemente in sede ADI …, ha manifestato la volontà di superare lo stato convenzionale della professione e di evolvere la propria opera in un atteggiamento affine al disegno industriale'. A. Rosselli, 'Grafici e industrial design', *Stile Industria*, 9:37 (April 1962), 13.

27 'Portare avanti delle iniziative nel settore da inserire nel quadro generale delle attvità dell'ADI'. AALS, D b. 14 fasc. 7, meeting minute, '1a Riunione della Sezione Grafici della A.D.I.', 8 May 1962, p. 1.

28 'Riconoscimento ufficiale (non solo formale o casuale)'. *Ibid.*

29 'Vorrei proprio che qualcuno mi spiegasse quali sono i limiti nella nostra professione determinando una volta per tutte cosa è e cosa fa realmente il grafico.' *Ibid.*, p. 2.

30 Reicher, 'The context of social identity', 929.

31 AALS, D b. 14 fasc. 7., archival document, 'Riunione del 7 Febbraio 1967', 7 February 1967.

32 'Usciamo dalla fase di tipo bozzetistico ed entriamo nella fase metodologica'. AALS, D b. 14 fasc. 7, meeting minute, '1a Riunione della Sezione Grafici della A.D.I.', M. Provinciali, 8 May 1962, p. 2.

33 M. Picasso (ed.), *1945–1995: cinquant'anni di grafica a Milano* (Milan: Centro Studi Grafici, 1996).

34 Fallan, 'Annus mirabilis', p. 258.

35 'Il processo di "creazione visiva" di una pagina, di un allestimento, o di una pubblicità è in sostanza il medesimo'. A. Rossi, 'Il nostro principio di scelta', *Linea Grafica*, 7:5–6 (May–June 1954), 127.

36 'Non consideriamo come a sé stante, ma sempre in funzione di quella unità fra produzione e propaganda che la rivista intende affermare'. A. Rosselli, 'Artisti italiani per la pubblicità', *Stile Industria*, 1:1 (June 1954), 31.

37 'Debolezza … prevalere dell'invenzione sull'analisi e la ricerca dei veri scopi del disegno'. A. Rosselli, 'Grafica tecnica', *Stile Industria*, 2:4 (April 1955), 47.

38 'Un errore dividere la pubblicità in due gruppi: pubblicità generica e pubblicità tecnica'. A. Rossi, 'Grafica non grafica tecnica', *Linea Grafica*, 8:9–10 (September–October 1955), 236.

39 'Affiancare i grafici nella loro ricerca, di aiutarli ad affermare una necessità ed un prestigio della loro professione, di stabilire una collaborazione con gli architetti ed i disegnatori industriali'. A. Rosselli, 'Grafica tecnica', *Stile Industria*, 3:6 (February 1956), 42.

40 'La grafica in linea di principio si può considerare nella stessa sfera d'azione del disegno industriale … le espressioni grafiche indirizzate in massima parte verso un'azione pubblicitaria, non permettono confronti e argomentazioni omogenei con il procedimento dell'industrial design. … Alla radice dell'evolversi della professione del grafico sta quindi un metodo nuovo di avvicinarsi e risolvere i molti nuovi problemi della grafica, ma soprattutto un preciso atteggiamento di "designer".' Rosselli, 'Grafici e industrial design', 13–14.

41 'Svincolare l'interesse del grafico dalla sola sfera della pubblicità e maggiormente lo immette nella sfera operativa dell'industria moderna'. *Ibid.*, 14.

42 G. Dorfles, *Il disegno industriale e la sua estetica* (Bologna: Cappelli Editore, 1963), pp. 15–16.

43 'Un lavoro di grafica applicato a un intero sistema comunicativo … quando la progettazione grafica non è solo bidimensionale e comprende tutto uno schema operativo che riguarda la comunicazione visiva in diversi settori, possiamo senz'altro considerare la grafica come un fatto di design'. G. Dorfles in F. Mataloni, 'Immagine aziendale e disegno coordinato', *Linea Grafica*, 21:4 (July–August 1969), 267 and 270.

44 G. Dorfles, *Introduzione al disegno industriale: linguaggio e storia della produzione di serie* (Turin: Einaudi, 1972), p. 41.

45 'Riscattato dal ruolo subalterno dell'addetto alla decorazione o alla cosmesi e si integra invece attivamente al processo produttivo'. R. Baldini, 'Grafica nella produzione', *Stile Industria*, 9:38 (June 1962), 33.

46 F. H. K. Henrion and A. Parkin, *Design Coordination and Corporate Image* (London: Studio Vista, 1967), pp. 36–41, 86–101, 124–35 and 148–53.

47 Bob Noorda was not the first graphic designer to be awarded the Compasso d'Oro. Max Huber had, in fact, received the award in 1954 for a geometric pattern on plastic he designed for the Stabilimenti di Ponte Lambro. Noorda was awarded the Compasso d'Oro again in 1974 for the coordinated image of Regione Lombardia that he co-designed with Pino Tovaglia and Roberto Sambonet.

48 G. Oropallo, 'This way to the exit: The re-writing of the city through graphic design, 1964–1989', in Lees-Maffei and Fallan (eds), *Made in Italy*, pp. 194–99.

49 J. Aynsley, A. J. Clarke and T. Messell, 'Introduction', in Aynsley, Clarke and Messell (eds), *International Design Organisations*, pp. 1–11; J. M. Woodham, 'Local, national and global: Redrawing the design historical map', *Journal of Design History*, 18:3 (2005), 257–67.

50 AALS, D b. 14 fasc. 7, archival document, 'Codice dell'A.G.I.'.

51 B. Bos and E. Bos (eds), *AGI: Graphic Design since 1950* (London: Thames and Hudson, 2007).

52 J. Lampel and A. D. Meyer, 'Introduction. Field-configuring events as structuring mechanisms: How conferences, ceremonies, and trade shows constitute new technologies industries, and markets', *Journal of Management Studies*, 45:6 (2008), 1026.

53 *Ibid.*

54 F. H. K. Henrion, *AGI Annals* (Zurich: Alliance Graphique Internationale, 1989), p. 102.

55 *Ibid.*, p. 103.

56 G. Facetti, in Bos and Bos (eds), *AGI*, p. 121.

57 R. Koolhass and H. U. Obrist, *Project Japan: Metabolism Talk* (Cologne: Taschen, 2011); J. Traganou, *Designing the Olympics: Representation, Participation, Contestation* (New York: Routledge, 2016), pp. 77–9; T. Iguchi, 'Reconsideration of the World Design Conference 1960 in Tokyo and the World Industrial Design Conference 1973 in Kyoto: Transformation of design theory', www.design-cu.jp/iasdr2013/papers/1183-1b.pdf, accessed 31 May 2023.

58 'La comunicazione visiva è diventata oggetto di una ricerca scientifica ... tuttavia la maggior parte dei designers pensa che la cosa più importante dei mezzi di comunicazione sia la creazione artistica e che il modo di comunicare sia solo un problema secondario'. T. Maldonado, in A. Rosselli, 'World Design Conference 1960', *Stile Industria*, 7:28 (August 1960), xix.

59 'Cattiva abitudine di spiegare la comunicazione limitandola al campo pubblicitario'. *Ibid.*

60 'Solo un uso coordinato e unificato ... di simboli chiari, visivamente immediati e comprensibili a chiunque, potrebbe migliorare sensibilmente le relazioni tra individui di lingue e di paesi diversi, individui che già stanno acquistando una mentalità internazionale'. M. Huber in Rosselli, 'World Design Conference 1960', xvii.

61 P. Kneebone, in J. Frascara (ed.), *Graphic Design World Views: A Celebration of Icograda's 25th Anniversary* (Tokyo; New York: Kodansha, 1990), p. 13.

62 *Ibid.*

63 F. H. K. Henrion, 'Graphic Design and Visual Communication Technology', in Anon., *2nd General Assembly and Congress Icograda*, n. p.

64 UBDA, Icograda Archive, ICO/1/1/2, archival document, 'Icograda Inaugural Meeting London April 26th–28th 1963', 26–28 April 1963, p. 3.

65 Anon., 'AIAP: il Presidente dell'Icograda in visita all'Aiap', *La Pubblicità: Bollettino Mensile della FIP e Associazioni Aderenti*, 20:12 (December 1966), 24.

66 UBDA, Icograda Archive, ICO/2/2/1, letter from M. Singer (Icograda) to G. Stoppino (ADI), 20 June 1984; UBDA, Icograda Archive, ICO/5/4/69, letter from M. Singer (Icograda) to V. Piozzi (Aiap), 2 October 1984.

67 L. Armstrong, 'Steering a course between professionalism and commercialism: The Society of Industrial Artists and the Code of Conduct for the professional designer 1945–1975', *Journal of Design History*, 29:2 (2016), 161–79.

68 Woodham, *Twentieth Century Design*, p. 167.

69 J. M. Woodham, *A Dictionary of Modern Design* (Oxford; New York: Oxford University Press, 2004), p. 76.

70 'Sono pochi per la verità ed è un peccato che la pigrizia, un malinteso individualismo bohémien o la errata interpretazione dello spirito dello Statuto associativo'. Benca, 'La migliore pubblicità potrebbe essere italiana', *Poliedro*, 5 (January–April 1968), 9.

71 'Prova della sua generosità e maturità, … simpatica dimostrazione di apertura mentale e di equilibrio … L'Aiap nell'occasione di presentare all'estero una intera categoria professionale ha dimostrato di avvertire i suoi doveri nazionali di ufficialità.' *Ibid.*, 10.

72 Fasce and Bini, 'Irresistible empire or innocents abroad?', 12.

73 Arvidsson, *Marketing Modernity*, p. 70.

74 Schwarzkopf, 'From Fordist to creative economies', 867. On the D&AD, see J. Myerson and G. Vickers, *Rewind: Forty Years of Design & Advertising* (London; New York: Phaidon, 2002); R. Stanley, *D&AD 50* (Cologne: Taschen, 2012); B. McAlhone, 'Twenty-one years ago, D&AD was a gleam in Bob Brook's eye', *Design &Art Direction* (June 1983), 10–17.

75 S. Nixon, 'Looking westwards and worshipping: The New York "Creative Revolution" and British advertising, 1956–1980', *Journal of Consumer Culture*, 17:2 (2015), 147–66; R. Poynor (ed.), *Communicate: Independent British Graphic Design since the Sixties* (London: Laurence King, 2004), pp. 17–22.

76 'Entrambe le strade propongono ricerche e indagini di tipo collettivo, scambio interdisciplinare, programmazione, progettazione di gruppo, quindi una precisa metodologia operativa molto simile nei due procedimenti creativi. Non a caso la più importante associazione inglese della categoria si chiama Design & Art Direction.' G. Iliprandi, 'Un prodotto di consumo', *Sipradue*, 2 (March–April 1968), 13.

77 Galluzzo, 'I grafici sono sempre protagonisti?', pp. 173–219.

78 *Ibid.*, pp. 168–71.

79 Mataloni, 'Immagine aziendale e disegno coordinato', 267–72. Participants in the roundtable were Tito Anselmi, Mario Bellini, Rodolfo Bonetto, Gillo Dorfles, Franco Grignani, Giancarlo Iliprandi, Ilio Negri, Pino Tovaglia and AlfredoTroisi.

80 'Il problema è dei grafici che vogliono restare in ADI'. *Ibid.*, 272.

81 'Affetti da una specie di complesso di inferiorità. … forse il disegno, se non proprio i designer, è affetto da un'altra malattia: la mitomania'. *Ibid.*, 271–2.

Conclusion: redrafting Italian graphic design

Italian graphic design was born in Milan in 1933, was it not? Well, the year 1933 was indeed a crucial date in the history of Italian graphic design. The temporal and geographical convergence of multiple factors – Antonio Boggeri opening his studio and hiring a Bauhausler, the launch of *Campo Grafico*, plus Paul Renner curating the German Pavilion at the 5th Triennale – all suggest that the time was ripe for a change. Counter to the narrative of existing historiography, this book has explored the emergence and articulation of Italian graphic design as an ongoing process of becoming. In doing so, it has identified the multiple players involved in this becoming. We have looked back into the past for the initial seeds of change and considered the socio-cultural, economic and political background that shaped the new professional figure of graphic designer in Italy.

As we have seen throughout the foregoing pages, the actual 'birth' of Italian graphic design happened neither overnight, nor out of the blue. It was, in fact, rooted in the tradition of Italian typography and poster art and enriched by the crossover between graphics, advertising, photography, exhibition design and industrial design. It was a long and uneven process that spanned the war years and never found a definite and uncontested outcome. In the late 1960s, Milan's graphic designers were still having discussions among themselves about their practice. They were still struggling to be officially recognised by the design community and society at large. They were also as uncertain as at any time previously as to what the most appropriate term to define themselves and their practice was. These clarifications are in line with the idea that guided my research: practices are in a constant state of formation and under continuous renegotiation.

Tell me your name and I will tell you who you are

Graphic design terminology persists as an issue without a simple solution. Throughout this book, I have used semantic shifts as keys to unlock the changes in the way graphic design practice was understood in Milan between the early 1930s and mid-1960s. Indeed, the efforts practitioners made to articulate a specialist vocabulary formed a thread that ran through all its five chapters. The often short-lived agreements around a shared terminology were indicative of a process that was anything but straightforward. The terms used to identify graphic design during the period under study, and for many years thereafter, were vague and interchangeable. The uncertain connotations of specialist terminology was a constantly recurring issue that signalled the continuous re-adapting of graphic design practice. As Jonathan M. Woodham observed, 'the widely felt uncertainty for the connotations of the terms ... reflected the inability of designers to establish a clear-cut professional identity or status'.[1] It follows that one can trace the struggle graphic designers had to construct an autonomous discourse by looking at their gradual articulation of a specialist language. In other words, semantic shifts were not accidental, but mirrored the changing definition of the status and identity of the practice.

Nowadays, vocabulary is as contested a space as it was during the period I have explored in this book. In 2012, the Aiap changed its name once again, this time to Associazione Italiana Design della Comunicazione Visiva (Italian Association of Visual Communication Design). Prior to this latest name change, back in 1980 it had already been retitled, Associazione Italiana Creativi della Comunicazione Visiva (Italian Association of Visual Communication Creatives) – where the word 'creatives' was still close to art-related creativity – and then in 1993 it had become, Associazione Italiana Progettazione per la Comunicazione Visiva (Italian Association of Visual Communication Design).[2] This ongoing uncertainty about the connotations of terms is by no means unique to Italy. The 'little agreement on the proper nomenclature' is an endemic issue, shared by every language, and it is faced by graphic design practice still in our day.[3] For example, Icograda was retitled, International Council of Communication Design in 2011, and it is currently named, ico-D, International Council of Design.

Is graphic design ... design?

As to the question of whether or not graphic practice is part of Italian design, in 2021 the Milan Triennale signed an agreement with the Aiap to exhibit on a rotating basis a selection of materials from the CDPG, Centro di Documentazione del Progetto Grafico (Graphic Design Documentation

Centre), within the permanent display of the Triennale Design Museum. A series of conversations and a temporary exhibition entitled 'Il mestiere di grafico – oggi' (The graphic designer's practice – today) marked this joint venture. If the inclusion of graphic design in the permanent display of the Triennale Design Museum seals its rightful belonging in Italian design, the conversations and the temporary exhibition are both evidence of graphic designers' self-awareness and recurring need to renegotiate their collective identity and practice.

Since spring 2021, the ADI Design Museum – Compasso d'Oro in Milan has been showing the historical collection of the Compasso d'Oro award. The presence of graphic design in the permanent collection is revealing of the subordinate position that the practice still holds within the association. A fair number of the exhibits fall under the category graphic design; however, magazines, advertisements, posters and packaging are not given any value on their own besides that of mediating the industrial design products awarded over the years. The section 'Career Manifesto: A tribute by Italian graphic designers to the Masters of the Compasso d'Oro' pays homage to the winners of the Compasso d'Oro Career Awards. Each winner is celebrated with a poster by a contemporary graphic designer that visitors can take home as a souvenir of their visit. Meant to present 'a virtuous snapshot of the state of the art of contemporary Italian graphics', the display illustrates yet again the somewhat self-absorbed interest of the ADI towards graphic design.[4]

Complicating narratives of modernism

The articulation of graphic design practice in Italy developed alongside discourses on modernism. Because of this focus on modernism, I found myself 'guilty' of what design historian Daniel Huppatz defined as the discipline's 'fixation on modernism'.[5] Yet, instead of attempting to construct an artificially unified and design celebrity-centred narrative, I here analysed modernism as the subject of debate among practitioners and critics involving strategies of negotiation, adaptation and resistance. My focus on local and transnational networks of design exchange and mediating channels that either promoted, or contrasted, modernism in Italy, enabled me to investigate the dissemination of modernism as a multidirectional movement. Moreover, I also brought out parallels with other design cultures and made comparisons with key protagonists of narratives of modernism. These stemmed from direct or indirect connections that I was able to trace through archival research, primary literature and interviews. Some connections, like Xanti Schawinsky working for Studio Boggeri, were already known, but taken for granted; others, like the thread connecting the Red Bauhaus and the Cooperativa Rinascita in Milan, passing through the TGP in Mexico City, were quite unexpected.

By analysing everyday design practices in context, I challenged the malleability of modernism as a vehicle of ideologies and values within and beyond the design realm. I problematised the connotative potential of modernist visual vocabulary and illustrated how modernism was often used in ways that cast doubt on its alleged left-wing stance and reveal, by contrast, its problematic ambiguity. This was the case, for example, with the modernist trope of the enlarged dots of the halftone screen. As a decorative element that foregrounded the printing technology and process of mechanical reproduction for aesthetic purposes, the enlarged halftone dots were used together with lowercase sans-serifs and photomontages for promotional purposes, in order to articulate the public image of the Scuola del Libro in Milan and Studio Boggeri. When associated with content of fascist propaganda, they provided the regime with a contemporary and cutting-edge appeal and established a parallel between the mass-produced image and the mass-acclaimed leader. Later in the post-war period, the enlarged halftone dots contributed to graphic designers' efforts to have their practice included within the design domain by highlighting the mechanical aspect, the series production and the reproducibility of graphic design.

Critical graphic design history

As I stated in the introduction, one of my main incentives for the writing of this book was to contribute to an outward-looking graphic design history in context, by showing that what is required in order to open the history of graphic design to, and engage, a wider audience, is a critical approach and historical analysis that goes beyond the largely self-celebratory tendency of histories from within the field.[6] 'The history of graphic design', graphic design historian Teal Triggs argued, 'is more than a history of graphic objects; it is also a history of narratives formulated around process, production, social interaction, and discourse.'[7] In this vein, the argument advanced in this book provides an interdisciplinary framework that neither posits graphic design as a mere intermediary, nor understands it as isolated from external forces, but rather takes into account its social significance and cultural function. In doing so, it demonstrates the potential of using graphic design as a starting point for thinking about broader research questions – such as design education and practice, designers' social responsibility, professionalisation processes and mediation strategies – and for speaking to a wider public.

This book provides a fertile terrain for considering graphic design as an integral part of the history of design and visual culture, both within and outside Italy. Here, a contextualised approach has enabled graphic design to reclaim its significance within the history of Italian design as an equal partner with other design fields, product design above all. As such, this book contributes to a more diverse, inclusive and contextualised understanding of Italian design, and offers a much-needed critical and historical analysis of the role that graphic design has played in Italian design culture.

An open-ended practice

Since the 1960s, graphic designers in Italy, as elsewhere in the world, have carried on adapting their practice and negotiating their professional identity in order to respond to changing social, economic and cultural contexts, shifting design agendas and discourses, and evolving technologies. Gender equality has yet to be achieved. Take the AGI as an example. Women graphic designers waited until the mid-1960s to be admitted into the international association. By the end of the 1990s, women constituted a minority of about twenty-five members.[8] Only two of twelve members of the current Italian chapter are women: Silvana Amato and Luisa Milani, who became members in 2018 and 2019, respectively.[9] Graphic designer and historian Silvia Sfligiotti offered the following reflection about the state of graphic design practice in Italy towards the end of 2010: 'Our profession is one that undergoes continual redefinition; within Italy it does not seem to have achieved a state of [what] one might call "consolidation". … In defining the myriad approaches within our profession, sometimes one feels the ground slip away from under one's feet.'[10]

Drawing attention to everyday design practices, educational issues, networks, organisational strategies and mediating channels, this book provides a working basis upon which to build a more comprehensive picture of the professional status of the graphic designer in Italy. Ongoing debate among the graphic design community suggests that graphic designers are yet again today asking themselves what graphic design is. This is an open-ended question that has been approached historically and critically in this book by looking into the articulation of graphic design practice in Milan from the 1930s to the 1960s.

Notes

1 Woodham, *Twentieth Century Design*, p. 167.
2 Grazzani and Guida, *AIAP 70×70*, p. 12.
3 McCoy, 'Education in an adolescent profession', p. 3.
4 L. Molinari, 'Career Manifesto. A tribute by Italian graphic designers to the Masters of the Compasso d'Oro', www.adidesignmuseum.org/en/exhibition/manifesto-alla-carriera/, accessed 31 May 2023.
5 D. J. Huppatz, 'Globalizing design history and global design history', *Journal of Design History*, 28:2 (2015), 188.

6 Lees-Maffei and Maffei (eds), *Reading Graphic Design in Cultural Context*.

7 Triggs, 'Curating graphic design and its history', p. 20.

8 Bos and Bos (eds), *AGI*.

9 Anon., 'AGI members', www.a-g-i.org/members, accessed 31 May 2023.

10 S. Sfligiotti, 'Being in the world: Some approaches to graphic design in Italy towards the end of 2010', in Camuffo and Dalla Mura (eds), *Graphic Design Worlds/Words*, p. 93.

Bibliography

Archival sources

AAA Smithsonian Institute, Archives of American Art, Washington, US.
AALS Archivio Albe e Lica Steiner, Politecnico di Milano, Milan, Italy.
APICE Archivi della Parola, dell'Immagine e della Comunicazione Editoriale, Università degli Studi di Milano, Milan, Italy.
ASB Archivio Studio Boggeri, Meride, Switzerland.
ASM Archivio Storico della città di Monza, Monza, Italy.
ASSU Archivio Storico Società Umanitaria, Milan, Italy.
ATM Archivi della Triennale di Milano, Milan, Italy.
BA Bauhaus-Archiv, Berlin, Germany.
UBDA University of Brighton Design Archives, Brighton, UK.

Primary sources

Alfieri, D. and L. Freddi (eds), *Mostra della Rivoluzione Fascista* (Bergamo: Officine dell'Istituto Italiano delle Arti Grafiche, 1933).

Anon., *Prima esposizione internazionale delle arti decorative: Consorzio Milano-Monza Umanitaria* (Milan: Casa Editrice Bestetti & Tumminelli, 1923).

Anon., *Seconda mostra internazionale delle arti decorative: catalogo* (Milan: Case Editrici Alpes e F. de Rio, 1925).

Anon., *IV Esposizione triennale internazionale delle arti decorative ed industriali moderne: catalogo ufficiale* (Milan: Casa Editrice Ceschina, 1930).

Anon., 'Fotografia tedesca', *Casabella*, 39 (March 1931), 48–9.

Anon., 'Fotografia tedesca', *Casabella*, 40 (April 1931), 52–3.

Anon., 'Fotografia tedesca', *Casabella*, 41 (May 1931), 57–8.

Anon., 'Il libro bello: occhio e fotografia', *Casabella*, 41 (May 1931), 57.

Anon., 'Fotografia tedesca', *Casabella*, 49 (January 1932), 60.

Anon., *V Triennale di Milano: catalogo ufficiale* (Milan: Casa Editrice Ceschina, 1933).

Anon., *V Triennale di Milano: Padiglione della Stampa* (Milan: 1933).

Anon., 'Das deutsche Buchgewerbe auf dem V. Triennale in Mailand', *Gebrauchsgraphik*, 10:7 (July 1933), 10–12.

Anon., 'Arti grafiche alla Triennale', *Campo Grafico*, 1:10 (October 1933), 171–2.

Anon., 'Ostacoli', *Campo Grafico*, 2:5 (May 1934), 101.

Anon., 'Ancora sulla Triennale: onestà e responsabilità', *Campo Grafico*, 2:9 (September 1934), 197–9.

Anon., 'La regolamentazione dell'apprendistato grafico', *Graphicus*, 23:6 (January 1936), 15–16.

Anon., 'Editoriale', *Campo Grafico*, 4:7 (July 1936), 1.

Anon., 'Documentari di Campo Grafico', *Campo Grafico*, 6:2 (February 1938), 36–51.

Anon., 'Documentari di Campo Grafico', *Campo Grafico*, 6:6 (June 1938), 167–73.

Anon., *VII Triennale di Milano: guida* (Milan: S.A.M.E., 1940).

Anon., 'Un elogio e un rimprovero', *Linea Grafica*, 3:9–10 (September–October 1950), 276–7.

Anon., 'Le arti grafiche alla Triennale', *Bollettino Centro Studi Grafici*, 5:31 (June 1951), 1.

Anon., 'Offene Stellen', *Chamäleon*, 25 (November 1954), 6.

Anon., 'I consigli direttivi della FIP e delle otto associazioni nazionali aderenti', *La Pubblicità: Bollettino Mensile della FIP e Associazioni Aderenti*, 9:12 (December 1955), 8.

Anon., 'La "giarrettiera" pubblicitaria a Carlo Dradi', *La Pubblicità: Bollettino Mensile della FIP e Associazioni Aderenti*, 10:10 (October 1956), 7.

Anon., *Società Umanitaria: relazione sull'attività sociale dal 1956 al 1960* (Milan: Società Umanitaria, 1960).

Anon., 'Congresso dell'ICSID a Venezia', *Stile Industria*, 8:34 (October 1961), 1–28.

Anon., *GraphicsRCA: Fifteen Years' Work of the School of Graphic Design, Royal College of Art* (London: Lion & Unicorn Press, 1963).

Anon., 'AIAP: il Presidente dell'Icograda in visita all'Aiap', *La Pubblicità: Bollettino Mensile della FIP e Associazioni Aderenti*, 20:12 (December 1966), 24.

Anselmi, A. T., 'Hochschule für Gestaltung, Ulm: documenti di una scuola di disegno industriale', *Stile Industria*, 6:21 (March 1959), 3–20.

Baldini, R., 'Grafica nella produzione', *Stile Industria*, 9:38 (June 1962), 24–34.

Bauer, R., 'Problemi vivi della istruzione professionale', *Linea Grafica*, 7:1–2 (January–February 1954), 17–20.

Bauer, R., *Scuola del Libro: programmi di insegnamento, anno scolastico 1954–1955* (Milan: Società Umanitaria, 1954).

Benca, 'La migliore pubblicità potrebbe essere italiana', *Poliedro*, 5 (January–April 1968), 9–14.

Bertieri, R., 'La Scuola del Libro in Milano: la "Vita Nova"', *Risorgimento Grafico*, 21:8 (August 1924), 329–37.

Bertieri, R., 'Orientamenti nuovi della tipografia italiana', *Risorgimento Grafico*, 30:2 (February 1933), 81–94.

Bertieri, R., 'Ad un collega che si astiene', *Risorgimento Grafico*, 30:3 (March 1933), 141–3.

Bertieri, R., 'Alcuni aspetti grafici della Mostra della Rivoluzione Fascista', *Risorgimento Grafico*, 30:6 (June 1933), 321–39.

Bertieri, R., 'Architetti del libro e tipografi artisti in Italia', *Risorgimento Grafico*, 35:4 (April 1938), 145–62.

Black, M., 'The Royal College of Art', *Stile Industria*, 8:32 (May 1961), 2–9.

Boggeri, A., 'Commento', *Luci ed Ombre: Annuario della Fotografia Artistica Italiana* (Turin: Il Corriere Fotografico, 1929), pp. 9–16.

Boggeri, A., letter to A. Rossi, *Campo Grafico*, 2:12 (December 1934), 271.

Boggeri, A., 'La fotografia nella pubblicità', *La Pubblicità d'Italia*, 1:5–6 (November–December 1937), 16–25.

Boggeri, A., 'Stampati pubblicitari per i medici', *La Pubblicità d'Italia*, 5:50–4 (August–December 1941), 28–35.

Boggeri, A., 'Advertising art in post-war Italy', *Graphis*, 18 (1947), 148–53.

Bona, E., 'Stampati dello stato', *Campo Grafico*, 3:4 (April 1935), 78–9.

Bona, E., 'Pubblico e grafici', *Campo Grafico*, 6:10–12 (October–December 1938), 245–8.

Bona, E., 'Del progettista grafico', *Campo Grafico*, 8:1 (January 1939), 3–5.

Bottoni, P. (ed.), *T8 catalogo–guida* (Milan: Meregalli, 1947).

Caimi, N., 'La pubblicità e l'industria grafica', *Risorgimento Grafico*, 28:5 (May 1931), 237–40.

Campo Grafico, 'Presupposti alla collaborazione con l'artista', *Campo Grafico*, 2:3 (March 1934), 52–5.

Campo Grafico, 'Il gusto del cliente', *Campo Grafico*, 2:4 (April 1934), 77–8.

Campo Grafico, 'Come si suscita il gusto grafico', *Campo Grafico*, 2:6 (June 1934), 124–5.

Campo Grafico, 'Fotografia e tipografia', *Campo Grafico*, 2:12 (December 1934), 269.

Campo Grafico, 'Tipografia e Triennale', *Campo Grafico*, 3:6 (June 1935), 126–7.

Campo Grafico, 'Le arti grafiche alla VI Triennale di Milano 1936', *Campo Grafico*, 4:5 (May 1936), 85–94.

Castelli, G., 'La I riunione dell'A.D.I. a Milano', *Stile Industria*, 3:7 (June 1956), 3 and 48.

Castelli, G., 'Le scuole di industrial design in Inghilterra', *Stile Industria*, 5:18 (August 1958), 37–8.

D'Errico, E., 'Lo spirito moderno e la tipografia italiana', *Graphicus*, 26:5 (May 1936), 9.

D'Errico, E., 'VI Triennale di Milano', *Graphicus*, 27:2 (February 1937), 14–15.

Doblin, J., 'Institute of Design Chicago', *Stile Industria*, 6:24 (September 1959), 1–5.

Ferrigni, M., 'Gli artisti grafici alla V Triennale di Milano', *Risorgimento Grafico*, 31:1 (January 1934), 21–41.

Ferrigni, M., 'Fotografia pubblicitaria', *Risorgimento Grafico*, 31:2 (February 1934), 88–126.

Ferrigni, M., 'L'insegnamento grafico in Italia', *Risorgimento Grafico*, 32:1 (January 1935), 23–31.

Ferrigni, M., 'Saggi di giovani rilegatori', *Risorgimento Grafico*, 33:10 (October 1936), 377–94.

Frassinelli, C., 'Utilità dello schizzo nel lavoro tipografico', *Graphicus*, 18:230 (August 1928), 11–12.

G. P., 'Contro l'arte del libro?', *Graphicus*, 17:219 (September 1927), 17.

Gropius, W., 'Razionalizzazione nella economia edile', *Quadrante*, 24 (April 1935), 7, 10–13, 15, 19 and 25.

Guyatt, R., 'The School of Graphic Design of the RCA, London', *Graphis*, 15:84 (July–August 1959), 290–307 and 398–9.

Henrion, F. H. K., 'Graphic Design and Visual Communication Technology', in Anon., *2nd General Assembly and Congress Icograda – International Council of Graphic Design Associations*, conference proceedings, 1966.

Hofmann, A., *Methodik der Form- und Bildgestaltung. Aufbau – Synthese – Anwendung/ Manuel de création graphique / Graphic Design Manual. Principles and Practice* (Teufen: Niggli, 1965).

Il Risorgimento Grafico, 'Per l'insegnamento professionale', *Risorgimento Grafico*, 20:9 (September 1923), 438.

Il Risorgimento Grafico, 'Per l'insegnamento professionale', *Risorgimento Grafico*, 20:11 (November 1923), 535–7.

Il Risorgimento Grafico, 'Per l'insegnamento professionale', *Risorgimento Grafico*, 21:5 (May 1924), 208–11.

Il Risorgimento Grafico, 'Per l'insegnamento professionale. Le conclusioni del referendum', *Risorgimento Grafico*, 21:7 (July 1924), 291–5.

Il Risorgimento Grafico, 'Le arti grafiche alla Triennale', *Risorgimento Grafico*, 30:9 (September 1933), 517–31.

Iliprandi, G., 'Un prodotto di consumo', *Sipradue*, 2 (March–April 1968), 13.

Jacobson, E., *The Color Harmony Manual and How to Use It* (Chicago: Container Corporation of America, 1942).

Ladelli, L. (ed.), *Catalogo della biblioteca della Scuola del Libro in Milano* (Milan: Umanitaria, 1931).

Lancelotti, A., *Storia aneddotica della réclame* (Milan: Riccardo Quintieri Editore, 1912).

Maldonado, T., 'L'insegnamento superiore e la crisi dell'educazione', *Civiltà delle Macchine*, 5–6 (May–June 1957), 82–9.

Maldonado, T., 'Scienza, tecnologia e forma', *Stile Industria*, 5:18 (August 1958), 44.

Maldonado, T., 'Le nuove prospettive industriali e la formazione del designer', *Stile Industria*, 6:20 (January 1959), XIX–XXIV.

Maldonado, T., 'Formazione e alternative di una professione', *Stile Industria*, 8:34 (October 1961), 21–4.

Mangiarotti, A., 'Institute of Design di Chicago: esperienze di insegnamento', *Stile Industria*, 2:4 (April 1955), 7–11.

Marzagalli, A., 'Pubblicitario, artista, tipografo: un trinomio inscindibile', *L'Ufficio Moderno*, 28:5–6 (May–June 1943), 84–6.

Mataloni, F., 'Immagine aziendale e disegno coordinato', *Linea Grafica*, 21:4 (July–August 1969), 267–72.

Mazzanti, A., 'Tipografi e clientela', *Risorgimento Grafico*, 25:5 (May 1928), 217–20.

Mazzucchelli, A. M., 'Stile di una mostra', *Casabella*, 80 (August 1934), 6–9.

Melino, M., 'I sergenti della grafica', *Pirelli*, 6 (December 1962), 100–4.

Meyer, 'Royal College of Art London', *Gebrauchsgraphik*, 30:10 (October 1959), 20–5.

Meyer, 'ARK: the students' magazine of the Royal College of Art in London', *Gebrauchsgraphik*, 31:4 (April 1960), 36–43.

Modiano, G., 'Situazione grafica', *Quadrante*, 11 (May 1933), 21.

Modiano, G., 'Padiglione della Stampa', *Campo Grafico*, 1:7 (July 1933), 121–2.

Modiano, G., (Un Astensionista), 'Parole, parole, parole', *Risorgimento Grafico*, 31:4 (April 1934), 159–67.

Modiano, G., 'Necessità pubblicitaria della confezione e dell'imballaggio', *L'Ufficio Moderno*, 9:7–8 (July–August 1934), 361–5.

Modiano, G., 'Cinque manifesti', *Graphicus*, 24:10 (October 1934), 21–3.

Modiano, G., 'La tecnica dell'annuncio VI: l'illustrazione', *L'Ufficio Moderno*, 10:3 (March 1935), 129–30.

Modiano, G., 'Manifesti', *Campo Grafico*, 3:11–12 (November–December 1935), 244–5.

Modiano, G., 'Triennale 1936', *Risorgimento Grafico*, 34:1 (January 1937), 21–30.

Modiano, G., 'Sulle tendenze costruttive grafiche in Italia', *Graphicus*, 27:4–5 (April–May 1937), 31.

Modiano, G., 'Quattro righe', *Campo Grafico*, 5:5–6 (May–June 1937), 14–15.

Modiano, G., 'Lettera aperta a Raffaello Bertieri', *Risorgimento Grafico*, 35:8 (August 1938), 333–40.

Modiano, G., 'Un posteggio e una vetrina nel commento di un tipografo', *Campo Grafico*, 7:3–5 (March–May 1939), 103–4.

Modiano, G., 'L'arte grafica alla VII Triennale di Milano', *Industria della Stampa*, 11:4–5 (July–August 1940), 191–8.

Modiano, G., (ed.), *La Mostra Grafica alla Triennale* (Milan: Società Grafica G. Modiano, 1940).

Moholy-Nagy, L., *Painting, Photography, Film* (Cambridge, MA: MIT Press, 1969 (1925)).

Moholy-Nagy, L., 'Su l'avvenire della fotografia', *Note Fotografiche*, 9:2 (August 1932), 59–60.

Müller-Brockmann, J., *Gestaltungsprobleme des Grafikers/The Graphic Artist and his Design Problems/Les problems d'un artiste graphique* (Teufen: Niggli, 1961).

Müller-Munk, P., 'Il design esiste come professione', *Stile Industria*, 8:34 (October 1961), 12–14.

Noi, 'Presentazione', *L'Ufficio Moderno*, 10:10 (October 1935), 437–8.

Pagano, G., *Le scuole dell'Umanitaria anno XVI E.F.: Quaderno n. 1* (Milan: Società Umanitaria, 1937).

Peviani, G., 'La necessità dello schizzo', *Campo Grafico*, 1:1 (January 1933), 4–5.

Pica, A. (ed.), *Nona Triennale di Milano: catalogo* (Milan: S.A.M.E., 1951).

Pica, A. (ed.),*Undicesima Triennale: catalogo* (Milan: Arti Grafiche Crespi, 1957).

Pifferi, E., 'Mostra della Rivoluzione', *Casabella*, 64 (April 1933), 38–41.

Pizzuto, G., 'Guido Modiano, ein Italienischer Drucker – Evoluzione della tipografia in Italia attraverso l'opera di Guido Modiano', *Druck und Werbekunst: Italienische Werbegraphic*, 1 (1942), 7.

Pomé, R., *Concezione moderna della pubblicità: lezioni tenute al Politecnico di Milano per il Corso di Dirigenti di Aziende Industriali (Aprile–Maggio 1936–XIV)* (Rome: Edizioni della Federazione Nazionale Fascista Dirigenti Aziende Industriali, 1936).

Prezzolini, G., *L'arte di persuadere* (Milan: Lumachi, 1907).

Provinciali, M., 'Institute of Design', *Bollettino del Centro Studi Grafici*, 8:53 (May 1953), n. p.

Provinciali, M., 'I martedì del Centro: elementi per una sintassi della forma', *Bollettino del Centro Studi Grafici*, 8:65 (May 1964), n. p.

Ricciardi, G. C. (ed.), *Guida Ricciardi: la pubblicità in Italia* (Milan: Edizioni L'Ufficio Moderno, 1933).

Ricciardi, G. C. (ed.), *Guida Ricciardi: pubblicità e propaganda in Italia* (Milan: Edizione Pubblicità Ricciardi, 1936).

Ricciardi, G. C. (ed.), *Guida Ricciardi: pubblicità e propaganda* (Milan: Edizione Pubblicità Ricciardi, 1942).

Roggero, E., *Come si riesce con la pubblicità* (Milan: Hoepli, 1920).

Romano, G., 'La ricostruzione dell'Umanitaria a Milano', *Casabella Continuità*, 214 (February–March 1957), 28.

Rosselli, A., 'Artisti italiani per la pubblicità', *Stile Industria*, 1:1 (June 1954), 31–7.

Rosselli, A., 'Grafica tecnica', *Stile Industria*, 2:4 (April 1955), 46–53.

Rosselli, A., 'Grafica tecnica', *Stile Industria*, 3:6 (February 1956), 42–7.

Rosselli, A., 'Per una scuola di disegno industriale in Italia', *Stile Industria*, 5:17 (June 1958), 1.

Rosselli, A., 'L'insegnamento del disegno industriale e la realtà produttiva', *Stile Industria*, 6:21 (March 1959), 1–3.

Rosselli, A., 'Design italiano a Chicago', *Stile Industria*, 6:23 (July 1959), 1.

Rosselli, A., 'World Design Conference 1960', *Stile Industria*, 7:28 (August 1960), xi–xxvi.

Rosselli, A., 'Grafici e industrial design', *Stile Industria*, 9:37 (April 1962), 13–27.

Rossi, A., 'L'evoluzione della tipografia in Italia', *Campo Grafico*, 5:9 (September 1937), 4–7.

Rossi, A., 'Il nostro principio di scelta', *Linea Grafica*, 7:5–6 (May–June 1954), 126–7.

Rossi, A., 'Grafica non grafica tecnica', *Linea Grafica*, 8:9–10 (September–October 1955), 236.

Ruder, E., *Typographie* (Sulgen: Niggli, 1965).

Salvadori, R., 'La nuova grafica inglese e il Royal College of Art', *Linea Grafica*, 17:3–4 (March–April 1964), 105–8.

Santini, P. C. 'La Scuola di Ulm: organizzazione e metodi di lavoro', *Comunità*, 72 (August–September 1959), reprinted in *Notizie AIAP*, 89 (May 1999), 14–19.

Santini, P. C. (ed.), *12ª Triennale di Milano* (Milan: Arti Grafiche Crespi, 1960).

Sarfatti, M., 'Architettura, arte e simbolo della Mostra del Fascismo', *Architettura*, 12:1 (January 1933), 1–17.

Schawinsky, X., 'Pubblicità funzionale', *L'Ufficio Moderno*, 10:10 (October 1935), 467.

Sinisgalli, L., 'Boggeri regista grafico', *Linea Grafica*, 5:3–4 (March–April 1952), 66–7.

Sinisgalli, L., 'La responsabilità della grafica', in A. Pica (ed.), *Undicesima Triennale: catalogo* (Milan: Arti Grafiche Crespi, 1957), pp. 121–2.

Soresina, M., 'Per una estetica grafica italiana', *Risorgimento Grafico*, 30:3 (March 1933), 145–7.

Steiner, A., 'La mostra a fine anno alla Scuola del Libro della Società Umanitaria', *Linea Grafica*, 16:7–8 (July–August 1961), 239–46.

Trevisani, P., 'Piccoli stampati', *Risorgimento Grafico*, 34:2 (February 1937), 65–79.

Tschichold, J., 'Die Opposition gegen Buchkunst und Buchkunstaustellung', *Die Literarische Welt*, 3:29 (1927), 3.

Tschichold, J., *The New Typography* (Berkeley; Los Angeles; London: University of California Press, 2006 (1928)).

Veronesi, G., 'Pubblicità', *Campo Grafico*, 5:5–6 (June 1937), 36–9.

Veronesi, L. and B. Pallavera, 'Del fotomontaggio', *Campo Grafico*, 2:12 (December 1934), 278–81.

Weiss, I., 'Il bello non è inefficace', *Pirelli*, 2 (April 1954), 55.

Weiss, I., 'Panorama della pubblicità italiana', *L'Ufficio Moderno*, 31:3 (March 1957), 437–41.

Zveteremich, R., 'Die italienische Werbekunst in der Gegenwart – Panorana attuale della pubblicità italiana', *Deutscher Drucker: Deutschland-Italien Heft* (July 1941), 386–9.

Secondary sources

Abbott, A., *The System of Professions: An Essay on the Division of Expert Labour* (Chicago; London: University of Chicago Press, 1988).

Adamson, G., G. Riello and S. Teasley, 'Introduction: Towards global design history', in G. Adamson, G. Riello and S. Teasley (eds), *Global Design History* (London; New York: Routledge, 2011), pp. 1–10.

Amari, M., *I musei delle aziende. La cultura della tecnica tra arte e storia* (Milan: Franco Angeli Editore, 1997).

Anceschi, G., 'Il campo della grafica italiana: storia e problemi', *Rassegna*, 6 (1981), 5–19.

Anceschi, G., 'Design di base, fondamenta del design', *Ottagono*, 70 (September 1983), reprinted in *Notizie AIAP*, 10 (June 2000), 18–28.

Anceschi, G. and P. G. Tanca, 'Ulm e l'Italia', in H. Lindinger (ed.), *La scuola di Ulm: una nuova cultura del progetto* (Genoa: Costa & Nolan, 1988), pp. 51–3.

Anon., *Onoranze a Raffaello Bertieri nell'ambito del quinto centenario dell'introduzione della stampa in Italia* (Milan: Centro Studi Grafici, 1966).

Anon., *Milano 70/70: un secolo d'arte, 1946–1970* (Milan: Museo Poldi-Pezzoli, 1971).

Anon., *Albe Steiner: comunicazione visiva* (Milan: Fratelli Alinari, 1977).

Anon., *Gli annitrenta. Arte e cultura in Italia* (Mazzotta: Milan, 1982).

Antliff, M., 'Fascism, modernism, and modernity', *The Art Bulletin*, 84:1 (2002), 148–69.

Armstrong, L., 'Steering a course between professionalism and commercialism: The Society of Industrial Artists and the Code of Conduct for the professional designer 1945–1975', *Journal of Design History*, 29:2 (2016), 161–79.

Armstrong, L., 'A new image for a new profession: Self-image and representation in the professionalization of design in Britain, 1945–1960', *Journal of Consumer Culture*, 19:1 (2017), 104–24.

Armstrong, L., *The Industrialized Designer: Gender, Identity and Professionalisation in Britain and the US, 1930–1980* (Manchester: Manchester University Press, 2024).

Armstrong, L. and F. McDowell, 'Introduction: Fashioning professionals: History, theory and methods', in L. Armstrong and F. McDowell (eds), *Fashioning Professionals: Identity and Representation at Work in the Creative Industries* (London: Bloomsbury, 2018), pp. 1–25.

Arthurs, J., M. Ebner and K. Ferris (eds), *The Politics of Everyday Life in Fascist Italy. Outside the State?* (New York: Palgrave, 2017).

Arvidsson, A., 'Between Fascism and the American dream: Advertising in interwar Italy', *Social Science History*, 25:2 (2001), 151–86.

Arvidsson, A., *Marketing Modernity: Italian Advertising from Fascism to Postmodernity* (London; New York: Routledge, 2003).

Augeri, N. (ed.), *I Convitti della Rinascita* (Milan: Edizioni Aurora, 2016).

Aynsley, J., *Graphic Design in Germany 1890–1945* (London: Thames & Hudson, 2000).

Aynsley, J., *A Century of Graphic Design* (London: Mitchell Beazley, 2001).

Aynsley, J. and K. Forde (eds), *Design and the Modern Magazine* (Manchester; New York: Manchester University Press, 2007).

Aynsley, J., A. J. Clarke and T. Messell (eds), *International Design Organisations: Histories, Legacies, Values* (London: Bloomsbury, 2022).

Aynsley, J., A. J. Clarke and T. Messell, 'Introduction', in J. Aynsley, A. J. Clarke and T. Messell (eds), *International Design Organisations: Histories, Legacies, Values* (London: Bloomsbury, 2022), pp. 1–15.

Barazzetta, G., 'Sede e scuole della Società Umanitaria', *Casabella*, 750–1 (December 2006–January 2007), 10–15.

Barbieri, C., 'Negotiating graphic design between national and international design organisations: The case of the Associazione per il Design Industriale in Milan', in J. Aynsley, A. J. Clarke and T. Messell (eds), *International Design Organisations: Histories, Legacies, Values* (London: Bloomsbury, 2022), pp. 205–22.

Barbieri, C. and D. Fornari, 'The lost typefaces of Xanti Schawinsky: From the Bauhaus to Italy', in O. Moret (ed.), *Back to the Future: The Future in the Past. ICDHS 10th+1 Barcelona 2018* (Barcelona: Edicions de la Universitat de Barcelona, 2018), pp. 296–9.

Barbieri, C. and D. Fornari, 'Speaking Italian with a Swiss-German accent: Walter Ballmer and Swiss graphic design in Milan', *Design Issues*, 37:1 (2020), 26–41.

Baroni, D. and M. Vitta (eds), *Storia del design grafico* (Milan: Longanesi & Co., 2003).

Bassi, A., R. Riccini and C. Colombo (eds), *Design in Triennale 1947–68: percorsi fra Milano e Brianza* (Milan: Silvana Editoriale, 2004).

Bastianelli, S. and B. Fabbri, 'CSAG di Urbino: la prima scuola italiana di graphic design', *Progetto Grafico*, 24 (2013), 58–64.

Bauer, R. (ed.), *La Società Umanitaria. Fondazione P.M. Loria Milano, 1893/1963* (Milan: Società Umanitaria, 1964).

Bayer, H., *Herbert Bayer: Painter, Designer, Architect* (New York: Reinhold, 1967).

Becarelli, A. (ed.), *A Scuola come in fabbrica: l'esperienza dei Convitti Scuola della Rinascita* (Milan: Vangelista Editore, 1978).

Becarelli, A. (ed.), *Diritto allo studio, dovere di studiare: cinquantennale dei Convitti-Scuola della Rinascita* (Novara: Istituto didattico pedagogico della Resistenza, 1994).

Beegan, G. and P. Atkinson, 'Professionalism, amateurism and the boundaries of design', *Journal of Design History*, 21:4 (2008), 305–13.

Ben-Ghiat, R., *Fascist Modernities: Italy, 1922–1945* (Berkeley; Los Angeles; London: University of California Press, 2001).

Ben-Ghiat, R., 'Italian Fascists and National Socialists: The dynamics of an uneasy relationship', in R. A. Etlin (ed.), *Art, Culture, and the Media under the Third Reich* (Chicago: University of Chicago Press, 2002), pp. 257–84.

Berezin, M., *Making the Fascist Self: The Political Culture of Interwar Italy* (Ithaca: Cornell University Press, 1997).

Betts, P., 'The Bauhaus as Cold-War legend: West German modernism revised', *German Politics and Society*, 14:2 (1996), 75–100.

Betts, P., 'Science, semiotics and society: The Ulm Hochschule für Gestaltung in retrospect', *Design Issues*, 14:2 (1998), 67–82.

Betts, P., 'The Bauhaus and National Socialism: A dark chapter of modernism', in J. Fiedler and P. Feierabend (eds), *Bauhaus* (Cologne: Könemann, 1999), pp. 34–41.

Betts, P., *The Authority of Everyday Objects: A Cultural History of West German Industrial Design* (Berkeley; Los Angeles; London: University of California Press, 2004).

Bianchi, A., 'Antonio Boggeri, fotografia modernista e pubblicità', *L'Uomo Nero*, 8:7–8 (2011), 275–91.

Bigazzi, D. and M. Meriggi (eds), *Storia d'Italia. Le regioni dall'Unità a oggi: la Lombardia* (Turin: Einaudi, 2001).

Bignami, S. (ed.), *1933: un anno del Novecento a Milano* (Geneva; Milan: Skira, 2001).

Blume, T., *Xanti Schawinsky: Album* (Zurich: Jrp Ringier, 2016).

Bogart, M. H., *Artists, Advertising, and the Borders of Art* (Chicago: University of Chicago Press, 1995).

Boggeri, A. 'Una B rossa fra due punti', *Rassegna*, 6 (1981), 20–1.

Bonini, G. and A. Scalpelli (eds), *Milano fra guerra e dopoguerra* (Bari: De Donato, 1979).

Bos, B. and E. Bos (eds), *AGI: Graphic Design since 1950* (London: Thames and Hudson, 2007).

Bosoni, G., 'Le Triennali del design', in G. Petrillo and A. Scalpelli (eds), *Milano anni Cinquanta* (Milan: Franco Angeli Editore, 1986), pp. 758–78.

Bosoni, G., M. Campana and S. von Moos (eds), *Max Huber* (London; New York: Phaidon, 2006).

Bossaglia, R. (ed.), *L'ISIA a Monza: una scuola d'arte europea* (Milan: Silvana Editoriale, 1986).

Bosshard, H. R., 'Concrete art and typography', in C. Bignens, H. R. Bosshard and G. Fleischmann (eds), *Max Bill: Typography, Advertising, Book Design* (Zurich: Niggli, 1999), pp. 56–106.

Bourdieu, P., *Distinction: A Social Critique of the Judgement of Taste* (Cambridge, MA: Harvard University Press, 1984).

Bourdieu, P., *The Field of Cultural Production* (New York: Columbia University Press, 1993).

Bourdieu, P. and A. Darbel, *The Love of Art: European Art Museums and their Public* (Cambridge: Polity Press, 1991).

Brändle, C., K. Gimmi, B. Junod, C. Reble and B. Richter (eds), *100 Years of Swiss Graphic Design* (Zurich: Lars Müller, 2014).

Branzi, A., *Introduzione al design italiano: una modernità incompleta* (Milan: Baldini e Castoldi, 1999).

Braun, E., *Mario Sironi and Italian Modernism: Art and Politics under Fascism* (Cambridge: Cambridge University Press, 2000).

Brosseau, L., M. Dalla Mura, C. Imbert and J. Sueda, *Graphisme en France 2018: Exhibiting Graphic Design* (Paris: Centre National des Arts Plastiques Graphisme en France, 2018).

Brown, R. and D. Capozza, 'Social identity theory in retrospect and prospect', in D. Capozza and R. Brown (eds), *Social Identity Processes: Trends in Theory and Research* (London; Thousand Oaks; New Delhi: SAGE Publications, 2000), pp. vii–xv.

Brünning, U., 'Herbert Bayer – Universal design for the National Socialist economy and state', in J. Fiedler and P. Feierabend (eds), *Bauhaus* (Cologne: Könemann, 1999), pp. 332–45.

Buchanan, R., 'Education and professional practice in design', *Design Issues*, 14:2 (1998), 63–6.

Calvera, A., 'Local, regional, national, global and feedback: Several issues to be faced with constructing regional narratives', *Journal of Design History*, 18:4 (2005), 371–83.

Camuffo, G. and M. Dalla Mura (eds), *Graphic Design Worlds/Words* (Milan: Electa, 2011).

Camuffo, G. and M. Dalla Mura (eds), *Graphic Design, Exhibiting, Curating* (Bolzano: Bozen-Bolzano University Press, 2013).

Camuffo, G., M. Piazza and C. Vinti (eds), *TDM5: Grafica Italiana* (Milan: Corraini Edizioni, 2012).

Camuffo, G., M. Piazza and C. Vinti, 'TDM5. Un museo per una storia ancora da scrivere', in G. Camuffo, M. Piazza and C. Vinti (eds), *TDM5: Grafica Italiana* (Milan: Corraini Edizioni, 2012), pp. 18–28.

Capozza, D. and R. Brown (eds), *Social Identity Processes: Trends in Theory and Research* (London; Thousand Oaks; New Delhi: SAGE Publications, 2000).

Cardioli, A. and G. Vigini, *Storia dell'editoria italiana: un profilo introduttivo* (Milan: Editrice Bibliografica, 2004).

Carli, M., *Vedere il fascismo. Arte e politica nelle esposizioni del regime (1928–1942)* (Rome: Carocci, 2020).

Carlotti, A. L., 'Editori e giornali a Milano: continuità e cambiamento', in F. Colombo (ed.), *Libri, giornali e riviste a Milano. Storia delle innovazioni nell'editoria milanese dall'Ottocento ad oggi* (Milan: Editrice Abitare Segesta, 1998), pp. 179–90.

Carotti, C., '"L'Ufficio Moderno" di Guido Mazzali e il G.A.R.: una presenza culturale democratico-socialista nella Milano degli anni Trenta', *Storia in Lombardia*, 2 (2001), 67–92.

Cassanelli, R., U. Collu and O. Selvafolta (eds), *Nivola, Fancello, Pintori. Percorsi del moderno: dalle arti applicate all'industrial design* (Cagliari: Editoriale Wide, 2003).

Castillo, G., *Cold War on the Home Front: The Soft Power of Midcentury Design* (Minneapolis: University of Minnesota Press, 2001).

Castillo, G., 'Design pedagogy enters the Cold War: The reeducation of eleven West German architects', *Journal of Architectural Education*, 57:4 (2004), 10–18.

Castillo, G., 'The Bauhaus in Cold War Germany', in K. James-Chakraborty (ed.), *Bauhaus Culture: From Weimar to the Cold War* (Minneapolis; London: Minnesota University Press, 2006), pp. 171–93.

Castronovo, V., 'L'economia milanese alla fine della guerra e il confronto sugli obbiettivi della ricostruzione', in G. Bonini and A. Scalpelli (eds), *Milano fra guerra e dopoguerra* (Bari: De Donato, 1979), pp. 7–34.

Cavalli, L., 'Editoria: un'età d'oro dell'editoria italiana', in G. Aghina and A. Marangoni (eds), *Anni Cinquanta: la nascita della creatività italiana* (Milan: Skira, 2005), pp. 51–5.

Cerritelli, C. and N. Ossanna Cavadini (eds), *Simonetta Ferrante. La memoria del visibile: segno, colore, ritmo e calligrafie* (Cinisello Balsamo: Silvana Editoriale, 2016).

Chiappini, C., 'Antonio Boggeri: considerazioni su un protagonista della grafica italiana', *Ricerche di S/Confine*, 3:1 (2012), 138–48.

Clark, M., *Modern Italy: 1871 to the Present*, 3rd ed. (London: Routledge, 2014 (1984)).

Clarke, L. and C. Winch, 'Introduction', in L. Clarke and C. Winch (eds), *Vocational Education: International Approaches, Developments and Systems* (London; New York: Routledge, 2007), pp. 1–17.

Colombo, C. A., '"Sapere, fare e sapere fare": la Società Umanitaria, un modello laico per la formazione e l'orientamento al lavoro', in A. Bovo, N. Pietro, M. Palmaro, V. Parisi, H. M. Polidoro and A. Santucci (eds), *L'alchimia del lavoro: i generosi che primi in Milano fecondarono le arti e le scienze* (Milan: Raccolto Edizioni, 2008).

Colonetti, A. (ed.), *Grafica e design a Milano, 1933–2000* (Milan: Editrice Abitare Segesta, 2001).

Conradi, J., *Unimark International: The Design of Business and the Business of Design* (Baden: Lars Müller, 2010).

Corner, P., 'Italian Fascism: Whatever happened to dictatorship?', *Journal of Modern History*, 74:2 (2002), 325–51.

Corner, P., *The Fascist Party and Popular Opinion in Mussolini's Italy* (Oxford: Oxford University Press, 2012).

Corner, P., 'Collaboration, complicity, and evasion under Italian Fascism', in A. Lüdtke (ed.), *Everyday Life in Mass Dictatorship* (New York: Palgrave, 2016), pp. 75–93.

Crinson, M. and J. Lubbock, *Architecture: Art or Profession? Three Hundred Years of Architectural Education in Britain* (Manchester: Manchester University Press, 1994).

Crowley, D., 'National Modernism', in C. Wilk (ed.), *Modernism: Designing a New World, 1914–1939* (London: V&A Publications, 2006), pp. 34–60.

Crowley, D., 'Europe reconstructed, Europe divided', in D. Crowley and J. Pavitt (eds), *Cold War Modern: Design 1945–1970* (London: V&A Publishing, 2008), pp. 43–65.

Crowley, D., 'Humanity rearranged: The Polish and Czechoslovak Pavilions at Expo 58', *West 86th*, 19:1 (2012), 88–105.

Crowley, D. and J. Pavitt (eds), *Cold War Modern: Design 1945–1970* (London: V&A Publishing, 2008).

Curtis, P., *Patio and Pavilion: The Place of Sculpture in Modern Architecture* (London: Ridinghouse Editor, 2008).

Dalla Mura, M. and C. Vinti, 'A historiography of Italian design', in G. Lees-Maffei and K. Fallan (eds), *Made in Italy: Rethinking a Century of Italian Design* (London: Bloomsbury, 2014), pp. 35–55.

D'Amico, N., *Storia e storie della scuola italiana* (Bologna: Zanichelli, 2010).

Decleva, E., *Etica del lavoro, socialismo, cultura popolare: Augusto Osimo e la Società Umanitaria* (Milan: Franco Angeli Editore, 1985).

De Fusco, R., *Una storia dell'ADI: 50* (Milan: Franco Angeli Editore, 2010).

De Fusco, R., *Made in Italy: storia del design italiano. Nuova edizione* (Florence: Altralinea Edizioni, 2014).

De Giorgio, M., 'Donne e professioni', in M. Malatesta (ed.), *Storia d'Italia. I professionisti* (Turin: Einaudi, 1996), pp. 439–87.

De Grazia, V., *How Fascism Ruled Women: Italy 1922–1945* (Berkeley: University of California Press, 1992).

De Grazia, V., *Irresistible Empire: America's Advance through Twentieth-Century Europe* (Cambridge, MA; London: The Belknap Press of Harvard University Press, 2005).

De Iulio, S. and C. Vinti, 'La Publicité italienne et le modèle américain', *Vingtième Siècle. Revue d'Histoire*, 101 (2009), 61–80.

De Iulio, S. and C. Vinti, 'The Americanisation of Italian advertising during the 1950s and the 1960s: Mediations, conflicts, and appropriations', *Journal of Historical Research in Marketing*, 1:2 (2009), 270–94.

Della Campa, M. and C. A. Colombo (eds), *Spazio ai caratteri. L'Umanitaria e la Scuola del Libro* (Milan: Silvana Editoriale, 2004).

Dellapiana, E., *Il design e l'invenzione del Made in Italy* (Turin: Einaudi, 2022).

Dellapiana, E. and D. N. Prina, 'Craft, industry and art: ISIA (1922–1943) and the roots of Italian design education', in G. Lees-Maffei and K. Fallan (eds), *Made in Italy: Rethinking a Century of Italian Design* (London: Bloomsbury, 2014), pp. 109–25.

del Pero, M., 'Containing containment: Rethinking Italy's experience during the Cold War', *Journal of Modern Italian Studies*, 8:4 (2003), 532–55.

Di Jorio, I., 'Pubblicità e propaganda durante il fascismo. Saperi e transfer di competenze fra mercato e politica', *Italia Contemporanea – Sezione Open Access*, 3:291 (2020), 209–36.

Doordan, D. P., 'In the shadow of the fasces: Political design in Fascist Italy', *Design Issues*, 13:1 (1997), 39–52.

Dorfles, G., *Le oscillazioni del gusto* (Milan: Lerici, 1958).

Dorfles, G., *Il disegno industriale e la sua estetica* (Bologna: Cappelli Editore, 1963).

Dorfles, G., *Introduzione al disegno industriale: linguaggio e storia della produzione di serie* (Turin: Einaudi, 1972).

Dower, J. W., *Embracing Defeat: Japan in the Wake of World War II* (London: Allen Lane, 1999).

Dradi, C., *Millenovecentotrentatre: nasce a Milano la grafica moderna* (Milan: Ufficio Stampa Comune di Milano, 1973).

Dradi, C., 'Appunti per una storia della comunicazione visiva', *Bollettino del Centro Studi Grafici*, 61:1–2 (March–June 2009), 18–19.

Drucker, J., 'Philip Meggs and Richard Hollis: Models of graphic design history', *Design and Culture*, 1:1 (2009), 51–78.

Dunnage, J., *Twentieth-Century Italy: A Social History* (London; New York: Routledge, 2002).

Ebner, M., 'Coercion', in J. Arthurs, M. Ebner and K. Ferris (eds), *The Politics of Everyday Life in Fascist Italy. Outside the State?* (New York: Palgrave, 2017), pp. 77–98.

Falabrino, G. L., *Effimera e bella: storia della pubblicità italiana, Venezia 1691–Roma 2001* (Turin: Gutenberg, 2001).

Falasca-Zamponi, S., *Fascist Spectacle: The Aesthetics of Power in Mussolini's Italy* (Berkeley; Los Angeles; London: University of California Press, 1997).

Fallan, K., *Design History: Understanding Theory and Method* (Oxford; New York: Berg, 2010).

Fallan, K., 'Annus mirabilis: 1954, Alberto Rosselli and the institutionalisation of design mediation', in G. Lees-Maffei and K. Fallan (eds), *Made in Italy: Rethinking a Century of Italian Design* (London: Bloomsbury, 2014), pp. 255–70.

Fallan, K., 'Milanese mediations: Crafting Scandinavian design at the Triennali di Milano', *Konsthistorisk Tidskrift*, 83 (2014), 1–23.

Fallan, K. and G. Lees-Maffei, 'Introduction: National design histories in an age of globalization', in K. Fallan and G. Lees-Maffei (eds), *Designing Worlds: National Design Histories in an Age of Globalization* (New York: Berghahn Books, 2016), pp. 1–20.

Fallan, K. and G. Lees-Maffei, 'Real imagined communities: National narratives and the globalization of Design History', *Design Issues*, 32:1 (2016), 5–18.

Fasce, F. and E. Bini, 'Irresistible empire or innocents abroad? American advertising agencies in post-war Italy, 1950s–1970s', *Journal of Historical Research in Marketing*, 7:1 (2015), 7–30.

Fiedler, J. and P. Feierabend (eds), *Bauhaus* (Cologne: Könemann, 1999).

Findeli, A., *Le Bauhaus de Chicago: l'œvre pédagogique de László Moholy-Nagy* (Sillery: Septentrion, 1995).

Fioravanti, G., L. Passarelli and S. Sfligiotti (eds), *La grafica in Italia* (Milan: Leonardo Arte, 1997).

Foot, J., *Milan since the Miracle: City, Culture and Identity* (Oxford; New York: Berg, 2001).

Forgacs, D., *L'industrializzazione della cultura italiana (1880–1990)* (Bologna: Il Mulino, 1990).

Fornari, D., 'Swiss style made in Italy: Graphic design across the border', in R. Lzicar and D. Fornari (eds), *Mapping Graphic Design History in Switzerland* (Zurich: Triest Verlag, 2016), pp. 152–89.

Fornari, D. and C. Barbieri, 'The Olivetti showroom in Turin: A fragment of the Bauhaus in Italy', in D. Fornari and D. Turrini (eds), *Olivetti Identities: Spaces and Languages 1933–1983* (Zurich: Triest Verlag, 2022), pp. 60–73.

Fornari, D., R. Lzicar, S. Owens, M. Renner, A. Scheuermann and P. J. Schneemann (eds), *Swiss Graphic Design Histories* (Zurich: Scheidegger & Spiess, 2021).

Fossati, P. and R. Sambonet (eds), *Lo Studio Boggeri: 1933–1973. Comunicazione visuale e grafica applicata* (Cinisello Balsamo: Pizzi Editore, 1974).

Foster, H., 'The Bauhaus idea in America', in A. Borchardt-Hume (ed.), *Albers and Moholy-Nagy: From the Bauhaus to the New World* (London: Tate Publishing, 2006), pp. 92–102.

Fournier, V., 'The appeal to "professionalism" as a disciplinary mechanism', *Social Review*, 47:2 (1999), 280–307.

Frascara, J. (ed.), *Graphic Design World Views: A Celebration of Icograda's 25th Anniversary* (Tokyo; New York: Kodansha, 1990).

Frayling, C., *Art and Design: 100 Years at the Royal College of Art* (London: Collins & Brown, 1999).

Freidson, E., *Professional Powers: A Study of the Institutionalization of Formal Knowledge* (Chicago; London: University of Chicago Press, 1986).

Freidson, E., *Professionalism: The Third Logic* (Chicago: University of Chicago Press, 2001).

Gambarelli, F. R., *Monza anni Trenta dall'Umanitaria all'ISIA* (Monza: Musei Civici Monza, 2001).

Gaudenzi, B., 'Press advertising and fascist dictates: Showcasing the female consumer in Fascist Italy and Nazi Germany', *Journalism Studies*, 14:5 (2013), 663–80.

Gaudenzi, B., 'Dictators for sale: The commercialization of the Duce and the Führer in Fascist Italy and Nazi Germany', in J. Rüger and N. Wachsmann (eds), *Rewriting German History: New Perspectives on Modern Germany* (London: Palgrave Macmillan, 2015), pp. 267–87.

Gaudenzi, B., 'Il fascismo in vetrina', in F. Fasce, E. Bini and B. Gaudenzi, *Comprare per credere. La pubblicità in Italia dalla Belle Époque a oggi* (Rome: Carocci, 2016), pp. 41–83.

Genovesi, G., *Storia della scuola in Italia dal Settecento a oggi* (Bari: Laterza, 2004).

Gentile, E., *The Sacralization of Politics in Fascist Italy* (Cambridge, MA; London: Harvard University Press, 1996).

Georgi, W. and T. Minetti (eds), *Italian Design Is Coming Home. To Switzerland* (Amsterdam: Polyedra, 2011).

Ghirardo, D., 'Italian architects and fascist politics: An evaluation of the rationalist's role in regime building', *Journal of the Society of Architectural Historians*, 39:2 (1980), 109–27.

Ghirardo, D., 'Architects, exhibitions, and the politics of culture in Fascist Italy', *Journal of Architectural Education*, 45:2 (1992), 67–75.

Gigli Marchetti, A., *I tre anelli: mutualità, resistenza, cooperazione dei tipografi milanesi (1860–1925)* (Milan: Franco Angeli Editore, 1983).

Gigli Marchetti, A., 'Impresa e lavoro. L'industria tipografico-editoriale Milanese dalla fine dell'Ottocento al Fascismo', in G. Montecchi (ed.), *La città dell'editoria: dal libro tipografico all'opera digitale* (Milan: Skira, 2001), pp. 23–37.

Ginsborg, P., *A History of Contemporary Italy: Society and Politics, 1943–1988* (London: Penguin, 1990).

Grassi, A. and A. Pansera (eds), *L'Italia del design: trent'anni di dibattito* (Casale Manferrato: Marietti, 1986).

Grazzani, L. and F. E. Guida, *AIAP 70×70: eventi, personaggi e materiali di una storia associativa* (Milan: AIAP, 2015).

Guerin, D. A. and C. S. Martin, 'The career cycle approach to defining the interior design profession's body of knowledge', *Journal of Interior Design*, 30:2 (2004), 1–22.

Guida, F. E., 'Giarrettiere, puntine e progettiste', in D. Piscitelli (ed.), *AWDA: Aiap Women in Design Award, premio internazionale design della comunicazione* (Milan: AIAP, 2015), pp. 34–6.

Guida, F. E., 'Donne della grafica italiana. Per una storiografia inclusiva', in R. Riccini (ed.), *Angelica e Bradamante: le donne del design* (Padua: Il Poligrafo, 2017), pp. 193–206.

Gundle, S., 'L'americanizzazione del quotidiano. Televisione e consumismo nell'Italia degli Anni Cinquanta', *Quaderni Storici*, 21:62 (1986), 561–94.

Gundle, S., *I comunisti italiani tra Hollywood e Mosca. La sfida della cultura di massa (1943–1991)* (Florence: Giunti, 1995).

Gundle, S., 'Un Martini per il Duce: l'immaginario del consumismo nell'Italia degli anni Venti e Trenta', in A. Villari (ed.), *L'arte della pubblicità: il manifesto italiano e le avanguardie* (Milan: Silvana Editoriale, 2008), pp. 38–62.

Gundle, S., 'Mass culture and the culture of personality', in S. Gundle, C. Duggan and G. Pieri (eds), *The Cult of the Duce: Mussolini and the Italians* (Manchester: Manchester University Press, 2013).

Gundle, S., C. Duggan and G. Pieri (eds), *The Cult of the Duce: Mussolini and the Italians* (Manchester: Manchester University Press, 2013).

Guyatt, R., 'Graphic Design at the Royal College of Art', in Anon., *GraphicsRCA: Fifteen Years' Work of the School of Graphic Design, Royal College of Art* (London: Lion & Unicorn Press, 1963).

Hall, S., 'Introduction: Who needs "identity"', in S. Hall and P. du Gay (eds), *Questions of Cultural Identity* (London: Sage Publications, 1996), pp. 1–17.

Hayward, S., '"Good design is largely a matter of common sense": Questioning the meaning and ownership of a twentieth-century orthodoxy', *Journal of Design History*, 11:3 (1998), 217–33.

Heller, S., 'Advertising: Mother of graphic design', *Eye Magazine*, 5:17 (1995), 26–37.

Henrion, F. H. K., *AGI Annals* (Zurich: Alliance Graphique Internationale, 1989).

Henrion, F. H. K. and A. Parkin, *Design Coordination and Corporate Image* (London: Studio Vista, 1967).

Hodgen, M., *Workers Education in England and in the United States* (London: Kegan Paul, 1925).

Hogg, M. A. and D. J. Terry, 'Social identity and self-categorization processes in organizational contexts', *Academy of Management Review*, 25:1 (2000), 121–40.

Hogg, M. A. and D. J. Terry, 'Social identity and organisational processes', in M. A. Hogg and D. J. Terry (eds), *Social Identity Processes in Organisational Contexts* (London: Taylor and Francis Group, 2001), pp. 1–12.

Hollis, R., *Graphic Design: A Concise History* (London: Thames & Hudson, 1996).

Hollis, R., *Swiss Graphic Design: The Origins and Growth of an International Style, 1920–1965* (New Haven; London: Yale University Press, 2006).

Horowitz, F. A., 'Albers the teacher: Design', in F. A. Horowitz and B. Danilowitz (eds), *Josef Albers: To Open Eyes. The Bauhaus, Black Mountain College and Yale* (London; New York: Phaidon, 2006), pp. 98–124.

Huppatz, D. J., 'Globalizing design history and global design history', *Journal of Design History*, 28:2 (2015), 182–202.

Iliprandi, G., A. Marangoni, F. Origoni and A. Pansera (eds), *Visual design: 50 anni di produzione in Italia* (Milan: Idea Libri, 1984).

Iliprandi, G., 'An Interview with Giancarlo Iliprandi', in W. Georgi and T. Minetti (eds), *Italian Design Is Coming Home. To Switzerland* (Amsterdam: Polyedra, 2011), pp. 18–20.

Jacob, H., 'A personal view of an experiment in democracy and design education', *Journal of Design History*, 1:3–4 (1988), 221–34.

James-Chakraborty, K. (ed.), *Bauhaus Culture: From Weimar to the Cold War* (Minneapolis; London: Minnesota University Press, 2006).

Jobling, P. and D. Crowley, *Graphic Design: Reproduction and Representation since 1800* (Manchester; New York: Manchester University Press, 1996).

Kinross, R., 'Introduction to the English-language edition', in J. Tschichold, *The New Typography* (Berkeley; Los Angeles; London: University of California Press, 2006 (1928)), pp. xv–xliv.

Koolhass, R. and H. U. Obrist, *Project Japan: Metabolism Talk* (Cologne: Taschen, 2011).

Koon, T. H., *Believe, Obey, Fight: Political Socialization of Youth in Fascist Italy, 1922–1943* (Chapel Hill: University of North Carolina Press, 1985).

Lacaita, C. G., 'Istruzione tecnico-professionale e modernizzazione fra Otto e Novecento', in C. G. Lacaita (ed.), *La leva della conoscenza: istruzione e formazione professionale in Lombardia fra Otto e Novecento* (Milan: Giampiero Casagrande Editore, 2009), pp. 9–19.

Lamm, L. and N. Ossanna Cavadini (eds), *Lora Lamm. Grafica a Milano 1953–1963* (Cinisello Balsamo: Silvana Editoriale, 2013).

Lampel, J. and A. D. Meyer, 'Introduction. Field-configuring events as structuring mechanisms: How conferences, ceremonies, and trade shows constitute new technologies industries, and markets', *Journal of Management Studies*, 45:6 (2008), 1025–35.

Lave, J. and E. Wenger, *Situated Learning: Legitimate Peripheral Participation* (Cambridge: Cambridge University Press, 1991).

Lazzaro, C., 'Forging a visible fascist nation: Strategies for fusing past and present', in C. Lazzaro and R. J. Crum (eds), *Donatello Among the Blackshirts: History and Modernity in the Visual Culture of Fascism* (Ithaca; London: Cornell University Press, 2005), pp. 13–31.

Lazzaro, C. and R. J. Crum (eds), *Donatello Among the Blackshirts: History and Modernity in the Visual Culture of Fascism* (Ithaca; London: Cornell University Press, 2005).

Lees-Maffei, G., 'Introduction: Professionalization as a focus in interior design history', *Journal of Design History*, 21:1 (2008), 1–18.

Lees-Maffei, G., 'Reading graphic design in the expanded field: An introduction', in G. Lees-Maffei and N. P. Maffei (eds), *Reading Graphic Design in Cultural Context* (London: Bloomsbury, 2019), pp. 1–13.

Lees-Maffei, G. and K. Fallan (eds), *Made in Italy: Rethinking a Century of Italian Design* (London: Bloomsbury, 2014).

Lindinger, H. (ed.), *La scuola di Ulm: una nuova cultura del progetto* (Genoa: Costa & Nolan, 1988).

Lupi, I., 'Italo Lupi', in A. Bassi, R. Riccini and C. Colombo (eds), *Design in Triennale 1947–68: percorsi fra Milano e Brianza* (Milan: Silvana Editoriale, 2004), pp. 136–7.

Lupton, E., 'Design and production in the mechanical age', in D. Rothschild, E. Lupton and D. Goldstein (eds), *Graphic Design in the Mechanical Age: Selections from the Merrill C. Berman Collection* (New Haven; London: Yale University Press, 1998), pp. 51–94.

Lzicar, R. and D. Fornari (eds), *Mapping Graphic Design History in Switzerland* (Zurich: Triest Verlag, 2016).

Maglio, A., *Hannes Meyer: un razionalista in esilio. Architettura, urbanistica e politica 1930–54* (Milan: Franco Angeli Editore, 2002).

Maldonado, T., *Disegno industriale: un riesame* (Milan: Feltrinelli, 2008).

Maldonado, T., *Arte e artefatti: intervista di Hans Ulrich Obrist* (Milan: Feltrinelli, 2010).

Malvano, L., *Fascismo e politica dell'immagine* (Turin: Bollati e Boringhieri, 1988).

Marchand, R., *Advertising the American Dream: Making Way for Modernity, 1920–1940* (Berkeley: University of California Press, 1986).

Margolin, V., 'Narrative problems of graphic design history', *Visible Language*, 28:3 (1994), 234–43.

McAlhone, B., 'Twenty-one years ago, D&AD was a gleam in Bob Brook's eye', *Design &Art Direction* (June 1983), 10–17.

McCarthy, F., *Gropius: The Man Who Built the Bauhaus* (Cambridge, MA: The Belknap Press of Harvard University Press, 2019).

McCoy, K., 'Education in an adolescent profession', in S. Heller (ed.), *The Education of a Graphic Designer* (New York: Allworth Press, 2005), pp. 4–6.

McLaren, B., 'Under the sign of the reproduction', *Journal of Architectural Education*, 45:2 (1992), 98–106.

Melino, M., *La Scuola del Libro di Milano: documenti e fatti* (Milan: Società Umanitaria, 1954).

Melino, M. (ed.), *Riccardo Bauer: la militanza politica, l'opera educativa e sociale, la difesa della pace e dei diritti umani* (Milan: Franco Angeli Editore, 1985).

Miliotes, D., *What May Come: The Taller de Gráfica Popular and the Mexican Political Print* (New Haven; London: Yale University Press, 2014).

Millerson, G., *The Qualifying Associations: A Study in Professionalization* (London: Routledge & Kegan Paul, 1964).

Molinari, L. (ed.), *La memoria e il futuro: I Congresso Internazionale dell'Industrial Design, Triennale di Milano, 1954* (Milan; Geneva: Skira, 2001).

Monguzzi, B. (ed.), *Lo Studio Boggeri: 1933–1981* (Milan: Electa, 1981).

Monno, S. (ed.), *Umanitaria: cento anni di solidarietà* (Milan; Florence: Edizioni Charta, 1993).

Montecchi, G. (ed.), *La città dell'editoria: dal libro tipografico all'opera digitale (1880–2020)* (Geneva; Milan: Skira, 2001).

Moret, O. (ed.), *Back to the Future: The Future in the Past. ICDHS 10th+1 Barcelona 2018* (Barcelona: Edicions de la Universitat de Barcelona, 2018).

Mucchi, G., *Le occasioni perdute: memorie, 1899–1993* (Milan: Mazzotta, 2001).

Mugnai, F., 'Il classico in una stanza. Il Salone della Vittoria alla VI Triennale di Milano', *Firenze Architettura*, 2 (2016), 50–7.

Muraca, D. (ed.), *Germano Facetti dalla rappresentazione del lager alla storia del XX secolo* (Cinisello Balsamo: Silvana Editoriale, 2008).

Myerson, J. and G. Vickers, *Rewind: Forty Years of Design & Advertising* (London; New York: Phaidon, 2002).

Natta, A. and L. Raimondi (eds), *Scuola e resistenza nei Convitti Rinascita* (Rome: ANPI, 1950).

Nerdinger, W., *Bauhaus-Moderne im Nationalsozialismus: Zwischen Anbiederung und Verfolgung* (Munich: Prestel, 1993).

Nerdinger, W., 'Bauhaus architecture in the Third Reich', in K. James-Chakraborty (ed.), *Bauhaus Culture: From Weimar to the Cold War* (Minneapolis; London: University of Minnesota Press, 2006), pp. 139–52.

Nixon, S., 'Looking westwards and worshipping: The New York "Creative Revolution" and British advertising, 1956–1980', *Journal of Consumer Culture*, 17:2 (2015), 147–66.

Noorda, B., 'Eravamo una squadra molto affiatata', in M. Della Campa and C. A. Colombo (eds), *Spazio ai caratteri. L'Umanitaria e la Scuola del Libro* (Milan: Silvana Editoriale, 2004), pp. 142–3.

Oropallo, G., 'This way to the exit: The re-writing of the city through graphic design, 1964–1989', in G. Lees-Maffei and K. Fallan (eds), *Made in Italy: Rethinking a Century of Italian Design* (London: Bloomsbury, 2014), pp. 193–207.

Ortoleva, P., 'A geography of the media since 1945', in D. Forgacs and R. Lumley (eds), *Italian Cultural Studies: An Introduction* (New York: Oxford University Press, 1996), pp. 185–98.

Otto, E., 'Designing men: New vision of masculinity in the photomontages of Herbert Bayer, Marcel Breuer, and László Moholy-Nagy', in J. Saletnik and R. Schuldenfrei (eds), *Bauhaus Construct: Fashioning Identity, Discourse and Modernism* (London; New York: Routledge, 2009), pp. 183–204.

Packard, V., *The Hidden Persuaders* (London: Longmans Green, 1957).

Pansera, A., *Storia e cronaca della Triennale* (Milan: Longanesi & Co., 1974).

Pansera, A., 'Gli ISIA. Da dove veniamo e chi siamo', in M. Bazzini and A. Pansera (eds), *ISIA design convivio. Sperimentazione didattica: progetti, scenari e società* (Milan: Edizioni Aiap, 2015), pp. 18–20.

Pansera, A., *La formazione del designer in Italia: una storia lunga più di un secolo* (Venice: Marsilio, 2015).

Pansera, A., (ed.), *1923–1930 Monza verso l'unità delle arti* (Milan: Silvana Editoriale, 2004).

Panza, P., 'Le istituzioni culturali', in A. Gigli Marchetti (ed.), *L'età della speranza: Milano dalla ricostruzione al boom* (Milan: Skira, 2007), pp. 81–9.

Pavitt, J., 'The bomb in the brain', in D. Crowley and J. Pavitt (eds), *Cold War Modern: Design 1945–1970* (London: V&A Publishing, 2008), pp. 100–19.

Petrillo, G. and A. Scalpelli (eds), *Milano anni Cinquanta* (Milan: Franco Angeli Editore, 1986).

Petropoulos, J., *Artists under Hitler: Collaboration and Survival in Nazi Germany* (New Haven; London: Yale University Press, 2014).

Piazza, M., 'Grafica: creativi negli anni cinquanta', in G. Anghia and A. Marangoni (eds), *Milano anni cinquanta* (Milan: Franco Angeli Editore, 1986), pp. 163–9.

Piazza, M., 'Le storie visive della triennale', in S. Annichiarico and M. Piazza (eds), *Come comete: annunci e messaggi nella grafica della Triennale* (Milan: Charta, 2004), pp. 11–45.

Piazza, M., (ed.), *La grafica del Made in Italy: comunicazione e aziende del design 1950–1980* (Milan: Edizioni Aiap, 2012).

Picasso, M. (ed.), *1945–1995: cinquant'anni di grafica a Milano* (Milan: Centro Studi Grafici, 1996).

Pigozzi, M., 'Grafica industriale', in Anon., *Gli annitrenta. Arte e cultura in Italia* (Milan: Mazzotta, 1982), pp. 467–76.

Pisano, G., 'La difficile ripresa dell'associazionismo di massa dopo il Fascismo', in G. Bonini and A. Scalpelli (eds), *Milano fra guerra e dopoguerra* (Bari: De Donato, 1979), pp. 445–51.

Pischedda, B., 'Editoria a Milano: 1945–1970. Gli anni dell'entusiasmo', in G. Montecchi (ed.), *La città dell'editoria: dal libro tipografico all'opera digitale* (Milan: Skira, 2001), pp. 125–39.

Pitoni, L., *Ostinata bellezza. Anita Klinz, la prima art director italiana* (Milan: Mondadori, 2022).

Poynor, R. (ed.), *Communicate: Independent British Graphic Design since the Sixties* (London: Laurence King, 2004).

Priarone, G., *Grafica pubblicitaria in Italia negli anni Trenta* (Florence: Cantini, 1989).

Provinciali, M., 'Nel regno della sperimentazione', in M. Della Campa and C. A. Colombo (eds), *Spazio ai caratteri. L'Umanitaria e la Scuola del Libro* (Milan: Silvana Editoriale, 2004), pp. 126–7.

Pruneri, F., *La politica scolastica del Partito Comunista Italiano dalle origini al 1955* (Brescia: Editrice La Scuola, 1999).

Pruneri, F., 'The Convitti Scuola della Rinascita (The Boarding Schools of Rebirth): An innovative pedagogy for democracy in post-war Italy (1945–1955)', *Paedagogica Historica*, 52:1–2 (2016), 188–200.

Puaca, B. M., *Learning Democracy: Education Reform in West Germany, 1945–1965* (New York; Oxford: Berghahn Books, 2009).

Reicher, S., 'The context of social identity: Domination, resistance, and change', *Political Psychology*, 25:6 (2004), 921–45.

Riccini, R., 'Disegno industriale in Lombardia: un modello per il Made in Italy', in D. Bigazzi and M. Meriggi (eds), *Storia d'Italia. Le regioni dall'Unità a oggi: la Lombardia* (Turin: Einaudi, 2001), pp. 1164–93.

Riccini, R., 'Disegno industriale italiano. La costruzione di una cultura fra istituzioni e territorio', in A. Bassi, R. Riccini and C. Colombo (eds), *Design in Triennale 1947–68: percorsi fra Milano e Brianza* (Milan: Silvana Editoriale, 2004), pp. 13–32.

Riccini, R., 'Tomás Maldonado and the impact of the Hochschule für Gestaltung Ulm in Italy', in G. Lees-Maffei and K. Fallan (eds), *Made in Italy: Rethinking a Century of Italian Design* (London: Bloomsbury, 2014), pp. 89–105.

Riccini, R., (ed.), *Angelica e Bradamante: le donne del design* (Padua: Il Poligrafo, 2017).

Richter, B., 'Zurich–Milan', in C. Brändle, K. Gimmi, B. Junod, C. Reble and B. Richter (eds), *100 Years of Swiss Graphic Design* (Zurich: Lars Müller, 2014), pp. 137–43.

Richter, B. (ed.), *Zürich–Milan* (Baden: Lars Müller Publishers, 2007).

Ritzer, G., 'Professionalism and the individual', in E. Freidson (ed.), *The Professions and their Prospects* (Beverly Hills; London: Sage Publications, 1971), pp. 59–73.

Rizzi, R., A. Steiner and F. Origoni (eds), *Design italiano: Compasso d'Oro ADI* (Cantù: Clac, 1998).

Rossi, A., '*Campo Grafico* al tempo di Bertieri', in Anon., *Onoranze a Raffaello Bertieri nell'ambito del quinto centenario dell'introduzione della stampa in Italia* (Milan: Centro Studi Grafici, 1966), pp. 207–26.

Rossi, C., *Crafting Design in Italy: From Post-war to Postmodernism* (Manchester: Manchester University Press, 2015).

Rössler, P., *Herbert Bayer: Die Berliner Jahre – Werbegrafik 1928–1938* (Berlin: Bauhaus-Archiv, 2013).

Sani, R., 'La scuola e l'educazione alla democraia negli anni del secondo dopoguerra', in M. Corsi and R. Sani (eds), *L'educazione alla democrazia tra passato e presente* (Milan: Vita e Pensiero, 2004), pp. 43–62.

Sarfatti Larson, M., *The Rise of Professionalism: A Sociological Analysis* (Berkeley; Los Angeles; London: University of California Press, 1977).

Scarpellini, E., *Il teatro del popolo: la stagione artistica dell'Umanitaria fra cultura e società* (Milan: Franco Angeli Editore, 2003).

Scarpellini, E., *L'Italia dei consumi. Dalla Belle Époque al nuovo millennio* (Rome; Bari: Laterza, 2008).

Schlemmer, T. (ed.), *Oskar Schlemmer: Briefe und Tagebücher* (Stuttgart: Gerd Hatje, 1977).

Schnapp, J. T., 'Fascism's museum in motion', *Journal of Architectural Education*, 45:2 (1992), 87–97.

Schnapp, J. T., *Anno XX: la Mostra della Rivoluzione Fascista del 1932* (Pisa; Rome: Istituto Editoriali e Poligrafici Internazionali, 2003).

Schwarzkopf, S., 'They do it with mirrors: Advertising and British Cold War consumer politics', *Contemporary British History*, 19:2 (2005), 133–50.

Schwarzkopf, S., 'From Fordist to creative economies: The de-Americanisation of European advertising cultures since the 1960s', *European Review of History*, 20:5 (2013), 859–79.

Scotford, M., 'Messy history vs neat history: Toward an expanded view of women in graphic design', *Visible Language*, 28:4 (1994), 368–88.

Scott, W. R., *Institutions and Organisations* (London: Sage Publications, 2001).

Scotto di Luzio, A., 'L'industria dell'informazione: periodici e quotidiani, giornalisti e imprenditori', in D. Bigazzi and M. Meriggi (eds), *Storia d'Italia. Le regioni dall'Unità a oggi: la Lombardia* (Turin: Einaudi, 2001), pp. 331–84.

Scrivano, P., 'Signs of Americanization in Italian domestic life: Italy's postwar conversion to consumerism', *Journal of Contemporary History*, 40:2 (2005), 317–40.

Seago, A., *Burning the Box of Beautiful Things: The Development of a Postmodern Sensibility* (Oxford: Oxford University Press, 1995).

Seddon, J., 'Mentioned but denied significance: Women designers and the professionalization of design in Britain, 1920–1951', *Gender and History*, 12:2 (2000), 426–47.

Seddon, J. and S. Worden, 'Women designers in Britain in the 1920s and 1930s: Defining the professional and redefining design', *Journal of Design History*, 8:3 (1995), 177–93.

Sfligiotti, S., 'Being in the world: Some approaches to graphic design in Italy towards the end of 2010', in G. Camuffo and M. Dalla Mura (eds), *Graphic Design Worlds/Words* (Milan: Electa, 2011), pp. 93–7.

Shaw, P. and P. Bain, 'Introduction. Blackletter vs. Roman: Type as ideological surrogate', in P. Shaw and P. Bain (eds), *Blackletter: Type and National Identity* (New York: Princeton Architectural Press, 1998), pp. 10–15.

Soresina, M., 'Raffaello Bertieri alla Scuola del Libro', in Anon., *Onoranze a Raffaello Bertieri nell'ambito del quinto centenario dell'introduzione della stampa in Italia* (Milan: Centro Studi Grafici, 1966), pp. 75–87.

Sparke, P., 'A modern identity for a new nation: Design in Italy since 1860', in Z. G. Barański and R. J. West (eds), *The Cambridge Companion to Modern Italian Culture* (Cambridge; New York: Cambridge University Press, 2001), pp. 265–81.

Spitz, R., *HfG Ulm: The View Behind the Foreground. The Political History of the Ulm School of Design 1953–1968* (Stuttgart; London: Edition Axel Menges, 2002).

Stanley, R., *D&AD 50* (Cologne: Taschen, 2012).

Steiner, A., *Il mestiere di grafico* (Turin: Einaudi, 1978).

Steiner, A., *Lica Covo Steiner* (Mantua: Edizioni Corraini, 2015).

Steiner, A. (ed.), *Licalbe Steiner: grafici partigiani* (Milan: Edizioni Corraini, 2015).

Stone, M., 'The anatomy of a propaganda event: The Mostra della Rivoluzione Fascista', *Carte Italiane*, 1:12 (1992), 30–40.

Stone, M., 'Staging Fascism: The Exhibition of the Fascist Revolution', *Journal of Contemporary History*, 28:2 (1993), 215–43.

Stone, M., 'The State as patron: Making official culture in Fascist Italy', in M. Affrom and M. Antliff (eds), *Fascist Visions: Art and Ideology in France and Italy* (Princeton: Princeton University Press, 1997), pp. 205–38.

Stone, M., *The Patron State: Culture and Politics in Fascist Italy* (Princeton: Princeton University Press, 1998).

Thompson, D., *State Control in Fascist Italy: Culture and Conformity* (Manchester: Manchester University Press, 1991).

Thomson, E. M., '"The science of publicity": An American advertising theory, 1900–1920', *Journal of Design History*, 9:4 (1996), 253–72.

Thomson, E. M., *The Origins of Graphic Design in America: 1870–1920* (New Haven; London: Yale University Press, 1997).

Tonelli, A., *L'istruzione tecnica e professionale di Stato nelle strutture e nei programmi da Casati ai giorni nostri* (Milan: Giuffrè Editore, 1964).

Toniolo G., 'An overview of Italy's economic growth', in G. Toniolo (ed.), *The Oxford Handbook of the Italian Economy Since Unification* (Oxford; New York: Oxford University Press, 2013), pp. 3–36.

Toniolo G., (ed.), *The Oxford Handbook of the Italian Economy Since Unification* (Oxford; New York: Oxford University Press, 2013).

Traganou, J., *Designing the Olympics: Representation, Participation, Contestation* (New York: Routledge, 2016).

Triggs, T., 'Designing graphic design history', *Journal of Design History*, 22:4 (2009), 325–40.

Triggs, T., 'Graphic design history: Past, present, and future', *Design Issues*, 27:1 (2011), 3–6.

Triggs, T., 'Curating graphic design and its history', in R. Lzicar and D. Fornari (eds), *Mapping Graphic Design History in Switzerland* (Zurich: Triest Verlag, 2016), pp. 18–44.

Triggs, T., A. Shaughnessy and A. Gerber (eds), *GraphicsRCA: Fifty Years and Beyond* (London: Royal College of Art, 2014).

Trozzi, G., 'Quelli di via Conte Verde: per una storia del Corso di Disegno Industriale e Comunicazioni Visive di Roma', *Progetto Grafico*, 1 (2003), 102–5.

Turi, G., *Il Fascismo e il consenso degli intellettuali* (Bologna: Il Mulino, 1980).

Turi, G., *Lo Stato educatore. Politica e intellettuali nell'Italia fascista* (Bari: Laterza, 2002).

Tymkiw, M., *Nazi Exhibition Design and Modernism* (Minneapolis; London: University of Minnesota Press, 2018).

Valeri, A., *Pubblicità italiana: storia, protagonisti e tendenze di cento anni di comunicazione* (Milan: Sole24Ore, 1986).

Ventresca, R. A., *From Fascism to Democracy: Culture and Politics in the Italian Election of 1948* (Toronto; London: University of Toronto Press, 2004).

Veronesi, G., *Difficoltà politiche dell'architettura in Italia: 1920–1940* (Milan: Christian Marinotti Editore, 2008 (1953)).

Vignelli, M., 'Umanitaria, anni '60. Un'aria nuova per la grafica', in M. Della Campa and C. A. Colombo (eds), *Spazio ai caratteri. L'Umanitaria e la Scuola del Libro* (Milan: Silvana Editoriale, 2004), pp. 134–5.

Vinti, C., 'L'estetica grafica della "nuova tipografia" in Italia', *Disegno Industriale Industrial Design*, 2:2 (2002), 6–30.

Vinti, C., 'Campisti a scuola. Come è nata l'avventura di *Campo Grafico*', in M. Della Campa and C. A. Colombo (eds), *Spazio ai caratteri. L'Umanitaria e la Scuola del Libro* (Milan: Silvana Editoriale, 2004), pp. 59–62.

Vinti, C., 'Modiano e la "Mostra Grafica" alla VII Triennale', *Progetto Grafico*, 4–5 (2005), 50–63.

Vinti, C., *Gli anni dello stile industriale 1948–1965: immagine e politica culturale nella grande impresa italiana* (Venice: Marsilio, 2007).

Vinti, C., 'Design & craft in the definition of the graphic designer: The debate in Italian graphic arts magazines', in J. Gimeno-Martinez and F. Floré (eds), *Design and Craft: A History of Convergences and Divergences. 7th Conference of the International Committee of Design History and Design Studies (ICDHS) 20–22 September 2010* (Brussels: VWK, 2010), pp. 446–51.

Vinti, C., 'Graphic designers, people with problems. Some thoughts from Italy', in G. Camuffo and M. Dalla Mura (eds), *Graphic Design Worlds/Words* (Milan: Electa, 2011), pp. 85–91.

Vinti, C., 'The New Typography in Fascist Italy. Between internationalism and the search for a national style', in M. Cortat and D. Fornari (eds), *Archigraphiæ: Rationalist Lettering and Architecture in Fascist Rome* (Renens: Ecal, 2020), pp. 49–66.

Vittoria, A., *I luoghi della cultura. Istituzioni, riviste e circuiti intellettuali nell'Italia del Novecento* (Rome: Carocci, 2021).

Voigt, K., *Il rifugio precario: gli esuli in Italia dal 1933 al 1945* (Florence: La Nuova Italia Editrice, 1993).

Wang, D. and A. O. Ilham, 'Holding creativity together: A sociological theory of the design professions', *Design Issues*, 25:1 (2009), 5–21.

Weisenfeld, G., 'Japanese modernism and consumerism: Forging the new artistic field of "shôgyô bijutsu" (commercial art)', in E. K. Tipton and J. Clark (eds), *Being Modern in Japan: Culture and Society from the 1910s to the 1930s* (Honolulu: University of Hawaii Press, 1994), pp. 75–98.

Wenger, E., *Communities of Practice: Learning, Meaning, and Identity* (Cambridge: Cambridge University Press, 1998).

Wilk, C., 'Introduction: What was Modernism?', in C. Wilk (ed.), *Modernism: Designing a New World, 1914–1939* (London: V&A Publications, 2006), pp. 12–21.

Wilk, C., (ed.), *Modernism: Designing a New World, 1914–1939* (London: V&A Publications, 2006).

Wilkins, A. T., 'Augustus, Mussolini, and the parallel imagery of Empire', in C. Lazzaro and R. J. Crum (eds), *Donatello Among the Blackshirts: History and Modernity in the Visual Culture of Fascism* (Ithaca; London: Cornell University Press, 2005), pp. 53–65.

Willson, P., *Women in Twentieth-Century Italy* (New York: Palgrave Macmillan, 2010).

Wolff, R. J., 'Italian education during World War II: Remnant of failed fascist education, seeds of new schools', in R. Lowe (ed.), *Education and the Second World War: Studies in Schooling and Social Change* (London: The Falmer Press, 1992).

Woodham, J. M., *Twentieth Century Design* (Oxford; New York: Oxford University Press, 1997).

Woodham, J. M., *A Dictionary of Modern Design* (Oxford; New York: Oxford University Press, 2004).

Woodham, J. M., 'Local, national and global: Redrawing the design historical map', *Journal of Design History*, 18:3 (2005), 257–67.

Worchel, S., J. Iuzzini, D. Coutant and M. Ivaldi, 'A multidimensional model of identity: Relating individual and group identities to intergroup behaviour', in D. Capozza and R. Brown (eds), *Social Identity Processes: Trends in Theory and Research* (London; Thousand Oaks; New Delhi: SAGE Publications, 2000), pp. 15–32.

Yasuko, S., 'Designing the morality of consumption: "Chamber of Horrors" at the Museum of Ornamental Art, 1852–53', *Design Issues*, 20:4 (2004), 43–56.

Zamagni, V., *The Economic History of Italy, 1860–1990* (Oxford: Clarendon Press, 1993).

Zanantoni, M., *Albe Steiner: cambiare il libro per cambiare il mondo. Dalla Repubblica d'Ossola alle Edizioni Feltrinelli* (Milan: Unicopli, 2013).

Unpublished secondary sources

Colizzi, A., 'Bruno Munari and the Invention of Modern Graphic Design in Italy, 1928–1945' (PhD dissertation, University of Leiden, Leiden, 2011).

Galluzzo, M., 'I grafici sono sempre protagonisti? Pubblicità in Italia 1965–1985' (PhD dissertation, IUAV, Venice, 2018).

Pastore, M., 'Il Corso Superiore di Design Industriale di Venezia 1960/1971: la comunicazione visiva nell'offerta didattica e il suo ruolo nella formazione di nuove figure professionali' (MA dissertation, IUAV, Venice, 2007).

Internet sources

Anon., 'AGI members', www.a-g-i.org/members, accessed 31 May 2023.

Anon., 'Aiap Women in Design Award', www.aiap-awda.com, accessed 31 May 2023.

Anon., *Constitution of the Italian Republic* (Rome: Senato della Repubblica), www.senato.it/documenti/repository/istituzione/costituzione_inglese.pdf, accessed 31 May 2023.

Barbieri, C. and D. Fornari, 'Xanti Schawinsky and the fascist plebiscitary elections of 1934: Everyday design practice and visual culture in early-1930's Italy', *Journal of Design History*, epad026, https://doi.org/10.1093/jdh/epad026.

Crowley, D., 'Advertising and history: Admen plunder the past – with no history to call their own', *Eye Magazine*, 15:57 (2005), www.eyemagazine.com/opinion/article/advertising-and-history, accessed 31 May 2023.

Iguchi, T., 'Reconsideration of the World Design Conference 1960 in Tokyo and the World Industrial Design Conference 1973 in Kyoto: Transformation of design theory', www.design-cu.jp/iasdr2013/papers/1183–1b.pdf, accessed 31 May 2023.

Molinari, L., 'Career Manifesto. A tribute by Italian graphic designers to the Masters of the Compasso d'Oro', www.adidesignmuseum.org/en/exhibition/manifesto-alla-carriera/, accessed 31 May 2023.

Poynor, R., 'We need more galleries that exhibit graphic design', *Print*, 64:2 (April 2010), www.printmag.com/featured/observer-we-need-more-galleries-that-exhibit-graphic-design/, accessed 31 May 2023.

Poynor, R., 'Out of the studio: Graphic design history and visual studies', *Design Observer* (1 October 2011), www.designobserver.com/feature/out-of-the-studio-graphic-design-history-and-visual-studies/24048, accessed 31 May 2023.

Index

Page numbers in *italic* refer to figures.

EU authorised representative for GPSR:
Easy Access System Europe, Mustamäe tee 50,
10621 Tallinn, Estonia
gpsr.requests@easproject.com

www.ingramcontent.com/pod-product-compliance
Lightning Source LLC
Chambersburg PA
CBHW080551270326
41929CB00019B/3258